DISCARDED

Beyond Universal Reason

DISCARDED

Beyond Universal Reason

The Relation between Religion and Ethics
in the
Work of Stanley Hauerwas

EMMANUEL KATONGOLE

UNIVERSITY OF NOTRE DAME PRESS
Notre Dame, Indiana

Copyright 2000 by
University of Notre Dame Press
Notre Dame, IN 46556
All Rights Reserved
Manufactured in the United States of America

Library of Congress Cataloging-in-Publication Data

Katongole, Emmanuel, 1960–
   Beyond universal reason : the relation between religion and ethics in the
work of Stanley Hauerwas / Emmanuel Katongole.
     p. cm.
   Includes bibliographical references and index.
   ISBN 0-268-02159-7 (pbk. : alk. paper)
    1. Hauerwas, Stanley, 1940– 2. Christian ethics. I. Title.

BJ1278.5.H38 K38 2000
241'.0404'092—dc21
                                         99-059787

∞ The paper used in this publication meets the minimum requirements of
the American National Standard for Information Sciences—Permanence of
Paper for Printed Library Materials, ANSI Z39.48-1984.

Contents

Foreword

Emmanuel Katongole is a philosopher, a Roman Catholic priest, and a Ugandan. He is also one of the most delightful people I have had the pleasure to meet (though that was only for a few days). Of course, one of the reasons I may find him so delightful is he has written this wonderful book on my work. Moreover, he has in many respects defended what I have tried to do better than I have ever been able to do. That he is able not only to understand as well as to defend what I have been about is not, I think, because he is such an agreeable person. Rather, I believe what he has done in this book has everything to do with his being a philosopher, a Roman Catholic priest, and a Ugandan. Let me try to explain.

That he is a philosopher means he is free of many of the debates that have surrounded Christian ethics as well as Catholic moral theology in this century. From my perspective, recent Protestant and Catholic thinking about ethics has too often been determined by the philosophical presuppositions of modernity. This influence was all the more pernicious just to the extent those influenced by modern philosophy were often unaware they had been so influenced. For example, consider MacIntyre's account of the effect of Kant on Kleutgen in *Three Rival Versions of Moral Enquiry*.

Because Reverend Katongole is a philosopher he provides a framework that makes how I try to do theology seem less idiosyncratic. As a philosopher he sees that when I say, "Outside the church there is no salvation," I am making a claim that those schooled by Wittgenstein may not find as outrageous as it first appears. I am particularly grateful for the comparison Katongole makes between my work and that of Sabina Lovibond because it should put an end (though it probably will not) to charges I am a fideist. I remain unconvinced by Katongole, however, that I must give up "realism." Wittgenstein's "Not empiricism and yet realism in philosophy, that is the hardest thing," I believe, must continue to haunt all of us, particularly if we are theologians.

Of course Reverend Katongole is not just a philosopher but he is also a Roman Catholic priest. Accordingly, not only does he understand the theological agenda that drives my work, but he has a wonderful ear for appreciating not only what I say but what I do not say. If you think the way I think, the problem is how to proceed without reproducing the dualisms that are simply accepted by so many as theological givens—e.g., religion and morality, personal and social ethics, faith and reason, facts and values. That Reverend Katongole is able to see why I must resist these conceits— conceits that are at the heart of the Protestant accommodation to modernity—has everything to do with his Catholicism. For no matter how tempted Catholics are (particularly in the West) to reproduce Protestant mistakes, Catholicism surely stands as the tradition that has not only named but resisted the philosophical and political "givens" that shape liberal social orders and their correlative intellectual formations.

I feel confident I am right about the importance of Reverend Katongole being a philosopher for his reading of me. I am less confident I am right about his Catholicism, and I confess I can only speculate about the significance of his being Ugandan. Yet I cannot help but think—as one who is trying to help Christians learn that "the West" is not the necessary home for Christians—it is not accidental that one of my best readers comes from a home in which Christianity has never been at home. Accordingly, Emmanuel rightly understands my account of witness not as an invitation for Christians to abandon politics but as our most determinative political act.

That Emmanuel Katongole is a philosopher, a Roman Catholic priest, and a Ugandan would seem to make unlikely that he would befriend me. I am a philosophical amateur, I am for good and ill a Protestant layman, and I am an American. In short, it would seem that we should be strangers barely able to communicate. Yet his book stands as a testimony that such "differences" can be the very resources needed for us to discover agreements in judgments—in short, to be friends. Anyone wishing to better understand "my work" can find no better place than this book and for that I am in his debt. But more important, I believe, is not what this book says about me but what Emmanuel and I both most care about—that is, the wonder of being made part of a community across time directed to the truthful worship of God. That Emmanuel Katongole exists and claims me as a friend is surely evidence that God is indeed great.

STANLEY HAUERWAS

Introduction

Indeed, to begin by asking what is the relation between theology and ethics is to have already made a mistake.

Hauerwas

Over the last decade or so, Stanley Hauerwas has challenged the main foundations of modern ethical and political theory. Writing mostly from a theological background, he has noted how the conception of moral reason operating in much of contemporary ethical reflection, as well as the dominant forms of political liberalism tend to obscure and distort ordinary moral experience and the conception of ourselves as historical and social agents. Although Hauerwas's authorship has been both extensive in its scope and content, and has appealed to a wide audience, the reader may not always find it easy to understand some of his specific claims or the general direction of his work. This is partly due to the practical and occasional nature of his writings (mostly essays), which may not provide the much-needed interconnection with previous arguments or a systematic conceptual framework. This fact alone has been responsible for much of the misunderstanding, and even (in some cases) frustration with, Hauerwas's otherwise provocative work.

This work itself is born out of such frustration, in relation to one specific claim by Hauerwas. In the Introduction to his 1983 *The Peaceable Kingdom*, Hauerwas claimed that to "start by asking what is the relation between ethics and religion is to have already made a mistake."[1] When I began to read Hauerwas six years ago, this statement struck me as a highly contentious, and greatly unsubstantiated claim. For, not unlike many others (especially in the analytic tradition), I had taken the 'problem' of the relation between religion and ethics as one of those"perennial" philosophical questions which has been, as Bartley puts it, "a matter of controversy amongst philosophers and theologians from the earliest times."[2] Hauerwas's attempt to dismiss the problem altogether, could not, therefore, but strike me as highly contentious. I was interested to take up this claim and investigate the basis and limits of its validity.

It soon emerged from my investigation that Hauerwas's reason for dismissing the philosophical problem of the relation between religion and ethics was created by, and at home within, the dominant Kantian tradition of ethics, which Hauerwas was calling into question. In its quest for objectivity, the Kantian view of ethics (Hauerwas claimed) is characterized not only by a certain bias against particularity, but by an attempt to turn morality into an institution whose form and mode of justification did not depend on any particular and contingent social forms of life. Such a view of ethics not only becomes highly formal, it does not do justice to the experience we have of ourselves as contingent and particular moral agents. What was needed, and what Hauerwas himself was contributing to, was a more historical and socially embodied account of the moral life and moral reason. Such an account would not only offer a more adequate characterization of our ordinary moral experience, it would not give rise to the traditional 'problem' of the relation between religion and ethics.

It therefore became clear that Hauerwas's claim that "to begin by asking the relation between religion and ethics is to already have made a mistake" makes sense only within the wider framework of his attempt to set aside the Kantian moral tradition. However, even beyond this specific conclusion, the investigation had led me to see that there was a need for developing a comprehensive theoretical framework for a better appreciation of Hauerwas's work. Hauerwas himself does not develop this comprehensive theoretical framework, given, as we noted, the practical and occasional nature of his writing. However, such a framework would not only make the various and disparate claims made by Hauerwas conceptually coherent, it would examine the various implications of, and at the same time deal with the key criticisms associated with, Hauerwas's constructive revision of Kantian ethics.

Taking the problem of the relation between ethics and religion as a starting point, this work attempts to offer such a theoretical framework. The work is divided into two parts. The first part, which consists of four chapters, is a reconstruction of Hauerwas's conception of the moral life around the three categories of *moral character, vision* and *narrative*. A chapter is devoted to each of these three categories. This reconstruction, however, takes place against the backdrop (chapter 1) of a genealogical survey of the 'problem' of religion and ethics. The latter takes, as a point of departure, modernity's attempt to overcome particularity in the wake of a crisis of authority and the ensuing Reformation polemics and religious wars. In this first chapter I show how the effect of this attempt within ethics was to create something like an "Institution of Morality," with a distinctive mindset—the Moral Point of View—characterized by rational autonomy and universality. I shall locate the 'problem' of religion and ethics as a distinct problem of this mind-set. For, once rational autonomy and universality have been assumed to be the normative status of ethics, a problem is already created—namely, how to relate the local, particular, contingent, and timely aspects of one's existence to the universality and timelessness of the Moral Point of View. On this reading, the problem of religion and ethics represents a belated attempt by philosophers and theologians to find a 'place' for particularity within the universal standpoint of ethics.

This first chapter, which should be read as an extended introduction, is doubly significant for providing orientation to the book. In the first place, the very method of genealogical investigation invoked is meant to show that the 'problem' of religion and ethics is not the "perennial" problem we have been made to believe it is by liberal-minded philosophers who have treated it as pertaining to the "very nature of ethics." Instead, what this genealogical survey confirms is that the 'problem' of religion and ethics pertains to an ethics of a particular time and historical circumstances. As historical, there is nothing inevitable about this particular conception of ethics, and it can therefore be put aside.

Second, but more specifically, this first chapter is meant to already draw attention to the problematic assumptions within the Moral Point of View. It is on account of these shortcomings that Hauerwas suggests that this particular conception of ethics not only can be put aside but that it, in fact, *should* be overcome. I shall, in this introductory chapter, gather up the shortcomings of this conception of ethics around three key areas, namely: (i) an ahistorical (transcendental) conception of the self, (ii) a truncated (quandary) view of the moral life, and (iii) a foundational account of moral truth and objectivity. Hauerwas's conception of the moral life around the categories of moral character, vision, and narrative becomes compelling against this background, as an attempt to overcome these various shortcomings.

In chapter 2, against a transcendental conception of the self assumed within much of modern philosophical and theological ethical reflection, as well as within liberal political philosophy, Hauerwas's notion of moral character is developed as an argument for a historicist conception of the self. What this conception of the self as moral character will seek to show is that the self cannot stand outside the flow of historical contingency. Rather, the very nature and identity of the self is the result of, and inscribed within, particular narrative configurations of agency and affective investment.

In chapter 3, I explicate Hauerwas's attempt to reimage the moral life as a life of vision. This metaphor of vision is consciously borrowed by Hauerwas from Dame Murdoch to provide a critical response to the conception of ethics which revolves around quandaries and the notions of "choice" and "decision." Against this prioritization of "choice" and "decision" within Kantian ethics, Hauerwas proposes that we view the moral life not so much as a matter of making decisions and choices, but a life of vision, i.e., an ongoing attempt to see reality truthfully. Central to this conception of the moral life as a life of vision, and what I shall set out to develop at length in this chapter, is Hauerwas's claim that vision is a *learned* skill that is acquired through participation in the social-linguistic practices of a way of life.

Chapter 4 develops Hauerwas's notion of narrative as an alternative pattern of moral rationality to the Moral Point of View. A key objective of this chapter is to show the specific appeal and prospects of this notion of narrative by establishing its affinity with Aristotle's concept of *phronēsis*. What this affinity actually confirms is the nondisposable nature of moral reason, i.e., the realization that moral truth and objectivity is not the perspective of an impartial spectator, but that it is inseparable from the character of the agent as well as from the stories, roles, obligations, and activities that bind one's historical existence.

This argument for a historically constituted and socially embodied account of the moral life raises critical issues. Primary among these is the concern that a conception (Hauerwas's) of ethics around historical and particular traditions involves sectarianism. I will take up this critical challenge in the second part of the book, where three strands within this sectarian challenge—an epistemological, a sociological, and a political strand—are isolated. A separate chapter will be devoted to examining each of the these three strands of sectarianism.

In chapter 5, the *epistemological* strand of sectarianism will be identified with the challenge of relativism. In this chapter, therefore, the assumptions involved in the notion of relativism are examined with a view of showing how the very language of relativism is created by the ahistorical and foundational conception of truth, which the affirmation of narrative tradition is meant to call into question. Constructively, the chapter elaborates how the notions of truth and objectivity are recast and still rendered intelligible in the absence of any tradition-independent criteria.

The related challenges of fideism and of sectarianism (proper) are taken up in chapter 6. Critically, this chapter, too, argues that these charges arise out of an ahistorical conception of religious reason. This conception of religion is what will be explicated, following George Lindbeck as the experiential-expressivism model. A great part of the argument in this chapter, however, is meant to call into question the dominant *sociological* tradition—the Protestant Liberal Metanarrative—which polices this ahistorical conception of religion by declaring any alternative conception of religion "sectarian." The purpose of this critical argument is to put out of play the notions of "fideism" and of "sectarianism," so as to appreciate a more historical (Hauerwas's) conception of religion as a cultural-linguistic system.

In chapter 7, I examine the criticism that Hauerwas's position involves *political* irresponsibility. Hauerwas's affirmation of the Church as a distinctive and particular tradition, it is feared, does not take into account the complexity of modern pluralistic societies but instead encourages a withdrawal (by the members of that particular tradition) into a tribal ghetto. By way of a critical response to this challenge I shall show how this appeal to "pluralism" both underwrites a liberal conception of politics and implicitly declares the liberal social-political arrangement to be inevitable. However, there is nothing inevitable about this liberal arrangement. In fact, the critical aim of this chapter will be to show how the liberal social-political order is itself a historical arrangement which only attempts to conceal (nearly successfully) its own historicity, and the "local" interests it serves, under the guise of "neutrality" and "pluralism."

Constructively, the chapter elaborates an alternative and historical conception of politics as the "conversation" within a given tradition for the discovery and pursuit of a particular and contingent vision of the (common) good. What will particularly become clear in this chapter is how, in the absence of a tradition of traditions, *witness* becomes the overriding political category as various local traditions seek to outnarrate each other by the richness of social praxis and moral character which their respective stories of "in the beginning" engender.

The combined effect of both the constructive (Part I) and critical (Part II) argument of the book will be to confirm how particularity is a necessary feature of the moral life which, as such, simply cannot be transcended. If ethical reflection would begin by taking this fact into consideration, then indeed the traditional 'problem' of religion and ethics would not arise. Instead, moral philosophy would be able to offer a more adequate characterization of the moral life than what has so far been provided by the standard

(Kantian-inspired) accounts. However, the only way that moral philosophy would be able to do so is by taking seriously and by invoking, as Hauerwas does, a historical account of truth and objectivity, of religion, and of politics.

A word about style and methodology. This work is best characterized as an exercise in what Jeffrey Stout calls *bricolage*.[3] It involves creatively integrating many sources with the rich resource of Hauerwas's scholarship in an attempt to defend a historical conception of the moral life in general and of moral rationality in particular. Accordingly, those who look for faithful extensions of the projects of the many authors engaged within this work will be disappointed. This is even true in relation to the views of Stanley Hauerwas himself. I have not sought to focus on the systematic coherency of Hauerwas's "position," but have consciously opted for what might appear as an eclectic reading of Hauerwas's work. This methodology is, in great part, demanded by the very nature of Hauerwas's work. Firstly, Hauerwas himself consciously draws upon, and makes references to, a great many other authors. In order to clarify or spell out key implications within Hauerwas's work, it will therefore be necessary to draw attention to, explicate, or cite extensively from these other authors. In this connection, the major secondary literature engaged within this work falls into three broad categories. The first category includes authors like Aristotle, Wittgenstein, Murdoch, and MacIntyre, who have been key influences for Hauerwas all along and on whom Hauerwas has heavily relied in developing a specific notion. At various places in the book it will be necessary to directly engage these authors or extensively cite from them where, it is felt, this will make Hauerwas's argument conceptually or contrastively more lucid. Then there is another category of authors who more generally reflect the ongoing nature of Hauerwas's reflection. This group includes key names like Milbank, Lovibond, and Lindbeck, whose positions Hauerwas has claimed a certain affinity to. However, since at times Hauerwas only makes general reference to these authors, it may not always be immediately clear why and what exactly Hauerwas finds so compelling about these authors when he endorses their work as "providing the sort of theoretical framework that my own work presupposes."[4] It will, therefore, be necessary, particularly in the fifth and sixth chapters, to develop the positions of these authors as a way of providing a more explicit theoretical framework to Hauerwas's work. The third category of key secondary literature includes authors like Stout, De Certeau, and Dunne, whom I myself introduce. The relation between this latter group of authors and Hauerwas's work is meant to be collaborative. These authors are introduced, therefore, solely on pragmatic grounds be-

cause they provide a helpful background to or amplify the specific thesis of
the book.

A second significant observation that justifies our option for the *bricolage* methodology is that Hauerwas himself does not share the kind of
grand and systematic design that we have learned to expect from most
scholarly authors. In this respect, he clearly belongs to the tradition of what
Rorty calls "edifying" as opposed to "systematic" philosophy.[5] As edifying
philosophy, much of Hauerwas's writing is occasional and tentative, a fact
he readily admits, and to which the predominant essay genre of his writing
bears testimony. Even though his work contains what can be called a
"thick" theoretical moment, he does not set out to propose new doctrines
and theories or to defend a 'position', even though much of his writing sets
out to unsettle the dominant representations within academic theology and
philosophy. In this Hauerwas claims affinity with Wittgenstein. Nevertheless, just like Wittgenstein, Hauerwas's main preoccupation remains concrete: to offer suggestive indications by which a particular community—in
Hauerwas's case, the Church—can understand its way of life and its specific
challenges as it finds itself within the dominant culture of liberalism. Because of this edifying and practical intent, any attempt to synthesize Hauerwas's work into a coherent "position," may easily lead to gross misunderstanding. Therefore, I hope that the very methodology and style adopted in
this book will offer readers of Hauerwas's work a helpful guide for decipher-
ing his complex mode of ethical reflection, a mode which defies conventional disciplinary arrangements.

Something about the method employed in making references to the various sources: All references appear as notes at the end of the book. This, it is
hoped, will make the text more readable. References to Hauerwas's works
are not preceded by the author's name, but introduced directly by an abbre-
viation (in case of books) or by a short title (in case of individual articles).
References to works of all other authors are introduced by the name of the
author and a short title, followed by page references (where applicable). A
listing of all the works consulted is included at the end of the work, while a
list of all the abbreviations used is given at the beginning.

And finally, a note of acknowledgment for the various debts incurred in
the process of working on this book. As it stands, the book is a revision of
my doctoral dissertation "Particularity and Moral Rationality" submitted
to the Higher Institute of Philosophy of the University of Louvain (Belgium)
in November 1996. I am deeply grateful to Professor Frans De Wachter, who
supervised the writing of the dissertation. I am grateful to my friends Jeff

and Angie Goh, Irene Ssannyu, Len Chrobot, Jeff Bloechl, John Ries, and Elvira Roncalli for their comments on the initial drafts of the dissertation. The collaborative effort of all these friends has been more than incidental in bringing the text of this work to a readable quality. My stay and research at the University of Louvain was made possible by a scholarship from the Inter-Faculty Council for Development Cooperation of the Katholieke Universitet Leuven, as well as by the financial support of my friends Mark De Wulf, Chester and Roberta Blais. To them I am most grateful. I am deeply grateful to Professor Stanley Hauerwas, whose continued interest in my work still amazes me. I thank him for his great assistance, and encouragement in the course of my research. This assistance, as well his willingness to write a Foreword to this volume, has indeed bound me in his "good company." I am similarly grateful to Professor Johan Verstraeten for his keen interest in the work, as well as for his friendship. And lastly, Jim Langford, Jeffrey Gainey, and Ann Rice at the Notre Dame Press have not only been kind enough to undertake to publish this work, they have rendered such competent and invaluable editorial assistance that I did not have to be bothered by the geographical distance that separates us. To them and to all their staff at the Notre Dame Press, I am more than grateful.

MASAKA (UGANDA)
FEBRUARY 1998

Beyond Universal Reason

I

Ethics and the Impossible Flight from Moral Particularity

1

Flight from Particularity:
Toward a Genealogy of the 'Problem'
of the Relation between Religion and Ethics

> All philosophers suffer from the same defect, in that they start with present-day man and think they can arrive at their goal by analysing him. Instinctively they let "man" hover before them as an *aeterna veritas*, something unchanging in all turmoil, a secure measure of things. But everything the philosopher asserts about man is basically no more than a statement about man within a very *limited* time span. A lack of historical sense is the congenital defect of all philosophers.
>
> Nietzsche, *Human, All Too Human*, 14

Jeffrey Stout is certainly right when he claims that every bit of knowledge is an act of historical understanding. That it is largely a matter of constructing narratives that locate one's topic meaningfully in a particular setting. This realization, however, seems to be at odds with the dominant self-understanding of academic philosophy. The latter has often taken, as its mission, the inquiry into eternal essences and/or universal conditions-of-possibility. This is one reason academic philosophy has more readily appealed to analytical tools and/or transcendental methods of investigation in its attempt to understand one or the other of its topics. But as long as philosophy has succumbed to this temptation—what according to Nietzsche in the epigraph above is the "congenital defect of all philosophers"—it has bestowed a certain timelessness and universality on philosophical problems and their sought-after solutions. This is what tends to give philosophical problems an aura of exaggerated importance and inevitability. Every serious-minded philosopher, it is assumed, must somehow address himself/ herself to them.

The problem of the relation between religion and ethics seems accordingly to have become such an *aeterna veritas*, which, it has often been assumed, belongs to the nature of ethics as such, or to "the very logic of moral discourse." Our goal in this chapter is to undermine this assumption by

showing how much of what we have been told about this 'inevitable problem' actually applies to a very limited period within a particular (local) history. In fact, one cannot understand the 'problem' of religion and ethics
without giving an account of how, in the first place, we came to talk of religion and ethics as distinct spheres. This by itself calls for a genealogical survey. This chapter attempts at reconstructing such a genealogy. The narrative develops in three sections.

In the first section, the 'problem' of religion and ethics is narrated, following Jeffrey Stout, as the outcome of the shifting relationship between
theism and culture within European history. Here the issue is decisively political. The section recounts how, in the wake of the Reformation, Christianity ceased to provide a vocabulary in terms of which matters of public
importance could be debated and decided by European Christians of different persuasions without resort to violence. It was this impasse which led to
the secularization of a substantial part of public discourse, which in turn al-
tered the relationships between Christianity and European culture, providing a space to new (liberal) political legitimation, and giving rise to the differentiation of morality as a relatively autonomous cultural domain.

In the second section, the 'problem' of religion and ethics is narrated as
the story of the quest for moral autonomy, understood as a certain "emancipatory freedom" from all traditional influence, and in particular the influence of Christianity. Our aim in this section will be to show that it is this
view of autonomy which is responsible for the "anthropological turn"
within the field of moral conduct. For, once autonomy has been achieved or
presumed, one is faced with a challenge, namely, to determine whether, and
how, God or Christianity still matters morally. This challenge is the preoccupation of contemporary theological and philosophical approaches in
their discussion of the 'problem' of religion and ethics.

The third section deals with the problem of religion and ethics as it results from an attempt by moral reason to transcend history by purifying
thought of historical contingency. In this section, we shall trace the emergence of this distinctively modern view of moral rationality to Kant's attempt at a philosophical justification of morality. The result of Kant's
philosophical attempt, however, was to establish something like an "institution of morality," which is characterized, both in its view of the moral
self and in its account of moral reason, by a certain flight from particularity.
The 'problem' of religion and ethics is at home within this conception of
moral reason. For when one begins by assuming that there is something
like an "institution of morality," then one has already created a problem of

how such an "institution" is or is not related to other "nonmoral" convictions (e.g., religion) that form one's life.

These three sections do not develop three separate stories, but different strands of the same narrative. This narrative has as its aim to trace the problem of religion and ethics in its various manifestations within the social, political, and philosophical spheres. The narrative is therefore unified by a single historical theme: Various events in sixteenth- to seventeenth-century Europe—the secularization of a substantial part of public discourse as well as the birth of secular political entities (nation-states) following Reformation polemics; the struggle for autonomy against traditional and ecclesiastical structures that had become repressive; as well as the philosophical attempt to provide a form of ethical justification that would not appeal to any concrete convictions and practices—all combine to loosen morality's connection not only with religion but with the language of "fact" and contingency in general.

Our isolation of these factors and events is meant neither to offer, nor does it lay claim to, any comprehensive *historical* reconstruction of events within sixteenth- to seventeenth-century European history. Our goal is primarily *philosophical.* In attempting a genealogy of the 'problem' of religion and ethics we seek to show its narratability, i.e., that it is a *historical* problem, and not the *perennial* problem that has "been a matter of controversy amongst philosophers and theologians from the earliest times." Thus, this historical placement is meant to have the strategic effect of showing that the 'problem' is not philosophically inevitable and can thus be overcome. Positively, such a relief is meant to free the imagination so as to begin to see the possibility of understanding and doing ethics in such a way that the question does not arise. It is hoped, therefore, that this genealogical survey will provide a useful background for appreciating why Hauerwas does not "waste time" with the problem of religion and ethics. Instead, he questions the foundational assumptions within the standard accounts of ethics, which assume the problem to be inevitable. The chapter ends with a short discussion of Hauerwas's critical appraisal of those standard accounts and an outline of his constructive revision of ethics.

1. The Birth of Liberal Politics: Christianity 'Placed' by Secular Reason

In a moving and highly significant study, Jeffrey Stout has shown how the history of Christian thought in the modern world takes its point of departure in the late sixteenth to early seventeenth century's *crisis of authority.*[1]

Prior to the introduction of statistical and evidential criteria for assessing a proposition's truth, Stout argues, probability essentially consisted of approval by authority, whether in the form of appeal to the right persons or the right books. However, "as competing authorities multiplied and began to diverge more and more sharply, conventional means for resolving disputes arising from such competition became less and less effective. Where probability is a matter of what the authorities approve, and the authorities no longer speak with one voice, it becomes anything but clear which opinions one should accept."[2]

This "problem of many authorities" was, according to Stout, the central social and intellectual difficulty of the Reformation. Not only would the Reformation reveal that the ecclesiastical tradition had become deeply fractured, the inability by Christians of different persuasions to agree on any authoritative text, conciliar ruling, or papal decree caused a special challenge to the possibility of cooperation. This lack of agreement would, moreover, be exacerbated when these differences turned into polemical and eventually violent confrontations within the furor of the religious wars.

As Stout's work shows, already during Luther's confrontation with the official Church (Wittenberg 1517–Worms 1521), it became increasingly difficult for him to give positive support to his conclusions by citing earlier papal decrees and conciliar rulings, since there were obviously other decrees and rulings that could be cited against his position. Such a frustration would reveal not only an internal lack of coherence within the authority of the Church, but also the need for hermeneutically independent criteria to decide on the probability of the authorities themselves. In fact, even Luther's strategy of contraction—narrowing down the number of authorities he would recognize to *sola scriptura,* and thus relegating Christian tradition to the realm of *mere* opinion—ended up by producing the contrary effect: "Who is right about Scripture: Luther, Calvin, Zwingli, or someone else? The Protestant appeal to the individual conscience and inner persuasion in effect produces yet another version of the problem of many authorities. But now we have far more authorities than before, for *every* man recognizes his own inner light. Every conscience constitutes separate authority."[3]

The most important moment in the Catholic response to this Reformation challenge was to come at the Council of Trent (1545–63), which reasserted the Church's power through definition of dogma and condemnation of the Reformation heresy. However, instead of helping matters cool, even this Catholic response would have the contrary effect. The intellectual standoff between Protestants and Catholics was soon to be played out

at another level. For over a hundred years, beginning roughly at the end of
the last session of the Council of Trent and continuing throughout most of
the seventeenth century, Europe found itself embroiled in religious wars.

A way out of the above impasse in terms of cooperation and peaceful coexistence was to grant, gradually, an important measure of autonomy to the
political—hence an autonomy specifically *from* religious authority. Quoting Skinner, Stout notes,

> The sixteenth-century reformers were entirely at one with their Catholic
> adversaries on this point: they all insisted that one of the main aims of
> government must be to maintain "true religion" and the Church of
> Christ. As we have seen, this in turn means that the religious upheavals
> of the Reformation made a paradoxical yet vital contribution to the crys-
> tallising of the modern, secularised concept of the State. For as soon as
> the protagonists of the rival creeds showed that they were willing to fight
> each other to death, it began to seem obvious to a number of *politique*
> theorists that, if there were to be any prospect of achieving civic peace,
> the powers of the State would have to be divorced from the duty to up-
> hold any particular faith.[4]

The birth of the nation-state as the key political actor within modern
history has been the object of many studies.[5] It is, therefore, not necessary
to rehearse the findings of these studies. However, we have drawn attention
to Stout's extraordinary and lucid reconstruction of its origins in order to
highlight the shifting relationship between Christianity and European culture. First, the emergence of a new political legitimation amounted to a
transition from a theological frame of reference to a secular one. A secular
"state policy" emerges to fill the social space that had been created by seg-
mented religious formations within the Reformation polemics. While the
Church formerly provided a "uniqueness" of frame of reference, the *local-
ized* churches, now divided among and within themselves, became signs of
contingent, local, and partial determinations, and thus incapable of providing the needed reference for the integration of social life. It is within this social space that state power is born, to take the place of religion in providing
the frame of reference for a society.

What is uniquely modern about this "displacement" is that unlike its
predecessor, which appealed to a notion of the good society and human
functioning sustained by a theological framework, the newly born state
power will now seek to order laws of behavior relieved of criteria and
frames of reference. In as much as the criteria and frames of reference are
hitherto tied up with a religious metaphysics and sociology (ecclesiology),

this "loss" in the frames of reference would indeed come as a relief to the warring religious factions. For, as Stout points out, "any point of view in which religious consideration or conceptions of the good remained dominant was, in the early modern context, incapable of providing a basis for the reasonable and peaceful resolution of social conflict."[6]

Something else is uniquely modern about this "displacement." Rather than just shed those theological frames of reference that had become contentious, or substitute them with less contentious frames, the new state power would seek to organize political activity without any frames of reference at all. The new politics would strive for a total loss in the frames of reference and seek to provide a merely procedural framework for the pursuit of individual conceptions of the good, but with no overriding social good. Herein lies the "liberalism" of the new politics.

Secondly, the displacement of theological frames of reference would at the same time affect the very conception of Christian faith and of the Church to the point where Christianity found itself inscribed within a secular economy—an order which it no longer had the power to direct but whose protection it took to be its religious and moral duty. As Michel De Certeau nicely portrays, the displacement would involve the framing of the very category of 'religion.'[7] Even though, according to De Certeau, other factors, like the discovery of other religions in the New World, in Africa, and in Asia were increasingly making the subject of religion an object of study of an enlightened anthropology, the fact that Christianity itself came to be regarded as a 'religion' meant that it had ceased to be for its subjects that which allowed them to think and behave—a living tradition—and was now perceived from the outside as "socioeconomic positivity bound to a body of abstract hypotheses."[8]

A significant development within this trajectory is the internalization or privatization involved in reducing the essence of religion to 'belief' and 'conviction'. The social integrative reality that Christianity had been, is now

> changed into a fact of "belief"; it is a "conviction" (that is, an opinion combined with a passion), or a "superstition"; in sum the *object* of an analysis built over autonomous criteria. In other words, ethics plays the role formerly allocated to theology. A 'science of mores' hereafter *judges* religious ideology and its effects, at the very point where a "science of faith" used to classify conduct under a subsection entitled "moral theology", which ranked behavior according to the codes of doctrine. There are many signs of the evolution: the epistemological primacy of ethics in

reflections on society; the appraising of religion according to "values" no
longer its own (the common good, the demands of conscience, progress,
etc.); the withdrawal of religion to "religious practices" or its alignment
with categories imposed by society; the marginalization of worship in respect to civil or moral law, and so forth.[9]

It has been necessary to cite at length from De Certeau's descriptive
analysis in order to note the shifting relationship between Christianity and
European culture, both in ordinary life and in academic settings. As faith
and theology are gradually 'privatized' and pushed from the center, state
power becomes more central and a "science of mores" emerges as an autonomous sphere within the university curriculum. In fact, when both De
Certeau and Stout refer to the newly carved out "science of mores" as autonomous, it is immediately clear that it is autonomous specifically *from*
religious authority and from religious conceptions of the good which had
rendered the attainment of rational agreement on a whole range of issues
impossible.[10] As Stout notes in a later work: "Early modern ethical theorists disagreed rather little about cannibalism, bestiality, and the like, but
as religious discord grew they found it necessary to devise a language in
which highly contentious social and cosmological categories and assumptions would no longer be presupposed."[11]

In this connection, the autonomy in question is defined specifically *in
view of* peaceful coexistence and cooperation, which had been rendered the
paramount social and political issue by the religious rivalries and conflicts.
"It is not surprising," writes Stout, "that modern ethical theorists tend to
view morality itself as an institution whose primary function is to resolve
something called 'the problem of cooperation' for the intuitions on which
such theorists depend were largely put in place by circumstances that made
cooperation seem more important than other values for which one could
strive."[12] This concern for cooperation should, in fact, draw our attention
to the fact that the autonomous Moral Point of View emerges together
with, and is at home in, a liberal political order. Between the two of them,
they manage the "problem of cooperation" set by the crisis of authority.
Nowhere is this alliance made more explicit than in Rawls, who, according
to Stout, is "the most prominent contemporary theorist of the Moral Point
of View." Commenting on Rawls's *A Theory of Justice*, Stout notes that, "it
is the priority of the problem of cooperation that leads toward a liberal theory of social life in which 'justice as fairness' plays the central role and in
which the concept of 'rights' is more basic than that of 'good.'"[13]

A most telling feature of the shifting relationship between Christianity and the new politics, which was already hinted at in an earlier citation from De Certeau, is the "politicization of [religious] conduct." By "politicization" De Certeau means that, within the new autonomous moral-political sphere, not only will the ascription 'religious' become narrowly confined to a specific domain of what comes to pass as "religious practices," but more remarkably, political institutions now begin to "*use* religious institutions, infusing them with their own criteria, dominating them with their protection, aiming them toward their goals."[14] "Politicization" thus points to the discovery by the new politics, confirmed by the new anthropology, of the *usefulness* of religious convictions, beliefs, or practices. Montesquieu's remark, "All religions contain principles useful to society," is representative of this general sentiment. And, long before Kant, Lord Herbert of Cherbury had proposed "virtue as the essence of worship."[15]

Even without anticipating the discussion in the coming section, it is interesting to point out how modern philosophers (and theologians) in discussing the problem of the relation between religion and ethics are, in effect, inquiring about the *relevance* or *usefulness* (if any) of one's religious convictions to the moral task. The fact that this assumption is shared by theologians no less than philosophers is an indication that the "politicization of religious conduct" does not happen solely as an 'external' domination of religious institutions by hostile moral-political goals. There is as well an inner transformation on the part of Christian self-understanding. Having lost the Constantinian political monopoly, religious beliefs and institutions themselves begin to 'work' differently and thus betray another kind of dynamic based upon another system, an order which they no longer have the power of directing, but whose protection they now take to be their moral and religious duty. The contemporary expression of this inner transformation is manifest in theology's often apologetic quest for "relevance" by uncritically underwriting the *humanum*, whether in the form of social and political strategies for peace and justice, or a personal quest for meaning or happiness.

This situation no doubt creates a special irony for many Western democracies, since the latter, while requiring a disavowal of the public role for religious convictions, nevertheless requires either a "civil religion" or the Church to underwrite and support the social and political order. This awkward situation of Christianity within modern (particularly Western) democracies—what Lindbeck has called a position of "having once been culturally established but not yet clearly disestablished"[16]—is particularly apparent in what De Certeau calls the "formality of practices" of liberal politics.[17] The expression is meant to show how not only the liberal social order is born from a religious matrix, but that modern practice continues to be patterned greatly along the lines of "formalities" which were at home within a theological framework. With the new liberal politics, the "formalities" of old practices and institutions—e.g., family, medicine, government, economics, etc.—are left in place, but are now "infused" with a new logic. This is one clear reason why modern practice is, in many instances, just a secularized version of formerly Christian manifestations: The state replaces the Church as the social mediation of common 'salvation', subjectivity and conscience (as moral instinct) replace Christian spirituality and pietism, and "progress [of reason] as a form of theology replaces Christian eschatological messianism."[18]

The upshot of the story we have reconstructed so far is to affirm the particular and historically contingent origins of the liberal social-political order. Thus, any attempt, as by positivist social theory, to present the liberal social arrangement as the culmination of universal history cannot but look both vacuous and misleading. John Milbank is thus right when he dismisses what has come to be recognized as the standard "secularization thesis" as just a spurious attempt to universalize a particular history. According to this thesis, society—any society— "evolves through a process of gradual differentiation into separate social sub-systems: . . . art is distinguished from religion, religion from politics, economics from private ethical behaviour and so forth." Social organization reaches a climax only when the "boundaries between these sub-systems are inviolable."[19]

Milbank's critical assessment of the sociological tradition will provide a handy foil for Hauerwas's argument in favor of a more substantive conception of 'religion'. We shall, therefore, return to it (chapter 6). For now, we have been keen to locate the rise of the 'problem' between religion and ethics within the new political formations of early seventeenth-century Europe, within which Christianity was privatized, while society was reconstituted along a nonteleological and autonomous order of reason which was applied *etsi Deus non daretur*. However, the displacement that brought Christianity to be inscribed within this civil economy—or, to use an expression that has become popular since Milbank, to be 'placed' by secular reason—is only one part of the story of the 'problem' between religion and ethics. Another (crucial) aspect of this story is the quest for moral autonomy, understood as a certain "emancipatory freedom" from all traditional influence in general and from the influence of theology, in particular. This quest for autonomy was to issue into something like an "anthropological turn" in the field of conduct, which, once established, could not but give rise to the question of whether God (or religion) still mattered morally.

2. The Quest for Moral Autonomy: Does Religion Matter Morally?

The question "Does Religion Matter Morally?" has recently been the topic of a symposium by the Interdisciplinary Centre for the Study of Science, Society, and Religion of the Vrije Universiteit in Amsterdam. The very title and subtitle of the publication following the symposium,[20] suggests that in attempting a "critical reappraisal of the thesis of morality's independence from religion," the symposium was here tackling one of the perennial problems of philosophy. We do not wish to examine the specific contributions of this symposium, although we shall, in the course of the work, make reference to one or another of the articles in this collection. Our aim in this section is to show that the importance of the question, "Does Religion (God) Matter Morally?" can only be understood historically. Contemporary theological and philosophical approaches to the question are, therefore, guilty of bad faith when, in complete disregard of historical awareness, they seek to *eternalize* the question. Constructively, we shall seek to show that the question "Does Religion (God) Matter Morally?" only becomes intelligible after the modern "anthropological turn."[21] Within the field of morality, this anthropological turn is historically associated with what the theologian Walter Kasper has called an "emancipatory view of autonomy."[22]

This modern—emancipatory—concept of autonomy must be viewed primarily as an act of self-assertion against a theocentric and ecclesiastical tradition which had meanwhile become oppressive. Different factors and events—e.g., the Renaissance of classical humanism, and especially the reversion to the Stoic doctrine of natural law, the Church's alliance with the *ancien régime* (particularly in France), its dispute with the newly developing natural sciences, its authoritarian and reactionary insistence on a world-picture that had meanwhile been superseded—all contrive to lead to an aggressively antichurch form of autonomy.

However, this part of the story, too, has its point of departure in the early seventeenth-century crisis of authority. For example, in his stand against the papacy, Luther had not only relegated Christian tradition to mere opinion, thus undependable in matters as important as faith, but had also shown that the Church, and to a less extent God, was dispensable in deciding important matters. Luther's act of self-assertion at the Diet of Worms, "Here I Stand," already betrays the autonomy and self-sufficiency of the individual characteristic of the anthropological turn within modernity. In Luther, however, this act of self-assertion is still founded on God's authority, confirmed by Luther's appeal to Scripture. However, this connection between God and the individual's act of self-assertion (autonomy) would, within the Enlightenment tradition, become less and less obvious, giving rise to the 'problem' of justifying whether and how God or religion still matter within a life defined increasingly by autonomous self-determination.

Moral Theology in the Wake of the Anthropological Turn

When contemporary moral theologians seek to address the question of whether God matters morally, they do so by inquiring into the distinctiveness of Christian ethics.[23] On the whole, however, this debate has been uninspiring, owing to the fact that, having assumed an autonomous starting point, most contributors see their challenge as one of simply discovering the "contribution" or "relevance" of Christian convictions to an otherwise autonomous morality.[24] Timothy O'Connell best exemplifies this dominant assumption of an autonomous morality within contemporary Catholic moral theology when he writes:

> the fundamental ethical command imposed on the Christian is precisely to be what he or she is. "Be human." That is what God asks of us, no more and no less. Imitate Christ, and do this by seeking to be faithful to the human vocation as he was. . . . Christian ethics is human ethics, no more and no less. . . . Thus in a certain sense, moral theology is not theology at all. It is moral philosophy, pursued by persons who are believers.[25]

Once the *humanum* has been accepted as an autonomous starting point, O'Connell's conclusion should not be surprising. In fact, it is typical. Richard McCormick comes to the same conclusion. Christian ethics, McCormick writes, "does not and cannot add to human ethical self-understanding as such any material content that is, in principle, strange or foreign to man as he exists and experiences himself."[26] However, if it is the case that Christianity cannot "add to human self-understanding," then one is inevitably faced with the challenge of justifying whether, and how, Christianity or even God can be said to matter morally.

The attempt at showing that Christianity is still morally relevant has often consisted in a combination of strategies. One obvious strategy has been to minimize the historical particularity of the Incarnation and regard it, rather, as an ontological affirmation and validation of the humanum.[27] It is this strategy that often leads theologians to talk less and less of the historical person of Jesus and more of the "Christ-event," which is meant to provide a theological status to the humanum. However, even when the historical life of Jesus is invoked, it is to show that in his life and mission, Jesus "experienced what it is to be *human* in the fullest way and at the deepest level."[28] In any case, his moral significance lies in having provided an example of what it means to live *humanly*, i.e., "a radical concretization of what we are called for as men."[29] Accordingly, the Church and Christian practices are accorded a "parenetic and maieutic" task—the double task of affirmation and explication of the most demanding *human* values and norms.[30]

It is clear, then, that these attempts to make theology relevant do not advance beyond the Cartesian or Kantian 'solutions' to the theological problem. Descartes needed the idea of God to underwrite the *cogito*'s search for certainty.[31] Kant needed it to ensure harmony and happiness within the kingdom of ends.[32] However, what is notable about Descartes's and Kant's 'solutions' is that they are belated attempts to account for God, but which, in effect, are ways of invoking God to underwrite the already assumed autonomous positions. Similarly, one wonders whether liberal theology's appeal to the "Christ-event," and to the "parenetic and maieutic" role of faith is not just another sophisticated way of invoking Christianity to underwrite the human (autonomous) search for happiness or love, for political strategies in search of peace and justice, for democratic and/or economic transformation, or for liberation and freedom.[33]

The problem with such "anthropologizing" of Christianity, however, is that it tends to confirm Feuerbach's claim that religion is the projection of mankind's hopes.[34] Moreover, as Hauerwas points out, one fails to see how a Christianity whose primary task is to provide an "affirmation and explication of human values" can ever be anticultural, since, in an attempt to remain "relevant," it usually ends up by underwriting the prevailing humanism in the name of "human values."[35] What is already excluded within this theological self-understanding is the possibility of theology itself offering an alternative reading of the nature and content of "human values." But to the extent that theology fails to offer this alternative vision or conversation, it unwittingly announces its terminal existence. Within modernity, the attempts (in Descartes and Kant) to make Christianity "relevant" finally came to grief in Feuerbach's diagnosis of religion as mere human projection—a conclusion Nietzsche was soon to exploit as confirming the "death of God."[36] Contemporary moral theology in its eagerness to make

Christianity "relevant" by showing that talk about God has always really been talk about being human, risks coming to the same dialectical result. Moreover, as Hauerwas has again noted, to the extent these strategies are successful, the more theology makes itself redundant: "For if what is said theologically is but a confirmation of what we can know on other grounds or can be said more clearly in a non-theological language, then why bother saying it theologically at all?"[37]

Philosophy and the Thesis of "Logical Independency"

Within philosophy, the discussion concerning religion's relation to ethics has been limited almost exclusively to philosophers within the analytic tradition.[38] When these analytic philosophers address the issue of morality's relation to religion, they make much of something called the '*logical* autonomy' of moral discourse. However, the reasons why the discussions have been limited to analytic philosophy and why the question of whether God matters morally has, within analytic philosophy, turned into one of examining "logical" relations between moral terms are closely related. They have to do with the very story of modern philosophy as a foundational quest for certainty that runs from Descartes through Kant and ends with analytical philosophy as a "successor subject" to philosophy.[39] It is this foundational drive within modernity—what Richard Rorty calls the epistemological turn—which puts epistemology at the center of the philosophical enterprise and frames "epistemic justification" as the primary goal of inquiry. Thus, by the time we meet the question of the relation between religion and ethics within metaethics it has already taken on this concern for epistemic justification:

> It is this talk of justification that makes talk of *logical* dependence seem the "natural" way to phrase questions about the relation between religion and morality. . . . a successful justification of moral knowledge would first establish a firm foundation of some kind and then show how ethical judgments can be connected logically to that.[40]

Within analytic philosophy, discovering the absence or presence of these "necessary connections" has been taken to be an aspect of linguistic analysis, namely, examining the logical relation between the various concepts.[41] It is this quest for "necessary connections" (that would link moral conclusions to an objectively factual [religious] base or foundation) which explains why the discussion of ethics' logical relation to religion has only managed to produce a theological version of the "is-ought" problem. Listen for example, to Bartley introducing the problem:

> The logical relationship between morality and religion has been a matter of controversy amongst philosophers and theologians from the earliest times and it continues to be a subject of lively debate. The 'is-ought problem', as it is called, becomes particularly acute in the present connection. How are religious beliefs about what God's will is logically related to moral judgements as to what men ought to do? Or is the *ought* groundless apart from the *is?*[42]

Framing the issue in terms of an "is-ought" problem partly explains why the debate concerning ethics' relation to religion has, to a great extent, been philosophically disappointing. In the first place, as typical of discussions in analytic philosophy, the topic often ends up suffering the death of a thousand qualifications through a "self-consuming" methodological and conceptual preoccupation.[43] Secondly, the framing of the problem in terms of "is-ought" cannot but legitimate bias in the very framing of the debate. It is, therefore, unsurprising that most contributions to the debate begin by assuming the "thesis of logical independency" to avoid committing the naturalistic or, in this case, "supernaturalistic fallacy."

What is perhaps the most disappointing feature of the debate is that the analytic philosophers' way of talking about "logical (in)dependency" or "necessary connections" is characterized by something like what Quentin Bell has called "bad art,"[44] in its tendency to obscure rather than reveal what is really at stake. For example, in a highly influential and widely discussed 1973 essay,[45] William Frankena announced that the thesis of morality's dependency on religion "is both vague and ambiguous."[46] Frankena proposed to initiate a refinement of reflection by "discussing with some care" one of the thesis's many forms—"the claim that morality is *logically* dependent on religion." It soon becomes clear, however, that Frankena's real aim is to undermine the thesis of logical dependency. And so, he argues that religious or theological premises are neither *necessary* nor *sufficient* to justify logically some or all ethical principles: "In fact, I believe, we would not and should not think that our ethical beliefs were justified by being shown to rest on and follow from certain religious or theological beliefs, unless we thought that these were themselves in some way rationally justifiable."[47]

All of these indications seem to give an impression that the problem of ethics' relation to religion is really one of sorting out the logical relations between the concepts of "religion" and "morality." However, it is only when one takes a closer look at Frankena's paper that one begins to see that Frankena's motives for rejecting the thesis of morality's *logical* dependence on religion are considerations other than the *logical* relations between concepts. For example, at the very start of his essay he notes:

> If morality is dependent on religion, then we cannot hope to solve our problems, or resolve the differences of opinion about them, unless and in so far as we can achieve agreement and certainty in religion (not a lively hope); but if it is not entirely dependent on religion, then we can expect to solve at least some of them by the use of empirical and historical inquiries of a publicly available and testable kind.[48]

Such an announcement at the start of Frankena's paper turns out to be a clear indication that all Frankena's talk about "necessary connections," "logical (in)dependency," "sufficient justification," etc., is really not about conceptual analysis and the *logical* relation between concepts, but that these are, in fact, a sophisticated (and misleading?) way of talking about "one of the central issues in our cultural crisis." This central issue is the historical problem we identified, of establishing peaceful cooperation in the wake of the crisis of authority and the ensuing interreligious controversies. Frankena betrays his concern for this central problem when he wonders whether "there is anything to be gained by insisting that all ethical beliefs are or must be logically grounded on religious beliefs. For to insist on this is to introduce into the foundations of any morality whatsoever all the difficulties in the adjudication of religious controversies, and to do so is hardly to encourage hope that mankind can reach, by peaceful and rational means, some desirable kind of agreement on moral and political principles."[49]

It therefore becomes abundantly clear that the decisive considerations for Frankena's rejection of the thesis of *logical* dependency are not logical but *historical*. These considerations go back to the Enlightenment hope that an agreement on moral and political principles could be reached by peaceful and rational means. As we already noted, it is precisely this assumption and hope which lay behind the framing of the autonomous Moral Point of View within the Enlightenment. Frankena not only assumes this same historical problem as the Enlightenment thinkers, he is, at bottom, dealing with the same challenge they had to face: If reason can discover universally valid moral principles and rational persons can agree on these normative matters, then does God matter morally? He does not advance beyond the classical (Kantian) solution when he admits:

I have not contended that morality is in no way dependent on religion for dynamics, motivation, inspiration, or vision. Nor have I contended that religion adds nothing to morality—it may add motivation, an additional obligation to do what is right, new duties, a new spirit in which to do them, a new dimension to already existing duties, or a sense of sin.[50]

We have taken time to examine Frankena's essay because it is a clear case of how the dominant (metaethical) philosophical approaches to the 'problem' of religion and ethics have been both uninspiring and unfruitful. The failure of these approaches to inspire any lasting insight is greatly due to the sophisticated attempts by which they conceal the *historical* problem by presenting the issue as one of inquiry into the "logical" dependency of moral terms. As Frankena's paper so acutely reveals, these approaches have either mostly ended with a restatement of the problem or with offering disguised versions of the Kantian solution. From this point of view, the dominant philosophical approaches have generated no genuine insights in the topic of whether, and how, religion (God) matters morally.

But what is fundamentally wrong with both the dominant theological and philosophical approaches to deserve their relegation to the margins of scholarly interest? Our contention is that both approaches are informed and infected by a deep lack of historical consciousness. For example, both approaches assume "autonomy" as an unquestionable starting point. In the dominant theological approaches this starting point is associated with an attempt to preserve the "institution of morality" or ethics *as such*, which, it is assumed, is realized independently of the specific convictions of a particular (e.g., Christian) existence. Within the dominant philosophical approach (metaethics), this starting point has been associated with something like "logical autonomy," presupposed as a timeless characteristic of moral discourse. Both approaches, by not examining the *historical* nature of this starting point but, instead, raising it to the level of a "timeless characteristic" of ethics (or moral discourse), succeed only in making a pseudo-problem out of what is, in fact, a genuine problem. While the pseudo-problem (e.g., logical dependency) may provide an academic forum to a very limited number of university "experts," it does not shed any light on "one of the central issues of our cultural crisis."

Instead, by bestowing a timelessness to the 'problem' of religion and ethics, both theological inquiry into the distinctiveness of Christian ethics and the metaethical preoccupation with the thesis of logical (in)dependency invite onto themselves Nietzsche's critical censure in the epigraph at the start of this chapter. In fact, Nietzsche's critique could be applied verbatim to these approaches, excepting, of course, that the topic of interest is no longer man as such but ethics: "They let 'ethics' hover before them as an *aeterna veritas*, something unchanging in all turmoil, a secure measure of things. But everything the philosopher asserts about ethics is basically no more than a statement about ethics within a *very limited* time span."[51]

The upshot of such ahistorical approaches by contemporary theology and philosophy is to already exclude, on *a priori* considerations, the possibility of overcoming a particular history. However, given the historical nature of any inquiry, particularly of the 'problem' of religion and ethics, it is difficult to see how any helpful inquiry into the question of whether God matters morally can start otherwise than by attending to those historical events, challenges, and solutions that gave significance to such a question in the first place. Only when these factors have been shown to be what they are, i.e., historical, can one begin to look for ways of overcoming the particular challenges that arise from them. At least then one allows for the possibility that there may be, indeed that there have been, other historical conditions which do (did) not allow such a question to arise at all. However, to begin ahistorically, as the dominant theological and philosophical approaches do, "by [just] asking what is the relation between theology and ethics is to have already made a mistake."[52] It is to have fallen into that "congenital defect" of academic philosophy that Nietzsche rightly worried about.

The critical realization that the 'problem' of religion and ethics involves a certain covering-up of history should draw our attention to the very ahistorical conception of moral rationality that informs the understanding of ethics within these approaches. Our contention is that the conception of moral rationality here is characterized by flight from particularity, as an attempt to purify thought of historical contingency. This is a distinctively modern view of moral reason, whose emergence can be traced to factors within the same European history we have been looking at. And so, in our third section, we need to focus specifically on that part of the story by which the conception of moral reason is transformed to the point of being characterized by a formal and universal perspective, as well as on the subsequent attempts by philosophers to find a place for particularity (religion) within this universal perspective.

3. Flight from Particularity: Religion outside the Boundaries of Reason

In the first section of this chapter, we noted how the problem of cooperation raised by interreligious rivalries gradually led to new political formations and to the differentiation of an autonomous sphere of conduct which was neither theological nor legal nor aesthetic. We also noted that one particular feature of the new political formations of this time is that they had to create this sphere of conduct, "relieved of the frames of reference," that is, without appealing to any conception of the good or human flourishing. While this 'solution' to suspend all appeals to (theological) conceptions of the good or human flourishing in debating matters of public interest might have provided a much-needed relief from the controversies surrounding these particular conceptions, it posed a major philosophical problem. It meant that the inherited moral content—the "formality of practices"—was now without any publicly shared rationale or justification. For it was by appealing to particular conceptions of the good and human flourishing within the by-now collapsed medieval *ethos* that the concepts of virtue and happiness were held together, giving an obvious point to the moral life. Suspending reference to a teleological framework in general, and to any definite conception of the good in particular, would leave a moral content whose relationship to the present state of the individual was not quite clear. The question of a recent title, 'Why Be Moral?'[53] had not only become meaningful, but was also one to which an answer had to be given. It is against this background that the project of an independent justification of morality became not merely the concern of individual thinkers but central to seventeenth-century European culture.[54] It was to this challenge that Kant responded with a rational justification of morality which would, in effect, create something like an "institution of morality" with a distinctive mind-set. Our interest in this development should be obvious. As an academic topic, the 'problem' of religion and ethics is at home in this "institution of morality." We therefore need to examine two aspects of Kant's attempt at a rational justification of morality to see how and why it gives rise to the 'problem' of religion and ethics.

Aspects of Kant's Rational Foundation of Morality

Kant's rational justification of morality involves grounding morality within the universal prescriptions of a *pure* practical reason, which effectively made the rational *individual* at once the autonomous and rational basis of morality. What must be underscored, however, is the type of individual the Kantian moral self is. Morality has always had strong links to the individual, and this is true even within the medieval-theistic tradition. However, as MacIntyre helpfully points out, in the previous traditions to be an individual and, thus, to be a moral self was "to fill a set of roles each of which has its own point and purpose: member of a family, citizen, soldier, philosopher, servant of God."[55]The Kantian *individual*, however, is a moral agent to the extent that he or she is able to abstract from any such thick descriptions. In the second *Critique*, Kant effectively denies the contingent factors of an individual's existence (inclinations, self-interest, prudential considerations) a place within the Moral Point of View. Any introduction of such considerations would, according to Kant, compromise the purity of reason and the autonomy of the will. Kant's central model, to ensure the purity of the Moral Point of View, involves his famous distinction between noumenal and phenomenal selfhood:

> Since it is as noumenal agents that we are capable of rational willing, and it is of our phenomenal character that the particularities of our spatio-temporal character can be predicated, we abstract in our role as rational agents from everything that differentiates one of us from another in the field of appearance.[56]

The story we have told up till now makes it clear why Kant would identify the Moral Point of View with the noumenal self. Any appeal to the contingent commitments of the self had been complicated by both the loss of a teleological framework and by the feuds and violence issuing out of any such attachments, especially in as far as these were associated with religious affiliations. Thus, in the interest of securing cooperation, Kant was willing to render "everything that differentiates one of us from another in the field of appearance" morally irrelevant. Once these differences had been 'bracketed', Kant assumed, moral argument and agreement would be possible on the basis of reason alone.

Nevertheless, such a flight from the phenomenal world did pose one problem. To leave behind all contingent commitments and engagements, such as being a father, a mother, a soldier or a student, etc., would be to leave behind any interesting reasons for acting one way or the other. There would be no reason for the autonomous rational will (noumenal self) to be moral at all. Kant seems to have been clearly aware of this problem and so tried to "save" the moral project by construing morality as part of the transcendental structure of the noumenal self. The rational autonomous will, he suggested, is committed to the rules of morality for no other reason except that these are such as any rational self would legislate for oneself.

Within Kant's formulations, therefore, not only must the Moral Point of View abstract from any concrete commitments and engagements, the noumenal self is without any history. In a remark concerning the rational origins of evil action, Kant notes that every such action must be regarded as though the individual had fallen into it directly from a state of innocence. For whatever his previous deportment may have been, whatever natural causes may have been influencing him, and whether these causes were to be found within him or outside him, his action is yet free and determined by none of these causes; hence it can and must always be judged as an *original* use of his will . . . Hence we cannot inquire into the temporal origins of this deed, but solely into its rational origin, if we are thereby to determine and, wherever possible, to elucidate the propensity, if it exists, *i.e.,* the general subjective ground of the adoption of transgression into our maxim.[57]

Although in the above citation Kant is specifically talking about the origins of moral evil, the description of the Good Will in the *Groundwork* assumes the same atomistic moral psychology.[58] No doubt for Kant this insistence on "an original use of [one's] will" was in view of advancing the autonomy of the will and thus moral responsibility. However, such a conception not only misleadingly assumes absolute freedom to be a condition for moral responsibility, it has been responsible for underwriting an occasionalistic conception of the moral life, with the correlative understanding of the moral self that is passive and atomistic. In the coming chapter, we shall note the extent to which this Kantian moral self—a self that is able to stand outside the flow of contingency and history—is largely still with us today and how it has been a great inspiration for liberal ethical, theological, and political reflection.

However, in order to see the full effect that Kant's conception of the moral self, as well as his overall project of providing a rational (autonomous) justification for morality, would have in giving rise to a new conception of moral reason, one would need to compare the role reason played within both the modern and the predecessor tradition. Within the medieval tradition, the presence of a teleological framework in general, and the appeal to particular conceptions of the good and human flourishing in particular, would render a certain logical and holistic background for assessing the epistemic validity of particular moral claims. Again as MacIntyre has pointed out, within this holistic teleological framework, to call a particular action just or right was to say that is what a good man would do in a particular situation. This means that within such a teleological framework, moral statements are at the same time factual statements, and can therefore "be called true or false in precisely the way in which all other factual statements can be so called."[59] What this means is that according to the medieval-theistic-teleological framework, moral judgements could be at once hypothetical and categorical in form. They were hypothetical insofar as they expressed a judgment as to what conduct would be teleologically appropriate for a human being. They were categorical in as far as they reported the particular contexts of the universal law commanded by God. Whatever their form, they were informed by particular convictions concerning the *telos* of man which had to be realized according to defined canons within a particular social setting.

The collapse of this *ethos* in general, and the loss of a teleological framework in particular, meant that moral judgments could no longer be hypothetical for Kant and his tradition. Indeed, how could they, since the very concept of reason had undergone a transformation to the point where it could not say anything about the nature of things anymore?[60] The loss of any reference to God also meant that moral norms could not be seen as deriving their authority from God. For how could appeals be made to God without reissuing the interreligious controversies? For the same reason, neither could moral rules derive their authority from tradition. Kant was responding to this dialectical challenge when he reinterpreted moral rules as imperatives the individual legislates for oneself. But what would make the individual's point of view rational? It must be, Kant offered, the purely formal characteristics of an imperative, as viewed from a strictly impersonal or universal perspective, that give a moral rule its authority.[61]

It is interesting to see what has happened between the predecessor tradition and Kant in terms of the conception of moral reason. Within the medieval-theistic tradition, to be rational one had to be right about the nature or order of things. For Kant, moral reason has to do with thinking according to certain canons. In the former tradition, moral reason generally took the form of contingent *reasons* in relation to concrete desires, goals, activities, and institutions, directing them to a socially available *telos*. In Kant, moral reason gains a procedural formality and purity that transcends the vagaries of particular concerns, desires, interests, and attachments. Whereas in the predecessor tradition to call something good was to make a factual *statement*, which could be true or false, in Kant it begins to appear implausible to treat moral judgments as factual statements. Rather, they must be *imperatives*, which as such are not susceptible to truth and falsity. An irreparable gulf now seems to lie between the world of "fact" and the Moral Point of View, between the "is" and "ought," between standpoint of the phenomenal (nonmoral) and that of the noumenal (moral) self.

This sketchy reconstruction is able to account why Kant, in many respects, is the converging point of the story we have told from three different angles. The secularization and redefinition of a formality of practices following the crisis of authority and Reformation polemics, the struggle for autonomy against traditional and ecclesiastical structures which had become oppressive, and the loss of a teleological framework, all contrived to loosen morality's connection not only with religion but with the language of fact and contingency in general. MacIntyre is accordingly right to note that Kant's problem would not have occurred if an earlier *ethos* had not, on account of these various factors, collapsed. In fact, Kant's positive contribution lies in his attempt to save this traditional *ethos* by rearranging its various elements into a new pattern fit for duty in late eighteenth-century Europe. The effect of Kant's philosophical contribution, however, was that in attempting to articulate a mind-set for this area of conduct, he was able to at once draw a relatively tight circle around morality (thus creating the "special institution"[62] morality is today), and to provide this "institution of morality" with something like a rational foundation.

The realization of this development is crucial for the argument of this book, since, as an academic topic, the 'problem' of religion and ethics presupposes Kant's contribution. For it is only when one begins by assuming that there is something like an institution of morality or a "foundation of morality" that one faces the problem of how such an institution or foundation is or is not related to other, nonmoral convictions which form people's lives. Specifically, the problem of ethics' relation to religion presupposes the distinctive conception of moral rationality operative within this Kantian institution of morality. Only when moral reason has been accorded the purity of the perspective *sub specie aeternitaties* does the agent's particularity—convictions (e.g., religious), conceptions of the good, reasons, desires, community belonging, and individual story—become a philosophical problem whose moral significance has to be justified. Only then does one have a problem of relating the concrete historical existence of the phenomenal self *(what is)* to the formal standpoint of the noumenal, and therefore, moral self *(the ought)*.

There have certainly been attempts by the Kantian-inspired standard accounts to justify the moral significance of the agent's particular story, convictions, and interests (and thus religion). These attempts, however, have been, on the whole, unsatisfactory. For one thing, the approaches have continued to uncritically assume the autonomy and putative purity of moral reason by confining the agent's particularity to what, in a memorable phrase, Toulmin has termed a role "outside the boundaries of reason."[63] Secondly, these attempts have often proceeded with a faulty moral psychol-

ogy that assumes the externality of agency and motivation. We need to substantiate the truth of these claims in a separate paragraph.

Religion "Outside the Boundaries of Reason"

Motivational accounts have often been offered by Kantian-inspired philosophers who have felt the need to account for the moral significance of the
agent's particular story. In this connection, for example, many have suggested that religion can make a (replaceable) contribution to ethics in terms
of motivation. Stephen Toulmin provides perhaps one of the most explicit
statements to this effect: "Ethics provides the 'reasons' for choosing the
right course; religion helps us to put our 'hearts' into it."[64] However, the
same position is found in Braithwaite, Nowell-Smith, and many others.[65] A
motivational account of private convictions and conceptions of the good is
also at stake when theologians portray, as noted earlier, the distinctiveness
of Christian ethics in terms of maieutic and parenetic discourse.

Other philosophers have made a general case for supererogation as a way
to account for the moral significance of the agent's unique story and particular convictions.[66] The claim made by these philosophers is that Kantian
ethics, concentrating on objective, universally determined rules and principles, leaves little room for realities such as friendship, loyalty, a sense of
fellow-feeling and community, personal attachment, sympathy, love, and
personality—realities which go beyond what is morally required. These realities, it is claimed, should be treated as constituting an independent category of morally meaningful, albeit optional, realities.[67] Some, like Strawson, Vivas, and Kupperman, go even as far as calling for a two-tier moral
system, comprising the moral (social, obligatory) and ethical (individual,
optional) realms, respectively.[68]

In the wake of this argument of supererogation, a number of authors have
been able to give a more liberal interpretation to "religion" and have framed
religion's moral significance in terms of self-awareness and the formulation
of personal values, goals, and ideals at an optional and supererogatory level
over and beyond the essential categorical morality.[69] Theologians, too, generally assume a supererogatory account when they locate the distinctiveness
of Christian ethics in terms of a Christian intentionality, explicitness, or
style.[70]

Even though these attempts to grant moral significance to the agent's
particular story and convictions in general, and to religious convictions in
particular in terms of motivation and supererogation, seem to expand the

limits of moral reason, these accounts do, in fact, respect and even confirm its autonomy and purity by assigning the particularities of the agent's biography to a role or category outside "the boundaries of reason," where they remain essentially *private,* and provide only an *added* motivation or an *optional* ideal.

Accordingly, these attempts are doubly problematic. First, they assume an unhistorical account of religion—the experiential-expressivist model—which reduces religion to a matter of private feelings, beliefs, and convictions. Secondly, the assumption that religion can provide only a *private* or *optional* motivation and ideal is grounded in a highly questionable moral psychology which assumes the externality of agency and motivation. We shall attend to the nature and shortcomings of the experiential-expressivist model of religion in the sixth chapter. For now, we need to say a little more on the questionable moral psychology which sustains the motivational and supererogatory accounts of religion.

The relegation of an agent's convictions and beliefs to the private ("outside the boundaries of reason") is often philosophically justified by invoking Hume's stricture against deriving "ought" from "is," according to which, one's feelings, convictions, or beliefs about what *is* the case cannot logically inform what one *ought* to do. Such a justification, however, is grounded in a faulty moral psychology that assumes the externality of agency and motivation, and leads to a distorted caricature of the relation between thought and action. The externality of agency and motivation assumes that the relation between thought and action is only casual since, it is assumed, the ought (good) can be determined and known independently of the particular convictions and beliefs, which only provide an "added" (therefore, optional) motivation.

However, as Hauerwas has shown, the relation between thought and action is not casual but necessary. He writes, "our beliefs [about ourselves, others and our environment], desires and intentions cannot be isolated as the 'motives' of our moral action where motive is understood to be independent of the description of the action as a moral action."[71] What Hauerwas helps us to see through the above citation, and what will be fully explicated in the coming chapter, is that the agent's intentions, convictions, desires, and reasons (in a word, the agent's intentionality) inform and determine what the agent does. To remove them from an action, or to render them external (or optional) to the determination of action, is to render the action itself unintelligible. In other words, what motivational and supererogatory accounts of the agent's biography miss is an adequate moral psychology that affirms the necessary connection between thinking and acting, between agency and action. This necessary connection is what is at stake in Hauerwas's prioritization of the notion of moral character within ethics.

This critical assessment of motivational and supererogatory accounts already reveals the questionable assumptions that sustain attempts to find a place for the agent's particular convictions and beliefs within the so-called universal perspective of the Moral Point of View. What the critical assessment in fact shows is that our and Hauerwas's uneasiness with the 'problem' of religion and ethics does not spring so much from the fact that philosophers (and theologians) have given the wrong answers and thus misconstrued the relation between religion and ethics. Rather, it involves a more primary contention, namely, that the very framing of the question is sustained by an unhistorical account of the moral life embodied within the Kantian institution of morality in general, moral rationality in particular.

This unhistorical account of the moral life and moral rationality cannot be sustained, owing to its shortcomings. In particular, Hauerwas has argued, this standard account distorts the nature of the moral life by: (i) placing the primary focus on "action," thereby obscuring any concerns of "being a moral self"; (ii) placing an unwarranted emphasis on particular quandaries, thereby encouraging an occasionalistic conception of the moral life; and (iii) requiring that the agent abstract from one's biography, attachments, interests, etc., thereby vacating the moral life of any substantive content. We need to briefly examine each of these shortcomings to find out how Hauerwas proposes to overcome them in his work. At the risk of anticipating this discussion, we note that the attempt to overcome these shortcomings constructively leads to the development within Hauerwas's work of the three key categories of *character, vision,* and *narrative.*

4. Hauerwas, Ethics, and Moral Particularity: An Outline

From "What Should I Do?" to Moral Character

Kantian ethics, Hauerwas has noted, tends to assume that the primary moral question is "What shall I do?" However, he has argued that such a concentration on 'action' within the standard accounts involves an occasionalistic understanding of the moral life, with a view of the self that is not morally engaged until it finds itself in a situation where it has to *act.* In fact, the very isolation of 'action' explains why standard accounts of ethics have provided few occasions for talking about *being* a moral self. On the contrary, these accounts have assumed that the answer to the question "What should I do?" can be determined in a way that does not appeal to the agent's particular convictions, beliefs or history, but in accordance with either universalizable (rational) principles or by the exigencies of the situation.

According to Hauerwas, this assumption that 'actions' can be determined in perfectly neutral terms is misleading, because action is always a narrative-dependent concept:

> action descriptions gain their intelligibility from the role they play in a community's history and therefore for individuals in that community. When 'acts' are abstracted from that history, the moral self cannot help but appear as an unconnected series of actions lacking continuity and unity.[72]

However, this is not the case. Rather, the action one performs, and indeed the very way one describes an action, is intimately bound up with the sort of person the agent is. Hauerwas has defended this necessary connection between what one is and one's actions or between agency and action through the development of the key notion of moral character. Moral character, he has argued, "is the category that marks the fact that our lives are not constituted by decision, but rather the moral quality of our lives is shaped by the ongoing orientation formed in and through our beliefs, stories and intentions."[73]

One must also realize that the attempt to establish a necessary connection between agency and action through the prioritization of moral character in Hauerwas's work involves, in the final analysis, a critique of the Kantian noumenal and atomistic self prevalent within the dominant liberal forms of reflection. As an "on-going orientation," character involves a realization that the self does not, and in fact cannot, stand outside the flow of history or contingency. One does not remain unaffected by what one does. Rather, in choosing and acting, one is already becoming a certain type of person, i.e., developing a certain moral character.

From "Decisions" to Vision

The prioritization of moral formation and character within Hauerwas's work already calls into question the preoccupation with 'decisions' within the standard accounts. The question of "What should I do?" within the standard accounts is sustained by the assumption that if one thinks clearly one should be able to come to the right decision. Critically, this quest for the "right" decision assumes that beneath the variety of human activity, there is one way of being moral and the same way of 'solving' moral problems available to everyone. But as we noted in the previous paragraph, there is no way to completely isolate a moral decision from the sort of person the agent happens to be since "the kind of decision we confront, indeed the very way we describe a situation, is a function of the kind of character we have."[74]

Secondly, the preoccupation with 'decisions' within the institution of morality presents the misleading impression that the moral life is a series of decisions. Already in one of his earliest works, Hauerwas critically noted how the moral life involves more than simply the decisions and choices about specific problems. Rather, it is a way of *seeing* the world:

> When we do make judgments about men, we judge not only their acts, "their solutions to specifiable practical problems, we consider something more elusive which may be called their total vision of life, as shown in their mode of speech or silence, their choice of words, their assessment of others, their conception of their own lives, what they think attractive or praiseworthy, what they think funny: in short, the configuration of their thought which shows continually in their reaction and conversation."[75]

Hauerwas's employment of the category of vision can be seen as an attempt to get away from a decision-based (occasionalistic) account of the moral life, a way of reaffirming that the moral life is an ongoing attempt to come to a truthful vision of oneself, others, and the world. What is crucial within this conception of the moral life as a life of vision is the realization that coming to a truthful vision of reality is not just a matter of thinking clearly, or making decisions by invoking general rules and principles. Vision requires training and formation. The self must be trained, if it is to see the world truthfully. This training, Hauerwas notes, is inseparable from the "kind of people [character] we are, and the way we have learned to construe the world through our *language*, habits and feelings."[76]

From "Pure Reason" to Narrative Rationality

The Kantian institution of morality is sustained by a foundational account of moral rationality which tries to secure for moral judgments an objectivity that frees such judgment from the particularity of the agent's history or community. This ideal of objectivity is what we have identified as the Moral

Point of View and with such metaphors as the Categorical Imperative, Universalizability, Ideal Observer, and the View from Nowhere. All these metaphors seem to share the assumption that reason is *moral* only if it is pure, i.e., if it is able to vacate the phenomenal world of contingent and particular reasons and ground itself in the noumenal world of universalizable maxims and of rationality *simpliciter*. Thus, according to a vulgarized version of these standard accounts, what one morally *ought* to do is not logically related to what one *is* historically as a father, or a daughter, or a teacher, or a doctor, or a Christian, or anything, but derives from reason *qua* reason.

Such a view of moral rationality, Hauerwas has argued, vacates the moral life of any substantive content which gives one's life meaning and moral particularity. For, as MacIntyre notes in a description which could as well have been made by Hauerwas:

> It is not just that different individuals live in different social circumstances; it is also that we all approach our own circumstances as bearers of a particular social identity. I am someone's son or daughter, someone else's cousin or uncle; I am a citizen of this or that city, a member of this or that guild or profession; I belong to this clan, that tribe, this nation. Hence what is good for me has to be the good for one who inhabits these roles. As such, I inherit from the past my family, my city, my tribe, my nation, a variety of debts, inheritances, rightful expectations and obligations. These constitute the given of my life, my starting point. This is in part what gives my life its own moral particularity.[77]

In as much as these aspects of one's story cannot be left behind, there is something ubiquitous in them. They are not a *mere* starting point that can be shed in pursuit of a more rational and objective (i.e., neutral) standpoint. In other words, there is no neutral *story* that ensures truth and objectivity in the moral life. If objectivity and truthfulness is to be found, "it will have to occur in and through the[se] stories that tie the contingencies of our life together."[78]

These are the claims at stake when Hauerwas calls for a narrative account of the moral life in general, moral reason in particular. Critically, use of the notion of narrative within Hauerwas's work is meant to dash the hopes of any attempts by reason to flee from historical contingency and particularity. Constructively, the notion of narrative is in itself a certain conception of moral reason, an alternative (to the standard Kantian) pattern of moral rationality.

The result of this thumbnail reconstruction of Hauerwas's project is to already make clear why Hauerwas does not waste time on the problem of the relation between religion and ethics. Rather, he undertakes a sustained critique of the assumptions embodied within the Kantian institution of morality, which assumptions create the problem in the first place. More specifically, through this reconstruction we have been able to identify the three key categories of moral character, vision, and narrative around which Hauerwas develops a historicist conception of the moral life. What, in our view, makes Hauerwas's re-conception of the moral life more cogent than the Moral Point of View is the ability to take seriously the realization that morally, the "world of appearances"—of contingency and particularity— cannot be transcended. It is the only world there is, and who we are, what we do, and our reasons for both, are inextricably bound up within it.

The implications of this claim for the moral life in general and moral rationality in particular still have to be worked out in detail. And with it, the defense of the central thesis of this work: namely, that from within Hauerwas's re-conception of the moral life along the categories of character, vision, and narrative, the problem of ethics' relation to religion does not arise. Indeed, from within this perspective, "to begin by asking what is the relation between religion and ethics is to already have made a mistake." This is the task awaiting us in the coming three chapters.

2

Moral Character: The Self and Agency within the Limits of History

> My real concern is philosophic: Not what we do or what we ought
> to do; but what happens to us in our wanting and doing.
>
> Gadamer

> Freedom is not a name for some real or ideal state in which we
> have absolute control of our lives. Rather, freedom is a quality that
> derives from having a well-formed character.
>
> Hauerwas

The goal of this chapter, which is divided into four sections, is to argue that
the notion of moral character within Hauerwas's work involves a conception of the self as radically historical. We show that his prioritization of this
notion of moral character within ethical reflection needs to be seen as a
critical response to the transcendental view of the self within much of contemporary ethical reflection. The latter has generally assumed an ontology
of identity, according to which the "I" is a self-existing and stable identity
which stands behind agency and thus remains unaffected by its actions and
decisions. Such an ontology in effect renders the self immune from the vicissitudes of historical contingency and particularity, and by this strategy
these contemporary reflections seek to protect the universality of moral
reason and provide a more stable foundation for the moral project.

In the first section, therefore, we shall trace Hauerwas's critique of this
Kantian self within the standard accounts of ethics and within liberal political philosophy. The goal of this critical exposition will be to show the extent to which liberal theories have tended to assume a defective moral psychology which depicts the self (agency) and action to be external. Such a
moral psychology, it will be pointed out, not only leads to a truncated view
of the moral life, it misconstrues the very nature of action.

Against this background, we will show, in the second section, how
Hauerwas's argument for the significance of the notion of moral character

is an attempt to present a more adequate moral psychology.[1] The goal of this argument will be to affirm an internal relation between the self and action. This claim is defended by both an appeal to action theory and to Aristotle's understanding of action *(praxis)*. Both of these key sources confirm the conclusion that the agent is not related to his action as an external cause or event. Rather, the agent *forms* his action by determining his beliefs, convictions, desires (in a word, intentionality) in one direction or another. This way, not only does one's action reveal the sort of person the agent is, the agent himself does not remain unaffected by what he does. In his doing and wanting he forms himself, he develops a lasting disposition, from which issue his actions. Understood as moral character, the self is thus fundamentally historical in as far as it is through historical agency that one's character is constantly being revealed, confirmed, or qualified.

In the third section, we shall show how this historical conception of the self calls into question any claims for self-sufficiency in the development of character. For, one's dependency in the formation of character on historically contingent factors and relations introduces elements of fragility, luck, and tragedy into the moral life. We shall particularly dwell on the passions and affective investment as one key source of this fragility. Against the background of Lewis's criticism (that Hauerwas betrays a commitment to the myth of the passions), we shall develop a comprehensive argument to show that an adequate appreciation of the passions and affective investment points to the centrality of the notion of *importance* within the moral life. And so, understood as the embodiment of the "importance of what we care about," the notion of moral character provides an even more pressing confirmation of the finitude and fragility of the moral life in general and the self in particular.

In the fourth and last section, we inquire into the implications that the notion of moral character spells for the meaning and nature of moral responsibility. We shall argue that a historical view of the self, in particular the awareness of the inherent sense of fragility and intertextuality involved in the notion of moral character calls for a revision of the standard foundational account (based on an ontology of identity) in favor of nonfoundational (narrative-based) account of responsibility. Such a narrative-based account of responsibility not only affects the meaning of freedom, it confirms that far from being a liability, the historical contingencies of the self provide a worthy resource for the moral life. Such contingencies are, in any case, unavoidable.

1. The Self beyond History in Contemporary Ethical Reflection

Much of contemporary ethical reflection, Hauerwas has consistently argued, assumes a problematic externality of agency and action. This 'alienation' of the self from its activities is underwritten by a problematic ontology of the "I" as a self-subsisting agent who stands outside the flow of history. Such a transcendental self, because he or she remains unaffected by what he or she does, is able to disengage from any concrete engagements and review them 'rationally': i.e., from a neutral perspective. This view of the agent is as at home within the philosophical standard accounts of ethics as within liberal political philosophy, and within a great deal of contemporary moral theological reflection.

The Self of Quandary Ethics

Already in his earliest work in the 1970s, Hauerwas was raising critical notes about the occasionalistic view of the moral life within the philosophical standard accounts of ethics. The latter, Hauerwas pointed out, in their overconcentration on quandaries, did not provide a coherent and convincing picture of the moral life. Rather, their preoccupation with quandaries gave the impression that the moral life was primarily concerned with hard choices and that ethics was a discipline primarily concerned with procedures for resolving conflict-of-choice decisions. Stephen Toulmin captures this standard conception well. Ethics, he writes, "is everybody's concern. . . . Everyone . . . is faced with moral *problems*—problems about which, after more or less reflection, a decision must be reached."[2]

   While such a concentration on moral *problems* and *decisions* is fairly widespread among the standard accounts, it does not offer any meaningful way to talk about "being a moral self." This possibility is, in fact, already excluded by the assumption, within such accounts, that a casuistry involving universal rules and principles is all that is needed to resolve these quandaries. From this perspective, one understands why Hauerwas welcomed the attempt, by both Situation Ethics[3] and Proportionalism,[4] to draw attention to the uniqueness of the situations in which the agent finds himself or herself, and the inadequacy of rules alone to do justice to it. However, as he has critically noted, these approaches themselves failed to address the challenge of "being a moral self." For, like the dominant tradition they criticized, they continued to assume that the moral life was primarily concerned with making 'decisions' and that the primary moral question was "What should I *do*?"

The primacy of this question within ethical reflection, as well as the isolation of 'actions', 'situations,' or 'problems' for primary consideration, offers no way to talk about the continuity of the self who acts in different situations. On the contrary, it gives the misleading impression that the self is not morally engaged until it has to make a *decision* or to *act*. Moral duties or obligations, on this account, appear as the sort of things that 'kick in,' and morality itself as a special sphere or institution which the self steps in and out of.[5] It is perhaps not surprising that such an assumption leads to the obliteration of the notion of moral character from ethical reflection. What the neglect of that notion amounts to, however, is a failure to take seriously the realization that one's life morally is not constituted by what one (sometimes) must do, but rather what one (always) is.

What is even more problematic is the realization that the preoccupation with decisions and actions within the standard accounts assumes and, in fact, continues to underwrite as normative a Kantian noumenal self, who must meet each new situation, decision, or action in a state of innocence in order to grasp the timelessness of the Moral Point of View. Such a self subsists in its own identity, remains unaffected by its agency, and thus has the ability to stand back from its concrete engagements and regard them 'objectively' as though he/she (the agent) were an outside observer, or an ideal spectator.

The Self in Liberal Political Philosophy

John Rawls's *A Theory of Justice* in many cases provides the most contemporary expression of this transcendental self within liberal political philosophy. Rawls's model, to ensure that citizens of a liberal state reach a fair *decision* concerning principles of justice, is that of the Original Position. Within this model, a 'veil of ignorance' is meant to deprive the members of the liberal community of "the knowledge of all the biases and prejudices associated with their contingent and particular history. Each is prevented, for example, from knowing his sex, race, physical strength, or intellectual capacity, the special circumstances of his birth, or the special ends or values one wishes to pursue."[6]

Following communitarians like Sandel, Hauerwas has pointed out that the moral psychology inherent in Rawls's Original Position entails a transcendental or unencumbered self—a self prior to and independent of any constitutive purposes, ends, and engagements.[7] This criticism is in fact sustained by indications in Rawls's own work in which he consciously associates the original position with Kant's kingdom of ends. In fact, when one attends to this Kantian reconstruction within Rawls's work, it becomes evident why Rawls's original position involves all the virtues and complications as those we noted in relation to Kant's transcendental (noumenal) selves. For example, Rawls, just like Kant, assumes that only such transcendental selves (of the Original Position) are the subjects of freedom and rationality. He writes,

> My suggestion is that we think of the original position as the point of view from which noumenal selves see the world. The parties qua noumenal selves have *complete freedom* to choose whatever principles they wish; but they also have the desire to express their nature as *rational* and equal.[8]

It is clear that the quest for absolute or complete freedom and rationality forces Rawls to adopt the same transcendental justification for the principles of ethics (fairness) as Kant. Kant did of course realize that by abstracting from its contingent commitments and attachments, the noumenal self was left without any interesting reasons for which to act one way or another. As we noted, Kant was only able to save the moral project by construing morality as part of the transcendental structure of this noumenal self. Similarly, once Rawls has, in the interest of fairness, abstracted the self from its contingent commitments and cast it into an Original Position, he realizes that the self so unencumbered is left without any reasons for preferring any particular set of principles arrived at under the veil of ignorance rather than any other set. To save the political project, Rawls has to resort to the same strategy as Kant. The "moral capacity," the perspective of eternity," the "veil of ignorance," the "original position," Rawls writes at different places, is arrived at "naturally" because it is part of the conceptual structure of every rational agent.[9]

Since the Dewey Lectures, Rawls has defended himself against this attack by denying that in *A Theory of Justice* he was developing a moral theory (or conception of moral reason), and certainly not a conception of the moral personality.[10] He has argued that his aim was to provide for a *political* conception of justice assumed by citizens within modern liberal societies. Such a conception of justice, Rawls has claimed, is detached from, independent of, and neutral in respect to, broader and inherently controversial philosophical, metaphysical, and religious commitments.[11]

However, even if one were to read Rawls on his strictly *political* terms, it is not clear how he would completely take the sting out of the criticism of the "unencumbered self." On the contrary, one wonders how Rawls is able to maintain a strict demarcation between the political and moral (and economical) spheres without at the same time assuming, or at least underwriting, a view of the self that is able to move smoothly back and forth between these spheres. The only way the self can do so is by standing independently of these spheres, and/or maintaining a superficial relationship to its engagements in any of these spheres. This means that although Rawls may not have intended to provide a theory of the moral self, he nevertheless assumes a Kantian noumenal self—a self that must abstract "from everything that separates us from another in the field of appearance." (More in chapter 7).

The Self in Theological Ethical Reflection

Perhaps nowhere is the relation between a view of the self and a conception of freedom clearer than in those theological approaches (predominantly Catholic) which have tended to use the language of *fundamental option*. Timothy O'Connell, for example, defends what he calls "an onion-peel view of the self." According to him, the self is analogous to an onion, comprised of layers, each with its own identity, but with no layer standing by itself. At the outermost layer, as it were, there is the environment, one's world, the things one owns. Moving inward one finds the actions, behavior, the things one does. And then the body, that which is the 'belonging' of a person and yet also *is* the person. Going deeper, there are moods, emotions, feelings. Deeper still are convictions by which one defines oneself. "And at the very center, in that dimensionless pinpoint around which everything else revolves, is the person himself or herself—the I."[12]

O'Connell notes that this 'I' cannot be an object, since if it were it would need another subject to know it as object. Rather, the 'I' is the condition of possibility of all else that is known. Thus, he concludes that as agent, as a *doer*, the self is changeable, but as a *be-er*, as a subject, the self must necessarily stay the same.[13] If O'Connell feels compelled to drive a wedge between *being* and *doing*, it is to ensure freedom for the 'I'. He assumes that such freedom can be guaranteed only by making sure that the self is not simply the product of history, biology, environment, or other contingent factors:

> The central core of myself, the "I" which is my personhood, is confronted with a reality that transcends all categories. . . . And from the perspective of my own core, the subjectivity that I am, this cosmically inclusive

objectivity presents itself for decision. A simple, singular decision: yes or no. The freedom of the human person, then, is not categorical freedom at all. Rather it is a freedom that transcends all categories, it is "transcendental freedom".[14]

Hauerwas has raised a number of critical points in relation to O'Connell's transcendental perspective, not least among them the observation that the relation between transcendental freedom and categorical freedom is never fully clarified by O'Connell, or by others who employ this distinction. Moreover, this distinction seems to involve all the complications of Kant's distinction between the noumenal and phenomenal worlds. Primary among these complications is the assumption that the self's real identity (what O'Connell calls "the central core of myself," the 'I') lies outside its history, in a self-defining stance or decision. Fundamental option is simply the name given to the *moment* in which this stance is assumed or emphatically renewed. What is ironic, however, is that even this "moment" cannot be in history, since its power lies exactly in its ability to transcend history.[15]

This critical review of O'Connell's work helps to show the extent to which the language of "fundamental option" involves a certain bias against history, a tendency to regard the self's concrete manifestations and engagements as limits to be transcended if the self is to take that fundamental stance in which it defines itself as a person. And so, to the extent the theologies of fundamental option have been popular, there has been a corresponding neglect of, and even pessimism about, the notion of moral character within contemporary theological reflection. For, contrary to the transcendentalism inherent in the theologies of fundamental option, the language of character encourages a historical conception of the self.

The various approaches above confirm the extent to which the Kantian noumenal self has been assumed in much of contemporary ethical, political, and theological literature. All the approaches surveyed above have assumed a self that is normatively characterized by the key virtue of abstraction from the contingent factors of the self's concrete historical existence. This flight from the historical particularity of the self is encouraged as a strategy to ensure either the universality of moral objectivity, absolute freedom, or political fairness. However, the result of this mistrust or bias against the historical and contingent manifestations of the self—what Gadamer has called the "prejudice against prejudice"[16]—has been to bestow an illusory timelessness to one's moral, religious, or political commitments. What one happens to be *(is)* is supposed to bear no logical relation to what one must *(ought* to) do, which can only be determined from the perspective of the Ideal Spectator, the Original Position, or as a Fundamental Option.

In terms of a moral psychology, it means that the agent (self) is not related to what he or she does. On the contrary, in order to realize 'objectivity', 'fairness', 'freedom', or 'authenticity', it is assumed that there must be an 'I' that somehow stands outside its actions, causes them, but itself remains unaffected by what it does. Only such an 'unmoved' (unaffected) agent is able to confront each new situation or action in a state of innocence.

But how can such an 'I', always determined by the demands of the moment, be a self, since it lacks any historical continuity? And in what sense can such a self be said to act? What is the relation between such a self and its activities? These and similar issues not only involve questions concerning a proper understanding of action and freedom, they call for the development of a moral psychology that would pay attention to the formation and continuity of the moral self and at the same time provide a convincing account of the relation between the agent (self) and its activities. We need to see Hauerwas's use of and arguments for the significance of the notion of moral character as in essence an attempt to provide such a moral psychology.

In a nutshell the argument for the significance of moral character attempts to show that in assuming the externality of agency and action, the approaches above have misunderstood the very nature of action.[17] The self cannot remain unaffected by what it does, since it cannot stand outside its actions and 'cause' them like one atomistic event causing another. Rather, in forming action, the agent forms himself. He develops a lasting disposition (character). Action is thus an agent-related concept. This internal connection between agency and action makes it impossible both to separate the self from his or her agency and to understand action without reference to the agent. Moreover, once an internal connection has been established between the self and action, then one has to give up not only a transcendental view of the self but also the quest for freedom understood as a quality by which an agent has absolute control over what he does. Instead, one begins to appreciate the sense in which freedom is an aspect of a well-formed character.

2. Moral Character and the Metaphysics of the Self: The Self as Agent

Already in his *Character and the Christian Life*, Hauerwas developed a comprehensive moral psychology in which he affirmed the necessary connection between thought and action. Drawing on key action theorists like Melden, Taylor, and MacMurray, he demonstrated how the connection between thought and action is not casual but internal, because such a connection is grounded in the very metaphysical constitution of selfhood. To be a self, he noted, is to be an agent, i.e., "an autonomous center of activity and [to be] the source of one's determinations."[18] The concept of agency in this early work by Hauerwas is premised on the realization that in order to act the self must be determined to act. This determination, however, does not come in terms of external causes. Human beings simply have the ability to determine themselves; to be a self is to be a self-determining being.

Although this realization that a human is a self-determining being is basic, it is also one that is easily overlooked. This becomes particularly clear when one notes the enthusiasm that the freedom-determinism debate has generated over the years. Although the debate has often been procured under the rubric of freedom and responsibility (either the self is free and, therefore, responsible; or the self is determined and, therefore, not responsible), what is at stake in the debate is the very understanding of the self and agent-causality. Both the libertarian and determinist assume that human beings must be moved to act. The libertarian, in an attempt to preserve responsibility, denies that a human is moved by motives, desires, or inclinations, for to do so would imply that one is not totally free. The libertarian thus posits a transcendental self (identified with an inner "free will") as source of one's determinations. The determinist rejects this transcendental self (internal cause) and instead explains human behavior in terms of the agent's physical and social conditions, or by an appeal to a particular set of dispositions.

From Hauerwas's perspective, which involves an affirmation of self-agency the 'quarrel' between these two positions is only superficial since both sides share fundamentally the same assumptions about agency. For example, both sides assume absolute freedom as a condition for responsibility. Secondly, though they differ on the how, both assume a Humeian metaphysics of causation that considers human behavior as one event causally related to another. Under this metaphysics, human actions are misleadingly regarded as independent pieces of reality which the agent "causes" in some kind of external and contingent manner.

However, when the self is understood as agent, the central problem of this debate (of explaining how the agent externally "causes" his actions, and yet remains "free") dissolves. For, the affirmation of human beings as self-determining agents implies that they are not related to what they do as one eternal cause to an event. What humans do is not separable from their agency. This means that once agency is taken as part of the metaphysical constitution, then there is "no need to posit a 'cause' of man's actions. Men simply have the ability to act; no further explanation is necessary. To be a man is to have power of efficient causation. The self does not cause its activities or have its experiences; it simply is its activities as well as its experience. I *am* rather than *'have'* . . . my activities."[19]

Once the full implications of this sort of claim are recognized, then at least two conclusions become inevitable. First, it becomes clear that through the affirmation of agency as part of the metaphysical structure of the self (self as agent), Hauerwas seeks to develop an account of the self that avoids both transcendental and behavioristic accounts. On the one hand, Hauerwas clearly avoids the need for a transcendental self (as procured, for example, by O'Connell and the libertarians), where, in order to 'cause' or 'own' its actions, the 'I' must stand over and beyond them. Contrary to the need for such a transcendental self, self-agency affirms that what the self does is not separable from its self-agency: "I am rather than have my activities." This, however, does not involve an affirmation of a behaviorist self (the other extreme). Such a self (as procured by the determinists) would be reducible to its many determinations. This cannot be the case with the affirmation of self-agency, since to be an agent is "to be an autonomous center of one's activities and the source of one's determinations."

Secondly, once it is acknowledged that the agent does not externally 'cause' his actions then it becomes clear why the freedom-determinism debate got off on the wrong foot by looking for the 'causes' of human actions. It makes no sense to look for the 'causes', since a human is a self-determining agent. Rather, the really crucial issue is to discover how one can determine himself to act in one way or another, which is tantamount to an inquiry into the structure of the agent's intentionality—the decisive factor in the formation of an action.[20] Action, Hauerwas notes, bears an internal and unavoidable reference to the agent, since the power of agency is nothing but "the efficacy or the power to produce the results that I *envisage.*"[21] The agent's power to "envisage" what he does simply means he has the power to determine himself to act with an end in view, that is, in line with his intentions, reasons, desires, and beliefs. Hauerwas also refers to this full range of intentional structure variously by shorthand references to the agent's 'intentions', 'reasons', or 'explanation'.[22] However, one must be careful not to imagine that Hauerwas is claiming that the agent's intentionality is the cause of his action. What must be given up once the intentional structure of action is noted is the very language of "cause" in relation to action. Accordingly, the agent's "volitions, motives, intentions, reasons do not cause or move men to act, but men acting embody them."[23] But neither do one's "reasons" merely provide an explanatory context for one's action. The agent's "reasons" are essential to the actual formation of one's action, as they inform *(in-form)* and influence *(flow into)* what one does.

This is a crucial realization, which means that in acting, "I, the agent, make something happen that would not have happened without my agency."[24] But it also means that the relation between one's intentionality and action is not casual, but that the very description of an action must bear an essential reference to this intentional structure. That is why action cannot be analyzed in purely physical, biological, or purposive terms. Purposive behavior, as is typical of animals, is behavior in which "in order to achieve this or the other result" explanations are given. Because this behavior bears no direct reference to an intentional structure, it can adequately be observer-determined in terms of biological and physical motivations or in terms of its publicly observable effects. Intentional conduct, on the other hand, requires "because of" explanations, which can only be given in terms of the agent's own 'reasons', 'intentions', and "descriptions."[25] The upshot of this distinction between purpose and intentional behavior is that while animals can have purposes only humans can be characterized as *intending* what they do. Only humans are "self-moving agents who can directly form our actions through our intentions."[26]

This observation means that unlike the case with purposive behavior, there is something characteristically internal and original about action, which renders action irreducible to independently specifiable motivations or publicly observable results. Action is an agent-dependent concept and must, therefore, bear an essential relation to the agent's intentionality. Thus, any attempt to explain action without reference to the agent's "description" by appealing solely either to general patterns of behavior or to its publicly available effects, renders action unintelligible. It is for this reason that Hauerwas grants primacy to the agent's perspective in the determination and description of action. This is not to deny that actions can have publicly recognizable effects which can always be known by an observer apart from the avowal of the agent. It simply means that insofar as what is done is an *action*, "it is still the agent who is the authority in defining what he has done." For, "'what' the action is, or even 'that' it is an action, can only be determined by the fact that [the agent] was acting under one description rather than another."[27] It is assumed that the agent can always supply a correct account of his or her action since as agent one has a direct knowledge of what one does. The knowledge of one's desires, beliefs, reasons, and intentions (i.e., of the description from which one is acting) is not something that one acquires. It is a non-propositional (Hampshire), non-observational (Anscombe), non-inferential (Melden) knowledge.

But does not this claim for the priority of the agent's perspective in the determination of action involve an exaggerated claim which, moreover, seems to underwrite a voluntaristic solipsism whereby the agent can do whatever he wants or describe his action anyhow?[28] This danger, although real, is certainly overstated, and tends to overlook the essential *sociality* of the agent.[29] As agent, one always finds oneself in a world already structured by language, institutionalized practices, and value systems. If the agent is to act in this world of structured meaning and symbolic value, he or she must 'find' the appropriate descriptions for what he or she does. Agency is thus fundamentally a social skill: "My act is not something I cause, as though it were external to me, but it is mine because I am able to 'fit' it into my ongoing story. My power as an agent is therefore relative to the power of my descriptive ability. Yet that very ability is fundamentally a social skill, for we learn to describe through appropriating the narratives of the communities in which we find ourselves."[30]

Later, in chapter 4 (notion of tradition), we shall explicate further how the agent forms his actions and thus his character within a community of shared meaning and interpretation. However, we must already note that the more Hauerwas has come to appreciate this narrative structure of action, the more he has affirmed MacIntyre's claim that it is a mistake to assume that by itself 'action' is a coherent and conceptually primitive concept. Rather, "the concept of an 'intelligible action' is a more fundamental concept than that of an action as such."[31]

Moreover, the realization that agency is fundamentally a social skill calls into question any hard dichotomy between self and community, between egoism and altruism, between the agent's description and the socially available descriptions. For,

> the first person singular is seldom the assertion of the solitary 'I', but rather the narrative of that I. It is exactly the category of narrative that helps us to see that we are not forced to choose between some universal standpoint and the subjectivistic appeals to our own experience. For our experiences always come in the form of narratives that can be checked against themselves as well as against others' experiences. I cannot make my behavior mean anything I want it to mean, for I have learned to

understand my life from the stories I have learned from others. . . . The language the agent uses to describe his behavior, to himself and to others, is not uniquely his; it is *ours*.[32]

It follows from the above quotation that the intelligibility of action has a noncontingent link with a common language and its norms. It also means that any explanation and justification for action takes place within such a social context. The latter, in fact, makes it possible for the agent's description to be checked (against publicly available descriptions), challenged, or even rejected. But the social context also explains why there is ordinarily no need to seek the agent's explanation, since so much of what the agent does is done in relation to social institutions and practices which make it immediately clear what the agent has done.

This social givenness, however, does not force the agent to adopt any description. It only points to the interactive horizon in which the agent forms his unique intentionality. In the final analysis, "when we are asked what we are doing, it is our description as agent that must be accepted as final."[33] As the foregoing discussion shows, this does not claim that the agent's avowal of what he has done and why he has done it is a sufficient or a satisfying one, but only that such an explanation is logically complete as an explanation of an action *qua* action.

Critical Implications

There are at least two critical implications which follow from the above affirmation of the priority of the agent's determination of action which bear directly on the main argument of our work. First, if action is an agent-related concept such that to remove the agent's "reasons" or leave them out of consideration renders action unintelligible, then there is certainly something problematic about the philosophical attempt to isolate the "moral significance" of the agent's biography. Such an attempt is premised on the assumptions that the agent's particular convictions and beliefs (e.g., religious convictions) are not essential in determining what the agent does (ethics). This is clearly the assumption behind motivational and supererogatory accounts of religion. These assume that the agent's convictions and intentions in general, and his or her religious beliefs in particular, provide only an "added" motivation or an "optional" dimension to the moral sphere. In light of the foregoing discussion, it becomes clear that these accounts assume a faulty moral psychology (of externality of action and the agents "reasons") which distorts the very nature of action.

Secondly, the realization that action is an agent-dependent concept calls into question attempts to provide assessment of action from an impartial spectator's (or ideal observer's) point of view. Such attempts continue to assume that the primary moral question is "What should I *do*?" As was noted earlier, the priority of this question tempts one to assume that the notion of action can be determined independently of the notion of agency (the sort of person the agent is), by appealing to universal principles, divine commands, or the exigencies of the situation. However, the realization that "action" is an agent-dependent concept means that ethics must not begin with the question "What should I do?" but with considerations related to the formation of the agent's desires, reasons, and intentions. And so, Hauerwas has argued,

> the question "What ought I to be?" precedes the question "What ought I to do?" If we begin our ethical reflection with the latter question we stand the risk of misunderstanding how practical reason should work as well as the moral life itself. For the question "What ought I to do?" tempts us to assume that moral situations are abstracted from the kind of people and history we have come to be. But that simply is not the case.[34]

It would certainly be misleading to conclude from the above citation that "What I ought to be" and "What I ought to do" are two separable questions of moral inquiry. This cannot be the case, since, as we have been arguing, action is an agent-related concept. A key advantage in giving priority to the notion of moral character within ethical reflection is that one is able to overcome such arbitrary opposition. Instead, one is able to preserve the internal link between intentionality and action, and thus, to account for the inevitable circularity between the self and its actions. We must, therefore, attend more directly to the significance, as well as inevitability of the notion of character for the moral life in general and for the conception of agency in particular.

Moral Character as the Form and Orientation of the Self

Hauerwas defines moral character as "the qualification of man's self-agency through his beliefs, intentions, and actions, by which a man acquires a moral history befitting his nature as a self-determining being."[35] This definition involves the realization that the agent cannot stand outside one's activity as though he or she were an external observer. Rather, something happens to the agent in his or her wanting, intending, and acting. The agent becomes a particular sort of person; he or she acquires a moral history or character. This moral history, which character denotes, is not something which the agent can leave behind or invoke at will in future engagements and activities, as if it is something one *has*. It is the very form, or embodiment of one's agency. In order to appreciate this connection between action and character, and its implications for the moral life, we need to attend to the Aristotelian background of Hauerwas's argument.

Aristotle on the Circularity between Action and Character

According to Aristotle, one does not acquire a virtuous character simply as a result of a natural inclination, or through an effortless inclination to the good (*NE* 1144b1–29; 1179b20–23).[36] Nor is the mere mechanical repetition of good acts sufficient to make one acquire good character, since people "may perform just acts without actually being just men." Virtuous character is a result of men repeatedly performing virtuous activities. However, for Aristotle, an act is not virtuous unless the agent has certain characteristics as he performs the act: "First of all, he [the agent] must know what he is doing; secondly, he must choose to act the way he does, and he must choose it for its own sake; and in the third place, the act must spring from a firm and unchangeable character" (*NE* 1105a27–32).

The requirement that a virtuous act must "spring from a firm and unchangeable character" brings one to the circularity at the heart of Aristotle's account of moral character. Aristotle expresses this circularity variously. He says that for an act to be virtuous it must spring from virtuous character; but one can have a virtuous character only as a result of repeatedly performing virtuous acts (*NE* 1105a27–35). Similarly, he notes that one can only become just by performing just acts, but in order to perform just acts one must be just, since he must perform "them *as* just and temperate men do them (*NE* 1105b5–9).

To understand the circularity in Aristotle is to understand the very nature of action, which involves paying attention to the distinction drawn by Aristotle between two kinds of 'activity', making *(poiēsis)* and acting *(praxis)* (*NE* 11040a2–5; 1104b1–4). This distinction clearly shows that Aristotle was aware that in *praxis* the agent is far more deeply invested in his action than the craftsman in his productive process. In *poiēsis*, (making an artifact, e.g., shoe), the craftsman stands somehow outside the productive process: it matters very little how the craftsman was internally formed in order to produce the artifact. Neither does the goodness of the product depend on how its making affected the artist's being. The criteria of success is the product itself. In *praxis*, however, the agent cannot stand outside his action, as if it were a 'product' separable from him. We shall return to this crucial distinction of Aristotle in our fourth chapter in the course of an inquiry into the role that knowledge plays in respect to each of these areas of 'activity'. It will be seen then how *phronēsis* and not *technē* is the type of knowledge proper to action. For now, however, the realization that the agent is deeply invested in his action confirms how in acting the agent not only reveals who he is, but is forming himself into a particular sort of person. Acting thus involves a flowing-out and a flowing-back into the sort of person the agent is. The action not only must "spring from a firm and unchangeable character," by acting "in a determinate manner . . . we acquire character and as a consequence, act in accordance to who we are."[37]

It is this dynamic flowing-out and flowing-in between action and character that mitigates against any idea of a fixed self.[38] We met this transcendental view of self in certain forms of Kantian and theological positions which, in order to safeguard the freedom of the agent, affirmed a self over and beyond any concrete determinations. However, the circularity between action and character confirms that such a transcendental self is simply a philosophical illusion, because one does not remain unaffected by what one does. On the contrary, something "happens to us in our wanting and doing." We become distinctive sorts of people. It is on this account that the self cannot be an ahistorically given and static identity. Rather, it is a historically (to use the ill-chosen phrase from Kupperman) "constructed self"[39] in virtue of its being constantly renewed and modified through one's historical agency.

The affirmation of a historical sense of the self partly explains why Hauerwas has since moved away from his original reference to character as the "qualification of one's self-agency" in preference to character as the "form of our self-agency."[40] The shift is meant to avoid any impression of a self that lies beneath or beyond agency, or any conception of character as something "added" to the self. There is no need to look behind agency for a self which character somehow projects, represents, or qualifies. As the "form of our self-agency," character "is not an accidental feature of our lives that can be distinguished from what 'we really are'; rather, character is a concept that denotes what makes us determinative moral agents. Our character is not a shadow of some deeper but more hidden real self; it is the form of our agency acquired through our beliefs and actions."[41] Hauerwas makes the same point even more sharply in another place when he notes:

"The idea of agency helps us to see that character is not a surface manifestation of some deeper reality called the 'self'. We are our character."[42]

The same flowing-out and flowing-in between action and character also suggests that character provides an "orientation to one's agency."[43] In this respect, the notion of character stands as a critique to the Kantian noumenal self whose every "action must be regarded as though the individual had fallen into it directly from a state of innocence."[44] We have met this noumenal and occasionalistic self within the standard accounts' preoccupation with quandaries. As an "orientation of self-agency," character suggests (contrary to the assumptions of the latter approaches) that in meeting any future event the agent does not start *ab initio*. One has already become something through one's past agency. By the present actions, one "acquires a moral history" which prepares one to meet the future in a particular way.

Although such a preparedness may be seen by some Kantian-inspired standard accounts as a limitation to one's freedom, it is a key aspect of freedom rightly understood—besides being, in any case, unavoidable. For, outside philosophical illusion, we do not exist as unencumbered selves who "come to each new moment as a mere cipher or blank sheet of paper. Rather, we come as those who are at once gifted and burdened, freed and enslaved, enriched and impoverished, included, directed and determined by the many earlier transactions we have made in the past."[45]

Thus, any quest for an original starting point, or a complete break from the past is just a philosophical illusion. So, too, is the idea that one can always completely "step back" from all one's prejudices and assumptions, or view one's engagements in the detached and disinterested way characteristic of the noumenal self. This inability to completely disengage from one's history does not, however, mean that the notion of character rules out any possibility for one to critically assess the sort of person one has become, or the possibility to "ask what we should do in order that we might do the morally right thing." Rather, it involves a realization that these possibilities are themselves dependent on, and limited by, "what we have become through the past."

It is in this sense of being the embodiment of "the many earlier transactions we have made in the past" or of a moral history that moral character is inescapable. Everyone, by dint of one's past attention and agency, whether one is aware of it or not, whether one likes it or regrets it, has already acquired a moral history. The latter not only sets a boundary and limit to one's interests and questions, it also provides a transition from the past to the future. Of course, this by itself does not mean that the character so acquired is able to provide this transition in a satisfactory way. In order to do so, a normatively well-formed character should be able to offer one the resources to "go on" in such a way that the future is neither unconditionally accepted nor prejudicially closed off.[46] But this observation already makes clear that in its broad usage character is a formal notion. To say someone has character does not tell us what sort of character one has.

3. Affective Investment: The Ancestral Roots of Character

So far, we have aimed at a fairly straightforward reconstruction of Hauerwas's argument for the significance and unavoidability of the notion of moral character for ethical reflection. By itself this reconstruction has aimed at defending a historical conception of the self by showing that the self does not, and cannot, stand outside history, since it is the very embodiment of historical agency.

The Intellectualism of Hauerwas's Account of Character

Although Hauerwas's account of moral character is, on the whole, compelling, many have pointed how it involves a certain intellectualism.[47] The effect of this intellectualism is that in his early work, particularly in *Character and the Christian Life* (1975), Hauerwas portrayed the formation of action and thus character as finally the result of a *deliberative process.* No doubt, this overstatement was, at least in part, an attempt by Hauerwas to preserve the role of the intellect in virtue (see chapter 4, below). In this respect, Hauerwas noted that even though for both Aristotle and Aquinas to say that one has character is to say that one has acquired certain kinds of habits called virtues, both Aristotle and Aquinas were clear that virtue is not any habit *(hexis)*, but a habit formed by activity: "Man's indeterminacy cannot be formed into virtue simply by just being passively habituated, for the fact that he is rational requires that he 'actively' shape and form his life by his activity through his desires and choices."[48] However, this desire to preserve the capacity to 'actively' order one's intentions and desires in accordance with one's own particular purposes must have led Hauerwas to claim that it is finally by *rational* "choice that a man is said to be the efficient cause of his action . . . since it is by choice that the 'reasons why' from which men act are translated into the actual formation of the act itself."[49] The result of this predilection for rational choice is that Hauerwas assumed (particularly in *Character and the Christian Life*) that as agent one is fully conscious of one's beliefs, convictions, and desires. This way, the agent remains "an autonomous center of activity and the source of one's determinations."[50] In the coming section we shall say more about how this preoccupation with rational control underwrites a modern conception of responsibility. For now, however, we need to examine more carefully its basis in Hauerwas's work.

Patricia Jung has rightly traced the intellectualism in Hauerwas's account of character to his reliance on action theory for his general conception of agency. Action theory, Jung has argued, "has an intellectualistic bias which cannot be overcome by the analytic methods that guide it. It does not account adequately for the ancestral roots of action which arise involuntarily from the body."[51] True, action theorists generally admit that much of human behavior is radically involuntary. For example, both Melden and Richard Taylor—two of Hauerwas's sources—cite cases of involuntary behavior, e.g., the movement of a leg when struck in the patellar region, the salivatory response to hunger, the act of perspiring, the twitching of eye, etc. However, these or similar cases of automatic responses are cited in order to distinguish these *acts of man* (events) from genuine *human actions*. In fact, it is on the basis of this distinction between happenings and actions that Hauerwas concludes that an unbridgeable gulf exists between the involuntary and the voluntary, between "what I do and what happens to me."[52] The force of this distinction is to affirm the priority of the agent's perspective in the determination of action by making clear that causal explanations are only relevant to the reflexive behavior and not to human *action:* "It is true that the observer never can determine with exactness what the agent has done, for 'what is done' is dependent on the agent's description."[53]

The result of this distinction between mere events and actions is that in the struggle to emphasize the voluntary and intentional qualities of human action (in opposition to determinists), action theorists in general, and Hauerwas in particular, fail to make clear that human willing and reasoning—and thus the formation of action and character—is not so tidy a process. Because the voluntary and the involuntary aspects of choice serve one another, the formation of character cannot be simply a matter of rational choice or the result of a fully deliberate process. Rather, it is equally the result of formation by which various voluntary and involuntary patterns are internalized and habituated.[54]

In a "New Introduction" to *Character and the Christian Life* (1985 edition) Hauerwas has acknowledged the basic validity of Miss Jung's criticism, and as a result, has noted suspicions about agency as an adequate basis for a theory of moral character.[55] He has accordingly underscored the significance of training, and the corresponding initiation into a tradition as key factors within the formation of character. We shall deal with this aspect of character formation more fully in our coming chapter. For now, it has been necessary that we precisely define the nature and origin of the intellectualism within Hauerwas's account of moral character. Such an analysis is especially called for in light of an assessment like the one of Paul Lewis.[56] The latter both misleadingly accuses Hauerwas of subscribing to the "myth of the passions" and traces this myth to Hauerwas's Aristotelianism.

Paul Lewis on Hauerwas and the Myth of the Passions

Lewis first notes that Hauerwas assumes the emotions to be the "stuff" which must be formed by reason. This is what seems to be at stake when Hauerwas explicitly acknowledges that character formation entails giving order to desires and affections. Or when he approves both Aristotle and Thomas for arguing that "our passions do not so much need control as direction."[57] In arguing against a view which understands emotions to be "controlled" by reason, in favor of one in which emotions "need direction," Lewis claims, Hauerwas still treats reason and emotion as two discrete entities, the latter to be formed by the former.[58] In this way, he still privileges reason over emotion. The effect of this rationalistic bias is that in Hauerwas's early conception, character remains primarily a matter of reason, albeit an importantly different, more chaste kind of reason than liberalism's. For Lewis, however, this means that

> Hauerwas does not take his critique of liberal rationality far enough. Criticizing disembodied, universalistic rationality, Hauerwas argues for a contingent, particularistic rationality. Though he exposes the pretentiousness of reason's claim to universality, he never questions the centrality given to reason in the moral tradition; he only questions the nature of reason.[59]

Lewis further argues that this shortcoming is not limited to Hauerwas, but is endemic to neo-Aristotelian approaches (he specifically mentions MacIntyre) to character ethics:

> The work of addressing or correcting the deficiencies of decisionism . . . is only half complete because neo-Aristotelian virtue ethics attacks only one of decisionism's errors. Decisionism erred not only in its one-

dimensional reduction of moral concerns to ethical principles, but also
by grounding its representation of morality in an excessively intellectualistic conception of moral agency. While neo-Aristotelian virtue ethics
has had profoundly salutary effects in addressing the first of these problems, it has been less effective in addressing the second. Its deficiency in
this regard is a function of its neglect of the affective or emotional dimensions of character.[60]

Lewis attributes this defect to what Solomon has called the "myth of the
passions."[61] The dominant feature of this myth is the conception of reason
and emotion as enemies of one another. Whereas reason represents the rational (thus positive) and distinctive feature of man, the passions are seen as
primitive and disruptive forces before which one is helpless. They well up
within one unbidden and have to be controlled, suppressed or vented. Passions are further said to lead reason astray through their treachery and
temptation. Solomon describes this myth as an enduring bias of Western
thought and thinks that it was already operative in the work of Aristotle. In
a passage cited by Solomon, Aristotle asserts that "the function of man is
activity of the soul which follows a rational principle . . . reason, more than
anything else, is man" (NE 1098a12–20; 1178a8).[62] It is this indication that
leads Lewis to suspect that Hauerwas cannot escape this "myth" since a rationalist bias is built into his Aristotelian heritage.

Lewis's criticism is both misleading and overly exaggerated since, in
light of Aristotelian scholarship[63] and Hauerwas's own explicit views, it is
absurd to ascribe the myth of the passions to Aristotle. For example, at various sections in Character and the Christian Life, Hauerwas is keen to emphasize the important role emotions play in Aristotle's account of moral
character. This is, in fact, the clear conclusion from Hauerwas's extensive
analysis of Aristotle's "extremely complex" concept of choice (proairesis),
namely, that Aristotle understood choice as a "unique blend of reason and
desire, involving not only our intellectual decisions but also our self's commitment to act in terms of its desire."[64] Hauerwas also approvingly quotes
Aristotle's conclusion to the effect that "choice is either intelligence motivated by desire or desire operating through thought, and it is as a combination of these two that man is a starting point of action" (NE 1139b1–5). This
quote, Hauerwas writes, "clearly reveals that for Aristotle a man's character is as much the result of his passions and desires as his reasons."[65] Hauerwas even suggests that the interaction of reason and desire, as it finally
leads to action through choice, is what is at stake in the deliberation within

Aristotle's practical syllogism (*NE* 1113a30–1139b5).[66] He only criticizes Aristotle for apparently limiting his understanding of desire too narrowly to ends which give pleasure.[67] It is, in fact, on account of this shortcoming in Aristotle that Hauerwas turns to Aquinas, whose conception of will and intention in the *Summa* (*ST* I–II) "provides a much better way of thinking about how reason and desire are interrelated."[68] These indications clearly show that Hauerwas is keen to defend Aristotle and Aquinas against "the intellectualistic view of man of which they are often accused." According to Hauerwas, "the basis of such accusations is Aristotle and Aquinas's 'faculty' psychology in which the animal desires seem to be sharply distinguished from human reason. However, if one looks at their analysis of human behavior, it is clear that they were aware of the interdependence of reason and desire."[69]

In relation to Lewis's claim that Hauerwas himself subscribes to the myth of the passions, we need to make at least two remarks. First, such a claim clearly overlooks passages in Hauerwas's work where he has categorically stated that "what must be rejected is what Solomon has called 'the myth of the passions' that interprets the passions as antithesis to 'reason'."[70] In this connection, Hauerwas approvingly quotes Solomon to the effect that "rather than disturbances or intrusions, these emotions, and the passions in general, are the very core of our existence, the system of meanings and values within which our lives either develop and grow or starve and stagnate."[71] In all these indications, Hauerwas endorses the work of Edwards in the manner that Lewis suggests. According to Edwards, affections "serve as the 'glue' which holds character or agency together. By participating in both understanding and will, affections unite these two powers and thereby constitute abiding character by providing a unifying, cohesive, organizing structure to the self, what we might call a 'center of gravity'." Affections are thus "the means by which we are engaged with the world, and they signal to us what is worth attending to at any particular point in time."[72] This is exactly the sense Hauerwas has in mind when he hints that our passions "make us what we are" and that emotions are "signals that are meant to remind us what sort of people we are."[73] In any case, contrary to Lewis's reading, Hauerwas does not regard the challenge of narrative or vision as primarily a matter of *understanding*,[74] but a matter of initiation into concrete practices embedded within narrative traditions, and of acquiring "sustained habits that form my emotions and passions, teaching me to feel one way or another."[75] These various indications clearly show that Hauerwas underscores the positive role of the emotions in the formation of character in a manner that rules out any commitment to the myth of the passions.

Secondly, the significance given to the emotions by Hauerwas does not, however, mean that the emotions are to be prized over and beyond reason. This is why Hauerwas rejects Solomon's prioritization of the emotions as just the flip side of liberalism's prioritization of reason.[76] What this rejection means is that any consideration that portrays reason and emotion in terms of "either-or" involves a false alternative. This false alternative seems to be assumed by Lewis when he criticizes Hauerwas for not questioning "the centrality given to reason in the moral tradition; he only questions the nature of reason."[77] What Lewis fails to see is that this is not necessarily a shortcoming, since what is crucial is not whether reason or emotion is more central, but the type of reason that informs the moral life in general, and self-agency in particular. In fact, once one begins with this false alternative, one stands the danger of misconstruing the very nature of practical rationality, which calls into question any strict demarcation between intellect and emotion. We shall attend more fully to this embodied nature of moral rationality in our fourth chapter. For now, we need to tease out some key implications which an adequate focus on the emotions bears on the historical conception of the moral life in general, the notion of moral character in particular.

Character, Narrative Emotions, and Finitude

What is specifically novel within Hauerwas's account of the emotions is that it is narrative-based. Thus to avoid any impression of the irreducibility, or 'naturalness', of emotions, Hauerwas points to the role of the various tradition-ed practices and habits in *forming* one's emotions and passions, *teaching* one to feel one way or another. Such a narrative account of the emotions[78] not only recognizes that the moral self (character) is located in its affective appeal, it affirms that the latter is itself grounded in the social-linguistic particularity of a given tradition. This observation by itself calls into question any exaggerated claim to the autonomy of the self or its ability to summon the various factors that constitute its existence. Rather, it shows how the status of the self is much more one of participation and belonging than of self-definition or self-constitution.

Although we shall attend more fully to the narrative nature of the self in our third and fourth chapters, it is already clear that the attention to narrative affirms a basic historicity and finitude to the self which is bound to frustrate any liberal claims for self-mastery or self-creation. This point becomes particularly poignant when a narrative account of the emotions is invoked, for the latter reveals even more clearly the extent to which the moral life in general, the self (character) in particular, greatly depends on factors beyond the agent's direct control. The conclusion Hauerwas has to draw from the affective investment in his concept of character bring him close to Frankfurt's idea of 'importance'[79] and to Nussbaum's idea of 'fragility'.

The notion of 'importance' involves at least two key implications for ethics. First, more than the standard notions of 'right', 'obligation', and even 'virtue', the notion of 'importance' connects the moral life directly to its affective dimension. As Hauerwas notes, "It is our nature, particularly in the form of our desires, that forces us to be moral. Lust, for example, certainly can be chaotic, but it can also set us on a way of life that makes us care about something. It is therefore a precious resource which we cannot do without."[80] Inasmuch as it points to the affective basis of care, the notion of importance thus calls into question the rationalistic biases of the standard account of ethics. To this effect, Hauerwas notes that the fact "that people appreciate the difference between right and wrong does not require in the first instance an intellectual skill, but an *inculcated* caring, a habit of taking certain sorts of things seriously."[81]

What the above indications show is that once the embodied nature of the moral agent is taken seriously, then morality cannot be a matter simply of following rules and obligations, but it must also and equally involve *learning* to feel one way or another, or *learning* to care about certain things, some more than others. It is, in fact, this aspect of care that connects the moral life to the pursuit of happiness.[82] Notice, however, that we have emphasized 'learning' in the above sentence and 'inculcated' in the citation before it. This has been to avoid any impression that there is something foundational about feelings that might underwrite a 'natural' morality. Rather, the stress is meant to underscore the fact that it is social-linguistic practices and habits which "*form* my emotions and passions *teaching* me to feel one way or another." In other words, the pursuit of happiness takes place within concrete practices of everyday life.

Secondly, the notion of "importance" points to a certain helplessness concerning the objects of one's care. Harry Frankfurt calls this helplessness, which is a result of affective investment, a strange experience of "volitional necessity."[83] Although Hauerwas does not employ the same terminology, he comes to a very similar understanding when he notes that, "if we are asked why is it we should care, the only response is to point out that in fact we do care and that it is hard to see how we could be people without caring."[84] It is significant that we note this helplessness in relation to the "importance of what we care about," since it shows that once the notion of importance is taken as a starting point, the question "Why Be Moral?" becomes totally absurd. That one cares about certain things more than others is part of the sort of person (character) one is, and it is hard to see how one would cease to care about these things without ceasing at the same time to be the sort of person one has become.[85] Thus, the really significant question is not whether to care or not to care ("Why be Moral?"), but what to care about. For, the particular objects of one's care not only reveal the sort of person one is, caring for them forms one into a distinctive individual.

However, to admit the centrality of the notion of "importance" is not only to deny self-sufficiency within the moral life, it is to open the moral life in general, and the notion of character in particular, to vulnerability through chance, reversal, or possible loss. Thus, prioritizing the notion of "importance" is one way of underscoring that the self (character) is in a great measure dependent on those contingent, thus unstable, goods and relations of one's care, the most important of which is friendship *(philia)*.[86] Here, however, it is important to note that when Hauerwas talks about friendship he does not limit it to the interpersonal relations between like-minded individuals. He defends the broader Aristotelian account of friendship which is co-extensive with the very notion of tradition or community. Contrary to popular impressions, Hauerwas argues, Aristotle does not assume that people must be strictly equal in status, power, or position, in order to be friends:

> For there seems to be a notion of what is just in every community, and friendship seems to be involved as well. Men address as friends their fellow travellers on a voyage, their fellow soldiers, and similarly also those who are associated with them in other kinds of community. Friendship is present to the extent that men share something in common, for that is also the extent to which they share a view of what is just. And the proverb "friends hold in common what they have" is correct, for friendship consists in community. (*NE* 1159b25–30)

It is in view of this broader conception of friendship as "fellow travellers" that character is said to be a "gift."[87] As a gift, the development of a truthful character is dependent on others with whom one happens to be bound, through tradition, into a common adventure. That is why, Hauerwas has argued, it is better to understand character not so much in terms of a prospective self-projecting or constant effort to realize an ideal, but more in terms of a retrospective acknowledgement of what one has become. This is what confirms the Aristotelian insight that the development of good character is greatly a matter of luck.[88] But also, this is what makes the moral good, inasmuch as the latter is inseparable from the development of character, both fragile and highly tragic. In this respect, Hauerwas has welcomed the basic thrust of Nussbaum's argument in *The Fragility of Goodness*, where she shows that excellence is impossible without vulnerability.[89] Nussbaum depicts this tragic sense of life by showing that Greek virtue was an attempt to live in a way that minimizes one's subjection to the unpredictable vicissitudes of life—that is, a way of being to some extent self-sufficient. However, as forms of excellence, the virtues make one's life more vulnerable, as the various Greek tragedies so dramatically portray. For, no one's character "is sufficient to embody the richness of the moral value and virtues of our existence. Our character is therefore the source of our strength, as it provides us with a history of commitment, but in doing so it also sets the stage for the possibility of tragedy."[90]

We have taken time to draw attention to the elements of finitude, 'importance', and fragility partly in order to show how once attention is paid to the embodied nature of the moral agent, there cannot be any straightforward ('rational') account of the moral life. Rather, the very formation of character, in as far as the latter is to a great extent an affective investment, is shown to depend on various external goods, which open it up to luck, constant vulnerability, tragic conflict, and to the possibility of reversal. Dependence on these contingent and external goods cannot but make the notion of character a source of constant philosophical frustration. For one reason, such a historically contingent starting point as character cannot but appear to many to be simply too fragile to build the moral project upon. Secondly, the elements of luck, tragedy, fragility, etc., make the notion of character resistant to any straightforward predictability, clarity, and control. This, according to Hauerwas, is one reason why the Kantian standard accounts have sought to get behind the language of moral character, in favor of a more 'rational' account of ethics based on universalizable principles and obligations. In fact, Hauerwas sees this Kantian quest for a more secure ground for the moral life as nothing but the modern equivalent of Plato's attempt (as described by Nussbaum) to overcome, through rationalization, unity, and commensurability, the role of fortune and tragedy in the moral life.

However, the very attempt to overcome the fragile and tragic nature of the moral life not only impoverishes human existence, it makes one more susceptible to violence since, in an attempt to overcome the historically contingent starting point, one takes flight into a false universalism of meta-narrative singularity. Theologically, this attempt, embodied within much of contemporary philosophy, is correlative to the sin of pride—an "attempt to live *sui generis,* to live as if we are or can be the authors of our own stories."[91] The sin here is a failure to realize the creaturely limits of the self, or, what amounts to the same thing, to realize that the self always finds itself as a 'character' in a drama not of its own making. In a lengthy citation from Reinhold Niebuhr, Hauerwas describes the sin both in religious and moral terms:

> Our unwillingness to face our contingency breeds insecurity which we seek to overcome by a "will-to-power which overreaches the limits of human creatureliness. Man is ignorant and involved in the limitations of a finite mind; but he pretends that he is not limited. He assumes that he can gradually transcend finite limitations until his mind becomes identical with universal mind. All of his intellectual and cultural pursuits, therefore, become injected with the sin of pride. . . . The Bible defines sin in both religious and moral terms. The religious dimension of sin is man's rebellion against God, his effort to usurp the place of God. The moral and social dimension of sin is injustice. The ego which falsely makes itself the centre of existence in its pride and will-to-power inevitably subordinates other life to its will and thus does injustice to other life."[92]

This homiletic diatribe fittingly brings us to the end of this long section. The section, it must be recalled, started by tracing the intellectualism within Hauerwas's early conception of character to his commitment to action theory, but which cannot be seen (contrary to Lewis) as an example of his subscription to the myth of the passions. Against this background, we have underscored both the role and narrative account of the emotions within Hauerwas's conception of the moral life. Our primary aim in this section, however, has been to show that an adequate attention to affective investment confirms the historical and fragile nature of the moral life in general and of the self (character) in particular. This is the case not only because of the involuntary springs of action, but also because the affective dimension of care points to the self's dependency on external and contingent goods through the notion of "importance." While such attachments certainly do contribute to the excellence of character, they do so by opening it to the possibility of luck, conflict, reversal, and possible loss.

4. Responsibility for One's Character: Beyond Freedom

The denial of any self-sufficiency in the development of one's character in the previous section raises a crucial issue concerning responsibility for one's character. Can one still be held responsible for developing a certain character, even when it has been acknowledged that character is dependent on a certain measure of luck, and on factors beyond one's direct control? How much freedom does one have in the formation of character, anyway? This section provides an answer to these and similar questions by exploring Hauerwas's conception of responsibility in general and responsibility for moral character in particular.

As a preliminary remark we need to note that throughout his work, Hauerwas makes it clear that the formation of character is the responsibility of the agent. There has been, however, a gradual shift in Hauerwas's understanding of responsibility from a simple modernist model of responsibility (in his earlier work) to a more sophisticated, tradition-dependent model of responsibility within his current thinking.

This section is divided into two subsections. The first is an exposition and a critique of the standard (modernist) conception of responsibility, which Hauerwas also inadvertently assumes in his early work. In the second subsection we note Hauerwas's attempt to overcome this standard conception of responsibility. We shall particularly note the role of tradition in this attempt, and how, by attending to the notion of tradition, Hauerwas comes to assume a nonfoundational conception of responsibility, i.e., a concept of "responsibility beyond freedom."

A Standard Conception of Responsibility

In his earlier work, Hauerwas's account of character involved the assumption that one is responsible for one's character in view of what Robert Audi has called the "traceability thesis."[93] According to this thesis, one is said to be responsible for one's character in the sense that one's character is traceable to responsibility for the actions that produced it, sustain it, or might alter it. At least three key assumptions sustain this specifically *modern* conception of responsibility. First, this model of responsibility assumes that the fundamental bearers of (normative) responsibility are *acts*. Secondly, the basis of this responsibility lies in the agent's capacity, ability, or faculty for *controlling* those actions. The agent's capacity to control his actions explains why, for example, Audi assumes that one can still be held responsible for one's character even if one may not have chosen on the social, psychological, or physiological factors that influence that character. One can nevertheless be held responsible for one's character because one can still "*monitor* it in ways that will lead to my trying to reform it if the need becomes evident, or to buttress it under conditions of impending erosion. The *control* I have over my traits derives from my *control* over my actions, which in turn affect my acquisition or retention of traits."[94] In a further complication, Audi even thinks that the "techniques" by which one can monitor or control one's character are primarily mental: "Many of these techniques involve sheer self-discipline, for example, *reminding* oneself what is right and exercising the will power to do it."[95]

Thirdly, this model of responsibility presupposes the existence of freedom. The latter, however, is understood in a specifically modern sense of *autonomy*. According to this model, ethical responsibility is imaginable only when "a *free* subject is set free from the enigmatic weight of the past and from all passivity, [and] is the initiator of his acts."[96] From this perspective, it becomes obvious that this model of responsibility is grounded in an ontology of identity that presupposes a self-existing or transcendental 'I' who stands outside its activities so as to 'own', 'control', or 'monitor' them, and serve as their 'condition of possibility'.

The presence of these three assumptions make this a characteristically *modern* conception of responsibility. In particular, the assumption of freedom as a condition-of-possibility for responsibility helps to explain why a great deal of contemporary literature on moral responsibility is either exclusively focused on, or assumes as of crucial importance, the freedom-determinism debate.[97] For, it is assumed that only if the will can be shown to be free, could a case be made for moral responsibility. The same assumption of freedom as a condition for responsibility helps to explain much of the frustration with a concept like moral character within modern ethical reflection. For example, Thomas Nagel argues that the notion of character is problematic for ethics because it compromises freedom.[98] Character, according to Nagel, is primarily a matter of what he, and Bernard Williams[99] after him, calls "constitutive luck," i.e., dependent on factors beyond one's control and conscious *choice* (e.g., biology and other "accidents of history").[100] Nagel's frustration basically springs from his failure to imagine, given his commitment to the modern conception of responsibility, how one can be held responsible both for the formation of character and for actions that flow out of what develops out of such luck.[101]

We have taken time to elaborate the features of this modern model of responsibility because it is the one that greatly governs Hauerwas's early account of character. In fact, his attempt to ground the formation of character in agency appears like a strategy in view of the "traceability thesis." In particular, his excessive concern for deliberative activity and rational "choice" as the basis of character in his early work[102] seems to have been, at least in part, a way to save character from a frustration like that experienced by Nagel, by ensuring the agent's integrity and control over what he does and, thus, over what he finally becomes. This is one reason why Hauerwas, in his early account of character, tends to play down Aristotle's and Aquinas's remarks on habituation, in favor of those that underline that man's rational nature "requires that he *actively* shape and form his life by his activity through his desires and *choices.*"[103] One is left without any doubt that Hauerwas then assumed a modern conception of responsibility when a passage like the one below is invoked. In it, Hauerwas makes it clear that it is finally by choice that we become the sort of people we are: "opinions do not qualify us in quite the same way as choice; for we can be good while still holding bad opinions, but we cannot be good and make bad choices. The reason for this seems to be that to choose means that we really commit or determine our self in one direction rather than another. . . . For this reason Aristotle says that choice is very closely related to virtue, for it is by our choices that we acquire character."[104]

However, by attempting to fit the formation of character within a foundational model of responsibility, Hauerwas easily overlaid his early account of character with a voluntaristic bias. As a result of this voluntarism, the formation of character in Hauerwas's early work appeared more like the agent's heroic achievement. Such a conception of character is indeed problematic, both theologically and philosophically. Theologically, an emphasis on character (so understood) would sit uneasily with some aspects of Christian beliefs, for example, grace and forgiveness, and might even seem to lead to a certain form of Pelagianism.[105]

From a philosophical point of view, the notion of character, especially in as far as it is marked by an overemphasis on self-determination, choice, the priority of the agent's perspective, as well as the claim that the primary moral question is "What should I be?" easily evokes the view of man the self-maker. In fact, such an emphasis seems to suggest a normative endorsement for an Aristotelian 'magnanimous man' or a Nietzschean *Übermensch,* who seems to be driven by a constant concern for self-improvement. What is particularly problematic is that such an emphasis on self-determination can easily give the misleading impression of a blueprint for character in the form of the "sort of person I should be" which one then sets out to realize.[106]

The traceability of responsibility for one's character to the agent's "choices" and "decisions" also introduces a subtle but unfortunate tension within Hauerwas's early account of the self. Hauerwas's insistence on man's self-agency was an attempt to get away from the transcendental, substantialist self of modern philosophy. As noted earlier, from man's nature as a self-determining agent, Hauerwas was to draw the conclusion (against libertarians) that there can be no self that stands behind agency in order to externally "cause," "own," or "control" its activities as if it were an external agent. However, his predilection for choice and decision as the bedrock of responsibility seems to require precisely this ontology of identity.

The Benefits of a Concept of Tradition

Hauerwas himself has become aware of these tensions in his early work, and has, in a "New Introduction" to *Character and the Christian Life* (1985), attributed them to his "then still lingering Kantianism."[107] The effect of this Kantianism, however, was that while he was keen to highlight those aspects that encouraged the agent's control, choice, and self-determination, he did not sufficiently attend to the more passive aspects of the agent's formation and habituation. This explains why, for instance, throughout his extensive analysis of Aristotle's notion of choice *(proairesis)* (*CCL,* 47–56), Hauerwas had failed to point out how the notion of choice in Aristotle was not foundational. Rather, for Aristotle the notion presupposes a wider context of settled habits and socially integrated goals. Without appealing to this wider context, there would be no way that the apparent dilemma involving Aristotle's notion of "choice" could be made sense of. In *NE* II, Aristotle makes it clear that virtues involve "choice." However, he is equally clear that there are two sorts of activities for which virtues are dispositions: actions and feelings (*NE* 1105b26; 1104b14; 1106b17; 1106b25; 1107a 9); the goal of virtue is not only to "act" well, but also to "feel," or be "acted upon" (affected) in the right way. The problem is that while actions are clearly chosen and have their *arche* within the agent, this cannot be said about the emotions and passions. How, then, can virtue be *proairetic?*

The only way that this dilemma could be avoided is by noting that *proairesis* for Aristotle does not have to do with simple "decision" or "with individual moments in an agent's life, nor with individual single actions, but with the practices of that life within the *larger context* of the character and intentions of a moral subject."[108] Only when this "larger context" is invoked does it become clear why Aristotle refers to virtues as dispositions *(hexis)* rather than "skills" or potentialities *(dunameis)* for action. As dispositions, virtues are cultivated and not chosen in any simple sense, for it is not as a direct result of calculation, deliberation, resolution, or any other relatively simple human activity that one becomes courageous, temperate, or wise. Rather, it is through a process of *ethismos*, or habituation, through the habitual acting out and embodying of those actualizations which the dispositions are dispositions toward, that virtue is acquired.[109]

It is this larger context that is at stake within the circularity we already noted at the heart of Aristotle's conception of character: "One can only become just by performing just acts, but in order to perform just acts one must already be just." The comprehensive political background and conventions within Greek society which are presupposed in Aristotle's ethical writings explain why Aristotle did not regard this circular argument as vicious but hermeneutic. This observation is significant since it clearly shows that the agent Aristotle had in mind is one who stood within (or had to be initiated into) a community of meaning and interpretation, in which he comes to discover that he is *already* connected in a network of social roles and practices that presuppose an operative conception of justice. It is for this reason that Aristotle thought that it does little good to argue with people who have not been "well-brought up," for they "do not have a notion of what is noble and truly pleasant, since they have never tasted it" (*NE* 1179b15–30).

Aristotle did not thereby imply that one could become virtuous simply by mechanical habituation. He is quite clear that the goodness or badness of moral character is due to the goodness or badness of the actions leading to its formation. And, as he argues at length (*NE* iii, 1–5), those actions are straightforwardly *voluntary*. It would, however, be a mistake to think that Aristotle's lengthy analysis of the conditions for the voluntariness of action was an attempt to establish the voluntariness of the states of character. Such a reading, although fairly widespread, seems to allow too smooth an interface between Aristotle's notion of voluntariness and the modern accounts of responsibility. The motive behind this smooth reading is to show that one is responsible for one's character because one is responsible for the actions that produced it.[110] True, Aristotle says different things at different times that may encourage this 'modern' reading. For example, his analysis in *NE* iii, 1–5 establishes that a voluntary action is one whose "origin" is in the agent, and makes it clear that the "origin" in question is the sort which makes it depend on the agent whether the action happens or not (*NE* 1110a15–17, 1111a23, 1113b17–19,1136b28–29, 1139a31, 1139b5). Moreover, Aristotle says that such an inquiry into the conditions under which one is the origin of one's actions is necessary because "we praise and blame people only for what they are responsible for." In this respect, only voluntary actions are praised and blamed (*NE* 1109b30–2//*EE* 1223a10–13). It is also true that Aristotle says that states of character are praiseworthy and blameworthy things (*NE* iii, 5). In one instance, he even seems to have thought that we acquire our states of character voluntarily (*NE* 1114a3–31).

These indications notwithstanding, nowhere in his account of voluntariness does Aristotle indicate that blameworthiness or praiseworthiness of states of character require that they are voluntary. On the contrary, although Aristotle thought that both actions and states of character were praiseworthy (or blameworthy), he seemed to assume that they are praiseworthy (or blameworthy) in apparently "different, although related ways: The latter are praiseworthy because they *produce* good actions and feelings, while the former are praiseworthy because they *are* good products produced by praiseworthy states."[111] In fact, once these two levels of responsibility are acknowledged, it becomes clear that Aristotle's account of voluntariness is not an attempt to establish conditions under which one is responsible for one's character, but to capture the conditions in which the agent's action is produced by, or a genuine expression of, his character. In Aristotle's view, only agents who have genuine character (a "firm and lasting disposition") are responsible for their voluntary actions.

It would require an independent study to reconstruct a complex notion of responsibility within Aristotle's ethical writings.[112] However, the foregoing remarks already help to show that Aristotle assumed an account of moral responsibility for character far more complex than what one gets from attending to his explicit analysis of the notions of "voluntariness" and "choice." According to this account, which Aristotle does not explicitly develop, the formation of, as well as responsibility for, one's character requires the wider and far more complex network of socially integrated goals and concrete practices. Without this context (and the presence of moral character) to begin with, the notions of "voluntariness" and "choice" would themselves remain unintelligible.

This point is crucial for at least two reasons. First, by assuming this "larger context," Aristotle ruled out any illusions that he had to, or even could, supply a foundational account of responsibility for moral character. On the contrary, by subsuming the formation of character within this larger context, he was aware that the self was always *already* morally implicated by one's participation in the various practices of concrete living, and as a result, the development of character will always already have started. Secondly, failure to invoke this larger context (as in the case with Hauerwas's early work) could not but leave the notion of character begging for a foundational basis. It is therefore only when Hauerwas "was 'forced' to see the importance of narrative,"[113] that he began to attend, through the notion of tradition, to the larger context of the formation of character. Only then did he begin to assume a more complex and nonfoundational account of responsibility in the development of character.

The discovery of the key notions of narrative and tradition brought significant developments in Hauerwas's conception. Primary among these developments was the realization that more than the notion of agency, "a community of character" lies behind the formation of the self and human character. What this development amounted to was a realization that more than being a "self-determination," the development of character is a "formation" or "transformation" through initiation into the practices of a community. Hauerwas has sought to preserve this insight by suggesting that character formation is best assumed under the metaphor of "journey."[114]

This metaphor of journey has at least two key implications for the conception of character. First, unlike a "trip," a "journey" precludes any idea of self-sufficiency or self-mastery on the part of the agent.[115] Understood as a journey, the notion of character, therefore, dispels any impressions for a voluntaristic blueprint in the formation of character and points to the communal (social-linguistic) adventure that sustains it. Secondly, the metaphor of journey confirms the ongoing aspect of character. This realization is crucial, for it both denies any ahistorical fixity (of self-identity) to the self and confirms that the formation of character is always going on whether one is aware of it or not.

Both of these implications of the metaphor of journey lead to an interesting but further qualification of Hauerwas's conception of the moral life and the task of ethics. Against the neglect of the formation of the agent within the standard accounts, Hauerwas had vehemently opposed the assumption of "What should I *do*?" as the primary moral question. With the metaphor of journey, he begins to see that his proposed starting point of

"What sort of person should I be?" was equally problematic (given the latter's voluntaristic implications). And so, more recently, Hauerwas has accepted that a more adequate way of understanding the moral project is to construct it around the question: "What sort of people are *we becoming*" through participation in a given social-linguistic practice?[116] The double shift within this novel formulation is significant: While the "we" is meant to draw attention to the social dimension of the formation of character, the use of the present "becoming" is significant for the realization that this formation is constantly going on. In our acting and wanting, in our descriptions and choices, we are becoming some sort of person, i.e., we are developing character.

The metaphor of journey has accordingly provided Hauerwas with a novel way of characterizing the relation between freedom and character. In particular, the realization that the formation of character is always underway means that such a formation has not even "awaited freedom." And so, freedom (especially understood as "choice") cannot be the basis for the development of character. Rather, "freedom is a quality that derives from our having a well-formed character."[117] The inversion of the relation between freedom and character involves nothing less than a rejection of the standard account of freedom and an affirmation of a narrative-based conception. Freedom, Hauerwas writes, "is not a name for some real or ideal state in which we have absolute control of our lives." Rather, it is the capacity to "claim as one's own" the various events and actions within one's biography. Such a capacity is not based on a substantialist metaphysics of the self, but is a narrative capacity; it does not primarily depend on one's "awareness" of what one is doing, it is an ability "to locate my action within an ongoing history and within a community of language users." However, such a narrative, which is able to provide one with skills to claim one's life as one's own, is "not the sort that I can simply 'make mine' through a decision. Substantive narratives that provide me a way to make myself my own require one to grow into the narrative." This is the sense in which freedom derives from a well-formed character, since character "is constituted by those skills of description which allow us to make both what we have done and what has happened to us part of an ongoing narrative."[118]

What has emerged from this chapter is not only the conclusion that the notion of moral character is a helpful starting point for ethical reflection, but that this notion is unavoidable if one has to offer a convincing account of the moral life. The notion of moral character particularly confirms the inherent temporality, sociality, as well as fragility of the moral life in general, and the self in particular. Understood as moral character, the self is not an ontologically self-existing identity or noumenal 'I' who stands over and beyond its various objects and relations, in the historical world. Rather, as character, the self is always embodied within various limitations—of its historical agency, its attachment to concrete objects and relations ("importance"), and of the hermeneutical horizons of a shared way of life (tradition)—all of which point to the extent to which the self owes its status and integrity to contingent factors, relations, and objects. As a result of these attachments, both the freedom and responsibility which such a historically embodied self assumes can neither be totally original nor absolute. It is a responsibility that preexists the self. One does not assume this responsibility by virtue of an ontological status. Rather, one 'discovers' this responsibility which is somehow 'already there' through participation in the various social-linguistic practices of a shared way of life.

In the last two sections of this chapter we have been particularly keen to point to the development within Hauerwas's thinking. This development is not limited to Hauerwas's views on moral character; it reflects the constantly developing nature of his thinking. No doubt, Hauerwas's readiness to qualify earlier views frustrates any attempt to build a "system" out of his thinking. However, it confirms that the main preoccupation behind his work is not to defend a certain position but to suggest categories that promise fruitful ways to think about the moral life. This attempt leads him to move on, or away from, earlier convictions as he critically rethinks these convictions, oftentimes in relation to the views of his critics. We have traced this intellectual development within the notion of moral character by noting how the emphasis on agency and self-determination (earlier work) gives way to an emphasis on the social linguistic basis of character. This focus on social-linguistic practice, in fact, helps to show how, although the notion of moral character continues to be central in Hauerwas's reflection, methodologically it is eventually subsumed under the (presently) dominant notions of vision and narrative.[119] We must, therefore, examine these two notions within his work (in our third and fourth chapters, respectively) in order to provide further defense of the historical account of the moral life in general, and the self in particular.

3

Re-visioning Ethics:
'Unselfing', Language, and Particularity

> We can only act within the world we can see and we can see the
> world rightly by being trained to see. We do not come to see just by
> looking, but by disciplined skills developed through initiation into
> a narrative. We cannot see the world rightly unless we are changed,
> because contrary to our assumptions, we do not desire to see the
> world truthfully.
>
> Hauerwas

Hauerwas's conception of morality as vision must be understood as a reaction to, and as an alternative for, "a far too narrow conception of moral experience accepted by many philosophical and religious ethicists."[1] This conception of morality as vision is one that Hauerwas adopts early in his work, by drawing on the writings of the Irish-born (Dublin 1919) novelist, playwright, and philosopher Dame Iris Murdoch.[2] The burden of this chapter is to survey Hauerwas's understanding of morality as vision. The chapter is divided into three sections. In the first section we shall survey the common ground between Murdoch and Hauerwas. The section particularly notes Hauerwas's positive appreciation of Murdoch's critical assessment of the contemporary ethics of autonomy, her account of the difficulty involved in seeing rightly, and her close identification of morality and art through the notion of *attention*.

The second section explores the distance between Murdoch's and Hauerwas's conception of vision. The goal is to point out the limitations of Murdoch's account of vision and of Hauerwas's advance over these "Murdochian muddles," particularly through his attention to the social-linguistic basis of vision. This particular aspect forms the distinctive contribution of Hauerwas to the understanding of vision. It is therefore taken over in the third section in an attempt to recast the metaphor of vision within his historicist conception of the moral life under the image of a craft. At stake within this section is the need for training and authority before one can come to a truthful vision of reality.

The purpose of the discussion is to advance the central argument of the book by making clear the inescapability of particularity within the moral life. Already in Iris Murdoch's re-imaging of the moral life around the key virtue of *attention* there is a return to the aspect of particularity within the moral life—an aspect which, however, tends to be theorized away by an exclusive identification of morality with an impartial and objective point of view within standard Kantian accounts. What is distinctive about Hauerwas's conception is that our vision (morality) is particular not so much because the objects of our attention are particular (though they certainly are), but because the skills by which our vision is trained are dependent on particular narrative traditions.

1. The Significance of Vision: Murdochian Themes

Dame Iris Murdoch began one of her essays in the '60s by noting that we live in a scientific and antimetaphysical age. We are, Murdoch noted, the heirs of the Enlightenment, romanticism and liberalism, traditions that have left us with a too shallow and flimsy conception of human personality.[3] This impoverishment, she suggested, ironically resulted from a too grand and too optimistic conception of the self: The modern self is rational and free, independent and powerful, autonomous and responsible. Kant, more than anybody else, has provided Western moral philosophy with its dominating image of the individual as a free rational will. By establishing the autonomy of reason, Kant at the same time repudiated the classical insight that the source of value and goodness lies outside ourselves. For Kant, nothing transcends the law of the individual's rational choice. Confronted even with Christ, Kant's autonomous and moral person must turn away to consider the judgment of his or her own conscience and to its universalizable reason.[4] After Kant, the autonomous individual becomes progressively stripped of even the meager metaphysical background that Kant was prepared to allow him.

One meets a version of this autonomous individual in Nietzsche, where the sovereign moral concept is courage in the sense which identifies it with freedom, will, and power. And as Murdoch pointed out, it is not such a long step from Nietzsche to existentialism, to analytic philosophy, and to phenomenology, where she traces versions of the modern autonomous self. In Sartre, the most influential of French existentialists, the autonomous self is solitary and free. Any suggestion of a transcendent background of values lies under suspicion of *mauvaise foi*. However, in the isolation of the individual will, the Sartrian authentic self remains condemned to itself and to complete freedom, a situation that rightly causes *angoisse*. One also gets a glimpse of the modern autonomous self in Heidegger, where, even in his ultimate possibility (of death), he is thrown back onto himself. If he must surrender, it must be to his own will and to his own possibilities. Heidegger is right, though, to point out the *angst* such 'transcendence' onto oneself causes. An even more refined picture of this modern autonomous self is encountered in analytical philosophy, where one is rational and totally free. The virtues fundamental to this analytic self are clarity and sincerity about intentions. Moral arguments are in reference to an empirical world of facts backed up by decision. One does not consult a standard outside oneself, but is "autonomous" in one's choices. One is not a "seer" of ethical truth, but a maker of it; not a character with certain virtues but a thin, abstract will that jumps from one decision to another.

Modern man's conception of himself, Murdoch surmised, is simply too grand. He optimistically combines a "simple-minded faith in science" with the assumption that he has the possibility of being completely rational and free. Moral philosophy, which, according to Murdoch, should present a realistic and accurate picture of the human condition and at the same time allow or show how one may improve morally, has only contributed to this consoling inflation of the self. Describing Murdoch's moral vision, Hauerwas writes:

> Rather than attempting to free each man from his paralyzing preoccupation with himself, modern moral philosophy has only increased and legitimatized this excessive self-concern. For our self-centeredness it only prescribes further self-reflection, since it has thought that our main moral errors result from adherence to illogical and confused moral reasons or arguments. Thus the primary responsibility for determining the reality of events still rests on the individual person. Both analytic and existentialist ethics share "a terror of anything which encloses the agent or threatens his supremacy as a center of significance. In this sense both philosophies tend toward solipsism"—i.e., just the condition that is the main cause of man's moral failure. "Self-knowledge, the minute understanding of one's own machinery, does not free the self; it only mires us deeper in our illusion of individual significance."[5]

Already in the early '60s, Murdoch saw the prevalent and popular trend in moral philosophy, under the dominant metaphors of autonomy and choice, to be both unrealistic and unambitious. Its voluntarism not only encouraged a certain noncognitivism in the moral life, but also spelled the loss of both the possibility and necessity of genuine transcendence and growth in the moral life. A key indication of this latter failure was how the classical moral-elitist concern of "How can I make myself better?"[6] had been replaced with a 'democratic' (and mediocre) preoccupation of "What should I do?" In Murdoch's view, genuine moral life should stretch one beyond this unambitious concern, towards the pursuit of some—albeit unattainable—*perfection.*

If moral philosophy is to assist in this goal, Murdoch suggested, then it needs to turn

> from the self-centred concept of sincerity to the other-centred concept of truth. . . . what we require is a renewed sense of the difficulty and complexity of the moral life and the opacity of persons. We need more concepts in terms of which to picture the substance of our being; it is through an enriching and deepening of concepts that moral progress takes place. Simone Weil said that morality was a matter of attention, not of will. We need a new vocabulary of attention.[7]

Murdoch was to find this "new vocabulary of attention" and the "enriching" of the concepts of morality in and through the metaphor of vision.

Murdoch on Morality as Vision

There are both critical and constructive aspects to Murdoch's use of the metaphor of vision. Critically, the use of the metaphor of vision by Murdoch is an attempt to get away from the language of choice and decision to a more comprehensive phenomenology of the moral life. The moral life, according to Murdoch, is not so much a matter of choice, as of vision, not of will but attention. More than thinking clearly or making rational choices, the moral life is a way of *seeing* the world. We differ, suggests Murdoch, not only because we choose different objects out of the same world but because we *see* different worlds. And when we

> assess people we do not just consider their solutions to specifiable practical problems, we consider something more elusive which may be called their total vision of life, as shown in their mode of speech or silence, their choice of words, their assessment of others, their conception of their own lives, what they think attractive or praise-worthy, what they think funny.[8]

This does not mean that Murdoch is oblivious to the necessity of making decisions, even hard decisions within the moral life. What she seeks to

capture here is the realization that what is needed if one is to make any decisions is not so much the "radical choice" of the existentialists, nor the
mental clarity of the analytic philosophers, but a kind of unselfish willingness to *see* the situation fairly, an *obedient* submission to reality. Similarly, at moments when situations are unclear, what is needed is not so
much a renewed attempt to specify the "facts," as a fresh *vision* which
may be derived from a story or from some sustaining concept which is able
to deal with what is obstinately obscure.[9]

Constructively, vision helps Murdoch to bring into focus two distinct
but related aspects of the moral life. First, against the background of existentialism, Murdoch used the notion of vision to focus ethics away from
the *self*-centered concept of sincerity to the *other*-centered concept of truth.
For Murdoch, this rethinking amounted to a key realization, namely, that
moral truth is not so much 'created' as 'discovered' by the self. The source
of moral goodness lies in a 'transcendent' object, i.e., an object outside one's
will. The moral task is to *see*, and respond to, this object fairly and justly,
without letting one's own needs, biases, and desires stand in one's way.

Secondly, the use of the metaphor of vision provided a way for Murdoch
to make a case for particularity as an inescapable dimension of morality
and of moral consciousness. This aspect is often "theorized away" by the
identification of morality with an impartial, impersonal, and objective
point of view. The moral task, under the metaphor of vision, is not a matter
of finding universalizable reasons or principles of action, but involves a true
and loving perception of particular, individual persons and situations.

In Murdoch, the central explanatory image which ties together these
two aspects of the moral life is the Platonic concept of the Good. When
Plato wants to explain the Idea of Good he uses the image of the sun (*Republic*, 503–9). In Plato's simile of the cave, the pilgrim emerges from the
cave and begins to see the real world in the light of the sun, and finally, the
sun itself. In "Sovereignty," Murdoch offers a re-reading of Plato's simile in
light of her understanding of the moral life as a life of vision. The main line
of her argument is straightforward: One becomes virtuous through forget-
fulness of self, and by focusing on something transcendent like Plato's idea
of the Good (sun). Like the Platonic sun, the good can only be seen at the
end of a long quest which involves a reorientation (the prisoners have to
turn round) and a gradual ascent out of the cave. Not only is the journey
long and tedious, the brilliance of its rays make the sun difficult to look at.
Looking at the sun is not like looking at other objects. Moreover, there are
false suns, easier to gaze upon and far more 'consoling' than the true one.

The fire in Plato's cave is such a false sun. For Murdoch, writing against the background of an inflated autonomous and rational will of the existentialists, the fire represents

> the self, the old unregenerate psyche, that great source of energy and warmth. The prisoners in the second stage of enlightenment have gained the kind of self-awareness which is nowadays a matter of so much interest to us. . . . They see the flames which threw the shadows which they used to think were real, and they can see the puppets, imitations of things in the real world, whose shadows they used to recognize. They do not yet dream that there is anything else to see. What is more likely than that they should settle down beside the fire, which though its form is flickering and unclear is quite easy to look at and cosy to sit by?[10]

The predicament of modern moral philosophy has been to mistake the self (fire) for the sun, self-scrutiny for goodness, sincerity for truth. Thus, the greatest moral challenge for the modern individual is to get away from the fire, to a contemplation and ascent towards the sun; to look directly out and away from self towards a distant transcendent perfection, a source of uncontaminated energy and goodness. For Murdoch, vision and virtue are but two aspects of this renewed challenge. After all, virtue is the attempt to pierce the veil of selfish consciousness to see the 'real' sun, to join the world as it really is.

Two characteristics (unity and indefinability) of the Platonic Good are particularly illuminating to the conception of the moral life. On one hand, the Platonic Good has power to unify other concepts such as courage, freedom, truth, and humility by being sovereign over them, and yet, on the other hand, the Good resists complete definition. The apparent tension between these two characteristics of the Good is instructive to explain, on the one hand, the transcendence that vision calls for, and, on the other, the particularity and individuality of the objects of vision. In Plato, the road from the cave towards the sun leads away from the world of particularity and detail towards the one transcendent idea of the Good. However, the (moral) pilgrim, once enlightened by the unifying idea of the Good (sun), must return to the cave, back to the sensible world of complexity and random detail. Because of this ascending-descending dialectic, Murdoch's "vision of the Good" clearly draws attention to the dialectical elements of random detail and intuited unity, of particularity and transcendence within the moral life.

A certain epistemological realism attends to the unifying and sovereign aspect of the Good. The Good (Platonic Sun) is real. It is (if you like) a 'thing' out there, and not a "mere value tag of the choosing will."[11] In fact, Murdoch's atheism seems to make the Good into God in disguise. The Good, Murdoch writes, is what "God was (or is): a *single perfect transcendent non-representable and necessary real object of attention.*"[12] It is this realism which partly explains the ethical intellectualism within Murdoch's metaphor of "vision of the Good." The latter is a form of 'contemplation'. And so, the moral life is understood by Murdoch as a continuous (but slow) ascent out of the darkness of *ignorance* (cave) to the light of *knowledge* (sun)—a kind of gradual exposing of the self to the 'illuminating' rays of goodness. Plato (and Murdoch, following him) pictures the pilgrim as ascending through four stages of 'enlightenment', progressively discovering at each stage that what he had been treating as realities were only shadows or images of something more real still. At the end of his quest, the pilgrim reaches a nonhypothetical first principle which is the Form or Idea of the Good. Only after this 'enlightenment' does the moral pilgrim descend and retrace his path, but moving only through the forms or true 'conception' of that which it previously 'understood' only in part. Concretely, this means that within the moral experience, "The 'mind' which has ascended to the vision of the Good can subsequently see the concepts through which it has ascended (art, work, nature, people, ideas, institutions, situations, etc., etc.) in their true nature and in their proper relationships to each other. The good man knows whether and when art or politics is more important than family."[13] Thus, through apprehension of the one idea of the Good, Murdoch argues, a certain hierarchy is introduced within the agent's manifold roles, obligations, and virtues, as well as within the various objects of one's attention.

Excusing the intellectualism as well as the assumption of unity and commensurability which marks the above Platonic conception (two shortcomings we shall attend to in the second section), Murdoch's "Vision of the Good" points to particularity as an aspect of the moral experience. One can have an experience of good persons, good actions, good situations, but the Good *qua* Good remains a perfection which "is never exemplified in the world we know." In its unmastered otherness, the Good resists any attempts at complete and determinate definition. As Hauerwas notes, "we do not necessarily come to understand the nature of the world; the strenuous moral task is to come to see the world as it is. Because the Good is indefinable this task can never be finished."[14] Vision of the Good thus depicts the moral task, which consists in an endless process of clarifying one's vision, thus evoking moral growth. A key aspect of this moral task is the very realization that the world, just like Plato's cave, does not come to us in a unity. One becomes moral by seeing and facing reality in its inexhaustible randomness and unsystematic and inexhaustible variety.

Hauerwas discovered Murdoch in the early 1970s, and immediately found her metaphor of vision highly instructive for rethinking the moral life. We therefore need to highlight, in the coming sections, some salient elements which Hauerwas has found particularly helpful in Murdoch's analysis and which he has appropriated in his own work.

The Difficult Task of 'Seeing': Contingency and Consolation

Throughout his analysis of morality as vision, Hauerwas leaves no doubt that learning to see clearly and realistically, which is the goal of the moral life, is not an easy task. One can only achieve it through training and discipline. In his earlier work, Hauerwas shared much of Murdoch's metaphysical and anthropological assumptions on why the task of beholding the Good is particularly difficult.[15] The world, Murdoch writes, "is aimless, chancy, and huge, and we are blinded by the self."[16] This means that the world is not only inexhaustibly random and particular, but, more, it lacks both unity and a *telos* to give it meaning. Similarly,

> human life has no external point or telos. . . . We are what we seem to be, transient mortal creatures subject to necessity and chance. This is to say that there is, in my view, no God in the traditional sense of that term; and the traditional sense is perhaps the only sense. . . . Equally the various metaphysical substitutes for God—Reason, Science, History—are false deities. . . . We are simply here.[17]

Confronted with this realization, "we are tempted to engage in fantastic reverie" or to "construct a veil to conceal the essential pointlessness of our existence." The result of this veil is that we fail to look at the world realistically or to *see* an individual object (say ourselves, a loved person, a lie) because we remain "completely enclosed in a fantasy world of our own into which we try to draw things from outside, not grasping their reality and independence, making them into dream objects of our own."[18]

The readiness by which the construction of this veil is accomplished confirms what both Murdoch and Hauerwas accepted as a key anthropological assumption, namely, that the human condition is characterized by 'sin'. Outside any theological context, Hauerwas, following Murdoch, describes this universal condition as an "inability to bear reality." He writes, "to be human is to create illusion."[19] Thus, contrary to the contemporary image of the self as rational, free, and powerful, "we are not isolated free choosers, monarchs of all we survey, but benighted creatures sunk in the very reality whose nature we are constantly and overwhelmingly tempted to deform by fantasy."[20] This is one reason why Murdoch appreciates Freudian psychology. The latter, she says, has been able to come to terms with the notion of 'original sin' by presenting "a realistic and detailed picture of 'the fallen man'." Freud sees, rightly in Murdoch's view, that the psyche is

> an egocentric system of quasi-mechanical energy, largely determined by its own individual history, whose natural attachments are sexual, ambiguous, and hard for the subject to understand or control. Introspection reveals only the deep tissue of ambivalent motive, and fantasy is a stronger force than reason. Objectivity and unselfishness are not natural to human beings.[21]

The picture that emerges in both Hauerwas and Murdoch is of a self that is not only naturally selfish, but that, "reluctant to face unpleasant realities," seeks *consolation*.

> Its [self's] consciousness is not normally a transparent glass through which it views the world, but a cloud of more or less fantastic reverie designed to protect the psyche from pain. It constantly seeks consolation, either through imagined inflation of self or through fictions of a theological nature. Even its loving is more often than not an assertion of self.[22]

This condition is so widespread that, in a particularly fascinating fashion, Murdoch plays the master of suspicion as she uncovers mechanisms of consolation in various fields. Philosophy itself, she suggests, can be a source of *consolation*. This temptation is nowhere more apparent than in the liberal moral philosophical tradition that combines "a consoling inflation of the self" with the assumption that "we can be completely rational and free." Such an idea of freedom simply encourages a consoling self-importance. Although Murdoch does not say so, it is clear that the same mechanisms of *consolation* can be detected in those philosophical meta-narratives that proceed with the self-assurance of having discovered the pattern of History, the essence of Reason; the evolution of Society; the nature of Truth, or the Story of stories.[23] Such philosophical pandering is simply an attempt to conceal the contingency of existence by imposing a pattern upon what is unavoidably particular.

Religion, too, can be a *consolation*. Prayer and sacraments may be 'misused' by the believer as mere instruments of consolation. In fact, for Dame Murdoch, Christian religion at its most popular level offers the most consoling moral framework by concealing the fact of death and the absolute contingency of existence which is a correlative of death. In so doing, however, it fails to *see* the human pilgrim: the supernatural background of its imagery provides an escape from the human condition rather than a realistic encounter with it. In this respect, "few ideas invented by humanity have more power to console than the idea of purgatory. To buy back evil by suffering in the embrace of good: what could be more satisfying, or as a romantic might say, more thrilling?"[24] Positively, however, Murdoch grants that at its less popular and more serious level, Christian theology is realistic. Thus, when it represents goodness as almost impossibly difficult to attain and sin as a universal characteristic of the human condition, theology reflects without consolation two fundamental aspects of human nature.

However, for both Murdoch and Hauerwas, human love can be the most compelling example of *consolation*. Most of our loving, both suggest, is a way of loving ourselves. We seldom love the other as other, but only as we make the other an aspect of our plan. "We [often] do not fall in love with a real person, but with the person we have created through our fantasy."[25] Murdoch's novels are full of characters who are so captured by pictures of another that they fail entirely to see the other as a distinct reality. Art, too, bears examples of the almost irresistible human tendency to seek consolation in fantasy. The talent of the artist can be readily employed to produce a work whose purpose is the consolation and aggrandizement of its author and the projection of his personal obsessions and wishes. For this reason, "almost all art is a form of fantasy-consolation and few artists achieve the vision of the real."[26]

The various mechanisms of *consolation* confirm not only the difficulty of "seeing" but also the realization that the chief enemy of clarity of vision is "personal fantasy: the tissue of self-aggrandizing and consoling wishes and dreams which prevents one from seeing what is there outside one."[27] If most of our moral decisions are shabby, Murdoch suggests, it is not because we do not "know enough facts" but because "our fat, relentless ego distorts our vision" by creating a fantasy world for itself which is far more consoling to behold than the particular, contingent, chancy, and tragic aspects of the real world. This is what makes the moral challenge one of vision, i.e., of a focus or gaze away from the self to the contingent and particular existence of the real world. The moral task is one of 'unselfing'.

The Task of Vision: 'Unselfing'

The 'unselfing' associated with vision is not limited to special occasions of the moral or mystic religious experience but is an everyday experience, as when one learns a foreign language. Murdoch's own example is learning Russian. Learning Russian leads the learner away from oneself towards something alien to one, something which one's consciousness cannot take over, swallow up, deny, or make unreal. The same can be said about the self-forgetful pleasure in observing the sheer pointless existence of animals, birds, trees, etc. In all these cases, an objective reality 'captures' one's attention. By submitting to the authority of these realities, one is involved in a form of self-forgetfulness, which clears one's mind of selfish care.

There is an element of transcendence associated with these ordinary experiences which provides a critical purchase to the existentialist conception of self as creator of moral value. It is, in fact, this 'unselfing' aspect of vision which reveals the helplessness the agent often feels with respect to moral situations. Even in a genuinely free moral response, one often experiences a certain helplessness in acting as one does. The metaphor of vision thus reveals how the moral life is deeply akin to the experience of love. It is pointless, beyond a certain point, to advise someone to stop loving, for falling out of love does not occur through a leap of the will (a matter of decision), but is an aspect of vision. It is only possible by "the acquiring of new objects of attention and thus new energies as a result of refocusing."[28]

The affinity between morality and love also shows how an understanding of freedom is connected with vision. For, freedom "is not the sudden jumping of the isolated will in and out of an impersonal logical complex," it is the "progressive and disciplined overcoming of self that allows for the clarification of our vision."[29] The virtue most necessary for this conception of freedom is humility, which "is not a peculiar habit of self-effacement, rather like having an inaudible voice, it is selfless respect for reality and one of the most difficult and central of all virtues."[30]

It could be objected that a conception of morality around the aesthetic metaphor of vision encourages a contemplative attitude on the part of the moral agent, whereas the point about this person is that he or she is essentially and inescapably an *agent*. Such an objection, however, fails to appreciate the priority of vision within agency and the fact that "we can only act in the world we see."[31] In fact, as Dame Murdoch notes, "our ability to act well 'when the time comes' depends partly, perhaps largely, upon the quality of our habitual objects of attention."[32] Besides, the metaphor of vision preserves the realization that the moral life is not so much a matter of active ordering of one's preferences as a response to one's situation. Much of the agent's moral commitment lies beyond one's direct choice and control, but is nonetheless incumbent on one, given the radical otherness of reality that one confronts. The primary moral challenge is to be able to see it all correctly and respond accordingly. Both Murdoch and Hauerwas cite many situations where the "fitting" moral response is a result of vision. Should I have an abortion? Should an unhappy marriage be continued for the sake of the children? Should an elderly relation be sent away to a nursing home? Should this retarded child be cared for or 'be sent to sleep'? In all these cases, as in similar others, coming to the 'right' answer "is an exercise of justice and realism and really *looking.*"[33] The challenge is to keep one's attention fixed upon the real situation and to prevent it from returning surreptitiously to the self with consolations of self-pity, resentment, fantasy, and/or despair.

In this attempt both Murdoch and Hauerwas make it clear that one does not "come to 'see'" just by looking, but through a certain discipline and training. In Murdoch, the concept that ties these aspects together is that of *attention.* This is a concept which Murdoch quite consciously borrows from Simone Weil, to express the idea that clear vision is a result of looking at reality, "not just any way" but through a "just and loving gaze."[34] This *virtue of looking* is not momentary. It is shaped by a habitual practice of attention, by which the quality and objects of one's attention themselves shape and reveal the sort of person one is, a realization that confirms that vision and the formation of character are simply two aspects of the same conception of ethics. Although Murdoch indicates that it is from within that complex fabric which is one's being that one sees or fails to see, it is Hauerwas who makes the dialectical relation between character and vision explicit. He notes how, while on the one hand, "a man's character is largely the result of [. . .] sustained attention," on the other, the objects and quality of one's vision, what one considers interesting, desirable, and praiseworthy, depend on the sort of person one has become through one's personal and societal narrative.[35] Accordingly, the work of attention continuously goes on and imperceptibly builds up structures of value around us and forms us into particular and distinctive sorts of individuals. This is why, even at crucial moments of choice, most of the business of choosing is, in fact, already over.[36] Thus, against the occasionalism of quandary and decision-based accounts of the moral life, vision and *attention* involve the realization that the moral life is something that goes on continually, not something that is switched off in between the occurrence of explicit moral choices.

For both Murdoch and Hauerwas, art provides an invaluable training in the *virtue of looking*. Murdoch's appreciation of art, especially literature, is perhaps not surprising. She has published more than fifteen novels, and acknowledges a personal debt to other authors as Jane Austen, Dickens, Tolstoy, Dostoevsky, George Eliot and Henry James. Hauerwas's own familiarity with literary characters in the works of authors as varied as Jane Austen, Trollope, Adams, and Murdoch has led him to appreciate how art, and literature in particular, can be a training in vision. Art is able to provide this training in at least three related ways. First, both Murdoch and Hauerwas note how art has the potential to develop a certain sensibility in the reader which is essential for any adequate moral understanding. By becoming "finely aware," through reading literary works, one becomes "richly responsible."[37] Art's great asset within this transformation is the ability to preserve and convey the enormous detail, variety, and contextuality of life, without succumbing to selfish obsession, fantasy, or conventional forms.[38] The good artist is thus characterized by an attentiveness to the otherness of reality and of his or her characters(s), seeing them in their radical particularity and contingency— whether they are sad, absurd, repulsive or even evil. This realism which marks a good artist transcends mere exact characterization. It is at once truth, pity, justice and love.[39] Thus, what is learned in the enjoyment of art, especially literature, is something about the 'real' quality of human nature as portrayed in literary characters. Thus, literature serves to *disclose* "our real situation" to us by enabling us to "focus attention" on this or that aspect of our experience. This is particularly needed since many aspects of one's tradition, because they have become so part and parcel of who one is, are difficult to discern in one's own life. It is impossible to "step out" of one's tradition so as to see it as a whole. It is therefore one of the functions of art to hold up a mirror to tradition in which such aspects of traditions and one's life may be reflected or revealed—not by abstraction—but in the full concrete texture of actual characters. It is also important to note that good art teaches how things and others can be looked at and loved without being seized and "appropriated into the greedy organism of the self."[40] Accordingly, the creation as well as the reading of various literary characters itself involves a basic forgiveness and humility, a letting be and appreciation of otherness.[41]

Secondly, art can provide insight into the peculiar sense in which the concept of virtue is tied on to the human condition. Murdoch has particularly developed this point in relation to her metaphysical assumption of an aimless and tragic world. Given the 'hope-less' nature of existence, Murdoch suggests, many of the stories people tell themselves are meant to console them and conceal the reality of death, chance, and contingency in their lives. Not so with good art, which has the power to break through conventional forms of consolation and reveal the 'unwelcome' aspects of existence, which one is often too timid to look at:

> It is the role of tragedy, and also of comedy, and of painting to show us suffering without a thrill and death without a consolation. Or if there is any consolation it is the austere consolation of a beauty which teaches that nothing in life is of any value except the attempt to be virtuous.[42]

For Murdoch, then, the absolute pointlessness of virtue revealed by the good artist, especially in the form of tragedy, is the pointlessness of human life itself.

We need not, and Hauerwas does not, accept Murdoch's extreme assumption of an aimless existence in order to appreciate the relation between virtue and art, especially in the forms of comedy and tragedy. In fact, Murdoch's assumption of both a metaphysically meaningless world and an anthropologically aimless life is questionable. If accepted, it would make the very exercise of virtue, which she calls for a dubious construction of value in a valueless world, an attempt to find meaning in an otherwise meaningless life! Wouldn't such an attempt be just another mechanism of the "consolation" she warns against, or the defense, at best, of ethics as a sort of pragmatism (and thus a return to the existentialist or modern subject able to choose for itself), which she begins by critically questioning.

It would therefore be more accurate for Dame Murdoch to speak of a metaphysically ambiguous world. The world exhibits both instances of teleology and aimlessness, of design and chance, of value and no-value (not valueless). Human life is equally ambiguous. Accordingly, the invigorating power of great art lies in its ability to portray this ambiguous otherness of reality. It does so, as Murdoch herself suggests, by "juxtaposition, almost identification of pointlessness and value," random detail and intuited unity, the permanent and the transient, charming beauty and revolting ugliness, comedy and tragedy. Given this basic ambiguity about life, the moral task is the ability to see it all realistically and to respond to it justly, which is inseparable from virtue.

Thirdly, both art and morality are other-directed. Good art, in both its genesis and enjoyment is totally opposed to selfish obsession. Thus, both morality and art are forms of 'unselfing', of a vision away from oneself toward the independent existence of something completely other. Both morality and art call for discipline (akin to some forms of spiritual exercises), which involves the checking of selfishness in the interest of seeing the 'real'. It is this attention to the real that makes both morality and art aspects of love. "Love is any relationship through which we are called from our own self-involvement, to appreciate the self-reality that transcends us."[43] For this reason, Hauerwas, following Murdoch, sees the artist to be the paradigm of the moral man, the lover who, being nothing himself, lets others exist through him.

> In the creation of a work of art the artist is going through the exercise of attending to something quite particular other than himself. The intensity of this exercise itself gives to the work of art its special independence. That is, it is an independence and uniqueness which is essentially the same as that conferred upon, or rather discovered in, another human being whom we love.[44]

It is on account of this close identification of art and morality that Hauerwas has argued that it is misleading to put the issue in terms of the relation between art and morality.[45] Such a formulation assumes the dominant Kantian view of morality and art as two separate spheres instead of seeing them as two aspects of the same struggle. This view is, according to Hauerwas, based on Kant's rationalist bias in characterizing art as a quasi-play activity, gratuitous, "for its own sake"—a sort of by-product of the failure to be entirely rational. However, given the complete pointlessness ("for its own sake") of art, it would be a clear mistake to regard our reference to art's great potential in sharpening vision, revealing reality, and strengthening judgment as an attempt to isolate the moral significance of art. If this were the case, one would be able to force art to serve some kind of "function." However, the artist cannot be said to write or paint for the sake of anything, not even for the sake of art, "any more than the man who enjoys conversation can be said to talk for the sake of talking."[46]

The "pointlessness" in these two examples of poetry and conversation makes it clear why both art and morality are affairs "we engage in for no end beyond the doing of them." It is therefore clearly a mistake to associate the moral life with the purposive aspects of our existence. We are not moral for reasons or ends beyond morality itself, which makes the question "Why be moral?"[47] something of a philosophical oxymoron. The only way such a question can be posed intelligibly is when the moral life has been reduced to the consideration of isolated actions which are abstracted from their narrative context of an individual's life and the sustaining tradition. However, understood as the life of a person rather than actions a person does, the moral life only begins when the complete pointlessness of morality is seen. The courageous person does not become courageous for any other reason than he or she "would not choose to be otherwise."[48] No doubt, there are many good reasons for being courageous, but they do not and cannot constitute the reason why one must be courageous any more than an artist can explain why he must write or paint.

The above affinity makes it all the more obvious why Hauerwas insists that the relation between morality and art "is not really causal but analogical."[49] The relation cannot be causal because the primary goal of art is not to convey information of facts, say about what reality is like or what kind of problems are involved in marriage. Rather, "the artist helps us to see 'facts' in a *new way*." What one gains from the artist's work is neither information nor new principles, but a *fresh vision*. Thus, the relation between art and morality is analogical, in that both are "modes of imagination." Art and morality are not

> separate modes of understanding that must be related, but they are rather equally rooted in the fundamental images that charge the imagination and allow us to understand at all—i.e., art and morality are equally dependent on metaphor. . . . Art and morality are therefore rooted in our language and involve the human endeavor not to have the imagination stilled by convention or distorted by fantasy.[50]

We reserve a discussion of Hauerwas's substantive understanding of the imagination for a later occasion. However, it is important to point out here how the introduction of the analogical conception of morality and art moves Hauerwas's conception of the themes of vision, imagination, art, and morality on a far more sophisticated level than Murdoch's. One clear advance in this direction is the social-linguistic context of the training in vision. This is an aspect that is completely neglected by Murdoch, but which becomes the centerpiece of Hauerwas's ethical reflection and is suggested already (in the citation above) by the reference to art and morality being rooted "in our language." It is particularly this important feature of vision that is at the heart of what has emerged as Hauerwas's "quarrel" with Murdoch. We must therefore examine more critically the differences between Hauerwas's and Dame Murdoch's respective conceptions of morality as vision. The goal of this examination will be to show how, in spite of his reliance on Murdoch's work, Hauerwas offers a far more adequate characterization of the moral life as a life of vision.

2. Beyond Murdochian 'Muddles'

Contingency, Hope, and 'Creatio ex nihilo'

More recently, Hauerwas has clearly distanced himself from some of Dame Murdoch's metaphysical views, particularly her assumption for the utter lack of finality (purpose) in the world.[51] We already noted how such an assumption of a metaphysically aimless existence renders the whole project of virtue which Murdoch calls for questionable: an attempt to find meaning in a meaningless world or to create value in a world devoid of value! Moreover, the very appreciation of chance, death, and contingency in life, which Murdoch calls for, can be destructive unless such a realization is sustained by hope. But this is precisely the element that is missing in Murdoch's world, where there is neither a *telos* nor any theological background, and where "'All is vanity' is the beginning and end of ethics."[52] Hauerwas has therefore noted how, from a Christian point of view, Murdoch's account of human existence is highly questionable:

> Christians believe that our lives are at once more captured by sin and yet sustained by a hope than Dame Murdoch can account. A Christian understanding of sin and hope is, moreover, correlative to an account of creation that sustains a teleological account of the world and our place in it.[53]

Hauerwas's quarrel with Murdoch is clear and well justified. While Murdoch has well attended to the element of contingency and 'sin' within human existence, the dialectical element of hope has been excluded by the denial of any teleological account of existence. Like Murdoch, Hauerwas notes the contingency of the world. However, the real challenge, according to him, is not just to see the "pointlessness" in the sheer existence of the contingent. A mere appreciation of contingency does not and cannot save one from the muddles of fantasy, egoism, self-deception and illusion so well described by Murdoch.[54] Rather, the challenge is to be able to see the existence of the contingent as a "gift," or more accurately, as contingent on "God's abundant love as reflected in the inner life of the triune God." Christians use the language of *creatio ex nihilo* to draw attention to this "graceful, contingent and finite gift of God, who was not in need of the world."[55] Such a theological framework does not mean that the otherness of the contingent is obliterated by being drawn up in a larger 'consoling' purpose, but it shows that the very language of contingency (contingent on what?) calls for, or at least implies, a teleological framework.

Thus, in contrast with Murdoch's account of the absolute pointlessness of existence, *creatio ex nihilo* means that Christians can locate the "purpose" of their existence in their being "creatures," i.e., within a wider story of God's ongoing engagement with creation. Creation names not just the source of the world's contingency but also God's continuing providential care over the world. Such a *telos* as implied in *creatio ex nihilo* is not that of a single overriding purpose that violently forces all we do into a preestablished hierarchy. Rather, it is a *telos* of *hope* that gives one the confidence to believe that one is not fated by the contingent (created) and finite character of one's existence. Without such, or a similar hope, sustained by some theological framework, Murdoch's world cannot be saved from cynicism and/or despair.

There is another crucial difference between Murdoch's and Hauerwas's conception of ethics as vision which we need to examine and which clearly shows that Hauerwas's conception of ethics as vision is far more historical than that of Dame Murdoch. The issue surrounds their respective philosophical heritage and how this affects their views concerning what they take to be (finally) the basis of a true vision of reality.

The Social Historical Context of Vision

Although Murdoch has noted that one does not see just by looking but through training and effort, still for her, *attention* is a form of mystical contemplation which leads to a direct apprehension of the Good.[56] This sort of Platonic mysticism is not only responsible for the highly individualistic characterization of vision in Murdoch's work, it tends to obscure the historical and social context of vision. For example, even though Murdoch rightly notes that the human condition is characterized by the inability to bear reality and the temptation to seek consolation, she fails to note that even the very realization that we are marked by such a 'sin' does not come naturally. It is only *learned* through training and initiation into a truthful narrative. For Hauerwas, only such a training can allow one to recognize the extent to which our lives are possessed by powers and narratives whose purpose is to hide from us the fact of our contingency and finitude.[57] A key test for a normatively adequate story (see chapter 4, below) is its ability to provide one with both linguistic and institutional skills, which are able to 'name' those powers that bind our contingent existence.

Similarly, one cannot simply will oneself out of self-deception, since such a willing may only mire the self deeper in fantasies of freedom. From this aspect, Hauerwas thinks that Murdoch is right to note that "our hedge against false consolation, against self-deception, cannot be found in ourselves," but rather comes externally. However, she is wrong to think that the 'salvation' comes in the form of mystical attention to an object. Even though such an attention might provide a much welcome moment of "unselfing," the needed 'salvation' is not mystical. Fantasy and illusion can be overcome, if indeed they are overcome, only through "being made part of a community with practices that offer the transformation and reordering of our lives and relationships."[58]

The above difference between Murdoch and Hauerwas has been more recently expressed by Hauerwas in terms of the linguistic basis of vision: "I thought the difference was as simple as her claim that 'we develop language in the context of looking', whereas I was convinced (and I thought I had learned this from Wittgenstein) that I can only see what I have been trained to say."[59] This way of putting the issue makes it obvious that the issue between Murdoch and Hauerwas revolves around their respective assumptions concerning the relation between experience and language. According to Murdoch, this relation is patterned on a clear "see-saying," or what we shall later (chapter 6) refer to, following Lindbeck, as the experiential-expressivist model. According to this model, experience is prior to its expression in language: "In seeing the world, one experiences the feeling—of awe, joy, fear, trust or presence of God, and then says it in word, deed, praise or service."[60] Thus, Murdoch is able to affirm: "we develop language in the context of looking."[61] This "see-saying" pattern seems to fit well Murdoch's Platonism and mystical conception of vision by ensuring the ineffability of certain types of experiences.

However, the instrumentalist (expressivist) conception of language behind this "see-saying" model has been rendered questionable in light of the later Wittgenstein's view on the relation between language and culture. According to Wittgenstein, the assumption of a pure experience is a chimera. Experience is always mediated through the social-linguistic schemes which partly constitute that experience. This means that social-linguistic schemes in general, and language in particular, are logically prior to, and serve as conditions of possibility for, any experience.

Hauerwas has adopted this Wittgensteinian "say-seeing" pattern as a more adequate characterization of the relation between language and experience. That is why, in the context of vision, he affirms: "I can only act in the world I can see, and my seeing is a matter of learning to say."[62] This means that social-linguistic schemes in general, and language in particular, is the final training ground for a clear and realistic vision of reality. This affirmation of the cultural linguistic context for vision offers at least two clear advantages over Murdoch's mystic conception of vision: First, it is able to account for the role of linguistic notions, and secondly, it sustains a substantive conception of moral imagination. We need to briefly survey each of these aspects of Hauerwas's conception of vision.

Linguistic notions as "Skills of Perception"

The historical-social context of vision points to the nature and role of language in general, and linguistic notions in particular. Part of Hauerwas's quarrel with the decision-based accounts of the moral life was that the latter had failed to "account for the significance of linguistic notions and how they work to provide us with skills of perception."[63] Instead, by extolling "decision" as the primary moral category, many of these standard accounts misleadingly assume the world to be independently given (made up of "facts" out there), about which one has to make a decision. However, according to the Wittgensteinian conception, there are no pure "facts." As facts they are always interpreted, arranged, and involve a "seeing as."[64] In terms of language, this not only means that social-linguistic schemes allow us to see the world, but also that the world we see is already structured by the same social, dynamic framework of linguistic possibilities. This structuring power of language is particularly located within the various notions within a language. The notions of a given language are therefore "skills of perception which we must learn to use properly."[65] We must survey a little more the two aspects of this conception of notions and their implications for the moral life.

First, notions are "skills of perception." The immediate implication of this realization is that learning the proper use of a language (which is not different from learning the use of various notions within that language) is correlative to learning to "see" the world in a given way. Moreover, such a "seeing" is not only a question of perceiving but of ordering one's life in that world. The "seeing" involves a normative requirement of how the self "ought" to be positioned if one is to see the world rightly.[66] One must note the self-involving nature of language at stake here. The real world is a world that language partly constitutes, and in order to see that world rightly, one must be in command of a certain vocabulary by which to describe that world. To do so, however, is to already have been drawn into that world. For example, getting immersed in the Hindu cultural-linguistic tradition (which is correlative to learning the use of its various notions like *karma, Atman, Samsara, Moskha,* etc.) is already to be drawn up in the world of the *Bhagavad Gita.* It is to begin to see the world as marked by endless regeneration and to order one's life accordingly in such a world, that is, if one really participates in the Hindu social-linguistic practice rather than merely learning about Hinduism. This observation is crucial, for it shows both the inescapability and intricacy of vision. As long as we are always using some language, we are being drawn into a particular vision and becoming particular sorts of people. In other words, "To see or not to see" is *not* the question. The question is, *which* language and *what* sort of people we are becoming by its use.

In any case, the observation that the use of language involves a normative transformation of the self exerts a critical strain on any attempt to provide a clear demarcation between moral and non-moral notions. This attempt has been sustained especially within analytic philosophy by the misleading (empiricist) opposition between "fact" and "value," "is" and "ought," and the corresponding demarcation of language into descriptive and evaluative usage. Such distinctions involve an illegitimate attempt to isolate, within a particular language, those notions which can entail the involvement (or formation) of the self and set them aside from those that merely describe the world. Already in his earliest work, Hauerwas relied on Julius Kovesi's analysis to undermine this evaluative-descriptive distinction.[67] Kovesi drew on the later Wittgenstein, particularly the latter's homogeneous or seamless conception of language in order to deny the presence of any metaphysical wedge between moral and non-moral notions.[68] This means that the notion of "table," for example, functions in the same way as the notion of "lie" in both describing and ordering one's life in the world. Even though these two notions order our relationship to the world in a different way, what a Wittgensteinian account must resist is the assumption that this different way is an aspect inherent within the notions themselves and can therefore be discovered formally through a clearly defined discipline of conceptual analysis. Rather, this different way is an aspect of the respective applications the notions acquire within a particular language game, or narrative context.[69] Otherwise, given the seamless conception of language, learning the notion "lie," just like learning the notion "table," is to know how the word orders that aspect of human behavior which it is about. Thus to learn moral notions is not just to learn about the world, but it is to learn how to order the world. To learn moral notions is in effect to act upon the world, as it trains our vision about the world.[70]

The interesting point, therefore, is knowing how to use the notion in question, which brings us to the other key aspect of Hauerwas's conception of notions, namely, that linguistic notions are skills of perception "which we must *learn* to use properly." In the *Philosophical Investigations,* Wittgenstein was able to show that one does not learn the meaning of a word or notion through ostensive definition. But, since notions are embodied in a way of life, the way to learn the meaning of words like "table," "lie," "abortion," "wheelbarrow," or "yellow," is by being introduced into the form of life in which the notions are at home. And so, learning to use various notions of a language is intimately connected to the history of interpretation (tradition) that informs that community in which the notions are operative. This is one reason why moral discussions across traditions, or between members of a given tradition who nevertheless hold different stories, are so irresolvable. For example, in the abortion debate, it is not that pro-life advocates know some "facts" about life that their pro-choice adversaries do not know and hope thereby to win them over by overwhelming evidence and argumentation. They both know the same "facts," but the issue turns on the story each one holds, within which they "see" the situation.

The foregoing discussion helps to make clear the intimate and dialectical relationship between vision, language, and community in Hauerwas's thinking. This intimate relation helps to locate the basis of vision and thus of particularity within a community's tradition. However, the dialectical nature of the relation between language and vision means that the notions within a given community both reflect and form a shared vision. While on one hand, the notions arise from the needs, convictions, and experiences of a common history, on the other hand, once instituted, the same notions direct, form, and make possible the community's experience. This dialectical relationship prevents a community's vision from becoming static or fixed once and for all. A key element within this dynamic poise of language and vision is the moral imagination by which a community's notions (and thus vision) is constantly challenged, extended or revised.

Metaphor and Moral Imagination

According to Hauerwas, moral imagination is a task correlative to the challenge of vision. As a task, imagination involves a "re-*vision*-ing" of the basic symbols and notions within a language, which provides new and richer visions of reality, away from the world of fantasy and social convention. To many, however, imagination, insofar as we often associate it with spontaneity, creativity, and unconstrained "free play," seems the most unlikely candidate for such a task. For, instead of providing a realistic vision of reality, imagination may simply draw the self into more fantastic illusions. Such widespread suspicion, in fact, seems to explain Murdoch's ambiguous view of the imagination. While she seemed to recognize, at least on one occasion, that "clear vision is a result of moral imagination,"[71] she nevertheless turns against that insight by noting that the task of morality is to see justly, to overcome prejudice, to avoid temptation, to "control and curb imagination."[72] The reason behind Murdoch's suspicion of the imagination should be transparent by now. Having noted that the greatest enemy of the moral life is personal fantasy: "the tissue of self-aggrandizing and consoling wishes and dreams which prevents one from seeing what is there outside one," she would not empower the "fat relentless ego" with yet another tool of fantastic reverie by extolling imagination.[73]

However, Murdoch's suspicion of the imagination betrays continued reliance on an account of the imagination created by rationalist assumptions of modern epistemologies.[74] According to this account, which has become the 'standard' conception since the Enlightenment, imagination is a power which somehow exists "in the mind." Hauerwas has found this conception of the imagination both abstract and disembodied. This is partly because [according to this view] the status of imagination is fundamentally an epistemological issue divorced from the practices of particular communities. He has therefore pointed out how a substantive and morally helpful appeal to the imagination points not so much to an individual's mental faculty of 'free-play', but to the narrative context of a community's practices and way of life:

> Imagination is not a power that somehow exists 'in the mind,' but is a pointer to a community's constant willingness to expose itself to the innovations required by its convictions. . . . Similarly, the world is seen differently when construed by such an imaginative community, for the world is not simply there, always ready to be known, but rather is known well only when known through the practices and habits of community constituted by a truthful story.[75]

Thus, against any individualistic conception, Hauerwas affirms that the type of imagination which is morally significant is a faculty which cannot be exercised in isolation, but only within an organic grouping of persons who are participants in a common mode of activity. Understood this way, imagination becomes an integral part of moral casuistry, by which a tradition "imaginatively tests the often unacknowledged implications of its narrative commitments."[76] However, in as far as imagination is capable of this, it can be a threat, because it "creates the unexpected or disrupts our normal way of seeing." That is why Hauerwas recommends that "the task of imagining, of skillful re-vision-ing, must be thoroughly disciplined by the virtues of hope and courage if it is to be sustained."[77] But this precisely is what makes the task of imagination a *moral* task: It is a task to the extent that it is "morally required because we refuse to allow the 'necessities' of the world, which are often but stale habits, to go unchallenged when they are in fact susceptible to the power of the imagination." It is moral in as far as the ability to imagine, "to notice and make use of the unexpected," is inseparable from the character of one who embodies the virtues of hope and courage in one's life. There is accordingly a dialectical relationship between character and moral imagination: "Imagination is the very means by which we live morally, and [yet] our moral life is in truth the source of our imagination."[78]

One final point that needs to be noted in relation to imagination as a moral task is that if "in order to see, our vision must be trained by our ability to say," then imagination is a linguistic achievement. As a linguistic competence, imagination is a "skillful re-ordering" of those basic symbols and notions which shape our vision through the mediation of metaphor. For, it is through the use of metaphorical language that one is able to creatively extend, enrich, or revise the limitations inherent in an inherited moral vocabulary. As Benedict Guevin remarks:

> The language of imagination therefore is essentially symbolic and metaphorical. Metaphor often enters into the development of vision, because it enables us to see that something can be other than what we had thought it to be. . . . It is metaphor which enables us to hold in tension our concrete grasp or reality concomitantly with the meaning of reality experienced imaginatively, i.e., non-logically, and non-empirically.[79]

The ability to engage in this "play of metaphor" no doubt depends on one's command of the language and one's already acquired experience with various situations. In other words, the world of metaphor, improvisation, spontaneity, nuanciation, re-description, etc., is made possible only by the settled mastery of linguistic usage which discipline and years of training makes available. The significance of this realization is that it points to the role and inescapability of training and authority within the moral life. In order to explore this connection between vision, language, and authority, we need to attend to the reasons behind Hauerwas's conception of morality as a craft.

3. Morality as a Craft: Vision, Training, and Authority

The discussions above have helped to make explicit the affirmation of the social-linguistic basis of vision as the key advance by Hauerwas over Murdoch in their attempt to conceive the moral under the metaphor of vision. Simply stated, against Murdoch's claim for a mystical and direct vision of reality, Hauerwas has rightly noted how our vision of reality is always mediated through the cultural-linguistic schemes of particular traditions. Accordingly, not only do notions function as skills of perception, but moral imagination itself is a linguistic ability. What these discussions have led to is the gradual realization of the need for training before one can come to a proper use of language (and thus a realistic vision of reality). It is finally this aspect of training, and the correlative need for authority that leads Hauerwas to conceive the moral life under the image of a craft. A key insight related to this craftlike nature of morality is the observation that vision (the moral task) is not so much about knowledge but formation, whereby one's vision is formed not so much by analytic tools of clear thinking as by participating in determinate practices within a tradition. A conception of authority is central to this view of the moral life.

Authority, Rationality, and Freedom

Contrary to modernity, Hauerwas argues, the moral good is not simply available to any intelligent person no matter what their point of view. Rather, in order to be moral, a person has to be made into a particular kind of person (character) if he or she is to acquire knowledge about what is true and good. In the language of vision, transformation is required if one is to see the world truly. This transformation, Hauerwas suggests, is like that of making oneself an apprentice to a master of a craft so as to be initiated into the art of, for example, football, baseball, bricklaying, quilting, farming, or parenting.[80]

This assumption, however, implies a critique of the optimism characteristic of decision-based accounts of the moral life. The latter assumes that being moral does not require initiation or training, but is a condition that accrues to us *qua* rational beings. On this reading, Hauerwas sees in Kant's formulations of the categorical imperative an attempt to get behind the need for authority. The primary moral challenge, Kant assumed, was to "think clearly, . . . to get the basic, universally fitting principles right."[81] To be sure, Hauerwas is aware that Kant's own views on both moral and political authority are more complex than is often acknowledged.[82] In fact, against the background of rival and irresolvable claims to authority, religious wars, and institutional dogmatism, Kant was (rightly) worried about the dangers of blind obedience to a person or institution. Unfortunately, this worry was to emerge within Enlightenment and post-Enlightenment rhetoric as a certain bias against, and distortion of, the very concept of authority. The *Sapere Aude* Enlightenment battle-cry, the dominant instrumental conception of reason within the Enlightenment, as well as the quest for emancipatory autonomy in the various spheres of life, all somehow combined to lead toward the somewhat negative conception of authority as being diametrically opposed to reason—as, in fact, blind obedience. But as Gadamer rightly notes, authority

> is ultimately based not on the subjection and abdication of reason, but on an act of acknowledgement and knowledge—the knowledge, namely, that the other is superior to oneself in judgement and insight and that for this reason his judgement takes precedence—i.e., priority over one's own.[83]

Hauerwas has affirmed the same conclusion by defending, alongside MacIntyre, the inevitability of authority as a necessary condition for rationality.[84] This conclusion will be explicated shortly. However, it already makes it clear that critical thinking is only possible against the background of unquestioned assumptions and presuppositions that tradition makes available.

Similarly, authority is a necessary condition for a genuine realization of freedom. Even a purely phenomenological observation based on the basic fact of sociality, as well as on the mimetic structure of intentionality would lead to this conclusion: We learn to "experience"—to see, hear, feel, know, fear, desire, etc.—only in relation to, and by imitating others.[85] However, within Hauerwas's work, the realization is connected to a Wittgensteinian observation to the effect that our experience is always mediated through social-linguistic structures:

> If it is true that I can act only in the world I see and that my seeing is a matter of my learning to say, it is equally the case that my "saying"

requires sustained habits that form my emotions and passions, teaching me to feel one way rather than another.[86]

We have already drawn attention to this passage (chapter 2) as a way of underscoring the key insight that emotions and feelings are themselves *earned* responses. What is significant here is for one to realize that in 'learning' "to feel one way rather than another," or in learning to "desire the right things rightly," we inevitably need the authority of others. As Hauerwas notes:

> The relation between "seeing" and "saying" makes clear that our seeing inextricably depends on others as what we see is known partly by how it can be shared. . . . To see, therefore, requires others to stand over against us to say how we have got it wrong.[87]

Once such a realization is granted, it becomes clear that the issue is not really one of either authority or autonomy, but of which authority to recognize, since the presence of some authority is inevitable, and "autonomy itself is a form of authority which can be as destructive as paternalism." And so, to say that there is no recognized moral authority within modern capitalistic societies is not to say that there is no moral authority, *tout court*. It is simply to blind oneself to the various 'authorities' of the media, commercial advertisement, peer pressure, the authority of one's arbitrary feelings and desires, etc., which continue to determine one's vision and reactions. However, to the extent that these are not explicitly recognized as authorities, they become easily manipulative, as well as domineering, while giving the impression that one is always free to make up one's mind.

There is, therefore, a need to rehabilitate a philosophical account of authority and in particular an account of authority within the moral field. In what comes close to a definition, Hauerwas notes that authority, by its nature, "involves a willingness to accept the judgments of another as superior to [one's] own on the basis of that person's office and assumed skills."[88] There is nothing particularly novel about this conception of authority, but in order to see how this sense of authority is central to the moral life, we need to turn to Hauerwas's account of the craftlike nature of morality.[89]

The Moral Life as a Craft: Training, Authority and Vision

As already noted, the moral good is not immediately available to anyone. A person has to be made into a particular kind of person (character) if he or she is to acquire knowledge about what is true and good. This transformation, Hauerwas suggests, is like that of making oneself an apprentice to a master of a craft. This close identification between morality and crafts is based on at least three closely related characteristics shared by both. First of all, morality, just like crafts, seeks the realization of goods internal to itself. Both morality and crafts are, therefore, what MacIntyre calls "practices." A practice, according to MacIntyre, is

> any coherent and complex form of socially established cooperative human activity through which goods internal to that form of activity are realized in the course of trying to achieve those standards of excellence which are appropriate to, and partially definite of, that form of activity, with the result that human powers to achieve excellence, and human conceptions of the ends and goods involved, are systematically extended.[90]

That the goods are "internal to the practice" simply means that these goods can only be specified within the practices themselves. Herein lies the key difference between a 'practice' and an 'organization'. The latter exists to serve extrinsic purposes. Thus, both the nature and standards of success of an organization can be precisely *determined* beforehand as the ends to which the organization is a means. With a 'practice' however, this ends-means framework completely breaks down. Both the nature of a 'practice' and the goods within it can only be *discovered* and specified within the practice itself.[91] That is to say, through participation in the particular history of the craft itself: "To share in the rationality of a craft requires sharing in the contingencies of its history, understanding its story as one's own, and finding a place for oneself as a character in the enacted dramatic narrative, which is that story so far."[92]

Our attention is already drawn, through the above citation, to the second aspect crucial to the understanding of morality as a craft, namely, the historical nature of crafts. This historical aspect, in fact, helps to advance Hauerwas's argument for the social-linguistic basis of vision. Because mastering a craft is at the same time a certain linguistic competency, in learning a craft one does not start *de novo*. Rather, one begins by learning the appropriate language that forms and is formed by the skills of the particular craft. As Hauerwas notes, one "cannot learn to lay brick without learning to talk 'right'. The language embodies the history of the craft of bricklaying. So when you learn to be a bricklayer you are not learning a craft *de novo* but rather being initiated into a history."[93] In this respect, Hauerwas indicates that being initiated into the history of a craft involves acknowledging the authority of those standards of excellence "realized so far," as well as the inadequacy of one's own performance as judged by them. MacIntyre makes this point more explicitly when he notes: "If, on starting to listen to music, I do not accept my own incapacity to judge correctly, I will never learn to hear, let alone to appreciate, Bartok's last quartets."[94] To learn a craft is thus to subject one's own attitudes, choices, preferences and tastes to the authority of the "masters," i.e., those granted authority insofar as they exemplify in their work the best standards so far.

Thirdly, the historical nature of crafts noted above, especially as it involves the acknowledgment of those "who exemplify in their work the best standards so far" shows that the notion of craft (and morality) involves the undemocratic, even elitist assumption that some people are better at it than others. The authority of these "masters"—i.e., those who "know how to go further . . . and how to direct others to go further"—is based on "the history of [their] accomplishment," on their "assumed [acquired] skills," on "their having experience and judgment gained (acquired) through their knowledge of the tradition."[95] These references to the historical basis of authority anticipate quite appropriately the Aristotelian conception of the "masters" as the *phronomoi*, those whom "because *experience* has given them an eye they see aright."[96] For this reason, Hauerwas contends, the authority required to sustain the temporal character of a craft differs markedly from the conception of authority within an organization, in that it is "experience" or "acquired skills" and not "technical expertise" or "managerial efficiency" that lies at the basis of authority within a craft. Unfortunately, partly under the spell of scientific mastery and bureaucratic efficiency, modernity has assumed as dominant the organizational conception of authority. The latter, whose paradigmatic embodiment is the "expert" and "manager," involves the rational determination and deployment of the most efficient means to independently conceived goals. While the goal of such a model is to achieve external goods, separable from the character of the agent, the goal of authority within a craft is toward achieving the internal goods of "education of individuals into certain practices and states of character."[97]

We shall pursue this crucial difference in the coming chapter as the difference between two forms of practical reason to which Aristotle gave the names of *technē* and *phronēsis*, respectively. What perhaps needs to be highlighted here is that the conception of authority within a craft involves a key element of obedience or a willingness to accept the judgments of another as superior to one's own. These judgments are not exercised in isolation but are embodied in what Sabina Lovibond calls "a system of material relationships," i.e., various socializing processes by which one is brought, through a "myriad of corrective cues," to participate in one or the other of the craftlike institutions, such as the family, the church, schools, universities, medicine, etc.[98]

What is particularly significant is that one realizes that the "obedience" within this conception of authority need not be seen as either authoritarian or as implying blind submission. Rather, it is based on a dynamic and dialectical master-apprentice relationship. Only by submitting to the master does the apprentice learn not only to attain the best standards so far but to extend them to new levels. There is, therefore, an aspect of "inner transcendence" within the very conception of authority which helps to advance both critical inquiry and objectivity. That is why Hauerwas thinks that there could be no more conformist strategy than the assumption within some extreme forms of liberal philosophy of education that the pedagogical task is to help students to "think for themselves," or "make up their minds." To encourage students to make up their minds, Hauerwas notes, is a sure way to avoid any meaningful disagreements, and "to ensure that they [students] become good conformist consumers in a capitalistic economy."[99] Against this liberal assumption, what must be said "is that most students do not have minds well enough trained to be able to think. . . . A central pedagogical task is to tell students that they do not yet have minds worth making up. . . . That is the reason I tell my students my first object is to help them think like me."[100] In a footnote to this claim, Hauerwas notes,

> . . . I am aware that such a claim appears authoritarian, but ironically I think it is just the opposite of authoritarianism. What does it mean to introduce students to think like me? It means I must introduce them to all the sources that think through me, and in the process they will obviously learn to think not only like me, but different from me as the different voices that think through me provide them with skills I have not appropriated sufficiently.[101]

The substance of Hauerwas's remarks here echo a Wittgensteinian observation to the effect that critical thinking can only emerge at the point where reason has been strengthened by implanting in the learner a system of beliefs for which no grounds are offered.[102] This makes it clear that Hauerwas is here not making a boastful reference to his personal authority, but is stating an epistemological claim, namely, that there can be no knowledge without appropriate authority. Rather, authority is a necessary condition for rationality in general, and moral rationality in particular:

Authority is that power of a community that allows for reasoned interpretations of the community's past and future goals. Authority, therefore,
is not contrary to reason but essential to it. Authority is the means by
which the wisdom of the past is critically appropriated by being tested by
current realities as well as by challenging the too often self-imposed limits of the present.[103]

A full appreciation of this citation depends on acknowledging the historical
and, therefore, traditioned nature of rational inquiry, a defense of which will
be undertaken in our coming chapter. For now, we need to bring this discussion concerning the craftlike nature of morality to a conclusion by making
explicit the relationship between vision, craft, and moral knowledge.

Vision, Character, and Moral Knowledge

When the moral life is viewed through the analogy of a craft, the need for
training and authority becomes obvious. This need is based on the appreciation that the moral life (just like a craft) is concerned with the realization of
internal goods. Such goods are not known by necessity, but are discovered
historically through concrete judgments. If moral knowledge were necessary and universal, then there would be no need for training and authority.
However, the temporal character of morality (crafts) has confirmed the realization that moral truth is not timeless. It is historical and, as historical, it
is inseparable from the education of individuals in certain practices and
states of character. In the language of vision, one cannot come to see just by
looking. Transformation is required if one is to see realistically. This is the
sense behind Hauerwas's already quoted claim to the effect that "in order to
be moral, a person has to be made into a particular kind of person if he or
she is to acquire knowledge about what is true and good."[104]

This observation points to a very close relationship between moral
knowledge and a person's character or between vision and the sort of person
one is. The presence of this intimate relationship requires, in fact, that we
qualify our observation at the start of this section, when we noted that the
moral life is not so much a question of knowledge as of formation. From the
consideration here, such a remark only misleadingly casts "knowledge"
and the "formation of character" into an undesirable dualistic polarity. The
point of the contrast then was essentially critical: a reaction against both
Murdoch's intellectualistic conception of vision, and the implied (modernist) gnostic reduction of the moral task to one of clear thinking. But now
that attention to the craftlike nature of morality has made obvious the pri-

ority and need for the formation of the agent, it becomes clear that the issue is finally not one of either knowledge or formation, but of the specific role played by knowledge within the formation of the moral agent.

Constructively, then, we need to highlight how the moral life, as a life of vision, involves knowledge. What the present section has made clear, however, is that the knowledge associated with vision is a special kind of knowledge which, like learning a craft, is only acquired through the very discipline and practice of the craft: "Truth in this sense is like a 'knowing how'—a skill that can only be passed from master to apprentice," where the "knowing how" (of a craft) is not different from the acquisition of excellence within it.[105] This nondisposable nature of knowledge within the moral sphere will become more explicit in our coming chapter, when we establish an affinity between narrative and Aristotle's concept of *phronēsis*.[106] Then, we shall show how the inseparability of this knowledge from the character of the agent is the special and distinctive feature of moral reason. Before we do so, however, a brief conclusion to the foregoing chapter is in order.

This chapter has explored Hauerwas's constructive attempt to re-image the moral life as a life of vision. Hauerwas's debt to Dame Iris Murdoch for this conception, as well as his 'quarrel' with some of the assumptions she associates with the metaphor of vision has formed a major part of the argument in this chapter. The main objective has been to show how the moral life is not so much about decisions and choices, but learning to *see* the world, oneself, and others in a particular way which requires a transformation of the self so as to sustain the vision.

The appropriateness of vision as a metaphor for the moral life has been made obvious by the extensive use to which the metaphor is amenable. The language of vision has been used to make at least five key interrelated observations concerning the moral life: (1) how difficult it is to accurately see the world as a whole and particular things, such as a desk, a red wheelbarrow, suicide, the telling of a lie, etc.; (2) how closely akin the moral life is to art; (3) how one's ability to see requires the development of linguistic skills; (4) how seeing involves a community (tradition) and authority in order to train us to see; (5) how the close relation between vision and character, truth and virtue points to a distinctive conception of moral rationality.

The exploration into Hauerwas's re-*vision*-ing of the moral life has been undertaken with a view of advancing the central thesis of our work, namely, the inescapability of moral particularity. What has emerged as a clear conclusion is the affirmation of our social and historical existence as the basis of moral life. In the language of vision, this means that what in the final analysis leads to the particularity of vision is not the irreducibility and uniqueness of the objects of *attention* (Murdoch). Nor is the particularity of vision premised on the assumption that morality has to do with something like an individual's "total vision of life."[107] Rather, the basis for moral particularity lies within those linguistic skills which train our vision. Since to refer to language is to refer to something traditioned, the final basis for moral particularity is the community whose various stories, metaphors, virtues, obligations, indeed the whole way of life, train one to see reality in a distinctive way. It is to this narrative context of moral truth that Hauerwas is referring when, in the words of the epigraph at the start of this chapter, he notes, "we do not come to see just by looking, but by disciplined skills developed through initiation into a narrative."

Such a conclusion, however, weighs critically against the assumption of a "neutral" ethics or a "neutral" vision. The attempt to neutralize moral philosophy (to dispense with "good" in favor of "right") is, therefore, not only misguided but also misleading, since would-be neutral philosophers cannot avoid appealing to concepts, metaphors, and notions—thus to the language—of a particular tradition. Moreover, it is this assumption that we can have a neutral ethics that artificially creates the problem of how such an institution of morality can be related to the 'nonmoral' convictions like religion, politics, etiquette, custom, etc. However, the fact that social-linguistic forms do not lend themselves to such a clear-cut demarcation between 'moral' and 'nonmoral' operations renders a philosophical attempt to determine the relation between religion and ethics highly suspect. On the contrary, Wittgenstein's views on the homogeneity of language provide a clear confirmation of how the various notions within a language work together to provide a unified vision of both how the world is and how the self is to be positioned if it is to see that world accurately. From this consideration, it becomes clear not only why every ethics is distinctive, but why Christian ethics is certainly distinctive. For, the language Christians use, its various stories, metaphors, doctrines, and practices (especially liturgy), train the Christian to see the world, oneself, and others in a distinctive way.

However, if the metaphor of vision seems to lead to this positive realization, it equally involves a challenge: The realization of the social-linguistic basis of vision seems to put us at a significant disadvantage morally, since one is never "free" to choose the language through which one learns to see the world. Rather, one discovers oneself already using language which determines the world in which one acts and thus the self. Truthful languages are those that help one to grasp that one has been so determined, but still give one the critical skills to challenge the boundaries of that language. Such truthful languages are not 'ready-made', but are the result of a communal and individual struggle against conventional forms of consolation by constant reappropriation of the language. The moral challenge which is inseparable from the formation of virtuous character is really one of skillful and imaginative re-*vision*-ing of the basic symbols, metaphors, and notions of that language as it forms one and as one learns to use it better.

4

Historicity and Contingency:
Narrative Identity and Moral Rationality

> [W]e offer a substantive explication of narrative as a constructive alternative to the standard account. Our penchant has been to rely upon the standard account as though it were the only lifeboat in a sea of subjective reactions and reductive explanations. To question it would be tantamount to exposing the leaks in the only bark remaining to us. In harkening to the narrative context for action, we are trying to direct attention to an alternative boat available to us. This one cannot provide the security promised by the other, but in return it contains instructions designed to equip us with the skills required to negotiate the dangers of the open sea.
>
> Hauerwas with Burrell

Hauerwas's use of the category of narrative is explicable from both a philosophical and theological background. Philosophically, narrative is employed by Hauerwas to articulate the form of rationality best suited for the craftlike nature of morality. Particularly, the notion of narrative is developed as a critical response to a scientific ideal of moral rationality and objectivity operative within the predominant Kantian accounts of ethics. Hauerwas has found such an ideal of moral rationality—associated with such titles as the Categorical Imperative, the Original Position, the View from Nowhere, the Ideal Observer, the Moral Point of View, the Universality Principle, etc.—alienating in its attempt to free moral judgments from the particularity of the beliefs, wants, convictions, (hi)story and community of the agent who makes them. However, what the craftlike nature of morality (previous chapter) has confirmed is that these historical particularities should not—and, in any case, cannot—be transcended, since the moral point or vision is always embodied within a community's practices and narratives. Hauerwas's appeal to narrative is thus an attempt to provide an alternative (to the Kantian) view of moral rationality and objectivity. It involves a methodological shift in thinking and talking about moral rationality and objectivity, a shift from a systematic-rationalistic account of the moral life to a narrative-based account, a shift from system to story.

There is also a very important theological stake in Hauerwas's attempt to recover the narrative account of moral rationality. In and through the category of narrative he seeks to "provide an account of moral existence and ethical rationality that may help render the convictions of Christians morally intelligible."[1] Part of Hauerwas's uneasiness with the non-narrative views of moral rationality is that the latter inevitably lead to a reductionistic account of religious beliefs. Since their point is to arrive at rules and principles which are universally valid and applicable, any religious beliefs justified by the appeal to the canons of these accounts are either stripped of their distinctiveness or rendered 'private'—and thus assigned to an optional motivational or supererogatory status. By invoking the narrative character of Christian faith, Hauerwas hopes to show that the Christian story is already a morality in itself, that is, a distinctive and truthful way of seeing (vision) and relating to the world.

The category of narrative or story has recently received so much attention in both philosophy and theology that "a virtual cottage industry of academic scholarship has grown up around it."[2] Narrative philosophies and theologies have been as varied methodologically and substantially as the appeal to narrative itself. From a more general point of view, the category of narrative has been used, among other purposes, to explain human action, to articulate structures of human consciousness, to depict the identity of agents, to explain strategies of reading, to justify a view of the importance of storytelling, to account for the historical development of traditions, to provide an alternative to foundationalist and/or other scientific epistemologies, and to develop a means of imposing order on what is otherwise chaotic.[3]

Within theology, "narrative theology" has been characterized by the same wide and nonuniform appeal to narrative, ranging from an explication of religion in human experience in general to the use of narrative as a heuristic category for explicating the basic substance of Christian theology, from a focus on biography (and even autobiography) as a way of displaying Christian convictions to a hermeneutics of biblical narrative.[4] It is therefore not surprising that there appears no agreement as to the precise meaning of narrative or its role in theology.[5] This might be one reason why Hauerwas, in spite of sharing the above renewed theological interest in "story" and narrative, has categorically denied that he should be understood as developing a "narrative theology" or "theology of narrative."[6]

There are, however, other equally compelling reasons why Hauerwas would wish to deny "narrative theology" or "narrative ethics" as an adequate characterization of his work. Firstly, Hauerwas does not set out to develop a substantive case for narrative either as a methodological category or as a theological argument in its own right. In any case, he has noted that it is "a mistake to think that my emphasis on narrative is the central focus of my position."[7] If he pays attention to narrative, it is because it clarifies "the interrelation between the various themes I have sought to develop in the attempt to give a constructive account of the Christian moral life."[8]

Yet an even more serious reason pertains to Hauerwas's suspicion of how "narrative" might easily become a faddish appeal to the importance of telling stories, which might moreover conceal an anti-intellectual excuse for avoiding the need to address the serious epistemological question of how narrative claims may be true or false, i.e., "you have your story and we have ours and there is no way to judge the truth of either."[9] For Hauerwas, however, the crucial appeal to narrative does not relate to the significance of "telling stories," though that may be part of it, but rather to the realization that "rationality, methods of argument, and historical explanation have . . . a fundamentally narrative form."[10] Thus, it is primarily an epistemological preoccupation—that of showing how moral and religious convictions can be true or false—which forces Hauerwas to see that narrative is indispensable for understanding the moral life in general and Christian moral convictions in particular.

In this chapter, we provide an extensive explication of Hauerwas's claim that narrative is "a crucial conceptual category for such matters as understanding issues of epistemology and methods of argument, depicting personal identity, and displaying the content of Christian convictions."[11] The chapter is divided into two sections. In the first section we shall examine why narrative is a crucial conceptual category for understanding the moral life, by attending to the narrative structure of both personal and social identity. Such a focus will help to show that human existence is not only accidentally historical but thoroughly so. This means that all our actions, including our search for the good and our inquiry into the truth, are themselves historical and particular, i.e., they depend on narrative traditions.

In the second section we shall examine Hauerwas's primary epistemological interest in narrative as a specific alternative (to the standard accounts) form of moral rationality. The argument here will try to show that to insist on narrative is not to rid the moral life of any rational basis, but that stories themselves develop a capacity for judging among alternatives. In any case, we shall show that the notion of narrative can provide an adequate conception of moral rationality, patterned on Aristotle's notion of *phronēsis*.

1. Historical Existence and the Inescapability of Narrative

Historical existence makes the concept of narrative inevitable for moral reflection. In its most ordinary meaning, narrative, Hauerwas notes, is a "connected description of contingent actions and events."[12] Such a description is needed to "catch the connections" between the various historical events and realities, which are inherently particular and contingent. He quotes L. O. Mink on this point:

> Surprises and contingencies are the stuff of stories, as of games, yet by virtue of the promised yet open outcomes we are enabled to follow a series of events across their contingent relations and to understand them as leading to an as yet unrevealed conclusion. We may follow understandingly what we could not predict or infer. . . . The features which enable a story to flow and us to follow, then, are the clues to the nature of *historical* understanding. An historical narrative does not demonstrate the necessity of events but makes them intelligible by unfolding the story which connects their significance.[13]

However, talk about this need for narrative to supply an intelligible pattern to historical occurrences must proceed with caution lest it give the misleading impression that narrative simply connects, or "configures and refigures human action which is already present on the level of *mimesis*."[14] This Ricoeurian characterization may misleadingly suggest a view of narrative as a structure imposed upon an otherwise non-narrative experience. But since (except in the case of fiction) stories are lived before they are told, narrative structure so pervades human existence, experience, and action that historical existence itself acquires the form of a story.[15] There is no way one can step out of this narrative configuration of historical existence, for there exists an inherent circularity between experience and narrative. Experience is already structured by a process of symbolization which is itself influenced by narrative traditions. In this section we shall try to make explicit this aspect of historical existence, with a view to showing how a narrative structure marks not only personal and communal identity but also all of our actions, including our moral and rational operations.

The Self as a Story

That the Self is a story is understood by Hauerwas in at least two related senses. According to the first sense, there is no other way to understand the self except through the story of which the self is the author:

> "*Who* somebody is or was we can know only by knowing the story of which he himself is the hero—his biography, in other words; everything else we know of him, including the work he may have left behind, tells us only *what* he is or was." What we must know how to do is to spell out in story form that a person is not like a type, but is a proper name. Indeed, a story can and does function like a proper name and vice versa.[16]

There might be a slightly misleading aspect to the above citation, which refers to Hannah Arendt. The basis of the distinction in Arendt is that *what* a person is, is settled in terms of attributes and qualities (e.g., professor, landlord, wife, priest, kind, etc.) that may be shared with others. *Who* one is, on the other hand, tells of the unique and rich individuality of the self, which is captured only by one's equally unique story.[17] The misleading part of this characterization is that it might give an impression that the two questions can be separated, as if the real self (*who* somebody is) always lies transcendentally behind the phenomenal self of agency (*what* he is). This, however, would contradict earlier conclusions about agency and character according to which the self does not stand over and beyond its activities but rather is constituted within these very activities.

The primary realization behind the above citation, however, is that each person *is* a story, a unique narrative. This fact has ethical ramifications, primary among which is the need for a person to discover, tell, and "spell out" the story of one's life. Although such a "telling" may include occasional explicit autobiography, this is not its primary meaning, for most of us do not write autobiographies or feel any urge to do so, and we may rarely or even never have occasion to give a comprehensive account of our life story. Rather, the "telling" involves a basic "attentiveness" to the factors within, and historical evolution of, one's life. Such an "attentiveness" leads not only to the discovery of who one is but also to the practice of occasionally "spelling out" (explicitly) the limits of one's story against inadvertent forms of self-deception.

Although we can tell stories *about* ourselves, on a more fundamental level there is no separation or distance between self and narrative. Therefore, the second, and philosophically more significant sense in which Hauerwas refers to the "self as a story" is that in which the self is coterminous with narrative identity. He suggests that

> descriptively the self is best understood as a narrative, and normatively we require a narrative that will provide the skills appropriate to the conflicting loyalties and roles we necessarily confront in our existence. The unity of the self is therefore more like the unity that is exhibited in a good novel—namely with many subplots and characters that we at times do not closely relate to the primary dramatic action of the novel. But ironically without such subplots we cannot achieve the kind of unity necessary to claim our actions as our own.[18]

At least two remarks need to be made concerning this narrative structure of the self. First, it is clear from the quotation above that a person's life needs an inner narrative to bind together the various contingent loyalties, roles, and events (subplots) that one confronts. Where such narrative fails in the life of a person, personal identity, intentional action, imagination of the future, grounding in social life, love, affection, as well as the feeling for the solid presence of things is all lost (as in the case of retrograde amnesia). In the resulting emptiness, as Richard Allen so aptly depicts, one ceaselessly invents and reinvents his self and world in a spate of a "narrational frenzy"— the endless and desperate concoction of story after story, none of which mean or matter more than any other, because all are equally detached from a "continuous inner narrative."[19]

Secondly, this "continuous inner narrative" (otherwise known as self-identity) is better characterized in terms of "self-constancy" or "coherence" than in terms of unchanging "sameness."[20] The link of this notion of self-constancy to narrative is constituted first of all by the fact that the temporal structure underlying this type of identity is more like the unity that is exhibited in a good novel. Such dynamic identity includes many contingent events (subplots and characters that we at times do not closely relate to the primary dramatic action), as well as changes (or reversals in fortune), where these events and changes are unified in terms of a narrative.

The self of this form of identity, which in our second chapter we identified with the notion of moral character, avoids both extremes of the transcendental self within modernity (on the one hand), and of the "death of the self" within certain forms of postmodern philosophy. First of all, the narrative self, characterized by "self-constancy" is clearly at odds with, and entails a great advance on, a transcendental conception of the self. The latter, whether in its Cartesian epistemological preoccupation (as the atemporal "knower who knows a known"), or in its Kantian moral endeavor (as the rational decision maker), is characterized by static identity. Unlike this substantialist and transcendental self whose identity remains unaffected by its agency or contingent historical fortunes, a narrative conception is well suited to capture the aspects of contingent history, openness for growth, and fragility in as much as the self necessarily remains exposed to the vicissitudes of history, dependence on others, and to the chronic possibility of conflict inherent in the plurality of its historical engagements.

This recognition of the historical nature of the self also provides a critical response to the other extreme of the "death of the self" celebrated within certain forms of postmodern ethics. One conclusion that has become synonymous with current (popular) conception of postmodernism is that the "self" or human subject is an effect of language, "constituted in and through self-narration."[21] This "death of the subject" has mostly been advanced through a (post)structuralist reading of Marx, which has sought to deconstruct the traditional self-conscious, self-determining, and knowing subject of modernity. Given the view that language is a social phenomenon that precedes the subject and that the self is an effect of language, many poststucturalists are led to see the self as but a form of social (cultural) production. Briefly stated, the thesis of the social construction of the self conceives the structure of one's thoughts and desires (and, therefore, subjectivity) to be "nothing more than a reproduction of the dominant ideology, i.e., the values and interests of the hegemonic bourgeoisie which direct human lives through . . . anonymous practices of social organization and control."[22]

However, reducing the self to a product of language, this postmodern celebration of the "death of the subject" ignores both the experience that we have of ourselves as self-determining agents and our desire to fashion our individual identities sometimes in opposition to aspects of the dominant culture. What must not be overlooked, however, is the realization that this possibility, too, where it exists, is made possible by, or dependent on, the sort of person (character) one is.

A key insight that pertains to a narrative display of self-identity is the realization that the self cannot simply be any story. The story of the self involves references to mythic, archetypal, or exemplary stories which unfold the larger-meaning horizons bounding human cultures: "We learn who we are through the stories we embrace as our own—the story of my life is structured by the larger stories (social, political, mythic) in which I understand my personal story to take place."[23]

The relation between the story of the self and these other stories is complex. Firstly, the individual's story is shaped by archetypal stories. In Hauer-was's own case, two such stories are Texas and Christianity.[24] "Texas" for Hauerwas is never meant to indicate simply where he happened to be born; it represents "a story that has for good or ill" shaped who he is. That he is a Texan "cannot be limited to being a description or an image. . . . For to claim that I am a Texan is to appeal to a narrative account that helps me bind to-gether a series of contingent events that create an intelligible pattern for my life . . . and at the same time supplies a way to form [my] future."[25]

Secondly, as the above quotation also makes clear, the wider stories pro-vide a future orientation by affecting the way one appreciates, adopts or re-jects other stories one confronts. The story of Texas, for example, contin-ues to influence Hauerwas's appreciation of the Christian story. As he notes, "being Texan is for many of us one of our most valuable lessons, as it has taught us how to be. I would have no idea what it might mean to be a Christian, as I would have no idea what it might mean to belong to a sepa-rate society."[26]

Another aspect of the archetypal stories is their normative significance. They can be normative in at least two senses. Firstly, archetypal stories help to define the moral problems one confronts, and even to determine in what sense something is or is not a moral problem. This is one reason why moral controversies are so difficult to resolve, since moral disagreements are not disagreements about "facts." Both pro- and anti-abortionists know the same biological facts about human life, just as the Israelis and HAMAS have the same "facts" concerning a bomb attack. Their disagreement con-cerning whether a certain medical intervention is no more than the re-moval of a "tissue" or an "abortion," or whether a recent bomb attack is morally justified or an act of "terrorism" turns on one's story, "and within which those 'facts' are known."[27]

Secondly, archetypal stories are normative by containing paradigms of what a person ought to become. They do this by suggesting or offering modes of vision of how one might "create and relate to a world":

> Stories, at least the kind of stories I am interested in, are not told to ex-plain as a theory explains, but to involve the agent in a way of life. A the-ory is meant to help you know the world without changing the world yourself; a story is to help you deal with the world by changing it through changing yourself.[28]

Unlike theories, then, stories provide one with a way of being in the world. This is why Hauerwas understands the archetypal stories to be morally significant but also potentially dangerous. If one's story is false or limited, so will be one's world and life, the reason being that "adopting different stories will unfold us into different sorts of people." Accordingly, there is a need to discriminate between stories in terms of their potential for forming truthful lives. We shall attend to this requirement more fully when we deal, in the next section, with the criteria for judging among stories. For now, however, we must note the circular movement involved in any such requirement.

The very ability to critically assess different stories in terms of their potential for truthful living is made possible by the fact that one has an adequate moral character. But acquiring such an adequate moral character itself is dependent on being able to identify a central story or a set of stories one takes as canonical. To so identify these stories would be not only to discover the shape of one's basic convictions, but also to understand the normative anchorage for one's character:

> we always find ourselves enmeshed in many histories—of our families, of Texas, America, European civilization, and so on—each of which is constituted by many interrelated and confusing story lines. The moral task consists in acquiring the skills, i.e., the *character*, which enable us to negotiate these many kinds and levels of narrative in a truthful manner.[29]

The circle here mitigates against any possibility of an unencumbered "original position" from which the self can assume the posture of an "ideal spectator" and so survey and choose which stories it wishes to accept. The self *already* finds itself 'placed' by, and within, wider stories not of its own making but which offer not only possibilities but also limits to what the self can be. This realization explains Hauerwas's positive appreciation of MacIntyre's work in general, the latter's argument for the inescapability of tradition in particular. For what MacIntyre's argument helps to show is that an individual's self-identity, as well as one's quest for the good, does not begin *de novo*, but with finding oneself part of a tradition:

> Our initiation into a story as well as the ability to sustain ourselves in that story depends on others who have gone before and those who continue to travel with us. "What I am, therefore, is in key part what I inherit, a specific past that is present to some degree in my present. I find myself part of a history and that is generally to say, whether I like it or not, whether I recognise it or not, one of the bearers of a tradition."[30]

We need to survey, under a separate paragraph, Hauerwas's concept of tradition, with a view to showing how this "specific past that is always present in my present" comes in the form of stories which an individual appropriates through socialization into a *community*. Such an examination will at once make clear why narrative is no less crucial for understanding issues of communal identity.

Concept of a Tradition

Tradition and community are coextensive notions in Hauerwas's understanding. At the basis of both is an appreciation for historical existence and the inescapability of narrative:

> narrative is the characteristic form of our awareness of ourselves as 'historical' beings who must give an account of the purposive relation between temporally discrete realities. Indeed, the ability to provide such an account, to sustain its growth in a *living* tradition, is the central criterion for identifying a group of people as a community. Community joins us with others to further the growth of a tradition whose manifold storylines are meant to help individuals identify and navigate the path to the good.[31]

At least two crucial observations need to be made in relation to the sense of tradition as developed by Hauerwas. First, there is an element of inescapability to tradition. As the citation at the end of the previous paragraph noted, "Whether I like it or not, whether I recognize it or not, I am one of the bearers of a tradition." Tradition is just the recognition of this historical and social aspect of human life. Thus, against any exaggerated autonomy, the notion of tradition involves the recognition that one's quest for the good is not one's to initiate or to define unilaterally. It is a quest that has already begun, that depends on others (past and present), and that the individual 'joins' through initiation into the already structured world of meaning and symbolization.

Secondly, for Hauerwas the notion of a 'living tradition' is far more basic than the notion of tradition. The notion of 'living tradition', in fact, involves a critique of the ideological appeals to "tradition" by conservative political theorists. The latter often assume a dichotomous but false contrast between tradition and reason. While reason is associated with criticism, innovation, and change, the attitude of tradition, it is assumed by these political theorists, is one of uncritical acceptance of the past. However, the notion of 'living tradition' confirms that change and continuity are two facets of the same process we call tradition: "Traditions by their nature require change. . . . And interpretation is the constant adjustment that is required if the current community is to stay in continuity with tradition."[32] Accordingly, any hankering for a "pure" tradition, whether in the form of a self-sufficient "deposit of faith" (as within some trends within the Catholic tradition) or a pure intratextual self-validation, is simply an illusion. Traditions are open to interpretations and reinterpretations. Moreover, the interpretations "may be quite diverse and controversial," as long as they "are sufficient to provide the individual members with the sense that they are more alike than unlike."[33] Following MacIntyre, Hauerwas therefore defines tradition as an argument, "an historically extended, socially embodied argument, and an argument precisely in part about the goods which constitute that tradition."[34] For this reason, tradition is not at odds with reason, but substantive ('living') traditions are themselves the bearers of rationality.

This is what makes the capacity of a tradition to sustain (rival) interpretations a normative requirement for any 'living' tradition, since it is this conversation itself which constitutes the common good within a given tradition. Accordingly, any normatively adequate tradition must "accept creative tension as a permanent feature of its life."

> [L]iving traditions presuppose rival interpretations. Good societies enable the argument to continue so that the possibilities and limits of the tradition can be exposed. The truthfulness of a tradition is tested in its ability to form people who are ready to put the tradition into question, or at least to recognise when it is being put into question by a rival tradition.[35]

However, the ability to sustain rival interpretations is just one key aspect that constitutes a 'living' tradition. One can identify within Hauerwas's work at least four other aspects that sustain a tradition in its search for the good: (i) the presence of relevant virtues and obligations; (ii) the use of linguistic notions, (iii) the need for stories, and (iv) the exercise of memory as a political and moral task. We shall explain each of these related aspects of a tradition.

Virtues and Obligations

Together, but in different ways, virtues and obligations sustain a tradition in the search for relevant goods. Quoting MacIntyre, Hauerwas notes that any community requires

> two distinct types of precepts to be observed in order to ensure the requisite kind of order for its common life. The first would be a set of precepts enjoining the virtues, those dispositions without the exercise of which

the good cannot be achieved, more particularly if the good is a form of life which includes as an essential part the exercise of the virtues. The second would be a set of precepts prohibiting those actions destructive of those human relationships which are necessary to a community in which and for which the good is to be achieved and for which the virtues are to be practised. Both sets of precepts derive their point, purpose, and justification from the *telos*, but in two very different ways.[36]

The respective contribution of virtues and obligations to the *telos* might be roughly characterized as follows: while the virtues are "dispositions which . . . sustain practices and enable us to achieve the goods internal to practices,"[37] obligations mark out the outer limits to communal self-understandings. They enjoin or warn against certain actions whose non-performance or performance would mean one is no longer living out the tradition that originally shaped one.

The relation between virtue and obligation cannot, therefore, be one of either conceptual, logical, or causal priority, but rather of mutuality and interdependence. The "recognition and performance of duty is made possible because we are virtuous, and a person of virtue is dutiful, because not to be so is to be less than virtuous."[38] This is clearly the reason why Hauerwas rejects any assumption that one must choose between an ethics of virtue or an ethics of obligation.[39] Such an either/or choice involves a false alternative between a "pure narrative" (virtue) and a "pure non-narrative" (obligation) account of the moral life.[40] As a false alternative it fails to appreciate that obligations, no less than virtues, are dependent on a particular narrative tradition. Abstracted from this tradition, they cease to be intelligible or compelling.[41] The same can be said about linguistic notions.

Linguistic Notions and Tradition: A Narrative Display

We have already explored Hauerwas's argument for the social linguistic basis of vision, as well as his claim that the notions within a language serve as skills of perception. What perhaps needs to be further clarified is how, as skills of perception, these notions work dialectically to at once reflect and shape a common vision. This means that while, on the one hand, linguistic notions are an embodiment of moral and social purposes of a particular tradition, on the other, they form both communal and personal vision by structuring reality within, and setting expectations according to, a particular *telos*. For this reason, the intelligibility as well as coherence of any notion depends on its place within a given narrative tradition and its *telos.* The notions of "family" and "marriage" provide an interesting test case.[42]

From within the perspective of the Christian tradition, Hauerwas has argued, marriage is a *political* act in the sense that "it requires a wider community," the Church, formed by a distinctive story of God's fidelity to His people.[43] It is this political purpose that provides a connection between the unitive and procreative ends of marriage. The requirement for both marital fidelity within and the permanence of marriage make sense because "our commitment to exclusive relations witnesses to God's pledge to his people, Israel and the Church, that through his exclusive commitment to them, all people will be brought into his Kingdom."[44]

It is on account of this story, and their belief in the Kingdom being inaugurated by God himself, that the early Christian community undermined assumptions about the naturalness of marriage by legitimating singleness as a form of life, symbolizing the conviction that "the Church grows, not through a socialization process rooted in the family, but through God's constant call to the outsider to be part of his Kingdom."[45] This is well served as a clear institutional expression that one's future "is not guaranteed by the family, but by the Church."[46] At the same time, however, the early Church also sponsored marriage and procreation as "the symbol of the Church's understanding that the struggle will be long and hard."[47] However, it is this same narrative context which explains why Christians "do not place their hope in their *children*, but rather that their children are a sign of their *hope* that, in spite of considerable evidence to the contrary, God has not abandoned this world."[48] Confidence in God's trustworthiness allows Christians sufficient confidence in themselves to bring new life into the world. Thus, Hauerwas notes, Christians regard it as their "joyful duty" to receive and welcome children into the world, "not as something that is 'ours', but as a gift which comes from another [God]."[49] Given such a hope, a refusal to have children can be an "act of ultimate despair that masks the deepest kind of self-hate and disgust," the fear that one's story is not worthwhile enough to pass on. Moreover, it might be a sign of unwillingness to participate in God's continuing creation, since "children are our anchors in history, our pledge and witness that the Lord we serve is the Lord not only of our community, but of all history."[50] In any case, from the Christian narrative, "marriage is a reality prior to any couple's decision to be married. It is a set of expectations carried by the community that offers an opportunity for some to be of service in the community."[51] This makes the family and marriage "heroic" political commitments by those involved, an invitation (vocation) to work together for something greater than themselves, greater than their love, or any love they could ever imagine.[52]

The accuracy of Hauerwas's account, or the validity of the particular normative conclusions he draws from it for Christian family life are beside the point here, even though one wonders whether the Christian understanding and use of the notions of "family" and "marriage" has ever been as coherent as Hauerwas portrays it.[53] What is significant, however, is to see how it is this particular narrative tradition and its *telos* that gives rise to, is served by, and provides intelligibility to, the notions of sacramental "marriage," "monogamy," "sex," and "having children."[54] The loss of this narrative tradition will, therefore, not only deprive these notions of any coherent conceptual intelligibility, it will render them practically ineffective, and eventually redundant. Hauerwas would agree that this, in many respects, is what has happened within modernity according to what De Certeau has called the "formality of practices." As was explained in our first chapter, the "formality of practices" for De Certeau represents nothing but the attempt by liberal politics to retain specifically Christian practices and notions (e.g., the "family" and "marriage"), without, however, appealing to Christian *telos* which these notions had been designed to serve and in whose narrative tradition they were at home. Such formalism involves nothing less than an attempt within liberalism to *depoliticize* the "family" and "marriage" by offering justification for them, not by appealing to any particular narrative tradition but in terms of so-called neutral notions of "rights," "natural feeling," "human nature," etc.

However, this "formality of practices" is highly misleading, since the very attempt to *depoliticize* the moral notions of marriage and family is itself highly *political*. Thus the appeal to the so-called neutral notions of a natural feeling of "love," "intimacy," or finding the "right person," as the basis of marriage turns out to be in the interest of liberal politics and economics, according to which the family becomes a "private" enclave which offers a much-needed emotional and social refuge away from the "public" realm of power-dominated relations and market agonistics. That is why, for Hauerwas, the significant issue between the moral posture of liberalism and that of any other (e.g., Christian) tradition is not that one appeals to "neutral" notions while the other to tradition-dependent ones. Such an alternative self-deceptively blinds one to the fact that all notions are tradition-dependent and how, in any case, the liberal tradition itself continues to shape people's vision and reactions through the employment and (re)appropriation of various notions. Once this conclusion is accepted, then it becomes clear that there can be nothing like a morally "neutral" notion. Rather, all notions are at the service of a given *telos* or politics, and abstracted from this narrative context, notions become unintelligible or, at best, receive a different meaning as they find themselves recast within a different narrative context—that is, at the service of a different *telos* or politics.[55]

Politics and the Need for Stories

A tradition's search for the relevant goods is not a theoretical quest, but one advanced through a community's politics. Hauerwas's understanding of politics is dependent on the realization that this search (for the good) is not a search for something already adequately characterized. What the goods are and the way to them is the object of much argument and disagreement: "for, politics is nothing else but a community's internal conversation with itself concerning the various possibilities of understanding and extending its life. In fact, the very discussion necessary to maintain the tradition can be considered an end in itself, since it provides the means for the community to discover the goods it holds in common."[56]

This conception of politics as everyday conversation (more in chapter 7) is clearly at variance with the liberal conception that understands politics in terms of interests, bureaucratic management, or power to determine social change. Politics in this modern sense is the province of a select group of technocrats, lobbyists, and politicians. From Hauerwas's point of view, this modern conception of politics misses the realization that "the most basic task of any polity is to offer its people a sense of participation in an adventure. For finally what we seek is not power, or security, or equality, or even dignity, but a sense of worth gained from participation and contribution to a common adventure."[57]

Stories are indispensable for this conception of politics, as Hauerwas demonstrates within the context of the story of the rabbits in Richard Adams's novel *Watership Down*.[58] As long as they continue to tell and hear the stories of El-ahrairah, the prince of rabbits, the rabbits in *Watership Down* sustain the sense of their common adventure. "Their stories serve to define who they are and to give them skills to survive the dangers of the world in a manner appropriate to being a rabbit." The implications are direct: Good and just societies, no less than the rabbits of *Watership Down* require truthful narratives if they are to maintain a sense of social identity as well as to "know the truth about existence and fight the constant temptation to self-deception."[59]

The loss of narrative art has a devastating effect, as becomes evident in Cowslip warren in *Watership Down.*[60] Cowslip is a warren characterized by peace, luxury, and unlimited freedom. Yet, behind this external satisfaction lies a tragic loss of the power to tell stories, which opens the rabbits of this warren to great self-deception and to subtle but serious dangers. Since they have unfortunately lost the art of narrative, the rabbits of Cowslip have equally lost the skills to recognize these dangers. Their inability to maintain the tradition (through the stories) of El-ahrairah results in the corruption, not only of their community, but their nature as well.

Liberalism, according to Hauerwas, faces a similar danger due to its substitution of a false security for narrative. In its various forms and versions, liberalism has presupposed that society can be organized without any narrative that is commonly held to be true, as long as there are efficient rules for the satisfaction of basic needs and services. Yet such an assumption is, according to Hauerwas, self-deceptive. For, as Hazel tells the members of the liberal warren of Cowslip: our need for narrative "hasn't changed. . . . After all, we haven't changed ourselves. Our lives have been the same as our fathers' and their fathers before them."[61] That is why, in spite of philosophically assuming the dispensability of narrative, the liberal social order still continues to be grounded on narratives of self-interest and a promise of security through economic self-sufficiency and technological positivism. Not only do such securities fail to provide adequate skills to deal with the tragic in human existence, these 'stories' become a more dangerous form of self-deception precisely because liberalism fails to recognize them as stories: "We thought that the way to drive out the evil gods was to deny the existence of all gods. In fact, however, we have found ourselves serving a false god that is all the more powerful because we fail to recognize it as a god."[62] We shall have occasion to examine the mythic nature of this liberal narrative in our seventh chapter. For now, the upshot of the realization that the liberal social order itself is founded on narrative makes it obvious that, descriptively, the difference between political configurations cannot be decided according to whether one form of politics is founded on story(ies) and the other not, but according to the *sort* of story.

Memory as a Moral/Political Task

The indispensability of narrative points to the centrality of memory as a moral and political task. A 'living' tradition primarily exists as a community of memory. And so, tradition is nothing but "memory sustained over time by ritual and habit."[63] Two remarks might help to make intelligible the irreplaceable role that Hauerwas accords to memory within a particular tradition. First, the memory that is at once moral and political cannot be an individual exercise. Hauerwas speaks of a "shared memory" that allows the foundations of a people's life together to be remembered, retold, and creatively reinterpreted. This is what makes memory a political task. For, the "shared memory" not only forms, but requires, a particular kind of community. This is the reason why "learning history is never really an act of *detached* scholarship, as academicians like to think. Learning history is, first of all, a rite of *collective identity.*"[64]

Secondly, as might be clear by now, the sense of memory here is not merely a matter of an intellectual "recalling" or "remembering of a past." Hauerwas uses various images and metaphors to characterize the dynamic sense of this memory and to qualify the usual intellectualistic and individualistic associations of memory. He refers to memory as a "creative force" which "truly shapes and guides a community"; it is a "presence" that "keeps past events in the mind in a way that draws guidance from them for the future"; it is a dynamic, but symbolic "re-enactment," not so much of "past events but of the character that produced them;" it is a "prophetic activity" determined not so much by 'fact' but "what kind of community we must be" in order to "remember the past and yet know how to go on in a changed world." It is memory "sustained through ritual and habit." In other words, it is a practical activity, embodied through the concrete practices and exemplary characters within a tradition. In order to remember, "we require not only historical-critical skills, but examples of people whose lives have been founded by that memory."[65]

To conclude, to exist as 'living' tradition—which is the same as to be a community of memory—means that not only a tradition's search for the relevant goods but also its very inquiry into the truth depends on that tradition's history and self-understanding. Human communities

> are communities of memory exactly because [our] existence is necessarily historical. "If they were founded as a 'truth' that could be known without remembering then they [communities] would be no more than philosophical alternatives. That they are fundamentally communities of memory, that is they depend on scripture, ritual, and holy people, denotes that the character of [our] understanding of the truth is particular and historical."[66]

A great deal has already been said about the narrative nature of the moral life. This is what was at stake in chapter 3 when we presented the moral life as a life of vision and insisted that this vision is a learned quality, which is finally dependent on the social-linguistic background. The effect of this argument was to confirm that our appreciation of what is morally desirable is fundamentally particular and historical and, therefore, requires narrative display. What we need to provide now, but which has all the while been assumed, is an extended defense of Hauerwas's claim that our inquiry into the truth (moral truth in particular) is likewise particular and historical, i.e., is dependent on tradition.

2. Narrative: An Alternative Pattern for Moral Rationality

All rationality, Hauerwas has argued, "depends on tradition, is based upon a view of the world, a story and a way of looking at things."[67] Those familiar with MacIntyre's argument might immediately recognize Hauerwas's debt to him for this claim.[68] Although Hauerwas does not rehearse the full argument of MacIntyre's defense of the traditioned nature of rationality, he consciously draws on MacIntyre in order to tease out implications for the nature and scope of moral reason. First, since all rational inquiry is tradition-dependent, Hauerwas argues, "methodologically, ethics . . . can only be carried out relative to a particular community's convictions."[69] Accordingly, there can be no ethics *qua* ethics:

> All ethical reflection occurs relative to a particular time and place. Not only do ethical problems change from one time to the next, but the very nature and structure of ethics is determined by the particularities of a community's history and convictions. From this perspective, the notion of "ethics" is misleading, since it seems to suggest that "ethics" is an identifiable discipline that is constant across history. . . . ethics always requires an adjective or qualifier—such as, Jewish, Christian, Hindu, existentialist, pragmatic, utilitarian, humanist, medieval, modern—in order to denote the social and historical character of ethics as a discipline.[70]

Any attempt, therefore, as by the standard accounts, to free moral reason from its historical and narrative context by grounding it on tradition-free norms of a universalizable Reason is doomed to fail, or at best to be misleading, since it must end by appealing to a particular tradition.[71]

However, it may not be hard to imagine why the standard accounts have attempted to free moral reason from its narrative context. The affirmation of the historical and social nature of *moral* reason involves a stubborn circularity which, from the point of view of the standard account, seems to compromise the clarity and 'purity' of moral reason. The circularity in question revolves around the realization that, while the truth of any story is judged by the sort of community or tradition it forms, it is only from within that same tradition that questions of the truthfulness of the story can be raised: "just as significant works of art occasion a tradition of interpretation and criticism, so significant narratives are at once the result of and continuation of moral communities and character that form nothing less than a tradition. And without tradition we have no means to ask questions of truth and falsity."[72]

This inevitable circularity between a tradition and truth gives rise to a number of significant questions. How are we to characterize this form of circular rationality in which truth and truthfulness (of community) seem to be bound up? Is this the form that "reason" necessarily takes within ethics? But given the circular nature of this rationality, how is one to avoid the danger of a tradition falling into complacency and solipsism about the truth of its story? Can a tradition-dependent rationality offer any useful criteria for judging between alternative stories? What form must moral reasoning *within* a given tradition take to ensure a sense of objectivity? And since there is no tradition-free vantage point from which questions of truth and falsity can be addressed, what sort of rational discussion can exist *between* two traditions? How are rival traditions themselves to be assessed short of relativism?

Answering these challenges is a crucial question for Hauerwas's advancement of narrative as "an alternative pattern for moral rationality." If Hauerwas is unable to provide a framework and articulate criteria by which narrative can supply an adequate sense of truth and objectivity within the moral sphere, then his appeal to narrative is just another fad that cannot survive serious epistemological inspection. But if, on the contrary, truth and objectivity can be shown to be attainable within narrative configurations, then a valid case will have been made for narrative as a form of rationality best suited for ethics. This is a key epistemological challenge that we shall take up both in this section and throughout the coming chapter. For the rest of this chapter we would like to survey Hauerwas's general understanding of the role of reason in morals. Specifically, we argue that Hauerwas's case for a "narrative moral rationality" is patterned on, and serves the same function as, Aristotle's notion of *phronēsis*. However, in order to appreciate this constructive argument for narrative as "an alternative pattern for moral rationality," we must first attend to Hauerwas's critical appraisal of the non-narrative conception of reason within the standard accounts of ethics.

The Standard Account: "Reason" as the Essence of Man

It has been the ideal of much of moral theory since the Enlightenment to secure for moral judgments an objectivity that would free such judgments from the subjective stories and traditions of the agents who make them, and base them on rationality as such. The appeal to "reason" or "rationality" thus plays a decisive role in the justification and validation of moral norms and judgments within the standard account. Hauerwas has noted at least three reasons. First, within the standard accounts, it is assumed that "reason" can be isolated from other characteristics, roles, virtues, and interests and postulated as *the good* "role," "mark," or "nature" of man. In this there is an affinity between the Kantian-inspired standard accounts and certain theological appeals to "natural law." Both are an attempt to provide a foundational account of the human good,[73] and thus determine principles of conduct which are not founded on any given set of convictions or historical roles but on a "natural" essence. This attempt to isolate "reason" as the essence of man assumes an essentialistic view of the self—a self that is able to stand back from its concrete (hi)story, particular convictions, and communal loyalties. Yet, given the comprehensive sense of our historical and traditioned nature which we have been defending, all our obligations, commitments, and roles, and the very notion of reason are community dependent: "'reason' is not committed to the idea that there is only one way to be rational—the variety of our rational activities is only limited by the language of our communities."[74]

Secondly, when "rationality" is claimed as the distinctive mark of man, undue emphasis is placed on the intellect as the sole source of moral commitment, which leaves one under the false tutelage of the "myth of the passions." This is perhaps one reason why, within many standard accounts, the moral life has tended to acquire a Manichean leaning, with an emphasis on rational self-control at the expense of forms of spontaneity often associated with the passions. Even when it is granted that one has passions, when "reason" is assumed as the essence of man, the supremacy of rational thought over the passions becomes an unquestionable ideal. But this leads to a distortion of the moral life in general and the virtues in particular. The latter appear to be the means by which to control the passions. However, as we argued in our second chapter, neither the passions nor reason can be isolated as the basis of morality, but both must be integrated within an ethics that prioritizes the formation of moral character.

Thirdly, when "rationality" is abstracted from other goods and relations which enhance life and is postulated as the "essence" of man, it readily acquires a formalistic role as a "technical instrument for man's attempt to secure survival."[75] Within a technological and capitalistic orientation, such a reason easily tends toward instrumental calculation to secure individual or societal survival. Indications for this tendency are noticeable from the assumption within certain philosophical justifications for the "need for morality,"[76] or for a functional justification of religion,[77] as well as for bureaucratic rationalization and managerial efficiency within liberal politics. These tendencies point to the predominance of an instrumental or techn(ē)ical conception of reason within modern Western philosophy in general, moral philosophy in particular.[78] Hauerwas's conception of moral rationality must be placed against this background. Against an instrumental view of reason within ethics, Hauerwas has insisted on a narrative conception of moral rationality which is patterned on an Aristotelian view of practical reason. In the next section, by showing the affinity between narrative and the Aristotelian phronēsis, both Hauerwas's quarrel with the view of reason within the standard account and his own substantive understanding of narrative as an alternative conception will be made more evident.

Narrative Moral Rationality as Aristotelian "Phronēsis"

Moral reason, Hauerwas has argued, cannot be abstracted from the narrative and social context of the manifold obligations, virtues, and roles the agent is involved in—as a father, teacher, husband, etc.[79] True, an individual often embodies various roles, a fact that may impose conflicting obligations and expectations. But this is precisely why the claim that the human being is rational is very significant. "Rationality," says Hauerwas, is not just "the technical ability to judge the best means to an end." More than this, it is the ability to deliberate, act, and give reasons for one's action and, very significantly, to order one's roles in the world.[80] This sense of 'rationality', Hauerwas notes, does not commit one to specify any one "essence," end, or purpose that dominates all others, but only that "we must have a story that gives direction to our character."[81] This observation means that moral rationality cannot be isolated from the character of the agent. Such a claim involves nothing but an attempt to relocate 'rationality', from a metaphysical determination or ascription of a 'mark', 'essence', or 'nature' to within man's agency. Thus Hauerwas has suggested: "To say that we are rational is to claim that as agents we can deliberate and plan our behavior. . . .

Rationality is for me, as I think it was for Aquinas, but another way of talking about agency."[82] In another highly significant paragraph, Hauerwas even suggests that this conception of narrative rationality is fully concomitant with Aristotle's notion of *phronēsis*. He writes:

> As Aristotle says, "There exists a capacity called 'cleverness', which is the power to perform those steps which are conducive to a goal we have set for ourselves and to attain that goal. If the goal is noble, cleverness deserves praise; if the goal is base, cleverness is knavery. That is why men of practical wisdom are often described as 'clever' and 'knavish'. But in fact this capacity (alone) is not practical wisdom, although practical wisdom does not exist without it. Without virtue or excellence, this eye of the soul (intelligence) does not acquire the characteristics of practical wisdom. Hence, it is clear that a man cannot have practical wisdom unless he is good."[83]

The full context of this citation in the *Nicomachean Ethics* must be made explicit if one is to appreciate why Hauerwas uses it here to claim affinity between his notion of narrative rationality with Aristotle's notion of *phronēsis*.[84] The quotation significantly appears at the end of chapter 12 of Book 6 of Aristotle's *Nicomachean Ethics*. Book 6 of the *NE* is devoted to an analysis of what Aristotle calls "intellectual virtues" *(aretai dianoethikai)*—i.e., virtues of a type which had already, in Book I (*NE* 1103a3–10), been distinguished from "ethical virtues" *(aretai ethikai)*. This structure by itself is very significant as it makes it clear that *phronēsis*, which occupies the bulk of *NE* Book 6, is an intellectual virtue.[85] There is, however, an interesting movement within the argument of chapter 12 of *NE* 6, from which the quotation above is drawn, which helps to make clear why Hauerwas invokes it in his argument for narrative moral rationality.

The whole chapter 12 of Book 6 of the *Nicomachean Ethics* is an attempt by Aristotle to show that knowledge is a necessary condition for virtue. However, no sooner has Aristotle carved out a place for knowledge (*NE* 1143b18–1144b20), than he immediately relativizes it, as we have seen, by arguing that "this capacity alone (cleverness) is not practical wisdom, although practical wisdom does not exist without it." And so *NE* 6.12, which opened, it had seemed, with the primary intention of demonstrating that knowledge, in the form of *phronēsis*, is necessary for virtue concludes by stating the converse: " Without virtue or excellence, this eye of the soul (intelligence) does not acquire the characteristics of practical wisdom. Hence, it is clear that a man cannot have practical wisdom unless he is good." This somewhat surprising conclusion shows that in trying to depict *phronēsis* Aristotle was at pains to show not simply that *phronēsis* is an intellectual virtue, but that it was a special type of intellectual virtue—specifically because it is a form of knowledge suffused with virtue. That is the reason why "without virtue, this eye of the soul does not acquire the characteristics of *phronēsis.*" In the context of Aristotle's argument, it then becomes clear that although *phronēsis* is an intellectual virtue, what differentiates it from the four other intellectual virtues *(technē, nous, epistēmē* and *sophia)* listed and discussed in Book 6 is precisely the intimacy of its relationship with ethical virtue.

Significant as this conclusion is to understanding Aristotle's argument in *NE* 6.12., it does not immediately make it any clearer why Hauerwas would use it to establish an affinity between his case for narrative moral rationality and Aristotle's *phronēsis.* In order to see this connection more clearly, we need to draw attention to two related arguments within Aristotle's analyses which help to explain why Aristotle would maintain that "one cannot have *phronēsis* without being good." The first of these related arguments involves the realization that *phronēsis* is knowledge operative within the field of action *(praxis).* The second involves Aristotle's understanding the moral life as a craft.[86] Drawing attention to these two related arguments will help to make clear why *phronēsis* has necessarily a historical and narrative character.

The first reason why Aristotle, in the passage quoted by Hauerwas above, resists the reduction of *phronēsis* to a formal and impersonal application of rational procedure (cleverness) has to do with the nondisposable nature of action for which this knowledge is required. We have already noted (chapter 2) how Aristotle delineates two forms of 'practical'[87] activity: making *(poiēsis)* and action *(praxis).* Aristotle was categorically clear that knowledge plays a different role in each case such that to the two forms of 'activity' corresponds two forms of 'knowledge', with *technē* (productive knowledge) as the form of knowledge which presides over 'making' *(poiēsis),* and *phronēsis* (practical wisdom) as the form proper to 'action' *(praxis).*[88] But how does 'making' and 'action' differ, and how does this difference not only determine the type of knowledge peculiar to each, but also provide *phronēsis* with a distinctively narrative aspect?

'Making', Aristotle suggests, has to do with fabrication or production, and therefore fits smoothly into a means-end framework. The standard paradigm of making is the artisan who stands outside his materials and allows the productive process to be shaped by a form which he has objectively conceived. Productive knowledge *(technē)*, therefore, lies in the ability to bring together, under the agent's rational direction, appropriate materials and means to the achievement of an end, say a house, a shoe, etc., which the agent has conceived. 'Action', however, involves a "fundamental modification" of this means-end framework.[89] For, "while making has an end other than itself, action does not. Good action itself is its end" (*NE* 1140b6–7). The absence of a substantial end-product separable from the agent (as well as the absence of any disposable materials to work on) not only makes action more elusive than making, it involves the presence of an agent who is invested in his action more completely than the producer in his product. As Hauerwas's own treatment of character (see earlier chapter 2) indicated, the agent is, in fact, constituted through his actions, which disclose him both to others and to himself as the sort of person he is. Compared with 'making', the field of 'action' requires not only a different configuration of knowledge, but also a different relationship between the agent and his action. Aristotle expresses this crucial difference by noting that while the relevant *technē* can be transmitted through instruction, a man possesses *phronēsis* not by 'knowing' but by acting (*NE* 1152a8–8).[90]

It is precisely this nondisposable nature of *phronēsis* that Aristotle is underscoring when he denies that "cleverness" is *phronēsis*. For, 'cleverness', just like *technē*, is merely the power "to perform those steps which are conducive to a goal we have set for ourselves" and which goal lies outside the agent. Such "executive ability"[91] employs detached knowledge about something, a knowledge whose significance resides solely in its content and is unaffected by the manner of its possession by the knower. *Phronēsis*, however, allows no distinction between the possession of knowledge and the application of the same knowledge.[92] *Phronēsis* is not a cognitive capacity that one has at one's disposal, but, rather, is closely bound up with the kind of person one is: "a man cannot have *phronēsis* unless he is good." In fact, it is by way of protecting this circle between moral character and *phronēsis* that, shortly before the passage cited above, Aristotle had categorically refused to consider action apart from its relation to the agent by maintaining, "some people who do just acts are not necessarily just."[93]

Once this comprehensive background of the passage that Hauerwas quotes from the *NE* is spelled out, then it becomes clear why Hauerwas claims affinity between his notion of narrative and *phronēsis*. In proposing narrative as an "alternative pattern of moral rationality," Hauerwas is simply reiterating the key insight that, he had contended, cannot be abstracted from the narrative and social context of the manifold obligations, virtues, and roles the agent is involved in—as a father, teacher, husband, etc. An even more specific and concrete expression of the narrative nature of moral reason is behind Hauerwas's claim: "Morally, there is no neutral story that insures the truthfulness of our particular stories. . . . If truthfulness (and the selfless characteristic of moral behavior) is to be found, it will have to occur in and through the stories that tie the contingencies of our life together."[94] Similarly, when Hauerwas (re)affirms, against Hartt, that "the truth demands truthfulness,"[95] the narrative nature of moral reason is at stake. The latter is simply a way of emphasizing that the truth of a story is inseparable from the truthfulness embodied within the lives of the people the story has formed. These indications in Hauerwas confirm why narrative rationality, just like *phronēsis,* cannot render itself to the same techn(e)cal and impersonal deployment as 'cleverness' or scientific knowledge. Even though both *phronēsis* and narrative provide for an 'intellectual' attentiveness within action, the fact that they are concerned with human *action* makes them a specific form of attentiveness.

Another key aspect which establishes an affinity between *'phronēsis'* and 'narrative' is the craftlike nature of morality, which both Aristotle and Hauerwas affirm. In order to explore the various aspects of this connection, it might be helpful to make explicit the Aristotelian background that informs Hauerwas's image of the "open sea" in the passage that serves as epigraph to this chapter. At the end of a sustained critique of the standard account of moral rationality, Hauerwas (with Burrell) writes,

> we offer a substantive explication of *narrative* as a constructive alternative to the standard account. Our penchant has been to rely upon the standard account as though it were the only lifeboat in a sea of subjective reactions and reductive explanations. To question it would be tantamount to exposing the leaks in the only bark remaining to us. In harkening to the narrative context for action, we are trying to direct attention to an alternative boat available to us. This one cannot provide the security promised by the other, but in return it contains instructions designed to equip us with the skills required to negotiate the dangers of the *open sea.*[96]

Even though Aristotle himself does not explicitly use the image of the open sea, his analyses provide sufficient background to support our case for an affinity between Hauerwas's notion of narrative and Aristotle's *phronēsis.* In *NE,* Book 2, in an analysis that clearly anticipates the distinction between *technē* and *phronēsis* in Book 6, Aristotle uses the cases of military strategy, navigation, and medicine in characterizing the moral life.[97] Although Aristotle continues to subsume the practice of these arts under the general category of *technē*, it is clear that they are a strange type of *technai*, if indeed they can still be referred to as *technai* at all. For, unlike the case of the more straightforward *technai*, e.g., building, their result is not so much a durable product (e.g., house), as a state of affairs. Moreover, rather than having disposable materials upon which he can impress a preconceived form, the soldier, doctor, or navigator "is more readily thought of as intervening in a field of forces, or as immersing himself in a medium, in which he seeks to accomplish a propitious end."[98] More importantly, however, while the master of *technē* ordinarily seeks to preside over his activity with secure mastery, the strange *technai* of navigation, military strategy, and medicine are marked by their distinctly close relationship with luck or chance *(tuchē)*: "they fall under one category, i.e., of opportunity *[ho kairos]*" (*NE* 1096a31).

The elements of opportunity and luck within these arts form a kind of penumbra around the clear light of rationality that one would expect within the more standard *technai*.[99] However, unlike the latter, these "philosophically orphaned *technai*,"[100] navigation for instance, gain their ends not so much by overcoming chance as by working around chance and opportunity. Since they are circumscribed by no fixed limit ("the open sea"), the play of chance is simply ineliminable:

> Being subject to chance, these latter technai cannot aspire to the same kind of mastery that obtains in the others. Success is to be achieved in them not so much by keeping one's gaze fixed on the preconceived form which one will impose on the material, as by a flexible kind of responsiveness to the dynamism of the material itself. It is sensitivity or attunement rather than mastery or domination that one strives for.[101]

It is precisely in this lack of mastery or complete security that Aristotle sees the affinity between these arts and *phronēsis*. The moral life, Aristotle shows, concerns realities that are by their nature contingent and variable, that is, realities that could be otherwise (*NE* 11094b–1527). And so, within the moral life, no less than in the cases we have been considering, "it is sensitivity or attunement rather than mastery or domination that one strives for."

Concretely, what does this mean for Hauerwas in claiming Aristotle as a fellow traveler in proposing narrative as "an alternative pattern for moral rationality"? First, it means that this Aristotelian background has greatly influenced Hauerwas's conception of the moral life under the image of a craft.[102] Although Hauerwas uses the somewhat different example of "brick-laying," he arrives at the same conclusions as Aristotle's analysis of the crafts of navigation and medicine, namely: that these crafts involve the pursuit of goods which are internal to the very practices themselves. In this respect, Hauerwas is fond of quoting Aristotle's conclusion to the effect that the moral life concerns "those things that admit of being other than they are."[103] This simply involves the realization that, as internal, the goods within the crafts are not only shifting and ambiguous, these goods cannot be clearly and strictly specified outside the very exercise of the relevant crafts. There is accordingly in the very determination and realization of these (internal) goods a certain lack of fixity ("the open sea") within crafts that renders the element of chance (luck) unavoidable.

Secondly, it means that in proposing narrative as an "alternative pattern of moral rationality," Hauerwas is aware that although the exercise of crafts requires deliberation and knowledge, it nevertheless cannot lend itself to precise measurements, exact calculation, or rigorous logic as that which is invoked where the determination of external goods is concerned. This in no way means that narrative is a substitution for general rules of conduct and universal principles. Narrative can no more dispense with these than the doctor or navigator (in Aristotle's case) with a theoretical training in the general principles that guide his craft.[104] That is why, for both Aristotle and Hauerwas, the *phronimos* is "a person of good character, that is to say a person who has internalized through early training certain ethical values and certain conceptions of the good human life as the more or less harmonious pursuit of these."[105] What, however, the proposal of narrative as "alternative pattern of moral rationality" simply shows is that Hauerwas has acknowledged Aristotle's conclusion that ethics, as the theoretical account of a craftlike domain, cannot aspire to the same conceptual closure, universal validity, and logical certitude as could be generated within mathematics or the standard forms of production *(technē)*. In comparing the moral life to the crafts of medicine and navigation, Aristotle writes,

> the accounts we demand must be in accordance with the subject-matter; matters concerned with conduct and questions of what is good for us have no fixity, any more than matters of health. The general account being of this nature, the account of particular cases is yet more lacking in exactness; for they do not fall under any art or precept *(technē)* but the agents themselves must in each case consider what is appropriate to the occasion, as happens also in the art *(technē)* of medicine or of navigation. (*NE* 1104a2–10)

It becomes clear from the above quotation that one key requirement for the exercise of both morality and crafts is that the agent "must in each case consider what is appropriate to the occasion." For this reason, when Aristotle comes to specify the kind of resourcefulness or knowledge required for conduct, he could not enshrine it within general rules and universal principles that would offset this requirement. And so, having offered one general indication that the resourcefulness would have to be a sort of mean between extremes,[106] Aristotle would offer no more specific guidance than to say that it is to be "determined by a rational principle, and by that principle by which the *phronimos* would determine it."[107]

Hauerwas's explication of narrative as a constructive alternative to the standard account must be understood as nothing but an attempt to preserve this same historical aspect of the moral life. In short, it is an argument to the effect that just like Aristotle's *phronēsis*, narrative moral rationality is inseparable from the story of the agent (his or her character). And just like the exercise of any craft, this sort of resourcefulness depends on one's initiation and training within the particular craft, on the various skills and experience acquired over the years, as well as on the history of one's accomplishments in the attempt to attain the ideals and standards realized so far within a particular craft. Moral reason, in as much as it depends on all these historical factors, has necessarily a narrative structure.

However, Hauerwas is aware that narrative, as the form of rationality best suited for craftlike nature of morality—just like Aristotle's *phronēsis*—"cannot provide the *security* promised by the other [Kantian accounts]."[108] Nevertheless, "it contains instructions designed to equip us with the skills required to negotiate the dangers of the open sea." What we need, therefore, is to look at some of these "instructions" in order to see how narrative can generate a "reasoned capacity" that can concretely and adequately guide the moral life. The "instructions" come in the form of criteria for distinguishing among various stories in terms of their potential for truthful living, which, to be sure, is no less precarious than negotiating the dangers of "the open sea."

Truth and Truthfulness: Judging between Stories

If, as Hauerwas says, "adopting different stories will constitute us into different sorts of people,"[109] then the truth of a story cannot be separated from the truthfulness embodied within the lives of those it has formed. And so, the one overriding criterion that Hauerwas offers for assessing the truth of various stories is that the truth of each story is finally known by the kind of lives it produces. The story embodied in any given tradition "directs us to observe the lives of those who live it as a crucial indication of the truth of their convictions. . . . At least part of what it means to call a significant narrative true is how that narrative claims and shapes our lives."[110] Truthful narratives "produce various characters necessary for the understanding and richness of the story itself. Just as scientific theories are partially judged by the fruitfulness of the activities they generate, so narratives can and should be judged by the richness of moral character and activity they generate."[111]

The nondisposable nature of moral truth, which both these citations confirm, shows how there can be no tradition-independent way to judge the richness of moral character. Accordingly, one cannot supply a universally valid and exhaustive set of criteria for judging the truth of stories. Such a list, if it existed, would have to be discovered *a priori* (independent of any narrative) and would have a "foundational" status in relation to all other stories. "There is no story of stories, i.e., an account that is literal and that thus provides a criterion to say which stories are true or false."[112] And so, whatever criteria one comes up with will have to be determined from within a particular tradition. From within the Christian tradition, Hauerwas has suggested a list of "working criteria," according to which a true story will have to offer:

(1) power to release us from destructive alternatives;
(2) ways of seeing through current distortions;
(3) room to keep us from having to resort to violence;
(4) a sense for the tragic: how meaning transcends power.[113]

We need not dwell on the applicability and concrete functioning of this particular set of criteria within the Christian tradition.[114] However, we need to focus on two formal conditions of narrative criteria for truth in general. The first concerns the moral necessity for a tradition to engage explicit criteria for truth in the struggle against self-deception. The second concerns the necessity for the presence of others for a fruitful engagement of the criteria within a given tradition.

We have already noted how Hauerwas accepts Iris Murdoch's assessment of the human condition. Human beings, according to this assessment, are not only finite, limited, and sinful, they live in an equally finite, limited, and divided world, one that is fraught with pain and suffering, loss and eventual death. It is a tragic world, full of unresolvable conflicts of goods, responsibilities, and obligations. This is precisely why individuals and communities are often tempted to erect a wall of illusion and self-deception, so as to protect themselves from looking at these disconcerting experiences of the "real" world. However, because Hauerwas recognizes this inveterate tendency toward self-deception, his defense of narrative is moderately sanguine. He is aware that stories, even good stories, conceal tendencies toward exclusiveness and self-deception. Such a tendency can only be checked by a constant ability to "step back" and "critically survey" one's story and engagements. The necessity for a tradition to develop explicit criteria for truth is to encourage this critical task.

The specific skill that Hauerwas associates with this critical ability to "step back"—a term he has since avoided because of its liberal associations[115]—is one of becoming explicitly conscious. However, consciousness here does not characterize a kind of mental mirror, but "the exercise of the (learned) skill of 'spelling out' some feature of the world we are engaged in."[116] The ability to 'spell out', therefore, is a sort of self-critical poise one (individual or tradition) adopts in relation to the story(ies) by which one is formed, and which allows one to see the limits of one's engagements.

As important as this skill is to avoiding self-deception, it is, nevertheless, readily avoided. Following Herbert Fingarette, Hauerwas identifies at least three reasons why a person (or a tradition) may expediently avoid spelling out some features or limits of one's engagements.[117] There is always the fear of injury that spelling things out could inflict upon one's loved ones. Also, many times societal roles provide a ready vehicle for self-deception, since one easily identifies with them (e.g., the narrow confines of one's profession) without any need to spell out what one is doing. In most cases, however, "self-deception results from an expedient policy of refusing to spell out our engagements in order to preserve the particular identity we have achieved."[118]

Whatever the source of the inability to "spell out" one's engagements, the result is self-deception, and the violence concomitant to allowing oneself to be morally formed by a limited story. One must recognize the circular nature of self-deception here. By avoiding spelling out some features and the limits of one's engagements, one self-deceptively fails to see the world in its totality. But this self-deception in turn ends up confirming one's limited vision and shaping the world in a way consistent with one's illusions. For example, the mother who insists against all evidence that her son is good, fails to recognize that she is not employing the ordinary criteria of right and wrong in his case. Even though her self-deception plays a supportive role by staving off the pain that would inevitably accompany spelling out what her son's behavior entails, at the same time it presents to her a world that seems to be in conspiracy against her son and herself—and to which she may seek to respond with hate and violence.

Hauerwas's anatomy of self-deception is descriptively powerful. However, even more powerful is the realization that "decision" and sincerity *alone* are not sufficient safeguards against self-deception. Avoiding self-deception ultimately depends on "the exercise of the *learned* skill of 'spelling out'." We stress 'learned' in order to underscore how 'spelling out', like any other skill, can be acquired only through participation in a community whose story is powerful enough to provide resources in terms of language, concrete examples, and institutions that habitually encourage and handle it in a nondestructive way. This explains why for Hauerwas forgiveness and humility are not only politically indispensable but are equally essential for historical objectivity, since only by forgiveness and humility can one avoid denying past wrongs or perpetrating an ideology that only continues to underwrite one's assumed righteousness.[119]

The priority of practices does not in any way mean a devaluation of the need to apply theoretical criteria for truth in the struggle against self-deception. Rather, it points to the nondisposable nature of any criteria operating within a tradition. These criteria cannot function as self-sufficient and isolatable fingertip principles with which one then confronts various traditioned practices. The criteria are themselves embodied within, and made available by, the concrete practices of a given tradition. There is, therefore, an inevitable circularity within the employment of the criteria to fight against self-deception. While they are made available through the practices of a given tradition, they are meant to test the truthfulness within those same practices. In terms of 'spelling out', the circularity is even more obvious. As a learned skill, 'spelling out' derives from a community's language, practices, and story. But the very existence of a community depends on the ability to form people willing to use this skill against the society's own story. The circularity is not vicious but points to the "creative tension" that Hauerwas makes one of the key requirements of a tradition normatively conceived. The truthfulness of a tradition, Hauerwas writes, " is tested in its ability to form people who are ready to put the tradition into question, or at least to recognize when it is being put into question by a rival tradition."[120] The circularity thus points to a movement of inner transcendence, or what we shall refer to in the next chapter as phronetic attentiveness—an inner dynamic by which a tradition's story and practices become objective. This self-reflectiveness by which a tradition learns to question its own engagements, is greatly advanced by the availability and explicit application of a tradition's criteria for truth.

Important as it is, self-reflexivity within a tradition's story and practices does not, on its own, lead far. In fact, if this were the case, both the criteria for truth and a tradition's practices would become internally self-validating, a fact that would easily lead to a solipsistic complacency or to a 'relativistic' "true for us," "true for you" cynicism. If such cynicism is to be avoided, there is a necessity for the dialectical presence of other stories. Of course, for Hauerwas there is no "story of stories." So, "what cannot be called for is a literal or perhaps a 'metaphysical' account." But in order to judge the truth and limits of any given story or tradition, "what may be called for is a better story."[121] This means that only coming in contact with an alternative story can provide an occasion to appreciate how the various criteria are met or fail to be met within or by one's particular story.

The necessity for the presence of others points to the hermeneutical nature of truth and objectivity in general and moral truth in particular. One cannot bring oneself to the moral point of view simply by a sort of Socratic self-inspection or a Cartesian methodical and systematic self-critique to see which of a person's convictions would pass a universalizable criterion. Important and necessary as such self-questioning no doubt is, it is not sufficient, since the path to moral truth and objectivity is decisively external. This externality comes not so much as a "face of the other" which imposes a singular and unconditional "ought," but as a hermeneutical contact with an alternative story with different criteria for truthful living. It is only by coming in contact with others who have been formed by a different story that a tradition is forced to test, reexamine, revise, or extend its own criteria of truthful living and success.

In the coming chapter, we shall pursue this crucial aspect of the hermeneutical contact with others under the category of "witness." For now, it is sufficient to note how there are two dialectical aspects (internal and external) for testing the truth of a given story. While a tradition's criteria for truth serve as an internal aspect, the latter dialectically depends on an external aspect, namely, the presence of other stories.[122] Without the challenging presence of others, there would be no need at all for a tradition to creatively revise, or even to engage in a critical self-examination in the first place. Thus, the presence of others is necessary to trigger this process of inner attentiveness which the criteria for truth provide.

Hauerwas recognizes that contact with others does not have to be personal. He therefore accords great epistemological and moral significance to

biographical, autobiographical, and fictional stories. The latter offers one a
way to experience concretely the sort of lives formed by different stories
without experimenting with one's life as well. For example, reading or lis-
tening to stories helps one to see oneself and one's world in different ways.
Also, one can learn to see a current ideology as distortion by watching what
it can do to people who let it shape their lives. And when one sees how various stories help persons to "go on," one is in a better position to determine
which ones best express truth about life and its possibilities.[123]

Hauerwas's own work contains extensive reflections on stories that help
to show how the various criteria might concretely be embodied or missed
by a story. Augustine's *Confessions*,[124] for example, narrates how Augustine was able to assess the Manichean, Platonic, and Christian stories and
how he came to see the practical truth of the latter, thus avoiding the rationalistic pretensions of Manicheanism.[125] Albert Speer's *Inside the Third
Reich*[126] shows how the dominant story Speer allowed to shape his life
failed to provide him with skills to see through the current distortions of
his engagements with Nazism, and so finally led him on a course of destructive self-deception. Thomas More's tragic confrontation with the king
of England is a paradigm of the hopeful life—a life lived truthfully and
therefore with a hope that truth is deeper than the optimism of those who
too quickly seek to resolve differences through the use of power.[127] A reliance on power readily resorts to violence, as the case of the warren of
Efrafa in Adam's *Watership Down*[128] shows.

Conclusion to Part I

This chapter, which has been an extended argument for the inescapability
of narrative as a category for meaningfully talking about the moral life in
general, and for conceiving moral rationality in particular, rightly brings us
to the conclusion of the first part of our work. This first part must be seen
as a constructive proposal for a historical conception of the moral life.
Hauerwas's reconstruction of the moral life around the three categories of
character, vision, and narrative has been shown to offer an alternative to
the standard ahistorical accounts of ethics (in which the question of the
relation between religion and ethics is at home). Against the background
of a flight from particularity assumed by the Moral Point of View, we have
sought to provide an elaboration of Hauerwas's central assumption, namely,
that given the very nature of a contingent and historical existence, all modes

of human existence and activity are historical and thereby marked with an irredeemable particularity. Thus, any sense of self-identity (character), one's conception of what is morally desirable (vision), as well as the very inquiry into truth (narrative) are all dependent on particular historical visions and canons embodied within the practices and stories of particular traditions. It is this inevitable sense of historical contingency and particularity that makes the claim at the beginning of this chapter intelligible, viz., that narrative is a crucial category for such matters as understanding issues of epistemology and methods of argument, depicting personal identity, and displaying the content of [moral] convictions.

However, once the inescapability of narrative has been established, then we can draw two key conclusions for the overall direction of our work. First, we have been keen to show how as a form of moral rationality, narrative involves a realization that moral truth is inseparable from the story of the agent. This conclusion has disastrous effects for the 'problem' of religion and ethics. For, if moral truth is inseparable from the story or character of the agent, then there is no way to get behind that story and ask what the moral significance of one's particular convictions (be they religious or otherwise) might be. To insist in asking the question is to persist in the misleading and impossible quest for a moral Reason which stands outside the flow of time and contingency. But it is this very quest which an appreciation of historical existence, and thus of the inevitability of narrative, totally undermines. As historical beings, we are so thoroughly historical that no human project, not even the quest for (moral) truth, stands outside the flow of history, outside the realm of narrative.

Secondly, if nothing stands outside the flow of contingency and narrative, then indeed life, and all its projects, is inscrutably fragile. The moral life remains tragically exposed to the vicissitudes of luck, to a dependence on others, to the chronic conflict inherent in the plurality of one's engagements, and to the affective depths within oneself. Kantian-inspired accounts have attempted, through a spurious promotion of reason to Reason (i.e., to the "essence of man"), to wrest some measure of control and reliability from this contingency. Unfortunately, this attempt to free moral reason from the particularities of historical existence involves a loss of substance as the price to be paid for rigor and apparent mastery. Moreover, it is this attempt to free moral reason from its historical moorings that has promoted the misleading picture of the moral life as a life of disparate decisions, as well as the illusory picture of the moral self as an indubitable and firm *cogito* who disinterestedly surveys the possibilities before him and makes a rational choice, based not on contingent considerations but on Reason as such.

Our intention in this first part has been to overcome this ahistorical conception of the moral life in general, and of the moral self and moral reason in particular. The self, its moral vision, and its claim to the truth, we have argued, all depend on historical events and realities, on others with whom it *happens* to share the journey, on others who have gone before, and on communities not of its own making but whose stories and practices it shares. Self-identity, moral goodness, and objectivity can only be attained within this contingent constellation of events by an attentive but constant struggle against self-deception through the application of skills and criteria for truth. Yet this, too, in the final analysis, depends not so much on the autonomous decision of the self but on the fortuitous presence of others, and on "finding oneself" part of a truthful tradition whose practices encourage and promote this quest for truth and moral goodness in a nondeceptive way.

II

Will the Real Sectarian Stand Up? Reason, Religion, and Politics within the Limits of History

In this second part of our work we intend to address the critical issues that a historicist conception of the moral life raises. We will seek to do so by attending to the criticisms that are often leveled against Hauerwas's work. The dominant criticism directed against Hauerwas is that his insistence on the distinctive nature of ethics in general and Christian ethics in particular is sectarian.[1] Although this criticism is usually not carefully developed, and even if its basic content is left unclear, it is almost always, more or less by definition, considered a deeply serious criticism that is supposed to show how his position is deeply deficient. However, it is not always easy to separate the various strands which this criticism involves. We isolate and treat three distinct strands in it: an epistemological (relativism), a sociological (fideism and sectarianism) and a political (tribalism) strand. These strands respectively form the content of the three chapters in this part.

As a preliminary remark we must note that Hauerwas's response (if indeed it can be called a response) to these charges takes a postmodern strategy, in the sense given to the term 'postmodern' by Nancey Murphy and James McClendon, Jr.[2] Murphy and McClendon describe postmodern philosophy and theology by contrasting it with three axes that can be used to describe positions taken in modern philosophy and theology: an epistemological axis (on which positions range from foundationalism to skepticism), a linguistic axis (on which positions range from representationalism to expressivism), and a metaphysical axis (on which positions range from individualism to collectivism). They define postmodern as "any mode of thought that departs from the three modern axes . . . without reverting to premodern categories."[3] As a postmodern or postliberal theologian, Hauerwas is proposing to leave behind these axes and the mutually contradictory polarities which these axes necessitate. What is peculiar to this strategy is that its preoccupation is not to offer a convincing defense against the various charges, but to question the epistemological, sociological, and political assumptions that set the charges in the first place. The goal of such a strategy will be to set aside a certain hegemonic conception of Truth, Religion, and Politics within which the charges are developed.

Each of the three chapters in this part progresses from a critical to a constructive assessment. The critical assessment will be intended to show how, by questioning the underlying assumptions, Hauerwas dispenses with the language and criticisms of relativism, fideism-cum-sectarianism, and tribalism. It is this dispensation that creates a space for constructively understanding Hauerwas's own conception of tradition-dependent objectivity, cultural-linguistic religion, and narrative-based politics.

5

Phronetic Particularity:
Moral Objectivity beyond Subjectivism and Relativism

But in fact (sometimes) our arguments do end, and (sometimes) they end in agreement. We ignore this fact because our craving is for ultimate argument-stoppers. We talk as if what we really want is philosophical argument that reduces our interlocutors to silence or, better yet, kills them if they refuse to accept our conclusion. And yet, even that is not enough, since some people might choose death. We seem to want arguments that close even that option, such that not even death could absolve the other person of the necessity of admitting our conclusion.

John Churchill

The tradition-dependent nature of reason, which we have defended in the previous chapter, makes it inevitable that truth and objectivity are themselves tradition-dependent concepts. Quoting MacIntyre, Hauerwas notes: "to be objective is to understand oneself as part of a community and one's world as part of a project and of a history. The authority of this history and this project derives from the goods internal to that practice. Objectivity is a *moral* concept before it is a methodological concept, and the activities of natural science turn out to be a species of moral activity."[1]

It is necessary to rehearse the Aristotelian background behind this citation so as to draw out the full implications for objectivity as a 'moral' concept. In the last section of the previous chapter, we noted why Aristotle assumed *phronēsis* to be the characteristic 'moral' concept and how this concept is characterized by a close identification between knowledge and virtue. Here, by referring to objectivity as a moral concept, Hauerwas is invoking the same Aristotelian conception and inviting us to cease to see objectivity primarily as a methodological and epistemological concept and instead view it as a phronetic concept, i.e., one in which questions of virtue and knowledge are inseparably linked.

To do so, however, is to already accept that the notion of objectivity is relative to a community's self-understanding and that it is inseparable from a community's history whose authority derives from the goods internal to that practice. But that is an invitation to give up the conception of objectivity as the ability to assume an external point of view—a "view from nowhere"—and to begin to see it as internal to the practices of a way of life.

Such a conception necessarily affects how one conceives the process of rational justification. The latter would equally be understood as internal to the practices and, therefore, one that takes contingent and particular reasons as the very practices needing justification. In any case, the final court of appeal in this process of rational justification is not some abstract, firm essence or external and self-evident proposition but the concrete practices of a particular community. This is the typical Aristotelian conception of moral justification and objectivity. As Nussbaum rightly notes:

> Aristotle asks us to look at our practices, seeing in the different areas, what sorts of judges we do, in fact, trust. This judgment about whom to trust and when seems to come, like the appearances, from us. We turn to doctors because we do, in fact, rely on doctors. This reliance, Aristotle insists, does not need to be justified by producing a further judge to certify the judge; it is sufficiently 'justified' by the facts of what we do. The expert, and our reasons for choosing him, are not behind our practices; they are inside them. And yet such experts do, in fact, help us to unravel puzzles.[2]

One is confronted, within the Aristotelian conception here, with a noticeable but inevitable circularity within the process of justification. What the circularity amounts to in fact, is the denial of any point of reference outside the concrete practices which could provide foundational validity to the practices, since "the expert, and our reasons for choosing him, are not behind our practices; they are inside them." The inescapable circularity within this Aristotelian conception makes Hauerwas's own appeal to historical justification suspect to many. The suspicions generally take the form of four criticisms. A tradition-dependent rationality, critics claim, (1) does not provide enough critical distance by which a tradition could avoid settling down into solipsistic self-validation or parochial complacency; (2) denies a standpoint beyond tradition, which deprives a tradition of any critical leverage for rational assessment. Concretely, this means giving up the notions of truth and objectivity in favor of concerns for narrative identity. A tradition-dependent rationality, it is further feared, (3) does not offer any possibility for making ontological claims—claims whose validity extends beyond any particular tradition. And lastly, it is claimed that (4) a tradition-dependent conception of moral truth ultimately involves a vicious form of relativism.

The present chapter examines the claims behind these four criticisms and provides a response to them. We shall take up each of these challenges in a separate section. In the first section we counter the charge of parochial complacency by showing how, given the various cues for phronetic attentiveness within Hauerwas's normative understanding of a tradition, the danger of practice settling down into solipsistic self-validation is over-dramatized. In the second section we examine how the notions of truth and objectivity concretely operate within a social-linguistic practice. We argue that with the affirmation of tradition what needs to be given up is not rational assessment or the notions of truth and objectivity as such, but certain connotations that these notions have acquired in the context of foundational epistemology. Once foundationalism is given up, we show, one can become reconciled to the fact that tradition or social-linguistic practices provide the sole context not only for justification but for a dynamic sense of objectivity as well.

The arguments in the third and fourth sections take up the implications for nonfoundationalism in responding to the two challenges here. In the third section, we show how, once foundationalism has been given up, it is possible to account for, and assess the truth of, ontological claims without reverting to a foundationalist quest for either a 'metaphysics' or 'an absolute conception of reality'. This conclusion will be extended into the fourth section, where we shall show that the demise of foundationalism requires setting aside the language of relativism altogether. Positively, this section will show that instead of developing strategies to respond to relativism, Hauerwas proposes a rehabilitation of "witness" as a decisive epistemological category.

Although we treat these criticisms separately, they are interrelated, since they all derive their critical force from within the same foundational epistemological tradition. This tradition is characterized by the dominant image of the mind as a mirror in direct contact with and thus accurately mirroring the basic structure of reality. However, it is this assumption of an immediate and direct contact with reality that the argument for the traditioned nature of all our activities, including rational inquiry, undermines. Our concern in this chapter, therefore, will be to show that once this foundational epistemological tradition has been set aside, we can continue to use the traditional categories of truth and objectivity without reproducing the specter of subjectivism or relativism.

1. Particularity and Phronetic Attentiveness

The Hauerwasian-Aristotelian conception noted above is at variance with the standard view of objectivity and justification. Whereas the former conceives justification as internal to practices, the latter has assumed that moral judgments, insofar as they can be considered true and moral, must not involve any special pleading from the agent's particular history, community identification, or concrete practices in order to establish their objectivity. On the contrary, their justification and objectivity is, so the standard conception contends, correlative to their ability to abstract from the peculiarities and limits of the above particularities. There is, therefore, within this standard view of objectivity, something of a dualistic polarization between the practices on the one hand and Reason on the other. In order to get a fair grip on the nature, extent, and problematic assumptions behind this polarization, it might be worthwhile to attend to Richard McCormick's criticism of Hauerwas's work. Since McCormick is a key voice within contemporary moral theology in general and Catholic moral theology in particular, attending to his criticism will expose the extent to which the standard account of moral objectivity has been uncritically assumed by much of contemporary moral theology.

The Standard Account: Origination-Justification Polarity

McCormick has criticized Hauerwas's emphasis on the distinctiveness of Christian ethics on the grounds that it tends to confuse Christian *parenesis* with the justification of moral principles and values.[3] McCormick recognizes that while moral theology has to do with *parenesis* (exhortation, character, and community formation, recognition and appreciation of moral values, etc.) it also has to do with moral deliberation and justification. According to McCormick, a clear distinction must be maintained between these two. While *parenesis* occurs in terms of the particular historical and "existential conditions" of the moral subject, the justification of any moral principle is "epistemologically separate from its story," i.e., it proceeds ahistorically and ends in the 'rational' (i.e., universal) determination of right and wrong. By insisting on the tradition-dependent nature of moral rationality, Hauerwas's ethics, McCormick fears, easily becomes "isolationist" and a form of "exhortation sectarianism." The danger that McCormick sees in such a position is that it unwittingly argues Christians out of public moral controversies "by presenting their convictions in terms of particular and often unshareable warrants."[4] We shall attend to the sociological and political implications of this sectarian challenge in our subsequent chapters. For now, our interest must be focused on the epistemological issues it raises.

The distinction drawn by McCormick between *parenesis* and *justification* is not novel within theological circles. It is, for example, invoked by James Childress[5] and drawn even more precisely by Bruno Schüller, as the distinction between the *origination* of moral principles on the one hand and their "truth value" or *validity* on the other.[6] In all these cases, what the distinction involves is a clear recognition that moral principles are not derived *a priori* but have, as their origin, the particular and historically contingent practices and vision of a community. However, for these principles to be *moral*, their validity, justification, or truth-value must extend beyond this historical starting point and be knowable and recognizable through *human* insight and reasoning.

This assumption, and the dualistic polarization of origination-justification it gives rise to, is quite at home within the standard moral philosophical tradition. It is, in fact, this same assumption which is responsible for setting the 'problem' of the relation between religion and ethics within moral philosophy. Moreover, this same polarization is reproduced within other standard dualistic formulations, for example, within the question of the relation between 'particularity' and 'universality', or between 'truths' and 'the Truth',[7] or between 'morality' and 'ethics',[8] or (within the analytic tradition) between 'is' and 'ought'. These various formulations not only share the same logical structure but are sustained by exactly the same epistemological assumptions as McCormick's (and Schüller's) origination-justification dualism.

Behind the various formulations in which the dualism is reproduced, one can recognize a specific conception of moral reason and objectivity which involves a certain denigration of the particular. The 'is', it is assumed by this conception, is an arational facticity, an opaque contingency, or a *mere* givenness which, left to itself, settles into solipsistic self-validation at best and ideological perversion at worst. That is why it is assumed that for an action to be *moral* ('ought'), it must be justifiable not from within the particular story or practices in which it is embodied, but from an external vantage point of a pure Reason or 'rationality-as-such'. In McCormick (and Schüller's) language, that is why the *justification* of moral principles must be set off against their *origination*.

This bias against the particular is simply misplaced. The 'is' or particular is not a mere givenness or an opaque positivity which awaits to be informed by, or translated into, an external rationality. The assumption that it is so is what constitutes particularism, the flip-side of a false universalism. For Hauerwas, the particular, whether as the self (character) or tradition (community) is always both concrete and dynamic. It is concrete, because it is informed by particularities of language and practices, and is dynamic in the Aristotelian sense of being phronetic.

In order to make this dynamic aspect within tradition explicit, we need first to recap on our earlier treatment of Aristotle's notion of *phronēsis* and see how the latter is coextensive with his (Aristotle's) account of 'experience'. Such an exploration will make clear that 'experience' for Aristotle does not denote some kind of informational knowledge preserved about this or that, but has the sense of "a non-objectified and largely non-objectifiable accumulation of 'understanding' which we can call wisdom."[9] And so, practices, according to this Aristotelian conception, are already suffused with this accumulation. In other words, Aristotle is able to grant that practices can and do provide a justification internal to them because he understands experience or the practices to be already phronetic.

The Dynamic (Phronetic) Element of Experience

It was noted that what differentiates *phronēsis* from the four other intellectual virtues that Aristotle discusses in Book Six of the *Nicomachean Ethics* is precisely its intimacy to ethical virtue. It is this intimacy, we pointed out, that partly explains the remarkable circularity in Aristotle's analysis of the relationship between virtue and knowledge. If one starts from the side of knowledge, one analyzes the need for virtue, and if one starts from the side of virtue, one analyzes the need for knowledge. Aristotle, in fact, does both in his dialectical critique of natural cleverness (*NE* 6.12) and natural virtue (*NE* 6.13), before he arrives at the daunting conclusion at the end of *NE* 6: "It is clear, then, from what has been said, that it is not possible to be good in the strict sense without phronesis nor phronetic without moral excellence " (1144b30–32).

Dunne, whose work we already referred to, delineates well this dynamic aspect of experience by noting how this circularity was significant for Aristotle as he (Aristotle) was at pains to make the point that virtue resists any strict conditionality on prior knowledge. It is not that one has *phronēsis* and *then* develops a good character, or that one first has a good character and *then* acquires *phronēsis*. In fact, the customary way of looking at *phronēsis* as a kind of (practical) knowledge that guides action is misleading. The circle points to the fact that *phronēsis* also arises from good action. One cannot have the knowledge to help one 'become' good unless one already 'is' good. "Being phronetic is itself part of what it means to be of good character."[10]

However, an even more significant point in this connection is the fact that Aristotle is able to avoid the circularity from turning vicious by pointing to the grounding role of "experience" in which both character and *phronēsis* stand as modalities.[11] Both character and *phronēsis* maintain a unique relation to experience that is missing in the case of the artisan and his *technē*. First of all, unlike *technē* that can be learned through a process of instruction, *phronēsis* is the result of 'experiential' learning. As Aristotle maintained: "we ought to attend to the undemonstrated sayings and opinions of experienced and older people or of *phronimoi* not less than to demonstrations; for because experience has given them an eye they see aright" (*EN* 6.11 1143b11–14).

Secondly, there is a rupture between *technē* and experience. The standpoint of the master of *technē* is that of third-person analyst who stands outside the experience from which he is generalizing. In fact, it is not essential that this experience should be his own rather than someone else's. Not so with *phronēsis*. There is no way the agent can stand outside experience, since there is no way one can stand outside the flow of activity, or in the case of a tradition, outside its own practices by which it is constituted.

This unique relation to experience means that *phronēsis* itself is a form of experience—according to Dunne, "the dynamic element of experience."[12] As the dynamic element, *phronēsis* maintains a dialectical poise *within* experience in such a way that experience is imbued with what Hauerwas calls a "creative tension."[13] *Phronēsis*, Dunne argues,

> arises from experience and *returns into experience*. It is, we might say, the insightfulness—or, using Aristotle's own metaphor, "the eye"—of a particular type of experience, and the insights it achieves are turned back into experience, which is in this way constantly reconstructed or enriched. And the more experience is reconstructed in this way, the more sensitive and insightful phronesis becomes—or, rather, the more the experiencer becomes a *phronimos*.[14]

The implications here are obvious. If we are looking for moral (which is to say phronetic) objectivity, it will have to be an objectivity that arises from experience (practices) and returns to the experiences. It will, in other words, be an objectivity internal to the practices. Moreover, the close link between *phronēsis* and virtue underscored by the last part of the citation means that only a virtuous person or community is capable of "phronetic experience." For Aristotle, the latter is to be clearly distinguished from what might be called "ordinary experience" in that, "while it [phronetic experience] retains familiarity with particulars, it still contains a greater pressure toward universalization."[15] There is need to emphasize 'pressure' in order to make clear how, for Aristotle, the emphasis does not lie with universalization as a final achievement, but with the "pressure toward," as the dynamic "process" of critical inner attentiveness or transcendence. This phronetic pressure not only "saves experience from settling down into mere routine," opaque contingency, or mere givenness, it points to a dynamic conception of objectivity as a process. There is always a chance of becoming more phronetic: "the more experience is reconstructed in this way, the more the experiencer becomes a *phronimos*" or the more a tradition becomes phronetic.

In any case, the discussion above makes it obvious that although there can always be a danger of a tradition growing complacent within its way of life, such danger is not necessarily inherent in the very nature of being a particular tradition. Hauerwas's gesturing to the Aristotelian conception of "justification internal to the practice" is premised on this realization that the form of life is not necessarily opaque to reason. As he notes, "substantive traditions are not at odds with reason, but are the bearers of rationality."[16] Moreover, given both the dynamic poise that *phronēsis* maintains within experience, and its close identification with virtue, a tradition can be seen as a dynamic form of life which not only aspires for moral rectitude but which will also already contain great pressure 'toward universalization'. That is, of course, if it is a phronetic tradition.

Hauerwas and the "Creative Tension" of Phronetic Attentiveness

In view of the above considerations, it becomes clear why Hauerwas's interest and argument is not just for character but for *virtuous* character; not just for story but for a *truthful* story; not just for tradition but for a *living* tradition; not just for community but for a *peaceable* community; and not just for particularity but for *moral* particularity. As *moral*, it must be *phronetic* to the extent it is marked by a habitual, but critical, "*attentiveness that makes the resources of one's past experience flexibly available to one* and, at the same time, allows the present situation to 'unconceal' its own particular significance."[17]

Evidence for such attentiveness is abundant in Hauerwas's work. One can, in fact, locate an internal and external (see previous chapter) moment as two dialectical sources or occasions of this process of phronetic attentiveness. The internal moment refers to the criteria for truth as well as other skills generated by, or from within, a given character or tradition. The external moment refers to the presence of others, as this presence occasions the same demand for phronetic attentiveness. In relation to internal elements that encourage phronetic attentiveness, one can point to the central role Hauerwas accords to deliberation and choice in the formation of character, which mitigates against any idea of character as passive habituation or uncritical interiorization of societal roles and expectations (see chapter 2). Concerning vision, we have noted how Hauerwas warns that coming to a 'truthful vision' of reality is not automatic, but requires "necessary skills of attention" to avoid fantasy and complacency. In this connection Hauerwas speaks of the need for an "imaginative [re]ordering of [our] basic symbols and metaphors" and of imagination as a moral task.[18]

Against the constant potential for a story to settle down into routine and easy self-justification he points to the need for constantly "rehearsing" or "spelling out" one's commitments. And one indication of a truthful story, we are told, is its ability to provide necessary "moral and intellectual skills" to yank their adherents out of self-deception that a blind identification with societal roles and descriptions may inadvertently provide. In any case, the whole point of suggesting criteria for truthfulness of a story is meant as an argument that the particular (in this case narrative) is not at odds with reason, but is itself capable of developing a "reasoned capacity" for judging among alternatives.[19]

All these indications show that the particular (character, story, or tradition) is normatively characterized by an inner attentiveness that charges it with a critical and dynamic orientation through which its own identity, possibilities, and limits are tested, confirmed, revised, or extended. This inner dynamic is what is captured by Hauerwas's reference to tradition, following MacIntyre, as "a historically extended, socially embodied *argument.*" Similarly, the realization that "living traditions presuppose *rival* interpretations" points to this normative aspect of inner attentiveness. This is the reason why "Good societies [must] enable the argument to continue so that the possibilities and limits of the tradition can be exposed." In fact, the truthfulness of a tradition "is tested in its ability to form people who are ready to put the tradition into question, or at least to recognize when it is being put into question by a rival tradition."[20]

It is for the same goal of advancing phronetic attentiveness and inner transcendence that Hauerwas insists on the need for, and a comprehensive understanding of, casuistry. Casuistry, Hauerwas notes, is not just "the province of a small group of 'experts'" as they attempt to adjudicate difficult cases, but the whole tradition is a community of discourse and casuistry. Casuistry is "the process by which a tradition tests whether its practices are consistent (that is, truthful) or inconsistent in the light of its basic habits and convictions or whether these convictions require new practices and behavior."[21] As a communal exercise of phronetic attentiveness, casuistry implies a reflexive ability on the part of a tradition, which enables it "to test imaginatively the often unacknowledged implications of its narrative commitments."[22]

Whatever else might be said about Hauerwas's understanding of tradition, it is never the cosy, uncritical, and 'faithful' passing on of a 'deposit' or form of life. On the contrary, any adequate tradition "must accept *creative tension* to be a permanent feature of its way of life."[23] The tension is "creative" not simply because it can expose the limits and possibilities of a tradition, but because in so doing it leads to those limits and possibilities being revised and extended in novel and creative directions. The tension thus exerts a certain "pressure toward universalization," that prevents the particular (character, story, or tradition) from settling down into mere routine or uncritical ideology.

The internal aspect of phronetic attentiveness is closely connected with, and even made possible by, the presence of other persons, stories, traditions, or forms of life. This dialectical presence of others underscores the hermeneutical significance of "witness" within Hauerwas's work. The key requirement that Hauerwas associates with witness is "openness" to the stranger.[24] This "openness to the stranger" signifies the need to allow the *questionableness* of one's convictions, or to be persuaded that the other's presence and convictions may enrich one's vision or even have to prevail over it. Within the formation of character, for example, the "masters" and "saints"—those who are recognized as embodying in a more nearly objective way the story of the tradition—play this critical function. It is therefore significant to note that Hauerwas has rightly continued to qualify his earlier understanding of character as a "heroic achievement" of the agent, by noting how "our character is a gift from others."[25] For the same reason, he has underscored how friendship is essential for the moral life if one has to achieve "a certain kind of self-knowledge, a practical wisdom,"which leads to the discovery of truths, commitments, and gifts one never knew existed.[26] That is why also, Hauerwas suggests, art, especially the novel[27] and even gossip,[28] may serve as helpful casuistry for the "imaginative testing of our habits of life against the well-lived and virtuous lives of others."[29]

This logic of inner transcendence explains why Hauerwas has rejected the traditional "particular versus universal" formulation—and its correlates of 'is-ought'; 'religion-ethics'; 'private-public' dualism. To begin in such an abstract manner—for instance, by seeking to determine the relation between particularity and universality, or religion and ethics—is to already have made a mistake. Such a starting point not only introduces false alternatives, it assumes foundational epistemological assumptions of external justification. In his work Hauerwas has avoided these abstract and reified formulations of "particularity" and "universality." For him, *particular* and *universal* are concrete adjectives that qualify concrete realities, e.g., particular tradition, universal church, etc. Concretely, this means that since there is nowhere to stand other than within a given tradition, then 'universal' is for Hauerwas not an ahistorical or metaphysical projection of pure meaning or eternal essences but a traditioned horizon of meaning and interpretation which is itself always being reconstituted and widened through contact with other particulars.

The synchronic structure of Hauerwas's key operative categories of character, vision, and story best exemplifies the dialectical interplay between the concrete particulars and the traditioned horizons, where it becomes clear that the interaction itself is not only the constituting moment of each but also the dynamic by which each is confirmed, widened, or even reconstituted. The formation of the agent's character and vision, for example, is made possible only as it is informed by, placed within, and yet also constantly challenged by, the wider horizon of the community's vision and tradition through the mediation of societal descriptions, practices, obligations, and virtues. But the latter, in turn, do not exist anywhere except in as far as they are embodied, accepted, challenged, and advanced by the exemplary or idiosyncratic particularity of the agent's character and vision. Similarly, the agent's particular story or narrative stands in the same "creative tension" in relation to the wider archetypal stories. Even without further elaboration, the implications for phronetic attentiveness are obvious. The presence of these 'traditioned horizons' and their interaction with concrete particulars is bound to advance the dynamics of inner transcendence within both particulars, thereby objectivizing[30] both levels of moral assessment.

The active sense of objectivity at work here involves a key realization associated with phronetic attentiveness, namely, that the "pressure toward universalization" can never lead to a state of complete transparency, or bring the particular into the realm of 'universality' *simpliciter*. This is exactly what Kantians like Herbert Schnädelbach find extremely disappointing about what, according to them, is "the ideology of *phronēsis*."[31] According to Schnädelbach, Neo-Aristotelianism, because it implies a "systematic harnessing of ethics to the yoke of some kind of existing ethos" can attain no more than a *mere* concrete historical action-context, a *mere* pragmatic universal. The best this Neo-Aristotelian "ethos-ethics" can realize are *merely* "hypothetical imperatives, which are nothing other than situationally specific rules of prudence, which Kant would scarcely have called moral."[32] The way to rescue the notion of *phronēsis*, according to Schnädelbach, is to reconstruct it within a Kantian perspective as 'practical' judgment. "This logically includes progressing from a *merely* pragmatic-general ethos to a principled-universal of practical reason."[33]

What Schnädelbach seeks, and what he would find sadly lacking in a Neo-Aristotelian conception like Hauerwas's, is some measure of security within the moral life. This is precisely the element he finds to be 'heroic' about Kant's project. The latter was able, through a progressive refinement of practical reason, to provide this measure of reliability by providing ethics with "an *ultimate* ethical *foundation*."[34] Throughout our work, we have been keen to show that Kant was able to do this only by granting to moral reason a purity and universality that it simply does not have. In the previous chapter we focused on two main reasons that mitigate against such purity. First, the very nature of action *(praxis)*, which is the domain of moral reason, resists the complete mastery, control, and generalization that is legitimately found within technical production. Secondly, our historical nature means that all our actions, including our rational deployment, are tradition-dependent. This means, as MacIntyre warns, that "particularity can never be simply left behind or obliterated. The notion of escaping from it into a realm of entirely universal maxims which belong to man as such, whether in its eighteenth-century Kantian form or in the presentation of some modern analytical moral philosophies, is an illusion. . . ."[35] In other words, given our historical nature, we have to be content with what, according to Schnädelbach, is "*merely* historical contingent ethos" *mere* hypothetical imperatives"; a "*merely* pragmatic" universal. For given the historical nature of existence and truth, we lack the high point from which to construct the much-desired "rational-universalistic" ethic. In Hauerwas's familiar formulation, we lack a "neutral story that insures the truthfulness of our particular stories. . . . If truthfulness . . . is to be found, it will have to occur in and through the stories that tie the contingencies of our life together."[36]

It now becomes clear why McCormick and Schüller's origination-justification dualism is not only problematic but, from the Aristotelian conception assumed by Hauerwas, must be resisted. The point of the polarization is to ensure a certain security and universality to the moral life by freeing reason from the contingent variables of a particular tradition and granting it moral validity only in as far as it is grounded in rationality-as-such. The affinity of both McCormick and Schüller with Schnädelbach is immediately obvious. For, like him, they both seek to progress "from a merely pragmatic-general ethos to a principled-universal of practical reason."[37] Like Schnädelbach, they are not content to let moral reason stand within the flow of "ethos-ethics" for, according to them, the latter is *mere* ethos, *mere* 'parenesis', *mere* origination, or *mere* religion, which, although morally significant, nevertheless still suffers from the opacity of its contingency. From such blindness it 'awaits' to be cured by some external Reason or Legality. Only the enlightened universalism of the latter, it is assumed, can translate (or summon up the 'reasons' implicit within) this *mere* ethos into *real* moral Reason.

A strong case can, and will, be made against the violence implicit within the pretentious self-understanding of such external and pure practical reason.[38] At this point, we need only establish the more modest observation, viz., that the quest for universal validity implicit within the origination-justification polarity is simply misplaced. The particular is not mere givenness, 'ordinary' experience, or opaque positivity, which 'awaits' being informed by external Reason. Rather, we have argued, truthfulness and objectivity do indeed "occur in and through the stories that tie the contingencies of our life together," for the particular, normatively speaking, already is a phronetic particular.

This objective has been achieved, first, by attending to Aristotle's understanding of phronetic experience; secondly, by elaborating the various internal and external cues that concretely depict Hauerwas's conception of phronetic particularity; and lastly, by pointing to the synchronic structure of Hauerwas's work in which the dialectical interaction between the particulars and traditioned horizons exerts a pressure toward universalization which helps to make both the concrete particulars and the traditioned horizons more objective and more truthful particulars.

What all these developments have shown is that the particular is never an opaque facticity; it is (normatively) suffused with enough creative tension and phronetic attentiveness to save it from settling down into parochial complacency. In fact, the very nature of phronetic attentiveness within a given tradition calls for a distinctive conception of moral objectivity. According to this conception, moral objectivity is not so much a static end point or status that is achieved but a process or 'pressure' by which a particular (character or tradition) becomes more attentive to the implications of one's story. This dynamic conception of moral objectivity still must be defended and its implications fleshed out.

2. Truth and Objectivity within a Social-Linguistic Context

The critical challenges within this section can be summed up briefly as follows: The claim that tradition-dependent rationality is all there is denies the presence of an external and neutral standpoint, which deprives a tradition of any critical leverage for rational assessment. Concretely, this means that a tradition gives up the traditional concern for truth and objectivity in favor of concern for narrative identity. The apparent seriousness of this sort of criticism can be made more concrete by attending to the key epistemological issues behind James Gustafson's critique of Hauerwas's work.

Gustafson: Farewell to the Concepts of 'Truth' and 'Falsity'?

Gustafson has criticized Hauerwas's affirmation of the distinctiveness of Christian ethics as a defensive posture which involves a fideistic and sectarian conception of theology, as well as a withdrawal of Christians into a sort of tribal ghetto where they cannot participate in the ambiguities of public choices and responsibilities.[39] Gustafson's worry is that such an affirmation of a distinctive tradition makes Christian convictions incorrigible. Moreover, because the emphasis on tradition is on "maintaining historical social identity," there is nothing to prevent this concern from becoming ideological, since an ethics grounded on a particular tradition simply demands "fidelity without further external justification."[40]

   Behind Gustafson's criticism is the worry that in the absence of an "external justification," one would have to give up the evaluative categories of truth and falsity and even the very notion of objectivity.[41] This fear, however, is driven by a foundational quest for contact with an "extra-linguistic givenness," to which could be contrasted the formulations within any given tradition in order to ascertain the latter's adequacy or truth. But such a guarantee is precisely what an appreciation for historical existence requires one to give up. All our actions and rational inquiry are so tradition-dependent that there is no way one can step outside historical traditions to come into a direct and immediate contact with reality. There is no 'theory of truth' as such—no story of stories that would guarantee the truthfulness of other stories. There are only particular configurations of reality, particular stories and canons of rationality, which are themselves tradition-dependent.

However, this does not mean that one has to give up questions of truth and falsity. On the contrary, tradition provides the very conditions-of-possibility for such questions, since "without tradition, there is no way we can start asking questions of truth or falsity."[42] This rebuttal does not provide any concrete or helpful explication of exactly how questions of truth and falsity make sense from within a given tradition. Hauerwas himself has not offered an extended or systematic formulation of this issue. He has, however, suggested that his position has a stake in a "qualified epistemological realism" similar to the one developed by Sabina Lovibond in her *Realism and Imagination in Ethics*.[43] Thus, by attending to Lovibond's work, we hope to be able to provide a more substantive explication to the conception of truth and objectivity that a tradition-dependent rationality involves. Such an explication will not only offer a sustained and adequate response to the challenge posed by Gustafson, it will also draw the reader's attention to the Wittgensteinian background that informs Hauerwas's work.

Sabina Lovibond's Realism and Imagination in Ethics

According to Lovibond, the lack of access to a tradition-independent description of reality does not mean that one has to give up the very notions of truth and objectivity. It only means that our traditional notions of truth and objectivity are in need of revision. In order to appreciate the meaning that these concepts take on within the affirmation of a social-linguistic background, we need, by way of introduction, to draw attention to the overall nature of Lovibond's argument, in particular to her Wittgensteinian background.

In *Realism and Imagination in Ethics*, Lovibond understands herself to be engaged in an attempt to realize in the field of ethics what Wittgenstein understood to be the difficult challenge for the whole of philosophy: "Not empiricism and yet realism in philosophy, that is the hardest thing."[44] The difficulty lies in the critical necessity to purge the concepts of truth, objectivity, and justification of the absolutist or transcendental connotations that have been accorded to them within the context of a foundational epistemology and yet show how these concepts can still be validly employed. This explains why her work has both a critical and constructive intent.

Critically, by using the later philosophy of Wittgenstein, in particular the latter's conception of language, Lovibond seeks to undermine the idea of an "extra-linguistic givenness" often associated with the correspondence theory of truth. The latter, Lovibond notes, is grounded in an empiricist metaphysical and epistemological tradition. This tradition is characterized by the dominant image of the mind in contact with, and thus mirroring accurately, the basic structure of reality. Sense impressions and feelings, according to this image, serve as the "primitive phenomena of consciousness"—original existents which force themselves onto us unbidden and which constitute a source of information from which we *infer* how things stand.[45] The aim, within this conception, of locating "primitive phenomena of consciousness," is to view sense impressions and feelings as so compelling that their accuracy cannot be doubted. These "privileged representations" are meant to serve as the foundation of knowledge, which is expressed under the key evaluative categories of "adequacy," "accuracy," and "Truth." All these notions do, in fact, point to a conception of knowledge as 'presence' or coming into direct contact with, and correspondence to, an extra-linguistic reality.

The above empiricist and foundational conception of truth gains much of its appeal from an instrumental view of language. Thought and feeling, according to this conception, exist prior to language, which is but a later arrival, an instrument for the communication of an otherwise 'pure' or 'primitive' contact with reality. Lovibond's critical aim in *Realism and Imagination* is to show how this empiricist view of language cannot be maintained in light of Wittgenstein's later philosophy, particularly his remarks on the relation of language and culture. Wittgenstein, Lovibond argues, was able to show that thought and feeling do not exist prior to language. Not only are they constituted in and through language, it is the social-linguistic practice which provides the conditions of possibility for any experience of reality.

We need to make two brief remarks here to set off Lovibond's project against possible misunderstanding. First, the realization that the social-linguistic practice which provides the context for the very concept of 'reality' is not equivalent to the idealistic claim that reality is the product of language. Nor is it a denial that our judgments are about reality. It is rather to recognize that because 'reality' itself is in part socially constituted, and the judgments socially constrained, there is no way to get behind the social-linguistic practice to an extra-linguistic "givenness," which would provide a justification for those judgments.

Secondly, the absence of any tradition-independent description of reality does not lead to the rejection of the very idea of rational justification of beliefs and actions. What is denied is the assumption that the process of justification is regulated by an external, absolute, or rationally irrebuttable end point. From within the Wittgensteinian conception, the process of justification is, instead, understood as relative to a "context and to the expectations of an audience."[46] In any case, the final point in this process of justification lies, not in providing a rationally self-justifying and indubitable proof, but in the shared way of life of a community:

> Demands for justification . . . tend to elicit the sort of response which the questioner will find relevant and plausible. . . . But if such demands are pressed beyond a certain point . . . the supply will run out and the questioner will be brushed aside with 'This is simply what I do'. And this response is not pig-headedness, but an essential feature of the use of language—which as we have seen, is represented by Wittgenstein as an activity interwoven with the total system of behaviour of a community.[47]

The major point scored by Lovibond from the proceedings so far has been critical. By drawing attention to Wittgenstein's conception of language, she has been able to confirm how (contrary to Gustafson) it does not make sense to "look for a source of authority external to human practice which would *certify* as true those propositions that we *call* true." Constructively, this conclusion involves nothing less than a relocation of the concept of justification from a transaction between the 'knowing subject' and reality (of the traditional epistemology) to a social transaction.[48] This depends, in the final analysis, on the conception of truth as an intersubjective agreement. We therefore need to examine Lovibond's positive argument for realism in ethics.

Once the idea of a 'primitive' or immediate experience of reality has been given up in the face of a social-linguistic affirmation, truth and objectivity cannot be seen to consist in an accurate mirroring of "the fabric of the world," but in intersubjective consensus. Lovibond writes: "the possibility of discourse about an objective world is determined by the fact of intersubjective agreement; and conversely, where such agreement exists, the particular discourse grounded in it can properly be called 'objective', regardless of its subject-matter."[49] The nature of this consensus is ultimately sublinguistic, i.e., it is a consensus not in the 'web of beliefs' but in the shared practices of a form of life. Quoting Wittgenstein, Lovibond notes, "the agreement of humans that is a presupposition of logic is not an agreement in *opinions*, much less in opinions in questions of logic. It is an agreement . . . in 'form of life'."[50] By noting how the intersubjective agreement is *ultimately* a consensus in the form of life, Wittgenstein sought to avoid giving the impression that we can *create* our own language game. Hence, although a language may look arbitrary, in that it is "just there like our life," it is not "as if we choose [or cook up] this language game."[51] On the contrary, the givenness of the language game which pre-exists the individual, calls for training and "induction" into the form of life if one is to participate in any rational inquiry such form of life occasions.

The notion of "induction" into a form of life allows for the possibility that within a given form of life (tradition), facts can obtain independently of one's present ability to recognize them as obtaining.[52] Or even the possibility of one being simply wrong about the moral truth of some other facts. As Lovibond notes, "the induction of an individual into a communal form of life is a gradual process: until it is complete, there will be some 'correct judgements' which escape him, and hence some moral facts which transcend his awareness."[53] Elsewhere, Lovibond grants that the possibility of making correct or wrong judgments is analogous to linguistic competency. Learning the use or meaning of a word is not a matter of sudden and total enlightenment. It is a matter of gradual familiarity. Thus, "while a speaker may master the use of a moral word adequately for the purposes of participation in a certain limited range of language-games involving that word, yet the same word may also figure in various other language-games into which he has not so far been initiated."[54]

These remarks already make clear why giving up the foundational quest for an extra-linguistic givenness does not result in either complete a-rationality or subjectivism. The notions of truth and falsity still retain validity. However, what a social-linguistic affirmation involves, at least within the ethical field, is a relocation of these notions from a connotation of "correspondence" with independently existing moral "facts," to a context of "participation" in the social-linguistic form of life. If, as Wittgenstein shows, learning the use or meaning of a word is not a matter of sudden and total enlightenment (like the sudden apprehension of a mathematical rule: 'Now I understand!'), then learning 'correct judgments' is not so much a theoretical challenge, as a practical challenge.[55] Learning correct judgments involves learning a particular mode of behavior. The correct use of moral concepts by individual speakers is grounded in an increasingly diversified capacity for participation in social practices.[56]

So also does the notion of objectivity retain its validity after undergoing the same relocation. Within a social-linguistic affirmation, moral objectivity has to do less with the foundational metaphor of "accuracy" (as measured against a fixed standpoint) and more with the metaphor of "induction" into a form of life.[57] But since the induction of an individual into a communal form of life is gradual, there is a very dynamic sense of objectivity at stake here. This dynamic conception of objectivity is made explicit by Lovibond in relation to Collingwood's notion of "culmination."[58] She writes,

> At any given moment in the life-history of the individual, his moral understanding will be complete in the sense that it will be a culmination—what he understands at that moment will sum up the whole evolution of his grasp upon moral concepts up to that point. This is the reflection in language of the fact that an individual's induction into the form of life of his community also partakes of the character of a scale of forms, each phase of which is a culmination: at each moment the individual will be a person who is intellectually complete as far as he goes. He will be a competent participant in various rule-governed practices, and will therefore possess an identity as a rational (social) being, even though other such practices exist in which he has *not* learnt to participate—perhaps because they have never impinged upon him. . . . The same can be said about the historical development of whole cultures.[59]

It has been worthwhile to quote Lovibond's own formulation at length in order to introduce a number of significant issues which will emerge in our discussion. To begin with, we need to focus specifically on the dynamic sense of objectivity which is implied by the notion of "culmination."

Both the idea of "induction" and the metaphor of "culmination" point to a conception of objectivity in Lovibond in an active sense as a "pull," or the "pull toward objectivity."[60] Just as was noted earlier in relation to the "pressure toward universalization," the emphasis is on "pull," which confirms an active sense of objectivity. In fact, Lovibond characterizes the "pull" toward objectivity as both material and intellectual. As material, it is effected through a socializing process, by which authority-relations embodied within the various social institutions bring one, through a "myriad

of corrective cues," "to see things in essentially the same way as ourselves."[61] As intellectual, it involves nothing less than the acknowledgment of certain intellectual authorities.[62] The latter, according to Lovibond, are perspectives and persons of "sound judgment." According to
Hauerwas, these are the "masters" and "saints" who, through their familiarity with the history of the tradition, have come to embody more nearly
what the tradition is all about.

In any case, the use of such active metaphors as, "pull," "culmination,"
and "induction" is highly instructive. It implies an explicit recognition by
Lovibond of the factor of growth and development in moral objectivity. Because this factor of growth is tied up with the elements of induction into a
form of life, linguistic training, culmination, authority, etc., the model of
the moral life it evokes is one not primarily concerned with the "what
should I do?" but with the formation of the agent (moral character) to come
to see (vision) reality in an objective way.

In other words, the model of the moral life inspired by this active sense
of objectivity is in great contrast with what Hauerwas has described as the
excessive "optimism" of the standard account. Modern moral philosophy,
Hauerwas has noted, has been written from the perspective of some last
stage, and with the assumption that everybody 'naturally' stands at this
stage, from which they face the same rational challenge: making up their
mind about the right thing to do. This assumption of everybody standing at
this last stage, however, makes the moral life discontinuous. Childhood, for
example, becomes morally uninteresting or some kind of "pre- or nonmoral" stage of development.[63] In contrast, the notions of character, vision,
and narrative provide useful ways to think about the self as involved in a
gradual and continuous journey of moral growth.

The goal of such moral growth is a continuous formation of one's vision,
leading to a *more* objective view of reality. However, one must not imagine
this objective view as transcendentally determined by a sort of "Ideal Observer."[64] The objective standpoint is a historical and contingent one. It is
objective, "not because [it] is *the* one which offers the best view of reality,
rather, it is because reality *is defined* as that which one apprehends when
one looks at the world from the standpoint in question. Reality is what is
observed by . . . the person of sound judgement."[65]

One cannot fail to notice, and perhaps even be disappointed by, the stubborn circularity within the above formulation, which we have noted elsewhere in respect to tradition in general, and to *phronēsis* in particular.
Here, the circularity amounts to a clear recognition that the determination

of objectivity, just like the determination of what counts as good reasons and convincing evidence is always contingent and local. In another helpful citation, Lovibond notes that what counts as an objective view of the world "is determined by the community of speakers in the same stipulative way in which, for example, they identify certain sorts of 'reasons' as compelling. . . . This does not, of course, mean that we are to imagine the relevant 'decisions' being made at a conference table. What it means is that certain canons of thought are upheld by a *shared way of proceeding*—for which, . . . there is, on Wittgenstein's view, no such thing as an absolute rational justification."[66]

Even without engaging Wittgenstein's comprehensive understanding of what it means to have a shared way of proceeding, it becomes clear that there is no need to give up the notions of objectivity and justification once the idea of an "extra-linguistic" reality and its promise of external justification is abandoned. Rather, one is led to realize the validity of Aristotle's conclusion (already referred to in a citation from Nussbaum), namely, that our reliance on doctors does not need to be justified "by producing a further judge to certify the judge." The practice is "sufficiently justified by the facts of what we do." In other words, there is no need to look for an external judge or point of justification. It is impossible to find one anyway. For, the absence of any story of stories means that any 'external' judge one finds will inevitably be standing within just another equally contingent social-linguistic practice.

This realization that reason has no standpoint other than within a given "shared way of proceeding" significantly means that reason lacks a leverage from which it would make its particular standpoint completely transparent. This is one important consequence of Wittgenstein's denial of an absolute rational justification. While the "shared way of proceeding" should be seen as the standard for any good reasons, "the standard has no ground."[67] This realization has both critical and constructive implications for philosophy in general and ethics in particular. Critically, for example, it calls into question a Cartesian preoccupation with seeking to make all one's prejudices rationally and transparently available. Constructively, it points to a certain measure of "gradualism" (moral and rational growth) that a nonfoundational position entails. The acceptance of a certain measure of gradualism is not a conservative strategy,[68] but is the recognition of the necessary boundedness of reason. To accept the boundedness of reason within tradition is not an abdication of reason. On the contrary: "The condition of 'doubting' all our beliefs indiscriminately does not belong within theoretical activity at all, but represents an abdication from such activity."[69] Accepting the boundedness of reason is thus simply to appreciate the only kind of reasonableness that is available to us as finite and historical beings.

It must be recalled that the immediate reason for our attention to Lovibond's work was to provide an extended answer to the challenge raised by Gustafson concerning the possibility of raising questions of truth and falsity from within a given tradition. Lovibond's nonfoundational argument has confirmed that the absence of an external umpire does not render questions of truth and falsity meaningless. On the contrary, the possibility within a given tradition of (moral) truths that transcend an individual's awareness, opens the possibility within a tradition for rational assessment (true/false), for the criticism and revision of one's beliefs, as well as for a dynamic concept of moral objectivity. What the latter has particularly amounted to is that both Hauerwas and Lovibond reject a founationalist view of moral truth and objectivity in favor of a historical and dynamic one. To use a mathematical idiom, they reject an algebraic, in favor of a geometrical model of objectivity. It is true, however, that compared to the foundational account of "objectivity" this phronetic understanding of objectivity appears as "something squashier and more dubious."[70] Nevertheless, it draws its philosophical validity from the realization that this is the only form of objectivity attainable within the field of *praxis,* and from an appreciation of *historical* existence. These are two factors that are unfortunately overlooked by "the algorithmic idealization" of moral rationality within the standard accounts, by which the concepts of truth and objectivity are abstracted from any historical embededness and reduced to calculable and static *termini* in a fully automatic process, in which their truth or falsity is, by dint of logic, absolutely necessitated.[71] The geometric model, on the other hand, evokes the idea of constructive and enlarging emplotment, which can only be assessed by taking into consideration the concrete sociallinguistic practices in which the agent—just like a geometer—stands.

3. Beyond Foundationalism: The Possibility of Ontological Truth Claims

The previous section has made explicit the sort of epistemological framework which underpins Hauerwas's ethics. What the argument in this section has amounted to is an invitation to give up any foundational quest for an external or tradition-neutral standpoint that would serve as the basis for epistemological justification or objectivity in the search for truth, value, and meaning. However, according to some critics, what may still be questionable about this antifoundational drive, is whether it does not leave us without any purchase on ontological claims. The challenge here concerns the status, as well as the very possibility, of making claims whose validity might extend beyond the bounds of any particular tradition. In the absence of theory-independent access to reality, how will the truth or falsity of such claims be assessed?

To get a fair grip on the assumptions behind this challenge so as to assess its validity, it is necessary that we begin by setting out Hauerwas's 'response' in contrast to the unsatisfactory positions of two people who have, in different ways, influenced Hauerwas or received his endorsement. Both Julian Hartt, Hauerwas's former teacher,[72] and Lovibond, whose work, we have seen, received Hauerwas's unqualified endorsement, seem to think that the possibility of ontological claims is compromised—unless we can have something like a "metaphysics" (Hartt), or "an absolute conception of reality" (Lovibond). Setting Hauerwas's position in contrast to the positions of these two 'mentors' will help to highlight the radical historicism which Hauerwas's position assumes. For, from a Hauerwasian point of view, it is possible to make and assess ontological claims. However, these truths cannot be made foundationally by appealing to some 'metaphysics' or to an 'absolute conception of reality' but, instead, must be made from within a particular tradition.

Beyond 'Metaphysics'

In an exchange with Hauerwas,[73] Hartt has expressed a fear that if narrative and tradition is all there is (à la Hauerwas), then there seems to be no way of avoiding historical moral relativism.[74] Behind this criticism lies Hartt's real worry, namely, that within a tradition-bound rationality, there is no way of sustaining "ontological cognitional warranties." The only way to ensure such ontological claims, he suggests, is through something like a "metaphysics," which would provide for a "more reliable bridge from tradition-community-history to actuality."[75]

What Hartt is looking for is a privileged standpoint outside any tradition or a mode of analysis that would provide a more direct and thus "more reliable" contact with actuality. Metaphysics for Hartt is such a foundational activity or discipline which can help one to get directly in touch with the "way things really are," what Hartt calls "an imperious engagement with actuality."[76] But it is precisely such a direct contact with actuality that an appreciation for historical existence deprives us of. No doubt, such contact, if we had one, would provide "a more *reliable* mode of transportation" than tradition. But given the historical and traditioned nature of existence it is not clear how one would construct such a 'metaphysics' without categories, modes of vision, absolute presuppositions, and conceptions of value and meaning—elements that only become available to one historically through the form of life that a tradition provides.[77] Our existence is so totally and thoroughly historical that all our modes of rational inquiry, including inquiry into what *we* consider absolutely necessary and universal or into what *we* regard as absolute conditions for meaning and value, are mediated through tradition. Human relation to reality is not accidentally symbolically mediated but necessarily so. Thus, to seek to go beyond language or symbolic systems generally, to come to the "Truth" as that which is universally valid, is just an attempt to transcend history. As historical, which is to say, traditioned beings, we lack such a "story of stories" or a tradition-independent "mode of analysis called metaphysics with its own peculiar subject matter called being, actuality, and so on."[78]

Apart from an appreciation for historical existence, methodological considerations also lie behind Hauerwas's denial of the possibility of a 'metaphysics'. The assumption of the availability of a 'metaphysics' has often led to reductionistic accounts of ethics, in which one seeks first to get one's 'metaphysics' straight and then go on to do ethics, i.e., draw ethical implications from it. For example, talk of "the moral significance of religious beliefs" is sustained by reducing Christianity into some kind of worldview (primitive metaphysics à la Comte) from which moral implications can be drawn.[79]

Methodologically, the inverse is the case, according to Hauerwas. It is not that ethical or religious practices are founded on a 'metaphysics'. Ethical or religious practices give rise to metaphysical claims. One always begins with the affirmation (explicit or tacit) of a particular moral or religious tradition and then extrapolates the metaphysical claims implicit within that tradition. This means that metaphysical thinking, in as far as it is a form of reflection, must concede to the priority of the social-linguistic practice, which is the condition for any reflection. Accordingly, metaphysical claims are not a sort of transcendental background for practices. They are embedded *within* those practices.[80] Hauerwas's rejection of a "metaphysics" should, therefore, not be seen as equivalent to the denial that traditions entail claims that may properly be called 'metaphysical'. All that is denied is that these claims "are known or best displayed by a clearly defined activity called 'metaphysics'."[81] An example might help to illumine the point here. Creation (that the world is created by a gracious God) and the Fall (that the world is marked by sin) are ontological claims made by Christian theology. What Hauerwas denies is that these claims "can be so isolated that they can be metaphysically construed separately from the [Christian] tradition" that embodies them through its concrete practices of pacifism and forgiveness. They arise out of, and therefore make sense only in the context of, a specific *praxis*. A Christian metaphysics is thus possible only because there are Christian practices. This is the reason why Hauerwas affirms (a conclusion which can validly be extended to all other disciplines) that "Christian theological reflection 'begins,' in as far as Christian reflection has a beginning, with ecclesiology [church *praxis*]."[82]

The practical genesis of metaphysical claims, it must be realized, is largely the result of what Hauerwas calls the "self-involving nature" of metaphysical claims. Metaphysical claims are self-involving because they create, and draw people into, a world. In other words, in order to affirm the theological claim of creation or the scientific-ontological claim of the "big-bang," one must already in some sense stand within the respective Christian or scientific *praxis*. The self-involving nature of these claims means that there is no transcendental ground from which one can gain access to them but through initiation into a particular way of life which they engender and regulate. This is the reason why metaphysical claims cannot, according to Hauerwas, be "displayed in a clearly defined [isolatable] activity called 'metaphysics'."

In any case, Hauerwas's denial of a 'metaphysics' and his affirmation of the methodological priority of practices amounts to affirming, contrary to Hartt, that there is no more reliable mode of transportation to get one in touch with actuality than the practice-generated reflection of a tradition. Both the genesis and display, as well as the justification of "ontological cognitional warrants," are tradition-dependent.

Beyond Universal Reason

Even though her Wittgenstein-inspired argument was positively appreciated (see previous section) as providing the sort of nonfoundational epistemological framework that underpins Hauerwas's work, Lovibond, nevertheless, like Hartt, betrays a lurking foundationalism when she comes to consider the cognitional status of ontological claims. In explicating moral knowledge as "culmination," Lovibond allowed the possibility of "truths" which might transcend the awareness of "whole cultures" or traditions.[83] Lovibond herself must have realized the epistemological difficulty involved in such an affirmation. For, if all knowledge is tradition-dependent and the final reference for the truth or falsity of one's beliefs is the intersubjective consensus within the form of life, how, then, does one come to justify claims whose truth transcends a particular form of life? And so when, at a later stage, she comes back to this issue, she suggests that the knowledge of these (ontological) truths is by way of a normative attitude of "transcendental parochialism"—a "condition in which the boundaries of our conceptual scheme will have to be pushed back, through critical reflection, to a *transcendental* limit."[84] In fact, Lovibond, just like Hauerwas, even recognizes the dialectical presence of other persons and traditions in this normative and critical effort (pressure to universalization) of pushing the tradition to the limits of its particular prejudices.

What is troubling, however, is Lovibond's assumption that a tradition will somehow transcend or "exhaust the supply of [this] dialectical material," and come to be said to know objectively only "insofar as knowledge is real for the whole human race *historically* unified in a single unified cultural system."[85] It is not clear whether by "single unified cultural system" Lovibond is expressing a political Esperantism for some sort of world community with a universal cultural and linguistic expression. In as far as no such community exists, one is right to see this "single unified cultural system" as a vague reference to the community of the autonomous rational moral agents—that fictive community into which many Kantian moral philosophers have sought to convert us. This suspicion would seem justified when one notes how the acknowledgment of the possibility of truths which transcend the awareness of a given tradition forces Lovibond to accept the "idea of an 'absolute conception of reality'," whose practical counterpart "would be a form of life which [is] in agreement, as the Hegelian idiom would have it, with 'universal reason'."[86]

Lovibond herself seems to be aware that her recourse to the terminology of 'transcendental' parochialism might be misleading. She therefore immediately cautions that the 'absolute conception of reality' must be interpreted "not in transcendental, but in immanent terms—not as conception of reality from which *all* traces of human perspective would be excluded, but as one in which the individual or local perspectives of *all* human beings would be able to find harmonious expression."[87]

Even with such a qualification, her assumption of, and confidence in, a Hegelian *Aufhebung* implicit within the notion of an 'absolute conception of reality' smacks of a residual foundationalism. For, it is precisely this assumption of knowing the common ground of all discourses that constitutes foundationalism. Hauerwas, for one, fails to point out this shortcoming within Lovibond's work. Part of the reason might be due to the fact that he simply enthusiastically endorsed Lovibond's nonfoundational claims without critically attending to the specific details of her overall argument.[88]

In our opinion, if Hauerwas is to remain consistent with his own presuppositions, he must stay clear of this specific aspect of Lovibond's argument. For, from a Hauerwasian perspective, Lovibond has both understated and sought to short-cut the necessity for witness by announcing an 'absolute conception of reality' as the point of rational commensurability of the various traditions. As Hauerwas would put it, such a tactic only achieves a "premature unity," an "artificial harmony," or an *a priori* resolution to the "divided character of the world," which only masks a form of violence and self-deception. For it is precisely the pretensions of grasping a universal beyond conflict that leads to exclusion and violence. As Kerry Whiteside has noted, "those who are confident of their grasp of ultimate truth, whether moral or historical, are too easily tempted to stifle differences of opinion. The assertion of universality itself . . . creates the conditions for an unreflective and often violent application of one's 'truths' on those who do not accept them."[89]

We shall return to this issue of violence as it is embodied within the false universalism of liberal politics and apologetics (chapter 7). For now, we are keen just to make the point that from Hauerwas's point of view, there is no need to posit a fictive Kantian community of rational ends or a Hegelian community of 'universal reason' to account for the possibility of ontological claims. The latter, just like any other claims, are made only from within a given tradition. But even more significantly, the truth or falsity of these claims is judged not against an ideal or "absolute conception of reality," but by the way these claims are embodied within the concrete practices, institutions, and characters they generate, and according to how they fare in confrontation (witness) with other contrary claims.

That is why "witness" is not simply a theological concept for Hauerwas, but a decisive epistemological category. For, only the "witnessal" presence of others can lead to the recognition of the limits of the claims embodied within a particular form of life. It is such witness or presence of other traditions and claims that dialectically exercises 'the pull toward objectivity', which is the source of revision, extension, confirmation, or even rejection of some ontological claims.

We shall say more about the dynamics of witness in our coming section. However, by way of concluding this section, we can note how our earlier use of the mathematical idiom of geometrical objectivity might help to clarify the central contention behind the analysis in this section. All that is being affirmed here, *pace* both Hartt and Lovibond, is that the truth of ontological claims, just as with other claims, is not algebraically calculated or measured against a determinate point through a 'metaphysics' that offers a rational contact with the way things 'really are' (Hartt), or through a 'cosmopolitan rationality' that provides an "absolute conception of reality" (Lovibond). Rather, their truth, like a geometric figure, lies in *being* constructed, and is always moving "toward an as yet undisclosed historical summing up that must [only] be narrated."[90]

4. Beyond Relativism: Historical Truth and Dialectical Witness

Perhaps the most often heard criticism raised against Hauerwas's affirmation of tradition-dependent rationality is that it involves a form of relativism.[91] Simply stated, the criticism runs: if all moral inquiry and objectivity is relative to intersubjective consensus within a particular form of life or tradition, then there would be no way for rational discussion and/or arbitration to proceed between two traditions that hold different conceptions of truth and rationality. In this section we shall seek to take the sting out of this challenge by showing how it is sustained by, and derives from, the same assumptions as the foundational epistemologies that the argument for tradition seeks to overcome. Hauerwas has therefore rightly learned to set it aside. The constructive side of this argument will be to show how a nonfoundational conception of the relation between traditions calls for the affirmation of witness as a decisive epistemological category.

Relativism as the Flip Side of Foundationalism

The apparent seriousness of the relativist challenge derives from the assumption that, in the absence of common canons of truth or procedure, dialogue between traditions breaks down or simply ends in polarized affirmations of a vulgar "true for us"–"true for you" cynicism. Such an impression, however, is so parasitic on a conception of truth and expectations for rational procedure within the epistemologies of the Enlightenment that one is right to see relativism as the flip side of foundationalism.[92] While Enlightenment thinkers have insisted upon a particular conception of truth and rationality, one in which truth is guaranteed by common canons and tradition-free methods of rational inquiry, relativism assumes that if that particular conception of truth and rationality cannot be sustained, then all rational inquiry between contending traditions completely breaks down. Relativism is thus created by what we have referred to as the false algorithmic ideal-ization of rationality which assumes *absolute* standards of truth as a con-dition for any rational discussion to take off. Either we have those *absolute* standards or we are left with no standards at all and thus no possibility for dialogue!

But do we really need *absolute* standards for meaningful and rational di-alogue to proceed? The epigraph at the beginning of this chapter draws our attention to both the misleading and coercive nature of the assumption that we need *absolute* and common canons of rationality for dialogue to be sus-tained. In a reference to Robert Nozick's remarks concerning the coercive aura surrounding talk about arguments, John Churchill writes:

> But in fact (sometimes) our arguments *do* end, and (sometimes) they end in agreement. We ignore this fact because of our craving for ultimate argument-stoppers. . . . What we really want is philosophical argument that reduces our interlocutors to silence or, better yet, kills them if they refuse to accept our conclusion. And yet, even that is not enough, since some people might choose death. We seem to want arguments that close even that option, such that not even death could absolve the other person of the necessity of admitting our conclusion.[93]

Churchill's insightful remarks help to make clear the foundational quest for certainty which lies behind the various epistemological criticisms peak-ing in the present charge of relativism. These remarks, in fact, confirm our claim that the fear (behind relativism) that rational dialogue between tradi-tions is impossible in the absence of tradition-neutral criteria is simply misleading. What foundationalism (and thus relativism) is looking for is not just dialogue but a certain type of dialogue—one in which agreement is guaranteed. And so the search for absolute standards—encountered through-out this chapter in its various versions as the quest for absolute justifica-tion, or for ahistorical objectivity, or for a 'metaphysics', or for an 'absolute conception of reality'—is a search for something that nobody could deny and at the same time still claim to be rational. It is an attempt to guarantee, before inquiry begins, that our various inquiries, if well-conducted, will be commensurate and will converge. Throughout this chapter we have been keen to show how the quest for such foundational guarantees must be given

up, because epistemologically it leads nowhere. In any case, such guarantees are simply unattainable. Given our historical and finite nature, we lack
a "story of stories" from which to secure the standard of rationality such
guarantees aspire for.

This means that rational dialogue cannot begin with an assurance of
commensuration and ultimate agreement. However, we need not see this
as a disaster which must only be accepted with an attitude of surrender or
capitulation on the part of philosophy. It should be received with a certain
therapeutic relief. The primary role of philosophy, as Wittgenstein noted, is
to describe, not to legislate or lay a foundation for, ordinary life.[94] And in
ordinary life, we *do*, in fact, proceed without such *a priori* guarantees of
success. Yet, we *do* engage in arguments, and "in fact (sometimes) our arguments *do* end, and (sometimes) they end in agreement."

This is why, once one has given up the foundational quest for "ultimate
argument-stoppers," relativism ceases to be the problem it is often feared to
be. Instead of trying to develop sophisticated defenses against relativism,
one puts it aside and concentrates on displaying concretely how contact
and dialogue between traditions can normatively take place. This is Hauerwas's mature position, which constructively has led to the affirmation of
witness as a decisive epistemological category.

"Excursus": Overcoming Foundationalism and Relativism

Hauerwas's realization of the above position has been only gradual,[95] which
indicates a development in his appreciation for the implications of tradition
and in his overcoming of foundational epistemologies. It is worthwhile to
provide a short "excursus" of this development, if only to offer a sense of
the evolution of Hauerwas's thinking, as well as the struggle, conceptual
confusions, and degree of eclecticism involved in his attempt to come to his
mature position.

In his earliest essays, in a bid to avoid relativism, Hauerwas posited "an
aspect of our moral activity which good societies exhibit, namely, that certain things should be required of all people irrespective of why they do what
they do."[96] One finds a series of attempts to characterize this "aspect of our
moral activity." For example, he considered Strawson's distinction between
"social morality and individual ideal."[97] He appealed to MacIntyre's argument that all societies necessarily involve basic virtues like justice, truthfulness, and courage.[98] He even toyed with the Universalization require-

ment and the Generalization principle as defended by R. M. Hare and Markus Singer, respectively.[99]

More recently, Hauerwas has admitted how this was all before the full discovery of the category of narrative. From Wittgenstein "I learned . . . to do philosophy in a therapeutic mode," and thus, "ended any attempt on my part to anchor theology [ethics] in some general account of 'human experience'."[100] With increasing attention to historical existence through the categories of narrative and tradition, he realized that, although people share important moral characteristics, "these shared characteristics are not of the sort that allows one to actually anchor morality in them."[101] Only then did he seek to develop an account of (narrative) rationality, in an attempt to defend the practical, historical, and social nature of moral reason.

This attempt, however, was to bring him face to face with the charge of relativism, since it involved admitting that any criteria for the truthfulness of a story would themselves have to be narrative-dependent. Hauerwas tried to get around this conclusion by affirming how narrative-dependent criteria could nevertheless have a validity beyond their narrative context, a realization that led him to adopt a soft-perspectivist position as developed by McClendon and Smith.[102] Even this position was, however, soon given up and, with it, attempts to defend himself against the relativist challenge. He had come to realize that relativism derived from the same assumptions as the foundational epistemologies he was questioning.

It is at this stage that Hauerwas came to realize, following Gilbert Harman,[103] that any epistemologically viable position must accept a certain form of relativism. This requires admitting the "dividedness of the world" as a basic phenomenological fact about which nothing can be done. Given our historical nature, cultures, languages, and communities are different. This is what Churchill has called "the fact of relativism" and about whose undeniability Geertz has written that it is "*merely* there, like Transylvania."[104]

Accepting this "fact of relativism," however, does not involve the nihilism of an "anything goes" or "one position is as good as any other" attitude, for which "radical skepticism" is only a euphemism. Neither does it involve the epistemological relativism of mutually inaccessible, unrelated, and isolated particularities of the "true for us"–"true for you" skeptic. Both of these forms of nihilism and cynicism, it must be noted, reflect an implicit foundationalism: unless we have absolute standards of truth, we are left with no standards at all! Both forms, in fact, show that the 'problem' of relativism is theory-dependent. It arises out of an attempt to deny the historicity of human existence by underwriting the contingency of the world through a theory—a "story of stories" that would supply a foundational account for knowledge and morality. Thus, accepting the "fact of relativism" involves realizing that "what we require . . . is not an argument that provides an *a priori* defeat of relativism, but an interpretation of and the corresponding skills to live in a world where others exist who do not share [our] moral history."[105] The need for 'an interpretation' and for 'corresponding skills' points to the moral and epistemological necessity of witness.

Witness as an Epistemological Category

In the absence of a "story of stories," rational contact between traditions takes the form of witness. As noted already, this hermeneutical sense of witness is not one that is explicitly developed by Hauerwas but is an extrapolation from, and an extension of, the theological use to which Hauerwas puts the term.[106] In the epistemological sense in which we use it in this chapter, witness involves the affirmation of the hermeneutical significance of the presence of others.

The hermeneutical inevitability of witness is premised on the nonfoundational realization that truth is historical. This realization means giving up the misleading assumption that we can go beyond language and symbolic systems in general, to the "Truth" as that which is universal and ahistorical. Because human beings are not accidentally culturally mediated, but necessarily so, truth does not come as a correspondence to an independently existing reality or the correspondence of language to an extralinguistic world. Rather, truth is an interpretative performance realized through and within the cultural linguistic practice.

This historical nature of truth mitigates against any epistemological singularity or self-sufficiency. Witness, as the form of contact between historically constituted traditions, affirms the realization that no one tradition is in possession of *the* truth. If that were the case, contact with other traditions would take the often preferred form of enforcement and imposition.[107] Instead, the historical nature of truth makes contact between traditions necessarily hermeneutical. As hermeneutical, it is a confrontation between historically constituted forms of truths—not as between versions (perspectives) of the same Truth—but as an interpretative dialogue which is capable of generating critical attentiveness by which truth is dialectically recognized, revised, or extended. To suggest witness as an epistemological category is to point to the normative aspect of this hermeneutical process.

Admittedly, this hermeneutical aspect might be related to the notions of 'dialogue' or 'conversation'. However, from a terminological point of view, witness is preferable to these more fashionable expressions because witness preserves the realization that, while contact with others may sometimes take the form of explicit argument and dialogue, the more primary form of hermeneutical contact is the mere presence of another—which leads to a 'display' of the richness of practices and character made possible by the other's particular story. In other words, the primary hermeneutical challenge is not to 'listen' to what the other has to say, but to 'see' who the other is, without attempting to reduce the other to an extension of one's self-understanding. This is why the contact must begin in silence.[108] Secondly, for reasons that we shall explicate shortly, only peaceful contact is, according to Hauerwas, hermeneutical. Witness carries an immediate association with this normative aspect of peaceableness in a way that dialogue and conversation do not. Thirdly, dialogue and conversation may tend to obscure the epistemological preoccupation of witness; dialogue by its association with political compromise, and conversation by the liberal aestheticization of communication. Witness, however, is primarily a reminder that the peaceful presence of others is essential for the very conception of historical truth.

Hauerwas's favorite characterization is that contact with the other often begins, and is effected, through the presence of the "stranger."[109] The use of this image indicates that the contact between one's familiar tradition and another tradition is initially a contact with a 'strange' story or with an alternative but 'strange' assessment or description of what is at stake. It is a contact between one tradition and what may initially appear as a 'strange' vision embodied within an equally 'strange' configuration of practices, virtues, and the account of practical rationality of the other. What needs to be made clear, however, is that the contact works dialectically and that, from each tradition's point of view, there is something 'strange' about the other's way of life.

Witness is epistemologically necessary for at least three reasons. First, self-knowledge requires witness. The presence of the 'stranger' can, and many times does, jolt a tradition into critical self-examination by which its own familiar story is examined in light of its various criteria for truth and success, as well as in the light of this other 'strange' alternative assessment. The epistemological necessity of this witness lies in a general observation that both individuals and traditions need the presence of others to *know* not only who one is, but also the limits and gifts (possibilities) one possesses.

Self-knowledge is not a solipsistic achievement on the part of an autonomous self. It is, in great measure, a gift through the presence of others
who are willing to listen to, confirm, or challenge one's story. This is at
least one way in which "one tradition might inform another of both its limits and possibilities."[110]

Secondly, the presence of the 'stranger' may serve as a helpful critic to
another's way of life. In fact, coming in contact with another story or form
of life might trigger the beginning of a MacIntyrean epistemological crisis—
the realization that one's story is either incoherent or not rich enough to ac-
commodate some aspects (e.g., tragedy) of existence. One must, however,
avoid understanding the epistemological crisis within an overly modern
and rationalist paradigm in which critique stands in service of a quest for
certainty. The critique associated with witness is neither an individuated
mental act nor a segregated portion of discourse isolated from the surrounding social practice and the intentionalities of human action. The sources of
critique reside in the interactive play of forms of praxis with and against
each other.[111]

It is through this 'witnessal' interplay between the familiar and the alien
that a tradition may discover in a particular configuration of its social practices (for example, a penal system, hierarchical organization, or allocation
of resources) new inadequacies, hitherto unrecognized incoherences, and
new problems for which there seem to be insufficient or no resources
within the established practice. That is why the recognition of such an epistemological crisis is always a great achievement on the part of any tradition. For, only then is a tradition able to start looking for innovative ways
to improve its story, or for alternative practical possibilities. For this reason, the possibility of recognizing an epistemological crisis—occasioned by
the presence of the 'stranger'—is considered by Hauerwas to be one of the
key normative requirements of a 'living' tradition. To repeat a citation
which must by now be very familiar: "the truthfulness of a tradition is
tested in its ability to form people who are ready to put the tradition into
question, or at least to recognize when it is being put into question by a
rival tradition."[112]

Thirdly, the presence of the 'stranger' may offer imaginative possibilities
to get a tradition out of an epistemological crisis. It is not enough that a tradition is able to recognize the limits of its own story. To be able to go on
peacefully, it requires innovative and imaginative readjustment.[113] Imagination is an epistemological necessity. However, as has already been noted,
in Hauerwas's substantive understanding, imagination has less to do with

an individual's capacity for fantastic re-imaging within a mental faculty for 'free play'. Imagination has more to do with the presence of another tradition whose concrete story, practices, and vocabulary provide 'real' options away from the self-imposed necessities of one's tradition. In other words, moral imagination is not so much the ability to flee from the concrete practices into a mental realm, albeit of sympathetic re-visioning, as it is the ability to flee from one set of concrete practices into an alternative, but richer, set of practices. Because such possibility depends on the concrete presence of another who provides this alternative, the key epistemological issue associated with witness is not only how one tradition can serve as a critic, but also how it can "be enriched by coming into contact with other traditions."[114]

Lest the above considerations portray an overly optimistic and smooth picture of the epistemological possibilities of the contact with the 'stranger', we should immediately add that witness offers no guarantee that contact with the 'stranger' will be successful, let alone peaceful. In fact, given the possibility that such contact may expose the limits of a tradition, or throw that tradition into an epistemological crisis, the 'stranger' is often seen as a threat. And so, contact between traditions has tended to be 'armed' with swords and/or defensive ideological self-justifications. This is clearly true, for example, in the case of a religious Constantinianism, which comes literally armed with an *extra ecclesia nulla salus* evangelizing mission. But it is equally true of a political and economic modernism which 'arms' itself with an evolutionary social theory whose *Geltungslogik* transcendentally plots traditions on a lineal superior-inferior scale, thus giving it an arrogant posture and mandate of modernizing inevitability. The self-justification can also take the form of a foundational epistemology which 'arms' modern man with an enlightened self-assurance of having discovered *the* Truth and *the* essence for universal Reason and Desire.

Whatever other forms it takes, both the self-justifications and the arming that is often involved in the contact with the 'stranger' are an attempt to determine beforehand the possibility, form, and outcome of this contact. They are, in other words, an attempt to deny the epistemological necessity of witness. However, an attempt to bypass the slow, uncertain, tentative (ad hoc) and contingent nature of witness in favor of the quick, certain, and smooth resolution of theory only mires traditions in ideological self-deception and violence. We need to briefly explain this conclusion.

To assume that the possibility, form, and outcome of the contact with the 'stranger' can be determined before any actual engagement is to deny the hermeneutical nature of truth. It is to assume that truth is given, and that one tradition could discover it and all the others would have to accept it. However, such self-assurance can only be seen as an ideological mechanism to stave off both the necessity and the pain that might come with accepting the limits of one's particular story, which the contact with the 'stranger' occasions. There is often a self-sustaining character to this process. The more a tradition is self-assured in its story, the less it feels the need to spell out, re-examine, or creatively re-adjust its story in view of the 'stranger's' presence. But the less it is willing to do so, the more ideological its story becomes, and the more a tradition is prone to violence to affirm what it self-deceptively takes to be *the* truth!

Thus, the denial of truth as hermeneutical is necessarily violent. Foundational epistemologies entail such a denial in their attempt to go beyond language and symbolic systems generally, to come to *the* "Truth," as that which is universal and ahistorical. This foundational quest not only overlooks the historical and contingent nature of truth, it essentially involves denying the otherness ('strangeness') of the other. Churchill's words in the epigraph at the start of this chapter once again ring with a chilling veracity. The assumption of having discovered *the* Truth reduces the other "to silence or, better yet, kills them if they refuse to accept our conclusion. And yet, even that is not enough, since some people might choose death. The assumption of having *the* truth on our side means that not even death could absolve the other of the necessity of admitting our conclusion."[115] The point here could perhaps be dismissed as mere rhetorical flourish were history not replete with unmarked graves of victims of such metanarrative singularity.

What is made clear by the above considerations is that as long as it is 'armed', contact with the 'stranger' cannot be hermeneutical. If this contact has to be epistemologically fruitful, it must be the sort of peaceful contact and presence that Hauerwas calls witness. In order to be peaceful, it requires a basic "openness" on the part of a tradition, an openness that stands between the two extremes of romanticism, on the one hand, and ethnocentricism, on the other. As has been already noted, this openness is nothing but a willingness to see the other as other and allow the questionableness of one's convictions or be persuaded that the other's presence and convictions may enrich one's vision or even have to prevail over it. This is the main reason why Hauerwas considers humility to be a key precondition for truth and the recognition of an epistemological crisis to be a great achievement on the part of a tradition. The latter indicates that to the extent a tradition (through the dialectical witness of the 'stranger') has had the humility to recognize the limits of its story and has realized the hermeneutical necessity of witness, it is on the road to (the contingent search for) truth.

In this chapter we have tried to defend Hauerwas's argument for a tradition-dependent rationality against four standard epistemological criticisms. The inevitable circularity involved within narrative moral rationality, critics had argued, (a) means that a tradition cannot avoid settling down into solipsistic self-validation or complacency; (b) involves the loss of a possibility for objective rational assessment; (c) makes it impossible to account for ontological claims; and finally, (d) leads to relativism. These criticisms are related. In fact, part of our goal has been to show how they all assume, and are set from within, the same foundational epistemology which is being questioned. We have therefore argued that once foundationalism is set aside these criticisms do not arise. The misleading impression which gives these criticisms their apparent strength is that the rejection of this dominant epistemological tradition casts the very notions of truth, rational justification, and objectivity into question. Our primary critical task has been, therefore, to show that the *notions of truth, rational justification, and objectivity themselves are not in question;* the problem is that the standards for their achievement have been set in the wrong place. However, even, with this critical point made, it still has been necessary to address the positive concerns behind the criticisms. And so, from a constructive point of view, our goal has been to show that (a) tradition (the particular) is normatively marked by a "creative tension"—phronetic attentiveness—which saves it from settling down into mere routine; (b) a social-linguistic affirmation can provide the context for rational assessment and a dynamic sense of objectivity; (c) it is possible to account for ontological claims in the absence of a 'metaphysics' or 'an absolute conception of reality'; and (d) that the nonfoundational realization of truth as historical requires the affirmation of witness as an epistemological category.

Given Hauerwas's reluctance to directly engage these epistemological issues, as well as the lack of conceptual closure generally within his work, our response to the above criticisms has been not so much an explication of Hauerwas's stated position, as a reconstruction of what could be an adequate Hauerwasian response.[116] While the need for such a reconstruction has emerged within the context of providing a response to the various criticisms, its value extends far beyond this critical interest. For one, the attempt has helped to set Hauerwas's operative categories within a wider and coherent theoretical epistemological framework. The latter has itself not only made explicit the Aristotelian and Wittgensteinian background to Hauerwas's work, it has shown the nonfoundational nature and the radical historicism of Hauerwas's thinking.

We have particularly noted how Hauerwas himself draws attention to the nonfoundational nature of his work by suggesting that his "Christian theology has a stake in a qualified epistemological realism," and that "Sabina Lovibond in her *Realism and Imagination in Ethics* . . . developed with rigor the kind of epistemological realism I have only asserted."[117] It was for this reason significant to show how Lovibond's Wittgensteinian argument provides confirmation and a well-needed theoretical expression to Hauerwas's less theoretically formulated argument.

These positive collaborations notwithstanding, we must note that Hauerwas's unqualified endorsement of Lovibond's work is misleading in at least two ways. First, from a Hauerwasian point of view, Lovibond is not historical enough and betrays (at least when it comes to the issue of ontological claims) a lurking foundationalism when she posits 'an absolute conception of reality'. We have already noted this shortcoming in Lovibond's work, and how Hauerwas's, unfortunately enough, fails to realize it. Perhaps what should be noted here is that this failure may point to a general limitation within Hauerwas's work. His readiness to claim affinity with other authors, but without engaging their work in sufficient detail, may leave him open to the charge of eclecticism. Moreover, by not taking time to critically engage these adopted positions, he risks inadvertently bringing on board aspects that sit uneasily with his own position. We have drawn attention to this danger in relation to Lovibond. A similar danger will be noted, in the coming chapter, in relation to Hauerwas's unqualified endorsement of George Lindbeck's work.

Secondly, within a nonfoundational affirmation, it is misleading that Hauerwas (following Lovibond) would still refer to his position as involving 'realism', albeit a qualified 'realism'. Both Wittgenstein's prioritization of social-linguistic forms of life, and Hauerwas's affirmation of tradition undermine the traditional opposition between subject and object. This in itself undermines the distinction between idealism and realism. This distinction, as Charles Guignon notes, has always been parasitic on the representationalist model (mind as mirror), according to which reality is either "out there" independent of us, or "in here" within our mind.[118] But if the representationalist model is discarded, as both Wittgenstein and Hauerwas believe it should be, then the assumption that we must choose either realism or idealism is misplaced. We can neither explain our activities by recourse to extra-linguistic facts, nor claim that language or mind is all there is. Giving up foundationalism requires leaving behind the very terminology of realism, qualified or unqualified.

However, this terminological oversight by Hauerwas should not blind us to the "therapeutic" effect of his anti-foundational theology, particularly for setting aside the 'problem' of the relation between religion and ethics. It becomes clear in the light of the developments of this chapter that the 'problem' is determined from, and set within, a foundational epistemological framework. The 'problem' of religion and ethics, which is nothing but an attempt to determine the moral significance of religion, involves nothing but an attempt to go beyond religious symbolic forms and language, to come to the "Truth," as that which is beyond particular historical and communal contexts. Such a foundational attempt, however, assumes a superficial view of social-linguistic forms by imagining truth as a correspondence to some extra-linguistic reality. However, from a Wittgensteinian background, no access to such extra-linguistic Reality is available, for human beings are symbolically mediated, not simply accidentally, but necessarily so. Therefore, the Moral Point of View does not lie beyond particular historical and communal contexts, any more than truth lies beyond tradition. To paraphrase Hauerwas, moral truth has to occur in and through those social-linguistic forms that constitute our historical existence. What perhaps needs to be made clear is the claim that religion is indeed such a social linguistic form of life. We, therefore, must examine Hauerwas's affirmation of a social-linguistic conception of religion and the criticisms such a conception generates.

6

Cultural Linguistic Prospects:
Religion beyond Sectarianism and Fideism

> Religion is not primarily a set of propositions to be believed or dis-
> believed; but a set of skills that one employs in living. Such skills
> are acquired by learning the stories of Israel and Jesus well enough
> not only to interpret the world, but to do so in specifically Christ-
> ian terms.
>
> Hauerwas

Hauerwas's insistence on the distinctive nature of Christian ethics has
often been dubbed a form of fideism.[1] The seriousness of this charge seems
to arise from an understanding that a fideistic position is caught up in a irresolvable tension: Either fideists proclaim their confession to the world
and have it fall on deaf ears, or they articulate only among themselves the
truth to which they bear witness. Either way, fideistic religion seems to be
doomed to an "in-house" affair, culturally marginal, and worst of all, lacking in any sort of robust rationality.[2]

These are actually two related but distinct dangers: The first involves the
fear that fideism lacks any sort of 'rational basis'. This fear is particularly expressed by Gustafson, who has aligned Hauerwas's position to that of certain
"Wittgensteinian fideists" (such as Holmer and Phillips) who take the language of science and the language of religion to be totally incommensurable.[3] Behind the appeal to Wittgenstein's "language games" or "forms of
life" by these 'fideists', Gustafson suspects a cowardly attempt to avoid testing religious language. From a fideistic position, it is thus feared, nothing
would "prevent doctrine from becoming ideology, since it "is difficult to see
how one can make any critique of the tradition, internal or external."[4]

The second, and equally serious fear is that the insistence (by Hauerwas)
on the distinctiveness of theology and ethics makes religion an "in-house"
affair, whose language becomes increasingly unintelligible to those outside.
Such a stance, it is thought, isolates Christians into a "sect"—an isolation
that is correlative to social irresponsibility—which encourages Christian

withdrawal from participation in the critical and ambiguous choices of public life. This perceived danger actually forms the center of the "sectarian temptation" and assumes a certain sociological understanding of the role of religion in public life.

These two dangers are certainly related, but it is important to separate them in order to draw attention to both the epistemological and sociological assumptions that sustain the language of fideism. For as Kenneth Surin notes, although critics are keen to make the charge of fideism, what they usually do not provide is a clear explanation of what fideism means. Critics assume that the meaning, content, and danger of 'fideism' is immediately obvious, and with that the burden to supply an adequate defense is shifted to the attacked position.[5] It would be possible for us to supply such a defense by showing either that critics have misunderstood Hauerwas's work or that it does not lead to those feared consequences—in any case that Hauerwas is not a fideist or a sectarian. Such an easy victory, however, would win the battle only by losing the war, since it would involve accepting the terms in which the charges are set, as well as the assumptions that underwrite these charges. What we need is a thorough examination of the usually unexamined assumptions that underwrite the very vocabulary of sectarianism and fideism.

The burden of this chapter will be to show that the charge of fideism trades on questionable assumptions in epistemology and sociology of religion. These assumptions involve a foundational understanding of "truth" and "religion" that is at odds with the basic historicity of human inquiry and social reality that we have affirmed in this work. The chapter is divided into three sections. In the first section we trace the language of fideism to the dialectical challenge of modernity, which involves the need to "explain" or to "translate" religious idioms into a neutral language accessible to all. This need, therefore, assumes the validity of the commensurability thesis, which has been shown to be problematic at best and mistaken in its foundational aspiration. In the second section we shall trace the genealogy of the sectarian language to the sociological tradition that runs from Max Weber through Ernst Troeltsch. The goal of this section will be to make explicit the questionable methodological and sociological assumptions within this tradition. The point of this critical attention will be to show how the language of sectarianism is a form of policing that is meant to underwrite both a particular social-political arrangement and a particular conception of religion as the only and inevitable possibility. The latter is what John Milbank critically refers to as the "Liberal Protestant Metanarrative." In the third section we show how, once this liberal Protestant metanarrative has been overcome, a more substantive conception of religion becomes possible. We therefore explore Hauerwas's understanding of religion by showing it to fit the cultural-linguistic model as developed by George Lindbeck.

1. Fideism: A Response to the Dialectical Challenge of Modernity

Fideism can certainly be a complex phenomenon.[6] The form we are interested in here is the one associated with a specific religious epistemology that assumes that in order for religious belief to be intelligible and respectable it *ought* to have rational justification, or (which we take to be the same thing) be able to account for the beliefs in terms of reasons, explanations, and evidence *external* to the beliefs themselves.[7]

We need to return to Jeffrey Stout's thesis concerning the crisis in authority within the early modern period to see how theism's traditional "mysteries" were gradually transformed into *paradoxes* of a kind that had either to be "explained" or else constitute possible grounds for disbelief. According to Stout, the emergency of full-blown skepticism about *scientia* and the working out of new canons of probability at Port Royal combined to make theology needful of philosophical support.[8] The significance of this development is found in the departure it represents from the previous conception of probability. Prior to the introduction of statistical and evidential criteria for assessing a proposition's truth, probability essentially consisted in approval by authority, whether in the form of an appeal to the right persons or to the right books. And this meant that even the most paradoxical beliefs were considered highly probable so long as they had the right imprimatur. Thus, the introduction of the new probability changed the religious situation drastically. With the connection between probability and authority broken, the religious believer was left with the task of attempting to supply new reasons for believing the central claims of theism. He had to prove the 'reasonableness' of his beliefs by appealing to new canons (of the probable) and to a set of concepts and a language in which, given the specter of religious rivalry, strictly religious explanations are reduced to the minimum.[9]

It is this newly arisen need to "explain" or "translate" religious phenomena in *secularized* language that is "the dialectical situation that is the fate of modern theism."[10] What makes the situation dialectical is that it seems to force the believer to choose between two equally unfortunate possibilities: Either believers reformulate their beliefs in a way compatible with modernity—in which case the beliefs lose their distinctiveness—or they celebrate the paradoxical nature of their beliefs, in which case the beliefs remain incomprehensible and hence socially irrelevant to the modern world. We shall briefly examine each of these options.

Deism and Liberal Protestantism

The first dialectical response is the one that takes the modern challenge seriously. Within the history of modern thinking, this response produced "reformulations of traditional theism like deism and liberal Protestantism."[11] Such reformulations should rightly be seen as an attempt to "explain" traditional mysteries of theism in a way understandable to modern, secular culture. While deism offered "natural" explanations for Christian beliefs and, as a result, declared any supernatural mysteries paradoxical, and therefore, improbable,[12] liberal Protestantism tried to soften the paradoxes with reductive interpretations. Kant, for example, reduced religious doctrines to moral allegories fit for the purposes of educating a fallible, sensuous humanity, ultimately to be overcome in pure rational faith. Schleiermacher subjected them to the equally reductive hermeneutic of emotive expressivity.

While such reformulations are clearly an attempt to make theism intelligible and "relevant" (and have been the dominant approach within modernity), the relevance is paid for with the great price of leaving theism socially indistinguishable.[13] The reformulations tend to shade off into "a thinly disguised atheism" and thus offers the atheist "less and less in which to disbelieve."[14]

Fideism

Fideism represents the other dialectical response to the modern challenge. The latter, as exemplified in Kierkegaard's and Barth's authorship, for instance, involves an insistence on the radical nature of faith, and how such faith "needs no justification from reason."[15] Both Kierkegaard and Barth would thus regard the positions of deism and liberal Protestantism as fundamentally distorting both the content and object of faith. As Stout describes their position:

> Attempts to place faith on firm grounding or to reach faith from a basis of human reason or experience are clearly an affront to God's otherness and bound to erode faith's essential content. Natural and liberal theologies

tend to sweep aside or soften the hard paradox of God's revelation in Christ from which faith must proceed. Faith, with God as its object, cannot help but be paradoxical.[16]

The result of this unwillingness to be apologetic about faith is a clear affirmation of the distinctiveness of the (Christian) thought and practice. However, this distinctiveness is bought at the price of displacing Christian thought and practice from the mainstream of social life (which is, per definition, secular) onto "the margins of public life and the recesses of private existence."[17]

What is perhaps even more problematic about the posture of fideism, but which often goes unnoticed, is the fact that fideism (e.g., Barth's and Kierkegaard's unapologetic theology) is a form of faith-foundationalism. As foundationalism, fideism shares the formal strategy of reason-foundationalism of the classical rationalists (deism and liberal Protestantism). Both classical rationalists and fideists respond to the dialectical challenge of modernity by constructing a foundation. They only differ both in the materials they use to construct their foundations and in whether people get access to that foundation basically through "reason" or "faith." While classical rationalists found that grounded in reason, fideism rejects this ground by insisting that theism needs no grounding from reason. Faith *grounds* itself in God's word. This attempt, however, to return theology to its "proper basis" in the foundational authority of God's word shares a fundamental but hidden agreement with the rationalist's search for foundations. We need to draw attention to this formal affinity now in order to show why, as a form of foundationalism, fideism (faith-foundationalism), no less than reason-foundationalism, has been rejected by Hauerwas.

Hauerwas's work cannot be said to involve a faith or fideistic foundationalism.[18] For one thing, Hauerwas's philosophical and theological agenda is not at all an attempt to find a secure foundation against skepticism or develop a "revelational positivism" like Barth's.[19] For Hauerwas, faith or theology requires "no foundation" at all, not even in revelation.[20] Which means that theology "does not, methodologically, have a starting point" but "must begin in the middle, that is, we must begin within a narrative."[21] True, Hauerwas has said, "if we have a *foundation* it is the *story* of Christ."[22] But one has failed to understand the meaning of this quizzical remark if one takes it as a confirmation of a fideistic starting point. In particular, one would have failed to realize that this remark comes at the end of a discussion whose aim was to display that truth (all truth) has no foundation at all. Moreover, the emphasis on 'story' in the above remark should provide a cautious interpretation, since stories (if they provide any foundation) are a queer sort of foundation. They point to no particular grounding claim, but involve contingent claims, "none of which could be isolated by themselves, but are intelligible only as they form a coherent narrative."[23]

Of a more serious challenge, therefore, is the criticism of fideism associated with reason-foundationalism, by which Hauerwas's work has been said to lack a robust rationality. Responding to this criticism requires a twofold strategy. First, we need to question the foundationalist assumptions that sustain this criticism. Secondly, we need to allay the fears behind this criticism by showing that Hauerwas's work involves sufficient resources to show that even in the absence of an overarching tradition or Archimedean ground, particular beliefs and convictions can still be criticized or revised, and questions of truth and objectivity raised about them. The last of these two objectives has already been undertaken in our previous chapter. However, we can rehearse its conclusion from another angle by questioning the foundationalist assumptions which underwrite the fideistic critique. One way Hauerwas has done this is by drawing attention to MacIntyre's "incommensurability thesis."

Fideism, 'Translation,' and the Incommensurability Thesis

We have sought to understand fideism as a failure to respond to the *modern* situation that sets the need for believers to reformulate, "explain," or "translate" their beliefs in a language understandable to modern secular culture. The possibility for "translation" assumes both the presence of some universal criteria for rationality and of some common language or, in its absence, the priority of a certain foundational discipline (science, epistemology, etc.) in which those criteria are at home. The language of this foundational discipline becomes the primary language into which other languages would need to be translated, justified, or naturalized if they are to be rendered intelligible. This assumption of translatability has been so much taken for granted that it even seems to be a key requirement for the very ascription of rationality: "If we can attribute a language to someone, his speech must be the kind of thing we could translate into our language."[24] Part of this hope has been reflected in the eagerness by which theologians have sought, at least since the Enlightenment, to demonstrate that theological language can be translated into terms that are meaningful and compelling for those who do not share Christianity's more particularistic beliefs.

However, the assumption that the paradoxes of theism can be "trans-lated" into a neutral language without losing any of their content rests on questionable philosophical grounds. In fact, once one critically attends to the notion of translatability, it becomes obvious that the very language and charge of fideism is caught up in the problems and perplexities of a mori-bund epistemological foundationalism. For, as recent antifoundational epis-temological treatises have shown, there is neither a "pure" and presupposi-tionless experience to serve as a faultless touchstone for translation, nor a 'privileged' field of inquiry (science, epistemology, or metaphysics) to get us in touch with this original experience.[25] Although Hauerwas has felt no need to rehearse these arguments, he has implicitly assumed them by en-dorsing MacIntyre's argument for incommensurability.[26]

Quoting MacIntyre, Hauerwas has noted how translatability assumes that there is something like "justice qua justice" or "rationality-as-such" in the same way it assumes English-as-such or Hebrew-as-such or Latin-as-such, languages which can be translated one into another: "but as Mac-Intyre argues, there are no such languages but only 'Latin-as-written-and-spoken-in-the-Rome-of-Cicero and Irish-as-written-and-spoken-in-sixteenth-century-Ulster. The boundaries of a language are the boundaries of some linguistic community which is also a social community.'"[27] MacIntyre's concern is actually with traditions and their particularity, an aspect of their unavoidable linguistic embodiment.[28] This forms part of his sustained ar-gument in *Whose Justice? Which Rationality?* against pretensions to uni-versalistic justification. Rational inquiry, MacIntyre argues, is a tradition-constituted and tradition-constituting enterprise. Central to MacIntyre's argument is the thesis that different conceptions of morality—exemplified by justice—are linked to different conceptions of practical rationality. Moral traditions differ not only in what they regard as values, virtues, and justified principles, but also in the very nature of their practical rationality. On account of such significant differences, the traditions are said to be in-commensurable,[29] because there are no common evaluative standards and because it is impossible to ascertain their correct translation into the lan-guage of that other tradition.

The critical and constructive validity of MacIntyre's argument should become compelling if we clear some misconceptions that are often associ-ated with the incommensurability thesis. First, the idea that traditions are said to be incommensurable does not lead either MacIntyre or Hauerwas to suppose that we live in radically different and conceptually irreducible tra-ditions. Such an assumption would not only make rational communication between members of any two traditions impossible, it would evoke "the very idea of a conceptual scheme,"[30] with the attendant complications of conceptual relativism and perspectivism. On the contrary, both Hauerwas and MacIntyre realize that traditions can be incommensurable only if at least a partial (minimal) translation between them is possible.[31] This minimal agreement, however, cannot be used as a basis to affirm, as Stout does, following David Davidson, that all discourses are in principle translatable.[32] Stout argues that nothing in the "nature of language itself" would keep his fictive communities of the Old World Corleones and the modernist Kantian explorers from translating each others' language.[33] However, this appeal by Davidson to "the very nature of language" is not convincing: ". . . Davidson tends to think of language fundamentally as a locus of belief. He thus fails to note that languages depend on what Wittgenstein calls 'agreements and judgements' that are only made possible against a background of skills and practices."[34] Thus, by attempting to "get behind the concrete skills and practices" to semantics ("the very nature of language") as a more reliable mode of resolution, both Davidson and Stout betray a residual foundationalism that makes their assumption for translatability inevitable.[35]

Secondly, incommensurability does not mean self-sufficiency. Both MacIntyre and Hauerwas recognize the necessary presence of the "other" in the process of the constitution and determination of a tradition.[36] Talking about a religious tradition for example, the "other" could be a scientific or secular tradition against which it can unambiguously set or define itself, or a *comparable* religious tradition whose presence critically helps it to come to a better appreciation of its own distinctiveness. In any case, incommensurability does not mean that traditions as a whole or concepts and practices drawn from different traditions are incomparable.[37]

Certainly, the argument for incommensurability does not render a tradition incorrigible, as Gustafson seems to think.[38] Both MacIntyre and Hauerwas have defended the critical resourcefulness of any 'living' tradition as well as the critical role of the presence of the "stranger." The latter can not only be an occasion for an epistemological crisis, but also provide critical witness and live options for a tradition. These claims have already been fully defended in the course of explicating Hauerwas's version of a qualified epistemological realism (chapter 5). There we showed how from the perspective of a particular tradition, and in the absence of any neutral language, beliefs and convictions can still be criticized, revised, and questions of truth and objectivity raised. For now, however, it should be clear that Hauerwas's appeal to MacIntyre's argument for incommensurability cannot be seen as a strategy for isolationist 'cocooning' or for a xenophobic puritanism. Rather, it is a reminder of the absence of a 'neutral' and high ground on which a normative engagement with the "other" takes place. It is a caution against excessive (liberal) optimism which uncritically assumes that because practices, beliefs, symbols, and actions from one tradition can be adopted by, and help to reshape another tradition, traditions are thereby commensurable, or that practices are the same.

There is something irksome, therefore, about the (stubborn) misconception that the affirmation of the distinctiveness of a particular form of life (Christian, for example) means rendering the beliefs and convictions of that tradition incorrigible or irreversible. Even in the face of Hauerwas's readily available indications to the contrary, critics seem determined to insist on making the charge and thus calling Hauerwas a fideist.[39] The presence of such widespread evidence that is so intentionally overlooked by critics should, in fact, lead us to suspect that the primary concern behind the charge of fideism is not, after all, the incorrigibility of particular convictions, but their revision in light of a *particular* language or discipline that happens to enjoy an overriding veridical status. That is why the core of Gustafson's argument for calling Hauerwas a fideist is the observation that insofar as religion is a rational activity it must be possible in principle to subject theological claims to correction and revision in light of *scientific* discoveries.[40] In a way, Gustafson's concern, in as much as it portrays a foundational logic, is not unique. He desires to find a common logic for all languages, to which religious language, in order to be public, must conform. However, the common logic he has in mind is nothing but the specific logic of scientific language. Of course, Gustafson may not think of scientific language as a *particular* language.[41] But this is precisely the foundationalist predicament. In the name of seeking universal criteria of rationality, foundationalists can do nothing but give preference to a particular community of ideas and claim universality for it.[42] Which is precisely what is called into question by the incommensurability thesis, namely,

> the idea of a foundational discipline that can determine the standards of rationality in every field. . . . Religious and theological claims are thus not immune to challenge, though they may be, like many other activities, not susceptible to definitive refutation or confirmation; they can nevertheless be tested and argued about.[43]

The full implications of this realization was explicated in the previous chapter. However, the present discussion has helped to confirm that nothing within the affirmation of a distinctive Christian practice makes theological convictions immune to challenge by considerations from scientific or other traditions. A closer look at the incommensurability thesis has cast doubts *not* on this possibility but on the excessive (liberal) optimism for "translation." This optimism uncritically bestows *a priori* veridical status on a particular language and seeks to naturalize all other languages within this one language.

The point above is still defensive. To put the issue more positively, we need to note that the incommensurability thesis confirms Wittgenstein's thesis that each language has its own logic and is to be understood in its own light.[44] Rather than give overriding veridical status to one language by seeking to translate religious vocabulary into the idioms of that language, the point is to view religious language as yet another language, another logic, to be understood in yet another way. And so, Christianity, if it is to be true to itself, will have to make ontological claims. But it cannot *defend* them in neutral or secular terms. Religious faith and practice, no less than science, generates reasons or warrants that are *internal* to the religious form of life itself.

This conception does of course assume a substantive understanding of religion in general, and Christianity in particular, as a language of its own, capable of generating its own logic and practice. It is precisely Hauerwas's determination to see Christianity in this way that has been branded "sectarianism," a form of social withdrawal, an attempt to isolate Christianity from the ambiguous demands and challenges of public life. We therefore need to devote specific attention to the assumptions behind the specific claim that Hauerwas's affirmation of the distinctiveness of Christian ethics is a form of sectarianism.

2. Sectarianism and the Liberal Protestant Metanarrative

The "sect" language has, to a significant extent, determined how Hauerwas is read by his contemporaries, especially those who see his emphasis on the particularity of the Christian story, ecclesial identity, and a distinctive Christian practice as compromising Christian social responsibility, or even a threat to it. Although this charge of "sectarianism" is often left unexplained, a central underlying assumption has to do with the inevitability and primacy of the state for public life. Because the state, it is assumed, "represents society acting as a whole," Christians share the responsibility "for managing it rightly."[45] Involved within this assumption is a specific

conception of the church-state relationship, in which the state is the primary social (public) actor, and the Church's significance or relevance is dependent on the ability to develop 'adequate' social or political implications
of its otherwise 'religious' message. Hauerwas's attempt to question the legitimacy of this *status quo,* or to conceive it differently, is seen as a sectarian withdrawal that involves social irresponsibility.

It is my contention in this section that the tradition that has legitimated
this *specific* church-state hegemony in which the language and charge of
sectarianism is at home weaves its narrative from questionable sociological
assumptions and methodology. Since the point of that narrative is to underwrite a *particular* social-political arrangement as inevitable, the full implications of this section will flow into the coming chapter. For now, however,
our aim will be to portray how the very language (and charge) of sectarianism is a strategy, among others, by which this narrative seeks to canonize
this particular social arrangement. We will do that first by tracing the genealogy of the sectarian language to Troeltsch's typology and Max Weber's
sociology, secondly by attending to Milbank's incisive analysis of the synchronic and diachronic elements within that sociology, and thirdly by
placing sectarianism alongside other 'policing' strategies whose effect is to
resist a substantive understanding of religion as a form of life or a cultural-
linguistic system.

Genealogy of the Sect-Language

In *The Church as Polis,* Arne Rasmusson traces the "sect" language back to
Max Weber's and Ernst Troeltsch's sociological accounts, where he (Rasmusson) shows how Troeltsch's more theologically related typological
analyses have been particularly influential in giving rise to the language of
sectarianism.[46] Since Rasmusson has provided an exceptionally concise and
clear formulation of Troeltsch's typology, it might be worthwhile to quote
him at length. In the *Social Teaching of the Christian Churches,*[47] Rasmusson notes, Troeltsch

> interpreted church history in terms of a typology of "church," "sect" and
> "mysticism," where particularly the opposition and dialectic between
> church and sect is constitutive of the church's historical and social devel-
> opment. The type "church" refers to the established type of organization
> that is conservative, accepts secular order, dominates the masses, has
> universal claims, and therefore uses (and becomes used by) the state and

the ruling classes to sustain and expand its domination and to stabilize and determine the social order. . . .

The sects, on the other hand, are comparatively smaller, and stress both a more personal and a more communal faith and practice. They are connected with the lower, or at least oppositional, classes, and do not try to dominate the world, but work from below and defend egalitarian views and practices. Separation from the world is stressed, as well as religious freedom and voluntary membership. Theologically they put the lordship of Christ and discipleship, and therefore also the life and message of Jesus, in the centre. . . .

Troeltsch argues "that both types are a logical result of the Gospel, and only conjointly do they exhaust the whole range of its sociological influence." . . . In the first centuries, the church vacillated between sect and church-type and it is first with the political establishment of the church and its developed hierarchical and sacramental theology, that we get clearly separated sects.[48]

It is significant to note that within Troeltsch's typology, "sect" is essentially a theological designation. This theological designation hardly makes any sense today, because it assumes one politically (Constantinian) established Church from which the 'sect' can be said to dissent. The current criticism of sectarianism is therefore essentially sociological and political, implying a withdrawal from public responsibility in relation to the 'world', and especially the nation-state.[49] Nevertheless, this pejorative sociological sense is still traceable to the assumptions behind the construction of Troeltsch's typology.

For example, even though Troeltsch's analysis, in the wake of Weber's religious sociology,[50] realized the exceptional social and political influence of the sectarian forms of Christianity in Western society,[51] he (Troeltsch) assumed the church-type to be normative. The reasons he did so, as Hauerwas notes, have to do with the (very questionable) assumptions behind the construction of the Troeltschian typology—assumptions inscribed within the Weberian sociological tradition that assumes that one can separate the "social" from the purely "religious," and treat them as separate dimensions of a 'religion'.[52]

Such an assumption explains Troeltsch's central thesis that the message of Jesus, as well as early Christianity was purely religious, lacking any social ethic. Which is the reason why Troeltsch (strangely) describes issues like how the Church is organized and how Christians live their everyday lives as purely "religious." There is no reason, according to Hauerwas, why

Troeltsch would make such a stupendous claim, except that he had accepted the Weberian legitimation of a specific sort of Christianity whose
'religious' base can be clearly isolated from its 'social' manifestation.

Contrary to such an assumption, however, Hauerwas has consistently
resisted any suggestions to treat the "social" (political) as something added
to the "religious" message of Christ: the story of Jesus is social and political in itself.[53] Troeltsch's (or any other attempt) to separate the "religious"
from the "social" message of Christianity is a modern dualism grounded in
political liberalism and epistemologically wedded to an ahistorical and
asocial account of religious knowledge. John Milbank has more extensively developed this criticism against Weber and Troeltsch, and the whole
sociological tradition that goes back to them.[54] Hauerwas has therefore
greatly welcomed Milbank's work as "providing the sort of theoretical
framework that my work presupposes."[55] Because of this recommendation,
and because Milbank's work provides a more cogent and sustained argument than Hauerwas's own work (given the occasional nature and essayis-
tic style of the latter), it is worthwhile to attend to Milbank's argument as a
way to question the assumption within the Weberian-Troeltsch sociological tradition that one can neatly separate the "religious" base from the "social" aspects of a religion (Christianity). It is precisely this assumption that
creates and sustains the language and charge of "sectarianism."

Milbank: Questioning the Weberian Sociological Tradition

Milbank refers to the sociological tradition which goes back to Max Weber
as "the liberal Protestant metanarrative."[56] The title is meant to capture
the shortcomings of the neo-Kantian methodological approach characteristic of this sociological tradition, most extensively set out in Weber, but
equally operative in recent sociology of religion. Such a method

> both enshrines and conceals a particular history, namely the emergence
> of Protestantism, liberal Protestantism, and the Enlightenment, and to-
> gether with these the rise of the bureaucratic state and capitalist econom-
> ics. Thus the retracing of this history acquires the status of metanarrative
> because, first, the whole of the rest of human history is emplotted with
> reference to it, and second, its main synchronic and diachronic structures
> cease to be regarded as items of a particular temporal sequence, but are
> elevated to the status of an eternal logic of social possibility.[57]

Thus, the title "liberal Protestant metanarrative" provides the essence
of Milbank's central argument that the dominant sociological tradition

takes only a particular, historical social-political arrangement and raises it to an inevitable working of social reason everywhere, a "rational account of universal history." In order to gauge the full force and extent of Milbank's attempt to debunk this sociological tradition, we need to follow a little more closely his argument as he analyzes both the synchronic and diachronic aspects within the "liberal Protestant metanarrative."

In treating its synchronic structure in Weber,[58] Milbank first notes how Weber was concerned, over against positivism and Marxism, to give a determinative place to substantive-value rational goals alongside instrumental rationality. The problem, and as Milbank sees it, is that Weber himself remained close to positivism in that he deemed processes of formal, means-end rationality to be the only thing that could be *directly* understood by the scientific historian (sociologist) with full objectivity. Thus, he assumed that "fully objective history (sociology) is *primarily* about economic rationality, formal bureaucracy, and Machiavellian politics."[59]

Thus, for Weber, whatever lies outside these categories—religion, art, traditional authority—do not "really belong to the realm of the factual at all; instead they belong to the 'irreal' realm of valuation, and they exist primarily as hidden, subjective forces." The result of this positivistic alignment was that Weber (in spite of himself) was able to discuss substantive value goals only negatively—as deviations from [instrumental] rationality. Here, however, Weber was already involved in an *a priori* determination of both what counts as "social"—thus rational—and of the "essence" of religion. It is this transcendental determination, Milbank thinks, that gives categories such as "charisma," "routinization," and "traditional authority" the important *(a priori)* role they play in Weber's sociology of religion as "ideal types," not just simple heuristic devices, and ensures their place in the "irreal realm of hidden, subjective forces."

> Any religious pattern of valuation which semi-permanently distorts the operation of pure means-end rationality cannot be acknowledged as a factual presence in terms of its symbolic ordering of the world; instead it can only be registered as an inertia, as a mechanical persistence of the effect of response to charisma, after the original has passed away.[60]

However, what these ideal types do in Weber's sociology is make religion, in its essence, an "extra-social" affair, but which, if the effect (charisma) persists, has to disseminate itself "socially" through narratives, doctrines, norms, and organization. The latter—conditions of social persistence as defined universally and *a priori* by Weber—are seen as only

'secondary' phenomena to religion for which he provides 'social explanations' (of more or less functionalist sort).

Machiavellian assumptions of modern political theory and modern economics are intrinsic to Weberian sociology and this for at least two reasons.
First, the necessity of "social factors" in which a religion can be dissemi-
nated indicates that for Weber an organization can survive only if it accom-
modates itself to the 'rational' self-interest that *always* and *everywhere*,
Weber assumes, is the essence of the public realm. Thus, according to Milbank, "Weber's *methodology* already rules out the idea that there might be
societies where conduct regularly assumed a more nuanced and less egotistic notion of 'self-interest'."[61]

Secondly, Weber's *Geltungslogik* establishes an *a priori* separation of the
economic and political spheres from the "religious," which ensures that
economical and political influences are, per definition, "extra-religious."
This is why Troeltsch, following Weber, regards the medieval town economy, partly influenced by substantive ethical and religious norms, as an
"improper economy—an economy that has not yet fully defined itself as an
economy" because it has not yet constituted itself as a 'separate' sphere
from morality and religion.[62] What is thereby denied by Weber and
Troeltsch's *Geltungslogik* is the historical realization that religion can be
so 'fundamental' (as is the case for traditional or Islamic societies) that it
would enter into the most basic level of the symbolic organization of society, and the most basic level of its operations of discipline and persuasion,
such that one would be unable to abstract a politics, economics, or ethics
behind and beneath it.

In successfully questioning the *a priori* distinctions between the political, economic, and religious spheres, Milbank seeks to question the very validity of Weberian sociology. Social differentiation, he argues, is "not the
outworking of rationality itself," but "a contingent historical event (albeit
both immensely widespread and persistent) in recent Western history." Weberian (and Troeltschian) sociology betrays and subverts this fact by taking
"as an *a priori* principle of sociological investigation what should be the
subject of a genuine historical enquiry: namely, the emergence of a secular
polity," where the differentiation of the political, economic, and religious
spheres is at home.[63] The latter can only be *narrated*,[64] but not turned into
general sociological explanations. Milbank continues, "It is only *after* the
modern event of differentiation that one can talk, in a more or less general
way, about economic influences on religion and vice-versa."

Once the *(a priori)* dualism between the "religious" and the "social" at the heart of Weber's (and Troeltsch's) sociology is questioned, then the whole notion of 'social explanation' of religion disintegrates. One can no longer talk about a final social base for religion, because "there is nothing 'social' which it could be reduced to." In the case of Christianity, one then is confronted with the Hauerwasian realization that the story of Jesus *is* itself a social ethic.[65]

When Milbank examines the diachronic component of Weber's sociology, he discovers the same betrayal and subversion of history at work as in the synchronic component. For example, Milbank does not find surprising the fact that the diachronic component in Weber's sociology has "as its main theme the emergence of formal-instrumental rationality." For, if instrumental rationality is "the norm for human knowledge and association, then sociology must come up with a plausible account of the long concealment and gradual emancipation of this norm."[66] However, the teleological and developmental reading of history within this theme helps to make clearly evident Weber's affinities with positivism. For, just as for Comte,

> the major problem for Weber is the role, in the emergence of reason, of the irrational, and primarily of religion. Like Comte also, Weber responds by erecting a three-phase theory of historical becoming: there is a first, 'magical' phase; a second phase of the great salvation-religions; and a third, modern, secular phase.[67]

Once this metanarrative (in which the third stage is really only exemplified in the case of the West) is set up by Weber as the inevitable history of religion, then it is (falsely) assumed that Western history could not have been otherwise; modernity must have been latent in the Jewish and Christian faith from the beginning! To Milbank, this is a clear betrayal and subversion of history by the "liberal Protestant metanarrative," which he sets out to deconstruct in sharp and lucid terms:

> There is a kind of hidden, diachronic functionalism at work here. If Christianity ushers in the modern world, then, right from the start, Christianity must be understood in these terms. Thus Troeltsch and Weber fail to see individualism, voluntarism, fideism, and Kantian ethicization as contingent *changes* in Christian doctrine and ethos, but project these things back into the beginnings of Christianity and even the Old Testament. The history of the west is turned into the always-coming-to-be of liberal protestantism or its secular aftermath, and this means precisely the always-coming-to-be of Weber's and Troeltsch's

methodology, their instrument of investigation. It is at the diachronic level therefore that method and ontological content are most seen to be locked in a mutually self-confirming circle.[68]

The result of the positivistic assumption and the self-confirming methodology, Milbank argues, is that Troeltsch and Weber create a "sociology" which is nothing but a spurious promotion of what they study—namely, the secular culture of modernity.[69]

Milbank devotes a full chapter of his work to critically expose the pretensions of this "liberal Protestant metanarrative" as it has been dominant in recent sociology of religion.[70] Three dominant 'sociological explanations' of religion are identified and treated by Milbank: (i) the functional ("where religion is subordinated to the social and deemed functional in relation to it");[71] (ii) the evolutionary ("where religion is described as evolving to a true self-recognition of its own marginality"),[72] and (iii) the ideological ("where religion is described as a later, 'ideological' legitimation of an earlier, purely social arrangement").[73] These sociological explanations, Milbank contends, are nothing but 'secular policing', whose "secret purpose is to ensure that religion is kept, conceptually, at the margins—both denied influence and yet acclaimed for its transcendental purity."[74]

Once one attends to the full effect of Milbank's critical appraisal of the synchronic and diachronic components of Weber's sociology, it becomes obvious that the language of sectarianism can only be sustained due to a double "illusion": First, the illusion that the particular political arrangement (Western) and its subsystems is inevitable,[75] and secondly, the illusion of a 'social fact', which can be contrasted with religion. Against the first illusion, for example, Milbank's exposure of the diachronic functionalism in Weber's sociology clearly shows that there is nothing inevitable about the particular social arrangement of Western capitalist societies. Rather, such an arrangement, with its differentiation of spheres, is a historical and, therefore, contingent development. In fact, once this realization has been accepted, one begins to harbor valid suspicions about evolutionary social theories in general. The latter presumes some dominant continuities over human history as a whole—continuities which portray trends of development which culminate (inevitably) in the emergence of modern, i.e., Western society.[76] Instead, one begins to take seriously a 'discontinuist' conception of history in which social formations do not represent an inevitable point on a progressive scheme of social development, but rather the *narratable* configuration of a number of historically contingent factors.[77]

Milbank's critical remarks on Weber's methodology similarly dispenses with the second illusion, namely, the assumption of a 'sociological explanation' of religion. The latter seeks to identify the 'functions' of a religion in relation to the more primary social reality. But if, as Milbank shows, religion itself can be so comprehensive (as in the case of Islamic and traditional societies), then sociology of religion assumes a problematic starting point by assuming that there is always a 'social fact' contrastable to religion. Given this illusion, Milbank concludes, the "special discipline called sociology of religion ought to come to an end."

> Secular reason claims that there is a 'social' vantage point from which it can locate and survey various 'religious' phenomena. But it has turned out that assumptions about the nature of religion themselves help to define the perspective of this social vantage. From a deconstructive angle, therefore, the priority of society over religion can always be inverted, and every secular positivism is revealed to be also a positivist theology.[78]

This is a crucial conclusion for the overall development of Milbank's argument in *Theology and Social Theory*, which moreover indicates the affinity between him and Hauerwas. The subtitle of Milbank's work, "Beyond Secular Reason," should already point to the observation that his attack on any reliance between theology and modern 'scientific' or humanist social theory (liberal protestant metanarrative) is driven by a more basic criticism of secular reason itself. The failure of social theory, according to Milbank's overall argument, lies in the very origins of social theory in a secular reason which at the beginning of the modern era sought empirical foundations for the social peace that theology had failed to provide. To do this, the social theories had to invent the "secular," as a realm of human aspirations resolutely devoid of ultimate commitments. That project, according to Milbank, could never be more than partly successful, for it remains, in important ways, parasitic on the religious consciousness which it sought to deny and, in spite of the secularist assumption, "frequently calls upon a stand-in for God, such as 'nature' or 'the market', to straighten out the messy details which resist description in rational human terms."[79] This is why, the secular "is revealed to be also a positivist theology" and all "'scientific' social theories are themselves theologies or antitheologies in disguise."[80]

Milbank (like Hauerwas) is particularly critical of the liberal and foundational illusions by which this secular order claims a "neutral" and "universal" assessment. There is no neutral, rational, universal account of society or history available, he argues. Accordingly, there can be no

Sociology—no 'social' vantage point from which one can locate and survey various 'religious' phenomena. Rather, theology is itself a social science (for Milbank, the queen of the sciences!). This, of course, does not mean that theology can claim any transcendental leverage over secular reason any more than the latter is able to claim one over theology. Theology is itself a contingent, historical construct "emerging from, and reacting back upon, particular social practices conjoined with particular semiotic and figural codings."[81] This is what opens up a space for a new *engagement* (critical *witness* according to Hauerwas) between theology and the secular, between the social realities of church and state, where neither can be transcendentally refuted but only "out-narrated" by the persuasive power of the alternative narrative.[82]

From this perspective, it becomes clear that both Milbank and Hauerwas are determined to present Christianity (church) as providing (an embodiment of) a substantive and critical account of society that offers a 'counter-modern' alternative—"historicist and pragmatist, yet *theologically* realist."[83] This means, according to Hauerwas, that the first social task of the Church is "not to make the nation-state system work," or "to make the world more peaceable or just. Put starkly, the first social ethical task of the church is to be the church. . . . As such, the church does not have a social ethic, the church *is* a social ethic." The church does not let the world set the agenda for what constitutes a " 'social ethic,' but a church of peace and justice must set its own agenda."[84]

Both the details and specific conclusion of Milbank's work deserve a more elaborate examination than can be undertaken within the scope of this work.[85] We have attended to it here in order to allow the reader to see why Hauerwas has found Milbank's argument so compelling that he has acknowledged it as the "sort of theoretical framework" that his own work presupposes. This is, accordingly, not the occasion to dwell on the one major reservation that Hauerwas retains against Milbank's project, namely, its abstract and metanarrative singularity that might, according to Hauerwas, conceal the same sort of violence as that inherent within the modern project which Milbank seeks to overcome.[86] This critical note, as well as Hauerwas's more positive appreciation of Milbank will be made more explicit in the coming chapter as we examine the prospects and limits of Hauerwas's politics of Witness. For now, however, we have drawn attention to Milbank in order to rehearse and provide conceptual amplification for Hauerwas's criticism of the assumptions within the Weberian sociological tradition—assumptions which underwrite and sustain the language of sectarianism. The result of this Milbankian excursus has been twofold: First, the "illusion" of a neutral framework or science (a sociology) that could assess the adequacy of a "religion" in terms of a more primary "social reality" has been challenged. In this connection, the language of sectarianism has been shown to be a form of 'policing' that seeks to confirm and sustain a *particular* social arrangement. Secondly, and as a result of this dispensation, one begins to appreciate that a religion can be so comprehensive that it "enters" all aspects of life and social organization. In this connection, "the liberal protestant metanarrative" from which the charge of sectarianism is framed is nothing but a 'policing' tactic meant to resist this substantive conception of religion. The combined effect of these two arguments is thus to make clear that the language and charge of sectarianism assumes a certain hegemonic understanding of "religion," which is, in effect, at the service of a particular social-political arrangement of the modern nation-state. In order to fully appreciate this conclusion, we need to critically draw attention to how "religion" is concretely policed in order to protect liberal politics.

Hauerwas and the "Democratic Policing of Christianity"

Hauerwas has been particularly critical of how theologians have, in their work, appropriated and (perhaps unwittingly, but uncritically) provided a justification for liberal democracy. Central to this appropriation, for instance, has been the assumption by theologians that "democratic societies and governments are the most natural expression of Christian convictions."[87] This explains why much of Christian "social ethics" has uncritically underwritten Christian involvement in the world as a way of sustaining "democracy as a universal achievement." The 'policing' implicit in such "social ethics" becomes evident by the assumption that "a world-affirming 'church' or world-denying 'sect'" are the only options open for Christians. This means that from the start, the Church's relation to the state is prejudicially determined by stark options of relevance or irrelevance; social responsibility or sectarian withdrawal. But what this all-or-nothing option (as implicit in Niebuhr's highly influential Christ-culture typologies),[88] concretely assumes is that religion can avoid being sectarian only by rendering itself "useful" through working out principles, social strategies, and pastoral guidelines, which prop up state action.[89] For Hauerwas, however, to the extent the Church has uncritically supplied such a justification, it has assumed a new Constantinianism, by failing to acknowledge the historical and contingent nature of the Church and of the liberal political arrangement.[90]

The liberal political arrangement also assumes a "gnostic" account of religion. The latter, which is a distinctly modern conception, reduces religion to a "form of knowledge"—a set of *beliefs* or *convictions*. Hauerwas is aware of the specific factors within the modern landscape that legitimated a new "formality of practices" and thus transformed Christianity from a set of practical rules attached to communal processes and practices into a set of *propositions* to which an *individual* gives assent.[91] However, what Hauerwas (just like Milbank) questions, is the liberal protestant metanarrative that seeks to obscure this history by declaring the gnostic conception of religion to be the true and normative essence of religion always and everywhere.

The gnostic conception moreover, assumes that religion is by nature 'private'. Such an assumption, however, tends to obscure the (hi)story of modern liberal society according to which, "with the triumphant rise of modern science, modern production, and the modern state," there is a felt need to distinguish the religious from the secular, thus shifting "the weight of religion more and more onto the moods and motivations of the individual believer."[92] As was narrated in the first chapter, the relocation of religion into "moods and motivations" did in effect confine Christianity to what Milbank calls the "irreal world of the sublime" (private value), while handing over the determination and control of practices to a secular state machinery and a 'neutral' ethics. Our point in 'narrating' these developments was to show this as a particular conception which cannot be raised to the essence of religion.

Moreover, we have already critically noted (chapter 2) how a privatized conception of religion assumes a questionable separation of beliefs and convictions ("moods and motivations") from practices. The constructive argument for character as a central moral category drew on the realization that there can be no 'neutral' determination of action, but that action and convictions are internally and conceptually related. It was this realization which led, in the third chapter, to a critical appraisal of the epistemological underpinning of the fact-value distinction on which the privatization of religion is premised.[93] By attending to Wittgenstein's understanding of language in general, the role of linguistic notions in particular, the centrality and homogeneity of language was affirmed and thus any ontological validity to a fact-value divide was denied.[94] The 'policing' involved in a gnostic and privatized conception of religion should be obvious. The privatization of beliefs means that religion gets consigned to an asocial sphere (value) of interiority, or in epistemological terms, to the realm of "truths but no Truth."[95] This strategy results into two effects. First, it means that religious convictions, having been rendered into 'opinions', lose the critical ability to challenge "the limits of our social orders," let alone to constitute any alternative social order. This is precisely why Hauerwas regards such liberal concepts as the freedom of religion to be "a subtle temptation." One is free to 'believe' anything as long one does not think that one's beliefs can be embodied.[96] Secondly, in view of the privatization, a "'public' sphere is cleared away for a counterfeit form of 'religion' to emerge that is said to be 'common' and thus becomes the 'religion of the nation'. What gets obscured in this arrangement is the possibility of a Christianity the material form of which is located neither in a private space nor in a general public space, but in the body of believers, in the church."[97] Such a possibility requires a social-linguistic conception of religion in general and of Christianity in particular.

In fact, Hauerwas critically notes, the very category "religion" embodies an Enlightenment essentialism that assumes that "the various historical faiths are but manifestations of a common phenomenon called *religion*.[98] This thesis is well elaborated by the social anthropologist Talal Asad, whom Hauerwas does not mention, but who clearly depicts how, as a historical category, "religion" emerged in the West only in the seventeenth century.[99] According to Asad's lucid thesis, it was "following the fragmentation of the unity and authority of the Roman Church and the consequent wars of religion, which tore European principalities apart, that the earliest systematic attempts at producing a universal definition of religion were made."[100] To be sure, this attempt coincided with the "discovery," through exploration, commerce, and, later, missionary work, of other (strange!) religions in the East, the South, and the New World. Factors such as these contributed to the emergence of a distinct field of study, an enlightened anthropology, whose *Geltungslogik* sought to extract an axiomatic, an essence, from the various religious particularities of belief and practice, just as Newtonian physics sought to isolate "real" unchanging patterns underlying the plurality of sensible phenomena. Whether that essence of the various religious patterns was seen to lie in virtue or social utility,[101] the direction of the transformation is unmistaken: "From being a concrete set of rules attached to specific processes of power and knowledge, religion . . . come[s] to be abstracted and universalized."[102] Once again, Kant provides one of the most eloquent expressions of this Enlightened essentialism:

There may be certainly different historical 'confessions', although these have nothing to do with religion itself but only with changes in the means used to further religion, and thus the province of historical research. And there may be just as many religious 'books' (the Zend-Avesta, the Vedas, the Koran, etc.). But there can only be 'one religion' which is valid for all men and at all times. Thus the different confessions can scarcely be more than the vehicles of religion; these are fortuitous, and may vary with differences in time or place.[103]

The reasons for Hauerwas's rejection of the category of "religion" will become more obvious when we treat its synchronic elements in the coming section. For now, however, it suffices to note that Hauerwas tries to stay clear of the essentialism within the category "religion" by preferring the more concrete designation "the church" or Christianity.

It is clear then, that the factors within the above Enlightenment essentialism that produce a functional, gnostic, and privatized version of "religion" form a single narrative. It is this narrative—the liberal protestant metanarrative—which sets the philosophical 'problem' of religion and ethics. For, only when Christianity has ceased to be a "fleshy embodiment" of specific practices and processes and becomes a set of beliefs (a 'gnosis') separable from practices, does one seek a way to draw moral (practical) implications from these beliefs, thus creating the question of the relation between practices (ethics) and beliefs (religion).

However, given the factors behind the framing of the category of "religion," one must grant a certain *historical* validity to the problem of religion and ethics. It arises out of, and reflects, a particular social situation. However, to raise this problem to the level of a 'perennial' question of philosophy should rightly be seen as a 'policing' strategy, meant to confirm and universalize this particular (historical) social arrangement: As Hauerwas notes, the setting of this question as well as "the predominance in theological and philosophical context of the motivational and supererogatory accounts of the relation between the religious and the moral is best explained in sociological terms."[104] As our treatment in this section has shown, these sociological terms provide a legitimation of Protestant liberalism. On account of the shortcomings that we have identified (following Milbank) within this metanarrative, it is not hard to see why Hauerwas does not address himself to the 'problem' but instead warns: "to begin by asking what is the relation between religion and ethics is to have already made a mistake."[105]

What we are actually confronting in Hauerwas's dismissal of the philosophical problem of religion and ethics is a rejection of a certain hegemonic conception of "ethics" and of "religion" in which the 'problem' is at home. Much has already been said about Hauerwas's critique of the standard account of ethics and his historical conception of the moral life. What remains (still) to be surveyed is his substantive understanding of "religion."

3. Religion as a Cultural-Linguistic System

The previous section returned us to Hauerwas's rejection of the distinctively modern category of 'religion'. However, apart from noting that such a category assumes a gnostic and privatized account of religious belief, the specific reasons for its rejection were not fully elaborated. What makes this account of religion internally questionable? Moreover, Hauerwas's own alternative conception of the phenomenon that is often characterized by 'religion' was left unexplained. How does Hauerwas understand 'religion'? The following section seeks to provide answers to these two questions by drawing attention to George Lindbeck's three models for studying religion.[106]

We draw attention to Lindbeck's analysis of the three models of religion because it provides a conceptually lucid framework for understanding the critical as well as the constructive conception of religion within Hauerwas's work. Even though Hauerwas himself has not elaborated this specific understanding of religion, he has endorsed Lindbeck's analysis in general, and his preference for a 'cultural-linguistic' model in particular, as "extremely helpful, as it allows me to make clear some of the primary presuppositions of my work."[107] Thus, in an introduction to *Against the Nations*, Hauerwas indicates that "the basic perspective" of his theological agenda is consonant with Lindbeck's cultural-linguistic model of religion and with postliberal, intratextual theology.[108] The primary motivation and goal of this section, therefore, will be to make explicit Hauerwas's understanding of religion as a 'cultural-linguistic' system, and to examine the prospects as well as the limits of such understanding.

Lindbeck: Three Models for the Study of Religion.

In *The Nature of Doctrine*, Lindbeck distinguishes three theoretical models for understanding religion: the cognitive-propositional, the experiential-expressivist, and the cultural-linguistic approaches.[109] The cognitive-propositional approach takes religion to be "essentially, but not necessarily exclusively, forms of speech and action focussed on a mind-independent sacred or divine reality."[110] According to this view, credal statements are factual descriptions offering information about states-of-affairs (most determinedly, the reality of a "god") largely external to the believer and his situation.[111] This approach is not given substantial coverage by Lindbeck, for, as he notes, in modern times this conception of religion has been on the decline in favor of the experiential-expressivist approach, which is favored by most contemporary theologians and philosophers of religion.

Proponents of the experiential-expressivist model, on the other hand, locate the essence of religion in "the pre-reflective experiential depths of the self and regard the public or outer features of religion as expressive or evocative objectifications (i.e., non-discursive symbols) of internal experience."[112] For his analysis of this model, Lindbeck follows Bernard Lonergan,[113] who identified in different religions a *common* core of experience at the prereflexive level which forms the source and norm of objectification (in religious language). This primordial experience is what is characterized variously as "the feeling of absolute dependence" (Schleiermacher); as "the dynamic state of being in love without restrictions" and "without an object" (Lonergan); or as "an experience of the holy" in the sense of Rudolf Otto's *mysterium fascinans et tremendum*; as "being grasped by ultimate concern" (Paul Tillich); as "consolation that has no cause" (Ignatius); as the experience "in which what is meant and the experience of what is meant are still one" (Rahner).[114]

Even though Lindbeck's characterization of the experiential-expressivist approach may at times tend to oversimplify the richness of this tradition,[115] the "experiential-expressivism" model seems nevertheless a fairly adequate formal characterization of the standard conception of religion within theological and nontheological circles. What is particularly significant is the realization that the experiential-expressivist model is a specifically *modern* approach, as it assumes both a privatized notion of religion and a conception of religion in terms of (private) feeling, convictions, and beliefs. Such a conception of religion works with what we characterized, following Loughlin, as a clear "see-saying" pattern. It is significant to note this point here, for it shows how the experiential-expressivism conceals a liberal tyranny: Only one's own 'religious experience', it is assumed, entitles one to believe![116] An even more basic issue with this approach is that it is premised on an empiricist and foundational epistemology that imagines some primitive phenomena of consciousness, a sort of "pure" experience that later finds expression in language. As was pointed out in the third chapter, both this empiricist ontology and the instrumentalist (expressivist) view of language that it involves trade on a content-scheme or experience-language dichotomy, which has been shown to be untenable in the light of a Wittgensteinian view of language.[117]

The cultural-linguistic model is Lindbeck's alternative to the above two models. According to this model, religions are seen as "comprehensive interpretative schemes, usually embodied in myths or narratives and heavily ritualized, which structure human experience and understanding of self and world."[118] Stated more contrastively, the cultural-linguistic approach perceives religion as essentially neither an attempt to map reality by means of truth-formulations corresponding to ultimate "reality" (cognitive-propositional), nor an external and objective expression of primordial inner experiences potentially shared by all humanity (experiential-expressivist), but as "a kind of cultural and/or linguistic framework or medium that shapes the entirety of life and thought."[119] Thus, religions, on this view, "are similar to cultures (. . . idioms for the constructing of reality and the living of life)."[120] Like a culture or language, religion is "a *communal* phenomenon that shapes the subjectivities of individuals rather than being primarily a manifestation of those subjectivities."[121]

Two crucial points need to be underscored about this understanding. First, the communal aspect of any cultural-linguistic system is based on Wittgenstein's denial of the possibility of private language.[122] Applied to religion, this does not mean the impossibility of personal religious experience, but it is to place the possibility of such experience within context of a community's life and action. Secondly, but related to the above, the cultural-linguistic conception of religion is based on a key anthropological realization that the structures of human subjectivity are themselves culturally formed.[123] Thus, the cultural-linguistic model is part of an outlook that stresses the degree to which human experience is shaped, molded and, in part, constituted by cultural and linguistic forms. Since

> expressive and communicative symbol systems, whether linguistic or non-linguistic, are primary—then, while there are of course nonreflective experiences, there are no uninterpreted or unschematized ones. On this view, the means of communication and expression are a precondition, a kind of quasi-transcendental (i.e., culturally formed) *a priori* for the possibility of experience, We cannot identify, describe, or recognize experience qua experience without the use of signs and symbols.[124]

Stated more technically, the identification of religion as a "cultural and/or linguistic framework" means that religion, just like any cultural system, "functions somewhat like a Kantian *a priori*." Like the Kantian *a priori*, Lindbeck notes, religious conceptual categories are logically prior to religious experience and serve as conditions of possibility for the same. However, significant differences with the Kantian idiom should also be noted. For unlike the Kantian *a priori*, a religious framework is [i] *not transcendentally deduced* (it is a "kind of quasi-transcendental") but is "a set of acquired skills" (acquired through practice and training), and [ii] *not universally necessary* but rests on "the foundational certainties of a form of life."[125]

By making reference to the Kantian idiom Lindbeck wishes only to adumbrate the Wittgensteinian denial of any experience which is not underpinned by language and thus of a "pure" or "primitive phenomena of consciousness" antecedent to, and independent of, language. The stress is important for showing, against the assumption of the experiential-expressivist approach, that there is no underlying unity of experience:

> Adherents of different religions do not diversely thematize the same experience; rather, they have different experiences. A Buddhist compassion, Christian love and—if I may cite a quasi-religious phenomenon—French Revolutionary 'fraternite' are not diverse modifications of a single fundamental awareness, emotion, attitude, or sentiment, but are radically distinct ways of experiencing and being oriented toward self, neighbor, and cosmos.[126]

The Church as a Cultural-Linguistic Tradition

Hauerwas has welcomed and endorsed Lindbeck's cultural-linguistic model for understanding religion. He notes, "as Lindbeck suggests, religion is not primarily a set of presuppositions to be believed or disbelieved, but a set of skills that one employs in living. Such skills are acquired by learning the stories of Israel and Jesus well enough not only to interpret the world, but to do so in specifically Christian terms."[127] This remark is clearly in line with Hauerwas's substantive understanding of a tradition as the very conditions-of-possibility for seeing the world. Thus, to refer to religion as a "set of skills" is to affirm the primacy of a religious tradition, since the only way to acquire the particular skills is through initiation into the language and practice of that tradition. If there is not first a community of faith, of word and of deed, there can be no religious experience.[128] The primacy of a community of faith and the need for training and initiation into this community explain the priority Hauerwas gives to everyday "practices"—liturgy, stories, and concrete lives—over "convictions" as the domain of religion.

All this helps to affirm that for Hauerwas religion is not so much about be-liefs, convictions, and doctrinal formulations, as it is about finding oneself as a member of a particular community, and living out (concrete practices, skills) one's life as a member of that community. In terms of knowledge, the primary knowledge is "not *about* the religion, nor *that* the religion teaches such and such, but rather *how* to be religious."[129]

However, one must note the self-referential aspect within this under-standing of religion as a tradition is significant: A 'religious experience' is only possible within the space of religious language and practice.[130] The cir-cle, however, is not vicious but hermeneutic, which, as we have noted, points to the necessity of training and initiation. However, it is such hermeneutic circularity that makes intelligible Hauerwas's contention that "outside the church there is no salvation."[131] For, away from the particular tradition that offers a training in the language of, and the particular skills that are associated with, the stories of God, one would not know what "sal-vation" is all about. Without these concrete practices and specific language one would not even 'see' that one is a "sinner," who thereby needs to be "saved." Thus the full critical force of Hauerwas's apparently conservative claim ("Outside the church there is no salvation") is to deny that "God," "sin," "salvation," etc., are natural categories, and to affirm how these cat-egories are arrived at historically through participation in a given cultural-linguistic way of life.

The upshot of this realization is that religions in general, and religious experiences in particular, are fundamentally historical realities. Thus, experiential-expressivist models of religion are mistaken in presenting categories like "God," "trust," "dependence," etc., as either "natural" or "core" experiences that are underived. To so claim is to protect a certain area of human activity (which religion is) from the fluctuations of history. Showing the futility of such an attempt has been a major preoccupation throughout our work. We can advance this objective here by drawing atten-tion to the prospects of the cultural-linguistic model of religion.

Prospects of the Cultural-Linguistic Model

Much debate has been generated by Lindbeck's analysis of the three mod-els, especially his argument for the superior efficacy of the cultural-linguistic model. It is beyond the scope of this work to revisit this debate, especially since it has taken place within theological circles and has gener-ally concentrated on the theologically related conclusions of Lindbeck's work.[132] In as much as our interest lies in Hauerwas's appreciation of the cultural-linguistic model of understanding religion, we can only note the anthropological implications that make this model preferable and point to a more adequate way than the one proffered by Lindbeck's in which the relation between experience and cultural-linguistic forms should be characterized.

As Tiina Allik has well noted, in its anthropology, the cultural-linguistic model "assumes and elaborates the radical materiality, historicity, and contingency of religious experience and of human experience in general."[133] Allik's argument hinges on seeing the notion of human finitude not only as a way to refer to the limits of human powers, but also as a way to characterize the *basic openness, vulnerability, and contingency* of all human capacities. Such a sense of finitude may either be valued or disdained, depending on how one conceptualizes human personhood. If one thinks of the goal of human existence as complete control and mastery over oneself and one's environment, then this openness is an undesirable vulnerability to contingent influences which may derail the best-laid plans for control and mastery. However, "if one sees openness, vulnerability, and contingency as the basis for the creativity and spontaneity of human existence, then finitude and materiality will be construed as positive boons, rather than as unfortunate obstacles in the way of the achievement of a nonhuman form of control."[134] Understood from this perspective, the cultural-linguistic approach involves an appreciation of human finitude in a way that the experiential-expressivist model does not.

Experiential-expressivist thinkers, by conceptualizing religious experience as having a "nonconceptual core" (in the prereflective experiential depths of the self), assume that the core of the self and of religious experience is invulnerable to events in the material, social, and historical world. To be sure, the affirmation by experiential-expressivism of this noncontingent invulnerable core of religious experience is motivated by a desire to affirm the adequacy of finite human persons as knowers of God, as well as "an epistemological desire to provide a sure foundation for the validity of religious experience and theistic belief."[135] However, by exempting an aspect of human persons from contingency and vulnerability, experiential-expressivism compromises the full finitude of human beings as open and contingent in *all* aspects of their being. Thus, against their own intentions, experiential-expressivist authors cast aspersions on the goodness of human creatures as finite and material as well as on the adequacy of finite human ways of knowing and being in the world.

In contrast, the cultural-linguistic approach, by conceptualizing human persons as dependent on their linguistic and cultural environments for the formation and maintenance of their capacities, affirms the full finitude (in the sense of openness, contingency, and historicity) of human persons and of both religious and nonreligious experience. To quote Allik again: "Theologically, this is a way of affirming that human selves and human capacities for particular kinds of experiences, including religious experiences, are dependent on the particular contingencies of an individual's cultural and linguistic environments or, in theological terms, on providence, not on the security provided by the concept of an inviolable core of human nature."[136]

Drawing attention to an affirmation of radical contingency and finitude makes the affinity between the cultural-linguistic model and the central thesis of our work obvious. In the first place, the realization that *all* human experience is dependent upon the particular contingencies of an individual's cultural-linguistic environment leads to an appreciation of a sense of *fragility* to our moral and religious projects that calls for the rehabilitation of the philosophical categories of luck and tragedy. Secondly, by vacating the moral and religious life of any foundational anchorage, a distinctive conception of the moral self as constituted in contingent, historical circumstances—that is, through the cultural symbols and linguistic forms of the communities in which one participates—is confirmed. Throughout our work, we have been keen to develop this historical sense of the moral life by noting how human experience—including who and what we become (character), how we come to see (vision), and the quest for truth and objectivity (narrative rationality)—is fundamentally historical. What we have been trying to make explicit in this chapter is the conclusion that this sense of historicity (contingency) extends equally to all religious experience. A cultural-linguistic model confirms that the experience of the holy is as historical as the experience of the good and of the beautiful. This by itself does not mean that God is a *product* of history. The cultural-linguistic model only affirms that the only way to have access to God is through historically contingent linguistic schemes and practices.

To note that linguistic and cultural systems are conditions-of-possibility for any experience at all is to rule out the possibility of an unmediated primary or core experience. However, this does not mean that we live in hermetic cultural-linguistic systems which do not allow radically "new" experiences to break through the limits of those cultural-linguistic systems. This would easily be the case if the relation between the cultural-linguistic *a priori* and experience followed a unilateral "say-seeing" scheme. Lindbeck's work at times unwittingly portrays this unilateral scheme.

It is true that Lindbeck explicitly notes that the relation between a cultural-linguistic system and experience is "not unilateral but dialectical."[137] However, when it comes to specific conclusions, his "intra-textual" theology tends to betray a residual Barthinian foundationalism. For example, on the relation between Scripture and the world, he announces: "It is the text, so to speak, which absorbs the world, rather than the world the text."[138] Such insistence not only seems to too narrowly reduce the rich Christian cultural-linguistic tradition to a scriptural core,[139] but also assumes a unilateral relation between the scriptural interpretative framework and any extra-textual realities. And so, within Lindbeck's theological program of intra-textuality, the scriptural text, its meaning as well as its interpretation, seems to be elevated into an ahistorical and surreal biblical world, well-shielded from contamination by the "acids of modernity"[140] as well as from any contingent human experience. This is why, for Lindbeck, the text absorbs the world, "not the world the text"; believers do not "find their stories in the Bible, but rather . . . they make the story of the Bible their own."[141] This linear characterization of the relation between text and reader has justifiably led critics to see Lindbeck's cultural-linguistic model as merely an inversion of the experiential-expressivist approach.[142]

Lindbeck is certainly right to claim that any appreciation of the cultural-linguistic model involves a form of intra-textual philosophy or theology. In this sense, intra-textuality is simply the affirmation of a valid insight, namely that the determination of goodness, truth, beauty is inseparable from particular narratives and cultural-linguistic practices. To put it differently, intra-textuality is the claim that meaning and truth are generated within the text, rather than being a correspondence to an extra-linguistic reality.[143] However, Lindbeck is mistaken when he assumes (unwittingly perhaps) a linear or "pure" intra-textuality. As Tilley notes, such an intra-textuality runs the danger of particularistic isolationism because it "stop[s] short of the radical implications of cultural-linguistic understandings of traditions and intratextual interpretations by positing a 'pure' text immune from shaping by ongoing conversation."[144] This shortcoming is only slightly hinted at, but not explicated by Hauerwas.[145] Hauerwas's enthusiastic endorsement of Lindbeck's project may, in fact, give the impression that his own work also retains these elements of Barthinian confessionalism. But this is not the case. On the contrary, in terms of intra-textuality, it is more accurate to see Hauerwas's work as involving a "dirty" or multiple intra-textuality.

A "dirty" or multiple intra-textuality rejects any suggestion of a linear relation between text and experience. Rather, it affirms creative tension between text and experience or between any one cultural-linguistic form and the experience it generates. It is this creative tension that 'saves' a given cultural-linguistic form (tradition) from settling down into parochial complacency or particularistic isolation. Instead, this creative (dialectal) tension initiates an ongoing conversation that leads to a given cultural-linguistic framework being shaped, challenged, or extended by elements from other traditions. In the previous chapter, we developed this element of creative tension as the normative requirement for dialectical witness.

A dialectical or 'dirty' intra-textuality is made possible by the very inner and dialectical unity between language and experience.[146] According to this inner unity, experience does not occur prior to language as a nonlinguistic datum for which one subsequently, through a reflective act, finds words. Linguisticality permeates the very being-in-the-world of historical man, insofar as experience, thinking, and understanding are linguistic through and through.

However, linguisticality, as the very condition-of-possibility of laying open a space in which a "world" discloses itself, does not mean that language thus becomes a prison, but "an open space that allows *infinite* expansion, depending on one's openness to tradition."[147] This means that a cultural-linguistic system or language is not fixed or "dogmatically certain," but is characterized by what Gadamer calls speculativity—a movement, suspension, and openness that wills new possible relations (experiences) to come into being.[148] We have already elaborated this capacity for speculativity as the 'phronetic attentiveness' characteristic of any 'living' tradition. However, it is significant to note that even this capacity and any "new" experience it issues is dependent on a given cultural-linguistic system which allows both its appearance and/or its recognition as new.

The full implication of the dialectic between language and experience is that it provides a fundamental critique to an instrumental (unilateral) conception of language on either side of the "see-saying"/"say-seeing" divide. Linguistic forms are not, *pace* experiential-expressivists, a mere objectification (descriptive or expressive) of a nonconceptual experience. But neither are they a fixed set of conditions-of-possibility that remain unaffected by the experience they structure. Lindbeck is right to insist on the priority of cultural-linguistic systems over experience, to affirm that there can be no experience outside a cultural-linguistic scheme. However, in his one-sided intratextual insistence that Scripture absorbs the world and not vice-versa, he misses the elements of phronetic attentiveness and dialectical witness. According to these dialectical elements, the richness of experience that the cultural-linguistic form makes possible, as well as the dialectical presence of other traditions, provide a dynamic by which the cultural-linguistic framework itself is constantly being formed, revised, or innovatively extended.

Two simple conclusions flow from this analysis of the dialectical interplay between language and experience. First, the unavoidability of cultural-linguistic schemes (Lindbeck), for any experience is tantamount to the inescapability of tradition (MacIntyre), prejudice (Gadamer), and particularity (Hauerwas). What all these complimentary approaches confirm is the inherent historicity and finitude of all human experience—including religious experience. Intra-textuality is simply a reminder that all questions of truth, beauty, the holy, and goodness are determined from within a particular tradition. Secondly, but very importantly, intra-textuality is always a dialectical (or dirty) intra-textuality because the cultural-linguist forms are themselves not static but are normatively characterized by a "creative tension" that allows for constant revision and development.

We note these far-reaching implications in order to dissociate the cultural-linguistic approach from Lindbeck's or any other particular theological agenda[149] and advance its appeal as a *formal* method for the study of religion. However, it remains only a formal method, whose limits must therefore also be briefly noted. As a formal method, the cultural-linguistic model, for instance, would not be able to inform us of the differences between traditions, say between Hinduism, Christianity, Islam, Azande witchcraft, and liberal capitalism, in as much as these are all cultural-linguistic systems! This means that a cultural linguistic model recognizes that different 'religions' are not based on a single foundational experience, but the similarities between them are a matter of family resemblances. These resemblances and differences, on account of the comprehensiveness, reflexivity, and complexity of any cultural-linguistic form, are simply a matter of narrative display or what Geertz has called "thick description."[150]

This is a crucial realization, which means that neither philosophy nor sociology (of religion) can claim to provide *a priori* criteria for distinguishing a 'religious' from a nonreligious cultural-linguistic scheme. For example, when Lindbeck refers to religions as "comprehensive interpretative schemes, *usually embodied in myths or narratives and heavily ritualized,* which structure human experience and understanding of self and world,"[151] one must realize that the same definition can equally apply to the Wall Street stock market. Ritualization and embodiment in myth and narratives is only a matter of degree, and Wall Street trading certainly enjoys its share of narrative mythology (statistics!) and ritualized performance. Thus the difference between it and Azande witchcraft is a matter of narrative display.

This is already to move the prospects of a cultural-linguistic conception of religion far beyond the limits of our work. From the perspective of our work, the substantive understanding of religion as a cultural-linguistic system renders the attempt to determine the "moral significance of religious convictions" absurd. The question arises only when one assumes, with the experiential-expressivist approach, that underlying the plurality of religious expressions there is a "core" religious experience which is variously expressed and from which moral implications can be drawn. But once one has accepted the cultural-linguistic approach, one also grants that a religion (in Hauerwas's case, Christianity) can be so 'fundamental' (tradition) that one does not (cannot) try to get *underneath* it (to a core experience) or *beyond* it (to its moral implications).

7

A Metaphysics of "In the Beginning": Politics beyond Tribalism and Liberal Agonistics

> Everything is dangerous as Foucault says; everything has the potential to create misery, to bring about disaster, to destroy institutions and relationships, to change who and what we are. Everything is risky. But the greatest danger occurs when forms of thought and practice persist without challenge, when one way of thinking becomes so powerful that we lose sight of all other possibilities, when one way of thinking totalises itself to the exclusion of all else.
>
> Ladelle McWhorter

> . . . all political and social theorists, I venture to claim, depend on some model of man in explaining what moves people and accounts for institutions. Such models are sometimes hidden but never absent, and the rise of behavioral political science has only enriched the stock. There is no more central or pervasive topic in the study of politics.
>
> Raymond Plant

The *political* formulation of the sectarian challenge goes like this: We live in pluralistic societies where there is no dominant community or tradition that shapes the lives and thoughts of individuals. By insisting on the distinctive language of any community, religious or otherwise, one would be calling for social withdrawal of the members into a tribal ghetto, away from responsible participation in the ambiguities of public choices. To many, Hauerwas's insistence on the distinctiveness of the Christian community, together with what he claims is the central conviction of that community, namely, nonviolence, makes him an "irresponsible tribalist" who fails to take into account the complexity of modern pluralistic societies.[1]

Constructively, this criticism trades on the assumption that while particular traditions may be helpful in the formation of individual characters and the shaping of private convictions and values, which might even strengthen democratic ideals and revamp the public ethos, the public space itself must remain neutral in respect to these traditions. Otherwise, given the pluralism characteristic of modern social reality, it is argued, cooperation and the determination of public policy becomes incessantly bogged down by irresolvable tensions of the sort of "Whose language? Which convictions? Whose vision?"

This "pluralistic" assumption has considerable descriptive appeal as Hauerwas himself recognizes. He is particularly aware of the historical circumstances (see chapter 1) in which the liberal social and political arrangement was born and the problem of cooperation that it managed. He even notes some of the positive aspects within the liberal social arrangement.[2] However, what he questions is the normative appeal to "pluralism" as it operates with the standard theological and philosophical discourse as a shorthand justification for the liberal social and political order.

In this chapter, we shall survey Hauerwas's conception of politics by moving from a critical to a constructive assessment. Critically, we shall seek to demonstrate that the appeal to "pluralism" is correlative to a "false universalism" at the heart of liberal social and political theory. As a result of this false universalism, liberal politics suffers from at least three shortcomings: (i) a failure to account for territoriality, (ii) a tendency to meta-narrative violence, and (iii) a Machiavellian rhetoric by which it masks the "local" interests it serves under the guise of "neutrality." The goal of this critical approach (section one) will be to confirm the historical and, therefore, optional nature of the liberal social-political arrangement.

Once the optional nature of the liberal social arrangement has been granted (and thus the language of "pluralism" and "tribalism" out of the way), we shall, in the second section, reconstruct Hauerwas's conception of politics around the metaphors of everyday "conversation" and the "common good." The objective behind this section will be to suggest the centrality of the imagination and witness as correlative political tasks. This will involve a redefining of the nature and meaning of so-called "public" responsibility.

The third section examines Hauerwas's pacifism as a form of politics against the background of a key challenge, namely, that the (re)conception of politics around historical traditions necessarily leads to violence, because there are no independent criteria by which competing local interests or visions can be arbitrated. Against such a fear, we shall argue that the assumption that difference, indeterminacy, and particularity necessarily leads to violence is founded on a *mythos*. To counter this *mythos*, one can put forward an alternative *mythos,* equally unfounded but nonetheless embodying an ontology of peace—which conceives differences as analogically related, rather than equivocally at variance. This is what is at stake in the Christian story of Creation, which, according to Hauerwas, generates a pacifist community and practice.

The fourth and last section takes up some of the implications of the previous sections with a view of providing a framework for a proper reading of Hauerwas's work. The section argues against a too hasty identification of Hauerwas with the recent return to virtue ethics, or with communitarianism. Nor should his work be seen as a form of political theology.

A note about terminology. Hauerwas himself acknowledges that liberalism is a complex and ambiguous reality.[3] Within this chapter, we adopt the most comprehensive definition of liberalism supplied by Hauerwas:

> In the most general terms I understand liberalism to be that impulse deriving from the Enlightenment project to free all people from the chains of their historical particularity in the name of freedom. As an epistemological position liberalism is the attempt to defend a foundationalism in order to free reason from being determined by any particularistic tradition. Politically liberalism makes the individual the supreme unit of society, thus making the political task the securing of cooperation between arbitrary units of desire.[4]

More specifically, Hauerwas follows Anthony Giddens in identifying the liberal social and political arrangement with the nation-state system, which, according to Giddens, is characterized by a fourfold "institutional clustering," namely, heightened surveillance, capitalistic enterprise, industrial production, and the consolidation of centralized control of the means of violence.[5]

1. Liberal Politics and False Universalism: The Optional Nature of the Nation-State

Liberal political thinking embodies a flight from the particular that is correlative to a false universalism. Hauerwas's response to this false universalism can be organized around three critical shortcomings. In the first place, Hauerwas has critically noted liberalism's inability to explain the territoriality of the nation-state. Much of modern political thought, for example, continues to rely for a justification of the state and liberal politics on seventeenth- to eighteenth-century political theorists and their universalistic and abstract notions of social contract, natural rights, and obligations.[6] These dominant accounts, however, trade on a false universalism that fails to account for the nation-state's history and its particularity. A case in point is the lack of attention to the nation-state's territoriality. Quoting O'Donovan, Hauerwas notes that liberal politics

> spring from a tradition of nation-states which have defined themselves in strictly territorial terms. But the political philosophies, which ought to offer us a conceptual structure for understanding this element of our political experience, have almost nothing to say about the territorial character of political units. On the contrary, it has been the preoccupation of European political philosophy since Hobbes, both in its liberal and collectionist traditions, to interpret society not in terms of its natural determinants, but in relation to the will, whether individual or common. This has resulted in a strange abstractness of intellectual political thought running counter to the strongly territorial instincts of pre-reflective political activity. . . . It is hard to comprehend the point of organizing our formal political discussion in purely placeless concepts—human rights, democratic representation, ideological pluralism, etc.—and treating those who want to talk about land as though they had sunk beneath the level of responsible discourse.[7]

The point of the citation above is that even though actual political experience and rhetoric betrays persistent concerns which people have for the *places* about which they care, such concerns are nevertheless either inadequately represented or systematically avoided in formal political discourse. The latter, in a typical Lockean or liberal tradition, continues to characterize political community as a legal and political pact between free and equal individuals, i.e., as the creation of the human will, unmediated by natural, physical, or cultural circumstances.

According to Hauerwas, this shortcoming is not unique to political theory, but endemic to the very Enlightenment project which attempted to "free all people from the chains of their historical particularity in the name of freedom."[8] However, the "placelessness" characteristic of liberal political theory is a noteworthy shortcoming, given, as we have just observed, the tradition of the nation-states, which have "understood themselves in strictly territorial terms." In fact, as Giddens has shown, "territoriality" is centrally unique to the nation-state.[9] "Borders" (in the sense of precisely defined territorial boundaries), he argues, are found only with the emergence of nation-states. Traditional states have "frontiers" (peripheral areas of the state in which the political authority of the center is diffuse or thinly spread) but not "borders."[10]

By failing to account for "locality," most liberal accounts of the nation-state make issues like patriotism or nationalism seem irrational, since "the very terms of the justification of the community are meant to deny that the goods we enjoy are particular to this land and history."[11] An even more determinate shortcoming is that although local instincts are at work as strongly as ever, by failing to recognize and acknowledge these local interests, the liberal political tradition deprives its subjects of the relevant skills with which to subject these local sentiments to an ordered and rational assessment. Recent outbreaks of nationalist violence and xenophobia in Europe following the collapse of communism bear significant witness to this shortcoming.[12]

The inability by liberal political theory to account for locality and particularity tends to lead to another key shortcoming of liberalism, namely, to an imperialistic self-conception and practice. It is this totalizing self-conception that we referred to, in the previous chapter, as the liberal protestant metanarrative. Then the concern was to show how the metanarrative effectively conceals the 'local' and 'particular', through a positivist social theory which portrays the nation-state as the inevitable climax of the progressive working out of social reason and political organization. In this chapter, we need to highlight the violence within this metanarrative. To be sure, this violence is not unique to liberalism; it is endemic to any metanarrative posture. It is, for instance, detectable within some versions of the natural law theory. As Hauerwas remarks, "violence and coercion become conceptually intelligible from a natural law standpoint. The universal presumptions of natural law make it more difficult to accept the very existence of those who disagree with us."[13] What is true of natural law theory is even more valid of the Enlightenment in its attempt to defeat the "particularistic obscurantism" of traditions in the name of the universal. But it is equally true of any attempt to overcome liberalism by offering an equally totalizing counternarrative. This is the key reason why Hauerwas, even as he remains impressed by and on the whole indebted to Milbank's work, feels uneasy about Milbank's metanarrative style. Such a grand narrative as Milbank's risks not only a relapse into what Loughlin has called a "new narratological foundationalism,"[14] it encourages a form of violence. Hence, Hauerwas's uneasiness:

> There is a very serious problem about the character of Milbank's whole project as he attempts to (out-narrate) supply a counter-narrative to that

of liberalism. Does he [not] reproduce exactly the violence of liberalism by trying to write such a grand narrative of how we have gotten in our peculiar straights today? In a sense his project is not unlike MacIntyre's project in *Whose Justice? Which Rationality?* Obviously in my own work I have tried to chip-away at liberalism one piece at a time.[15]

The coerciveness inherent within such a metanarrative style is often the attempt to render certain and necessary what are just contingent stories and commitments:

> Our attempt to rid our life of luck is the source of our greatest violence. The word Christians use to describe how our lives are constituted by such luck is grace. Yet grace does not remove, as the Greeks [and the Enlightenment] tried to remove through theory, the contingency of our existence.[16]

Within liberalism, the potential violence of her foundational and metanarrative quest is made even more real by liberalism's affiliation to a capitalistic economic philosophy, which portrays the individual atomistically as a unit of desire—a stranger and self-interested competitor against other self-interested units in the struggle for survival and over limited resources. Historically, this struggle for survival has often taken the familiar forms of domination and extermination of the other, to which the merciless killing of Native Americans[17] and the Jewish holocaust[18] stand as ready historical lessons. The same domination continues to take physical, economic and symbolic forms in the so-called Third World. Even the very naming of a "Third World" assumes the power to determine memory in how the social, cultural, economic, and political story of that part of the world should continue to unfold.[19] It is therefore ironic that within liberalism's logocentric positivism and market hegemony, tolerance (often celebrated with panache as the key virtue) turns into a subtle form of intolerance.[20] From this perspective, it becomes clear that the accusation of "tribalism" often leveled against Hauerwas and others who seek to question the validity and coherence of the liberal metanarrative is nothing but an *ad hominem* attack meant to protect this social-political arrangement. For, as Harvey notes, following De Certeau, "ethnological isolation is also a fundamental move in the hegemonic discourse of modernity."[21] The problem is that as an *ad hominem* attack, the charge of tribalism spares those who make it from seriously and frankly dealing with the false universalism of liberal theory and practice.

Any serious attempt to overcome such false universalism must start with an adequate attention to particularity: "Without the recovery of such locality, of such particularity, we will find that we lack the means . . . to challenge those that would make war in the name of universal ideals."[22] Although Hauerwas makes this remark in relation to the particularity of the ecclesial community, its wider implications are obvious. Without a proper recognition of the locality and particularity that marks *all* our projects and undertakings, those projects will continue to be marked by a structural potential for violence.

The realization of the historicity, contingency, and particularity of *all* our commitments and stories should not be seen as undermining their validity and significance. On the contrary, a proper appreciation of contingency and particularity provides a critical self-consciousness that can enable one to survey the limits of one's stories and engagements. What should be noted, however, is that a mere intellectual acknowledgment of contingency or particularity is not enough to generate this attitude, as Rorty seems to assume.[23] Only by finding oneself in a community whose practices and story generate sufficient moral skills and openness can one finds the means to live with finitude and contingency in a way that avoids both extremes of enlightened essentialism/metanarrative, on the one hand, and frivolous fascination, on the other.[24]

The third shortcoming of liberalism follows from the above two considerations. For, once this limited character of liberalism is exposed, then it becomes clear that the charge of "tribalism" raised against any positive argument for historical traditions may be nothing but liberalism's attempt to hide its own particularity, what Hauerwas calls the very "tribalism of the West or Europe or the First World."[25] If such an indictment sounds strange, Hauerwas suggests, it is because

> we are not accustomed to thinking of the voice of the empire as a sectarian voice. But so it is when it serves only a narrow interest. 'Empire as sect' is a theme worth pursuing in our own situation because it may be suggested that the voice of American power, for example, claims to be the voice of general well-being and may in a number of cases be only the voice of a narrow range of economic and political interest. The ideological guise is effective if large numbers of people can be kept from noticing the narrow base of real interest.[26]

That is why, for Hauerwas, the assumption of the primacy or the inevitability of the nation-state arrangement is "the most nefarious brand of tribalism of all. . . . Tribalism is not the church determined to serve God rather than Caesar. Tribalism is the United States of America, which sets up artificial boundaries and defends them with murderous intensity."[27] The point of the above criticism is of course mostly critical: to cast aspersions on the moral legitimacy of the nation-state, particularly on the assumption of a "neutral" politics which provides a justification for a democratic pluralist society. For, as Hauerwas has noted, within the liberal social-political arrangement, the so-called neutral sphere is already colonized (to use Habermas's language) by substantive liberal and market values which, under the rubric of "neutrality," effectively deny a voice to other substantive conceptions and values. That is why anyone who steps outside of that space, by appealing to other considerations, say religious values, is not regarded as a fully enfranchised participant in "public" discussion, over which reason is supposed to preside.[28]

This realization that the appeal to "neutrality" always serves particular interests has led Hauerwas to question the normative appeal to pluralism:

> I do not like the language of pluralism. Where are you standing? Pluralism is rabbis arguing the Torah. That is pluralism, that is genuine disagreement, within a tradition. What we live in is not pluralism. . . . It is very interesting that MacIntyre used the language of "fragments" to refer to our situation. He did not describe it as pluralism. We live amid fragments. I don't think we live in a pluralistic world. Pluralism presupposes knowing where you are standing when you are characterizing the diversity.[29]

And so, the appeal to "pluralism," just like the claim for "neutrality" and, negatively, the accusation of "tribalism" or "sectarianism," operates as a policing tactic which simply exerts a rhetorical drag in the so-called liberal direction. Accordingly, these policing tactics assume the priority of the Western-inspired nation-state and the Western-inspired capitalistic economy. In this way they mask a "local" agenda and pass it off as the agenda of everyone. Moreover, by assuming a hegemonic position, the appeal to "pluralism" domesticates genuine conflict and makes any meaningful disagreement impossible.

There is a need to slightly recap the foregoing argument so as to amplify the critical force which Hauerwas's case against liberalism's false universalism might play within a historical conception of the moral life. Both the traditional way of posing the question of the relation between religion and ethics, and the charge of political tribalism raised against any attempt to set aside the 'problem' of religion and ethics, have been shown to involve and assume the primacy and/or inevitability of the liberal social-political arrangement. By critically noting how a "false universalism" marks its very self-conception and operations, Hauerwas shows that the "nation-state, especially as we know it today, is not an ontological necessity for human living."[30] In our treatment, this optional nature of the nation-state has been pursued indirectly by pointing to (i) its own "locality" or territoriality (to which liberal political theory remains conspicuously blind), (ii) its limited story (which it tries to supplant by metanarrative singularity), and (iii) the "local" interests it promotes (but ideologically hides under the guise of "neutrality"). This indirect critique not only helps to make obvious the philosophical shortcomings of liberal political theory and practice but also confirms the historicity of this particular social arrangement. As historical, there is nothing inevitable about this social-political arrangement. Rather, its special features as well as any widespread appeal it may currently enjoy derive from contingent factors.[31]

Where does the optional nature of the liberal social-political arrangement leave us in terms of political discourse? One immediate realization is that it dispossesses us of the dominant political vocabulary and metaphors of struggle for "power," "interest," or "rights" through "neutral" procedures, and involves us in a novel and distinctive conception of politics as an attempt to live out a shared conception of the good life. Hauerwas's preoccupation with witness and the imagination as correlative political tasks becomes intelligible only within this comprehensive understanding of politics as a "conversation" embodied within the practices of everyday life. It is to this (re)conception of politics that we now turn.

2. Politics, Imagination, Witness, and "Public" Responsibility

Politics as Conversation

In order to appreciate the critical role that the notion of witness plays as a political category in Hauerwas's reflection, one needs to place it within his overall (re)conception of politics. Politics, according to Hauerwas, "is the conversation necessary for a people to discover the goods they have in common."[32] Two mutually inclusive aspects—conversation and the common good—pertain to this understanding of politics. First, the common good is not an abstract, philosophical idea. Rather, the very nature and pursuit of the common good is embedded within the concrete practices of everyday life. Secondly, the common good is theoretically undefinable. Hauerwas has used the metaphor of journey to underscore this aspect of the common good. Just as people on a journey do not have an exact knowledge of where the journey will lead, so "the *telos* in fact is a narrative, and the good is not so much a clearly defined 'end' as it is a sense of the journey on which that community finds itself. In political terms it means that the conversation of community is not *about* some good still to be realized, but the conversation *is* the good insofar as it is through the conversation that the community keeps faithful to the narrative."[33] What this MacIntyrean reconstruction confirms is the conception that politics is grounded in a "shared way of life." It is this common vision within a particular narrative-tradition that makes possible a conception of politics as a conversation—with a possibility of pluralistic interpretations and genuine disagreement.

However, such a conception of politics as a "conversation" for the discovery of the goods held in *common* seems to be in fundamental tension with liberal politics, which continues to rely on the Hobbesian and Lockean assumption of self-interested individuals without any agreed upon conception of the good. Such an assumption not only explains the liberal penchant for procedural formality, power brokerage, and interest-balancing, it also, in a self-fulfilling manner, ends up forming people into precisely that: "aggregates of self-interested individuals" who relate to each other as either complete strangers or interest bearers and bargainers rather than as participants within a shared process of discovering goods.[34]

It could be argued that such a critique represents the standard cliché communitarian attack formulated in contrast to liberal theories of the 1970s, which neither attends to the complexity of any particular liberal theory nor faces the changed and diversified nature of more recent liberal theories.[35] Rasmusson, for one, points out that more recent liberal theories have abandoned the idea of liberalism as a neutral option in the absence of any common conception of the good, and defends it in terms of its own specific conception of the good—institutions and practices that support this good (forms of government, economic institutions, etc.) and a set of virtues, e.g., equality, courage, liberty, law-abidingness, independence, tolerance, etc.[36] More recently, Musschenga, following Stout (who himself follows Rawls), has even defended "overlapping consensus" as the common good of liberalism.[37] According to Musschenga, liberalism is a tradition whose good is moral pluralism. His argument is that both comprehensive moral traditions and liberalism need each other. "Liberal morality is as the soil on a hill in which all kinds of trees grow. For their flourishing all the trees are dependent on the same soil in which they are rooted. At the same time the soil needs the trees. Their roots keep it together. Otherwise erosion would take place. Erosion will only not occur if there are enough trees planted in the soil."[38]

There is a positive element in the above attempts to defend the common good of liberalism. Such attempts seem to signify that liberalism has given up its false universalism and come to accept its own status as a historical and particular tradition with a particular vision and *telos*. The problem with these attempts, however, is that they fail to see that once the historical particularity of liberalism has been accepted, then there is no ground from which one can claim that the good of liberalism lies in its being a "tradition of all traditions," or "master tradition" which provides commensuration for other historical traditions.

Moreover, it is not clear whether such defenses of a liberal common good can be sustained within liberalism itself without sacrificing a central liberal commitment to fair (because neutral) procedural social arrangements. Accordingly, liberal apologies fail to get to the heart of Hauerwas's critique, which is, in the final analysis, directed to liberalism's pretensions of "neutrality." According to Hauerwas, the liberal claim to devise procedural mechanisms that are neutral in respect to any particular conception of the good greatly undermines the conversation that politics is meant to be. For, as Benjamin Barber has more candidly noted, "it is neutrality that destroys dialogue, for the power of political talk lies in its creativity, its variety, its openness and flexibility, its inventiveness, its capacity for discovery, its subtlety and complexity, its potential for empathetic and affective expression—in other words, in its deeply paradoxical, some would say dialectical, character."[39] Rather than ensuring 'fairness' for all the voices, the claim of neutrality simply creates an inherent bias and rids the conversation of room for any meaningful or substantial disagreement. As has been shown, the very claim of "neutrality" is a policing tactic which effectively denies a voice to all substantive conceptions—with the exception of those arising from or serving the market economy or liberal ideals. In other words, liberalism, *pace* Musschenga, cannot be a "neutral" soil equally hospitable to all trees!

Imagination as a Moral and Political Task

The pretensions to "neutrality" partly explain the predominance of the liberal social arrangement. For, the more substantive conceptions of the good are privatized or denied public expression under the guise for "neutrality," the more the liberal metanarrative becomes dominant and self-fulfilling. The result has been the lack of a conceivable alternative for public philosophy. What has been consistently denied throughout this work is that one should see this inability to conceive of an alternative as a vindication of the inevitability of the liberal arrangement as such. Rather, the lack of alternative conceptions has been shown to be due, in large part, to the various policing cues by which the liberal story has successfully concealed its own particularity and the local interests served by its arrangement.

It is at this point that liberalism becomes hegemonic to the point of becoming pernicious, as the first epigraph of this chapter suggests. In it, McWhorter aptly warns: "Everything is dangerous . . . everything is risky. . . . But the greatest danger occurs when forms of thought and practice persist without challenge, when one way of thinking becomes so powerful that we lose sight of all other possibilities, when one way of thinking totalizes itself to the exclusion of all else."[40] It is against this background that Hauerwas suggests that the greatest challenge of moral and political philosophy is not to devise realistic solutions. It is to liberate "man's imagination so that it can build new utopias different from all current models of society and therefore capable of contemplating the liberation of the world. When utopias are not imagined, ethics is reduced to solving problems within the established system."[41] From this perspective, the reasons for Hauerwas's incipient quarrel with Situation Ethics in particular and quandary ethics in general, become all the more apparent. By framing their ethical preoccupation around quandaries of the sort "What would you do if . . . ?" these accounts not only abstract agency from one's character and personal history, but they stifle and freeze one's imagination within the range of narrowly determined options. Admittedly, much of the attraction within these standard accounts of ethics draws from their "realistic" solutions. And so, by radically questioning them, Hauerwas is questioning the very appeals to moral and political realism.

Hauerwas's rejection of realism is significant for at least two related reasons. "First, it reveals the nakedness of the king, for too often 'realism' has been used as a magic incantation to avoid analyzing what ethically is at stake. The appeals to 'realism' are sometimes nothing more than the assertion of the facticity of the status quo and its necessary acceptance."[42] Secondly, in line with Hauerwas's pacifist stance,[43] the uncritical acceptance of the *status quo* very often means that we remain captured by the self-imposed necessity of violence: "The problem is not that living in a more peaceful world is not attainable, but that our imaginations have long been schooled out of such a hope by a false 'realism'."[44] In other words, the call to be realistic is often intellectually constraining, as the imagination too quickly surrenders to the current alternatives, which often are nothing more than ameliorative strategies developed to solve specific problems without providing resources for thinking critically about what a morally substantive society might look like.

In the final analysis however, both reasons for calling an end to "realism" are unified within, and made possible by, Hauerwas's substantive understanding of ethics as vision:

> more importantly, the rejection of 'political realism' reminds us that our political philosophy and ethics is and always has been an attempt to learn a way of 'seeing' political phenomenon, not just in the sense of seeing what it is, but in the sense of being able to evaluate the 'what is' in a wider context of significance.[45]

The "wider context" here must be understood as a reference to a social vision of one's narrative tradition. Bringing an end to "realism" is thus a call for moral/political philosophy to help people "learn to think in utopian terms,"[46] which is nothing but to learn to think imaginatively. For Hauerwas, there is no more urgent moral/political task than this:

> I am not simply trying to give new answers to old questions, but I am trying to change the questions. That forces me to develop new, or at least different, ways of putting matters that are not easily learned. . . . To change the questions involves nothing less than learning to speak differently.[47]

Much has already been said about imagination as a moral task (chapter 3). What we need to underscore here is how a substantive response to the challenge of tribalism requires the defense of imagination as a political task. In the coming section we shall provide a concrete display of Hauerwas's understanding of how such a task can be realized by the Christian story through its concrete social vision and the community and the practices it engenders. Before we do so, however, we need to rehearse Hauerwas's understanding of imagination so as to provide a transition from the hither-to theoretical argument of our work to its more concrete display.

As was noted, moral and political imagination is not so much "something we have in our minds. Rather, the imagination is a pattern of possibilities fostered within a community by the stories and correlative commitments that make it what it is."[48] Accordingly (and as we have already noted), moral imagination is not so much about the *fantastic* reimagings of a mental faculty, but as a "pattern of *possibilities*," it is fostered by the "concrete habits and language of a community." One, of course, realizes that here the stress is not so much on the individual but on the *community* whose "story and correlative commitments" make available these possibilities. At stake in this understanding of moral imagination is the affirmation of a community or tradition as a cultural-linguistic form which becomes a source of imaginative possibilities in two ways: first, for the members of the community, by situating their imaginative self-expression within the range of a community's vision and language. To the liberal ear such 'situating' might sound like an unjustified curbing of an individual's unbounded 'free play', but given what was noted of the dialectical tension between language and experience within a living tradition (chapter 6) the 'placing' is a condition of possibility for the very exercise and extension of one's imagination. Secondly, to those within another community, the presence of an alternative community with distinctive practices provides 'live options' in terms of novel possibilities, patterns of life, language, and self-understanding. Only from within this second sense of identifying imagination with a community and its story does Hauerwas's priority of "witness" become intelligible as a political category.

Imagination and the Critical Role of Witness

In the first section, we were able, through a theoretical account, to expose liberalism's false universalism and thus to make the optional nature of the liberal arrangement a bygone conclusion. Important as this theoretical strategy is, it must give way to the critical and decisive role of 'witness'. For, ultimately, the optional nature of liberal politics cannot become obvious "unless there is another conversation behind the wall which gives critical distance and standing ground for an *alternative assessment.*"[49] That is, unless one comes in contact with concrete communities which embody an alternative story which engenders an alternative conversation [politics] prioritizing an alternative set of commitments and practices, there can be no imaginative fostering of new utopias and possibilities for a societal vision different from one's own. In other words, only by the existence of, and one's contact with, an alternative set of practices, can one's imagination be enabled to 'see' new and live options for what had been hitherto resignedly accepted as 'realism'.

That is why for Hauerwas,

> the church does not exist to provide an *ethos* for democracy or any other form of social organization, but stands as a political alternative to every nation, witnessing to the kind of social life possible for those that have been formed by the story of Christ.[50]

However, it is only by being a distinctive community that the Church can provide an "alternative assessment" to the liberal story of what, and how, it means to be human.

Three important innovations pertain to this use of witness in Hauerwas's reflection. First, it must be noted that "alternative assessment" does not and cannot mean that Hauerwas is suggesting that we replace the state with church bureaucracy, the market with charity, and rights with love. That would be to substitute one false universalism with another. At stake within the call for an "alternative assessment" is the priority of local politics—the existence of particular and contingent social visions that provide one another, without the security of one commensurating 'tradition of traditions', with alternative possibilities and witness.

Secondly, even though the notion of "witness" is developed by Hauerwas within a primarily theological context, and specifically in relation to the Church community, there seems to be no reason why, formally, it cannot validly be employed as a political notion, in relation to various imaginative and alternative possibilities offered by "communities of witness" to the liberal social arrangement. One thinks of, for example, those 'local' traditions which, because they remain recalcitrant to the liberal logic, can bring the latter to recognize its limits by "witnessing," i.e., embodying an alternative social vision.[51]

Thirdly, just as with the case for imagination, Hauerwas is able to wrest the notion of witness away from its usual individualistic connotations and place it within the context of a community's vision and practices. Granted, a personal sense of witness on the part of the individuals of a given tradition is irreplaceable, especially in as much as it dialectically confirms and extends the practice of a community. However, since the former is grounded in, and only made possible by, the communal practice, witness for Hauerwas does not so much denote a personal religious mission as a social embodiment of a particular vision, which is able to provide an *alternative assessment* to other equally particular visions.

An even more positive and comprehensive sense of "witness" is the one that coheres with the all-pervasive sense of politics within Hauerwas's reflection. In the absence of any neutral assessment or high ground (not even within liberalism), everything turns into politics—not in the liberal sense of regulating the unbidden struggle for power,[52] but in the sense of a tradition seeking, through its everyday practices, to live out the vision entailed by its narrative. This explains the social and political significance Hauerwas accords to the small acts of everyday life—of taking time to enjoy a walk with a friend, to read Trollope's novels, to maintain universities, to have and care for children, to worship God, to grieve at illness and death, to talk to a stranger, etc. Such "gestures" are, according to Hauerwas, a far more "determinative *political* challenge" than power struggles and large-scale social strategies.[53]

The appreciation of the ordinary and of the everyday confirms the sense of politics as a conversation. We rehearse this conception here for two reasons: first, to underscore its antiliberal nature; politics in this sense is not primarily about deciding between competing interests, but about nurturing a particular kind of life, "an attempt to implement some partisan [traditioned] vision."[54] The novelty within this conception lies in the transition from "interest" to "vision" as the central metaphor for politics. Concretely, this transition involves a reassessment of the nature and role of political philosophy. On this approach, political philosophy does not only provide a justification or foundation for political society and activity, but narratively "clarifies and concretizes given normative contents," i.e., the reasons within the *ethos* of particular socities.[55]

Secondly, since between the different traditioned visions there is no neutral adjudication, the issue of "Whose vision? Which tradition?" finally turns into one of witness, by which the various traditions attempt to "out-witness" one another through a display of the richness of their story, which, in the final analysis, can only be known by the variety of practices and the richness of character each engenders. This is the sense in which witness can be said to cohere with the all-pervasive sense of politics in Hauerwas's reflection. Next, we shall try to make more explicit the prospects and limits of this sense of witness by anticipating three challenges that could be raised against Hauerwas's reduction of everything to politics.

Politics and Witness: Critical Issues

The first challenge concerns the claim to substitute "vision" for "interest" as the primary metaphor for politics. It could be argued that Hauerwas might have recognized that partisan politics is what is at stake in liberal politics even within the so-called "neutral" public sphere, but by turning all politics into an attempt to implement a partisan vision has he advanced beyond 'interest politics'? One might suggest that whatever Hauerwas set out to accomplish, he ends up legitimating a new form of pluralism: one that shifts the strategic focus from the individual subject to the "semiotically coherent" tradition or community, thus legitimating a pluralism similar to what Lowi has called "interest group liberalism."[56]

Such criticism would be grossly unfair, since it fails to realize that "interest politics" is largely determined by a liberal anthropology that sees community as an aggregate of individuals. We have already observed that this is an anthropology Hauerwas tries to overcome. Liberal anthropology, we have seen, is tied up with an unqualified view (psychology) of individual separateness and self-responsibility. As Sheldon Wolin notes:

> interest politics dissolves the idea of the citizen as one for whom it is natural to join together with other citizens to act for purposes related to a general community and substitutes the idea of individuals who are grouped according to conflicting interests. The individual is not first and foremost a civic creature bound by preexisting ties to those who share the same history, the same general association, and the same fate. He is instead a business executive, a teamster, a feminist, an office worker, farmer, or homosexual whose immediate identity naturally divides him or her from others. As a member of an interest group, the individual is given an essentially anticivic education. He is taught that the first duty is to support the self-interest of the group because politics is nothing but a struggle for advantage.[57]

The view of the person that emerges from this conception of interest politics is one of an unencumbered self which can objectively survey its interests, desires, and goals and thereby *decide* to form a community with other selves who might happen to share the same goals. With these two assumptions of "self" and "interest" as the starting point, the community that is formed by interest politics can be neither constitutive nor permanent, but only an occasional gathering (group) of like-minded individuals.[58]

Hauerwas's (re)conception of politics, on the other hand, is dependent on his substantive understanding of persons as constituted through a tradition not of one's direct choosing but which, nevertheless, constitutes a shared way of life and interpretation. What is at stake within such a tradition is not the pursuit of "interest" as if it were an advantage or a determinate set of objectives, but the social embodiment of concrete skills and possibilities made available by its central narrative(s). Thus, the substitution of "interest" with "vision" as a primary political metaphor involves at the same time leaving behind a liberal psychology and anthropology.[59]

The second and perhaps even more formidable challenge would be whether this talk about "alternative assessment" or "witness" could be simply a sophisticated attempt by Hauerwas to evade the crucial question of whether (and how) the Church should be involved in the "public" life.[60] This would seem to confirm the fear that Hauerwas, at best, provides Christians with no skills to deal with complex public choices and, at worst, encourages their withdrawal from public responsibility.[61]

Given Hauerwas's affirmation of particularity, one would have to realize that to begin by asking whether and how the Church should be involved in "public" life is to have already made a threefold mistake: a descriptive, a sociological, and an epistemological one. First, from a descriptive point of view, it is not clear that any practice can fail in some sense to be public, given that any action or practice is socially determined. Practices, therefore, have a public character, as the case of Christian worship may help to illuminate. Even though it is said to be private in that it is likely only to make sense to people with some familiarity to the practices, worship is public in more than one sense. It is public in the sense that people come together to worship; it is public in that coming together makes a statement that others can interpret; and it is public in the sense that outsiders can sit in.[62] And so, from a descriptive point of view, the question is not 'public or not public', but "What sort of public?"[63]

Sociologically, as was shown in the previous chapter, the question of "public" involvement accepts the questionable Weberian assumption of a Christianity whose purely "religious" base can be clearly isolated from its "social" manifestation, or a Christianity from which base implications can be drawn for influencing the more primary "social" reality. This standard conception of "public" also seems to be wedded to a foundational epistemological dualism of particularity and universality. That is why the question of whether theology should have a "public" character not only has the same formal structure, but also shares the same substantive content as the philosophical questions of the relation between *is* and *ought*, or between *religion* and *ethics*, or the corresponding question of the relation between *particularity* and *universality*. Positively, it must be acknowledged, though, that these questions are motivated by a recognition of the importance of particular and historically contingent convictions, practices, and community visions which inevitably (in)form one's ideals. Their problem, however, is to assume that this positivity is *only* a starting point that can and must be transcended because it is assumed (with a moribund epistemological foundationalism, it turns out) that, in as far as any perspective is an *ethical* one, its truth value and validity must be justified by publicly (universally) accessible reasons and warrants.

In chapter 5 we explored the problematic assumptions behind these epistemological dualisms. The goal of this exploration was to affirm the inescapable contingency and particularity not only of our starting point, but also of any forms of justification. Since there is no way to transcend or escape the particular, "public" can never be understood as a topologically higher plane of engagement with others, managed by some "conversational restraint" by which one is bound to agree in advance to "say nothing at all about" fundamental disagreements.[64] Nor is "public" an invocation of a philosophical attitude (Categorical, Universalization, etc.), which one adopts by stripping one's reasons and arguments of any particular associations. "Public," just like universality, is a name of a *direction* rather than a *terminus*, a mission rather than a clear picture of the goal. "Public" is the very *process* by which one allows the practices of a particular tradition or polity to act as a critic as well as be enriched by coming into contact with different peoples and histories.

Thus, the crucial question is how to be a 'living' tradition, i.e., a community suffused with a normative creative tension and sufficient openness to allow such contact with the other. Such contact or 'witness' cannot promise the same neat and secure, albeit false, resolution as one finds in the universality promised by a "shared conception of rationality" (including the universality covertly operative within some forms of postmodernism, under the disguised forms of "the very nature of language," "communicative competence," or "ideal speech situation").[65] In the absence of these or any other foundations, there is just no way to escape the permanent hermeneutical predicament of particular languages, communities, and traditions.

In relation to the question of public responsibility, what must therefore be realized is that Hauerwas is engaged in a *redefinition* of the public itself. According to this redefinition, the opposition is not between public and private, church and world, but between different communities—different stories, different forms of politics: "alternate social configurations which afford very different possibilities for being and becoming human in the world. It is precisely for this reason that Hauerwas argues that the Church does not develop a "public" theology, but in her very 'tactical'[66] existence in the world, as well as by her ability to carry on a conversation attentive to the concrete, contextual, complex, and all-too-often conflictual circumstances of everyday life, she provides a publicly available "alternative assessment" of what it means to be human.

The third, and to many the most formidable challenge, has to do with Hauerwas's apparent inability to realize that to (re)conceive politics around the particular is to mire the political landscape with irresolvable conflicts and violence. How is one to manage the violence that arises out of the confrontation of partisan visions? There is no easy solution to the problem of violence, but we need to question, as Hauerwas does, the two assumptions on which this challenge is premised.

First, the challenge of violence is premised on the assumption that if there is no place outside the various histories we inherit to "ground" an ethic, then we shall inevitably be caught in a web of warring communities with no possibility of rational agreement. But there is no reason to despair of peace once it has been shown that there is no "ground" outside the particular commitments and traditions. What makes an ordered peace possible is not some *a priori* universal principles of reason, but "people being in contact with one another."[67] We are thrown once again to the slow, uncertain but unavoidable demand for actual dialogue and witness.

Secondly, following Milbank, Hauerwas has more recently come to realize that the challenge of violence is premised on the assumption that difference and indeterminacy necessarily imply violence. However, to so assume is to already subscribe to a particular form of political realism—one that is grounded in an ontology of violence. What is needed is an alternative politics in which, because it is grounded on an ontology of peace and communality, difference and indeterminacy do not necessarily imply violence. The ontology at stake is what is implied by Hauerwas's central conviction for pacifism. These are significant, if still unsubstantiated claims that need to be concretely argued and defended, and whose implications still need to be spelled out in a separate section.

3. *Mythos*, Politics, and a Metaphysics of Nonviolent Witness

This section serves three purposes. In the first place, it is an extended and sustained response to the challenge of violence identified at the end of the last section. In outline, the response runs as follows: Hauerwas's (re)conception of politics in terms of particular and contingent visions and witness need not necessarily lead to violence. The assumption that it does is dependent on a particular metaphysics that reads indeterminacy, contingency, and difference as necessarily conflictual. But as Milbank (and following him, Hauerwas) has shown, such reading of reality is tied up with, and based on, a *mythos*—a particular narrative of "in the beginning." Once such a narrative is accepted, it legitimates a particular form of politics (liberalism), in which conflictual relations and assumptions are reproduced and confirmed, while being declared inevitable. Hauerwas's pacifism is an attempt to supplant this politics with an alternative politics which is equally founded on a *mythos*. However, unlike the liberal *mythos*, this (Christian) alternative is able to generate nonviolent political expectations and practice because it assumes a harmonious sociality of differences "in the beginning."

Secondly, the section helps to tie together the critical and constructive parts of this chapter, and helps to advance one central argument: The difference between any two forms of politics (liberal and ecclesial) is not that one is based on *mythos* and the other on "realistic" considerations—all politics is founded on *mythos*—but rather, a matter of different practices generated by the respective narrative or *mythos*. In other words, the differences between social and political configurations is a matter that can only be decided contingently, by narrative superiority.

Thirdly, the specific novelty within this argument lies in fleshing out the implications of *mythos*, metaphysics, and vision for political philosophy. The immediate interest in such explication, however, will be to develop Hauerwas's pacifism as a coherent intellectual and social-ethical position. And, given the lack of any serious attention given to pacifism within the philosophical tradition, it will be necessary to dedicate a little more time and space to this point.

Pacifism as a Form of Politics

Pacifism, according to Hauerwas, is "any position that involves the disavowal of violence as a means to secure otherwise legitimate ends."[68] Hauerwas's pacifist position has only gradually developed, reluctantly at first, through the key influence of the Mennonite John Howard Yoder.[69] At present, however, pacifism determines Hauerwas's whole theological reflection, both methodologically and substantially. As he says, "nonviolence is not just one implication among others that can be drawn from our Christian beliefs; it is at the very heart of our understanding of God."[70]

Like Yoder's, Hauerwas's pacifism is not based on some vague and rather sentimental appeals to the essential goodness of man, the nature of love, or on an ideal for universal brotherhood. Neither is it based on some absolute commitment to life as an end in itself, nor on some pragmatic calculations or absolute principles of an ethical ideal. "Pacifism based on such principles not only tends to be legalistic and self-righteous," but, abstracted from wider communal and/or theological convictions, often, this pacifism enlists violence as a way to achieve its ideals.[71] By assuming that Hauerwas's pacifism is founded on such an ethical ideal, critics have found Hauerwas's pacifist position both "naive," and "extraordinarily confused in [its] approach to politics."[72] Such a pacifist stance, it is often pointed out, is "frustrating at the level of guidance to action" in a world where the issues of "how much butter" must be balanced against "How many guns?" Some even suspect that behind this pacifism lies a puritan attempt to withdraw from public responsibility, which, given our contingent existence, must necessarily remain tragic, as evil must sometimes be tolerated as the price for achieving a relative good.[73]

This charge of social withdrawal is particularly misleading. How can one claim that pacifism involves withdrawal from public responsibility, Hauerwas has responded, unless one believes that "all politics is a cover for violence." Moreover,

> it is my contention that politics only begins with such a disavowal [of violence], for only then are we forced to listen to the other, thus beginning conversations necessary for discovering goods in common. From my perspective, far from requiring a withdrawal from the political arena, pacifism demands strenuous political engagement.[74]

In any case, the validity of all of the above criticisms is based on a serious misunderstanding of both Hauerwas's ethical project and the nature of his pacifism. First, the criticisms seem to be an indirect way of forcing Hauerwas to be "realistic." But that is precisely what Hauerwas has resisted all along by insisting that his work should not be seen as "simply trying to give new answers to old questions," but an attempt "to change the questions," so as to imbibe the moral imagination with new narrative possibilities.[75]

Secondly, such criticisms assume pacifism to be an ethical ideal or posture (optional) that one adopts within liberal politics. To so conceive it, however, is to abstract Hauerwas's pacifism from its wider theological context of the story and concrete practices of a particular community (Church), and is thus to miss its primary political intent. Hauerwas's pacifism is rooted beyond the question of whether we should or should not use violence, but in the deeper question of "what sort of people" we must be to embody a particular story. As Hauerwas notes, "Christian nonviolence or pacifism does not name a position; rather, it denotes a set of convictions and corresponding practices of a particular kind of people."[76]

Pacifism thus embodies a form of politics, which points to a particular kind of community, formed by a particular kind of story or vision, namely, the story of a nonviolent "in the beginning" or creation:

> The reason I believe Christians have been given the permission, that is, why it is good news for us, to live without resort to violence is that by doing so we live as God lives. Therefore pacifism is not first of all a prohibition, but an affirmation that God wills to rule his creation not through violence and coercion but by love. Moreover he has called us to be part of his rule by calling us into a community that is governed by peace.[77]

We wish to highlight the sense involved in the claim that pacifism is a form of politics by attending to two central aspects within the above citation, namely, the political (ecclesial) context of pacifism, and the significance of "creation" as an indication of the narrative that sustains this nonviolent community. Only by understanding the interconnection between these two aspects can one appreciate the novelty, as well as the far-reaching implications of Hauerwas's claim for the Church as an alternative (pacifist) witness, a "contrast model" to liberal politics.

For, abstracted from the existence of a community and its practices, pacifism is unintelligible. That is why for Hauerwas, pacifism is not, in the first place, a spiritualistic or moralistic program of individual convictions, but a political ethic concerned about the life of the *polis* called the Church. This is also the reason why he (Hauerwas) does not base a pacifist theology on the individual sayings of the Bible or on the teaching and acts of Christ abstracted from the wider significance of the person and work of Christ in founding the Church, the new messianic community. Jesus' Sermon on the Mount (Mt. 5:1ff.), for example, cannot be read as an invitation for the cultivation of an individual attitude of nonviolence, but as a blueprint for a politic ethic, i.e., for the life of a new community called Church: "the Sermon does not generate an ethic of non-violence, but rather demands the existence of a community of non-violence so that the world might know that as God's creatures we are meant to live peaceably with one another."[78] In fact, when the Sermon (indeed Scripture as a whole) is divorced from this ecclesial context, it cannot appear as a 'law' to be applied to and by individuals. However,

> individuals divorced from the community are incapable of living the life the Sermon depicts. . . . The sermon is only intelligible against the presumption that a new eschatological community has been brought into existence that makes a new way of life possible.[79]

This is what makes the Sermon more than just a series of moral injunctions, but a political vision of a new eschatological community, a community sustained by the key virtues of hope and patience, and by concrete ecclesial practices of peaceableness, Eucharistic *koinonia* and *diakonia*, reconciliation and forgiveness: "Christian nonviolence, in short, does not begin with a theory or conception about violence, war, 'the state or society,' and so on, but rather with practices such as forgiveness and reconciliation."[80]

However, what makes the life of a nonviolent community possible is commitment to a particular story. In the case of the Church, it is the tragic story of the life and work of Jesus. According to Hauerwas, the Cross in Christian theology, therefore, cannot be interpreted (as is often the case) in a pietistic, spiritualized, and individualistic sense, as an example of total self-giving or a symbol for individual sacrifice. Rather, it is a decisive political event which, by challenging the powers that be, inaugurates a new community based on the firm faith that a "morally worthy social order is not built on power and violence" but on nonviolent love.[81] What is ironic in this vision is that it is the Cross, a violent and tragic event, which provides an "interruption" of the history of the nations, which, according to Hauerwas, is the history of violence.[82] The Church, by remembering and retelling this story, generates a social praxis sustained by the conviction that peace is ontologically more basic than violence, because that is the way "God wills to rule his *creation.*"

Understood from this perspective, the Christian story of creation forms one continuous story with Christ's death on the cross. The latter, as well as any other form of violence, turns out, according to this account, to be an attempt to deny God's sovereignty over his creatures, as well as our contingent and creaturely status: "Violence derives from the self-deceptive story that we are in control—that we are our own creators—and that only we can bestow meaning on our lives, since there is no one else to do so."[83]

This extensive onto-theological background calls for two observations: First, it now becomes clear why, for Hauerwas, "creation" cannot work as a theological doctrine that could be heuristically used to underwrite an autonomous natural theology or natural morality.[84] Creation, even while remaining a central metaphysical claim, is unintelligible apart from the community whose existence and way of life it informs. Creation points not only to what the world is (created and contingent), but also to how the self must be (creature) and through what sort of social-linguistic practice (peaceful) the self must learn to "see" the world rightly. Secondly, it means

that the pacifism of the ecclesial social-linguistic practice depends ultimately on this particular story of creation or "in the beginning." This, however, does not mean that this story (and the pacifist practice it underwrites)
can be lightly dismissed as merely a story or *mythos*. Not only is it the case
that, given our contingent status, *mythos* (story) is inevitable, the fact that
pacifism is founded on *mythos* provides a partial response to the challenge
of violence. For, the assumption that difference, indeterminacy, and historical particularity necessarily imply violence is itself based on another
mythos. This has been shown most clearly in the work of John Milbank,
which, as we have already seen, Hauerwas has appropriated with considerable approval.

Excursus: Mythos, *Politics, and "In the Beginning"*

Against the background of a positive appreciation of postmodernity, especially in its critical exposition of "the pretentious arrogance" of universal
reason within modernity, as well as in its positive affirmation of particularity, absolute historicism, and celebration of difference, Milbank argues,
there is still a 'problematic' within postmodernity, namely, the assumption
that difference and indeterminacy implies violence. According to Milbank,
the postmodernists, with their roots in Nietzsche, assume that violence is
inescapable. Lyotard, for example, notes that a plurality of discourses cannot exist peacefully alongside each other but that the conflict must be nego-
tiated through, and mitigated by, "a set of formal rules of engagement such
as is provided by the market bureaucracy."[85]

This, according to Milbank, is postmodernity's predicament: it remains
in continuity with liberalism and the Enlightenment. For the latter assumed "some naturally given element of chaotic conflict which must be
tamed by the stability and self-identity of reason."[86] It is a 'problematic' in
the sense that postmodernity continues to assume, just like the modernism
it sought to overcome, an "ontology of violence."[87] Such ontology, namely,
that violence "is always what is going on," or that difference is "necessarily
conflictual," is based on a *mythos*, an unfounded narrative of "in the beginning." For example, Milbank argues, it is only by accepting "*agon* or play-
ful, competitive struggle . . . to be [the] universal condition . . . of primitive
humanity," that Nietzsche suggests that "domination and the will to
power operate necessarily" to control and manage this primordial "chaos."[88]
But the very move by Nietzsche of positing an *a priori* warfare, which Milbank also calls, "ontological violence," is nothing but a *mythos*. To counter

this *mythos*, Milbank suggests, "one can try to put forward an alternative *mythos*, equally unfounded, but nonetheless embodying an 'ontology of peace', which conceives differences as analogically related, rather than equivocally at variance."[89]

We will explain the full meaning of this citation shortly. Before we do so, however, we need to note that we have drawn attention to Milbank's work in order to recruit his insight that much of the assumption that once one has accepted a plurality of traditions violence is inevitable, turns on what one declares to be present 'in the beginning'. According to Hauerwas, it is the liberal *mythos* of 'in the beginning' which underwrites a social order in which violence is inevitable. To counter this ontology of violence, Hauerwas puts forward an alternative *mythos* of "in the beginning." Thus, what is at stake in Hauerwas's pacifism is the confrontation or witness between two forms of politics that are generated by two different ontologies— Christian nonviolence and liberal agonistics—that are enshrined within two respective stories of 'in the beginning.'

Before we specifically attend to these respective ontologies, we need to note how this reference to *mythos* already points to the extent to which politics is, in the final analysis, determined by stories. Accordingly, the difference between any two forms of politics is greatly a matter to be decided, theoretically at least, by attending to their respective *mythoi*. This is necessarily the case because, as was noted earlier, stories structure individual as well as collective (social) experiences in ways that set a horizon for human expectations and functioning. This is even more true in the case of those mythical stories of 'in the beginning', which enshrine a *telos* in the form of a vision of human nature and a hope for human flourishing. This realization is crucial for it confirms how any political theory can be said to be at once metaphysical, ethical, and to a great extent, theological.[90]

Creation Nonviolence and Liberal Agonistics

Creation, which is the Christian story of 'in the beginning', is, according to Hauerwas, essentially peaceful. In order to substantiate these claims, Hauerwas has more recently turned to "the extraordinary manner Milbank interrelates reflection on the trinity, creation, contingency, truth, and nonviolence."[91] At the center of this reflection is the argument that creation is nonviolent because it is the work of the Trinity.

In order to understand why the Trinity is at the center of both Milbank's and Hauerwas's "specifically Christian onto-logic," one must appreciate their argument that much of the violence within the modern and postmodern tradition is due to what Milbank calls the "nihilistic univocity" within these traditions. According to Milbank (and Hauerwas, following him), it is the predilection for univocity within the modern and postmodern tradition that leads thinkers to suspect that the only 'beyond' to *being* is nothing and that, in the absence of unity, differences must be equivocally at variance (war). What the modern and postmodern tradition lacks, according to Milbank, is an ear for analogy. The latter allows for existence to be at once present and absent, for differences to be grounded in a surplus of Being in such a way that Being itself contains "ontological difference."[92] Nowhere is such analogical reconciliation of difference more concretely displayed than within the relations of the Trinity itself. Within the Trinity, difference and sameness, "infinite realized act, and infinite unrealized power" mysteriously coincide. This is to say that the differential relations of the Trinity "are analogically related, rather than equivocally at variance." And so, because it is the work of the Trinity, creation is the "ongoing actualization of a sociality of harmonious difference displayed in the Trinity."[93]

Besides, as the work of the Trinity, creation is not only essentially peaceful, it is perfect. This, however, does not mean that it is a finished product. As an ongoing process, creation remains "God's continuously generated *ex nihilo* in time." This means that Christians do not assist God in creation,[94] but only participate in the musicality of God's peaceful and perfect creation by becoming part of "those practices of perfection" that constitute the Church community, in which the Sabbath is not just one day, but her very *form of life.*[95]

Christian practice is thus essentially pacifist because it is "the coding of transcendental difference as peace."[96] This transcendental difference is structurally grounded in an ontology of the peaceful and harmonious relations of the creating Trinity, in which violence is only a "secondary willed intrusion" that is known only because of a more profound peace. This theme, in fact, explains both Milbank's and Hauerwas's interest in Augustine. The idea of a peaceful creation is such a basic ontological affirmation that it leads Augustine to postulate two forms of politics, which he metaphorically casts as the *Civitas Dei* (marked by nonviolence and virtue, because it is based on the story of creation, and thus God's sovereignty), on the one hand, and the *Civitas terrena* (which, because it refuses to acknowledge God's sovereignty, is marked by coercion), on the other.[97] It is this Augustinian theology of the two cities which forms the bedrock of Hauerwas's own attempt to characterize the Church and liberalism as embodying two forms of politics generated by two different narratives. The social posturing of each of these forms of politics (just like any other politics) depends on their respective creation *mythos*, i.e., what one declares to be present "in the beginning." To both Augustine and Hauerwas, the Christian story of creation engenders a peaceable community and praxis. This is necessarily the case because, as the work of the Trinity, creation exposes the "non-necessity of supposing, like the Nietzscheans, that difference, non-totalization and indeterminacy of meaning *necessarily* imply arbitrariness and violence. To suppose that they do is merely to subscribe to a particular encoding of reality,"[98] i.e., to another story of the "in the beginning." For Augustine, this alternative is embodied within the *Civitas terrena*. For Hauerwas, the alternative is the story of liberal agonistics.

Liberal creation stories are not only responsible for such encoding, but ensure that the "very creation of the 'secular' is implicated in an ontology of violence."[99] Although Hauerwas has not taken time to specifically dwell on any liberal *mythos*, his writings provide more than sufficient evidence to build a strong case against the liberal "creation" narratives that provide agonistic accounts of existence. For example, the Hobbesian and, to a lesser extent, the Lockean versions of the creation of society assume that difference is irreducible and conflict unavoidable. According to Hobbes, for example, the State of Nature ("in the beginning") is a state of self-interested individuals ("Hobbesian appetites") set in competition and struggle with other self-interested individuals for limited resources. However, once such an ontology of competition and struggle is posited as what is always going on even "in the beginning," then the best hope for society is a cooperative collection of friendly strangers whose best peace is "the mere absence of war." It is this ontology that underwrites the inevitability of violence within liberal modernity and postmodernity. It is not surprising, therefore, that liberal virtue remains teleologically ordered to competition and war.[100]

Moreover, by anticipating capitalistic production and market economics, the liberal *mythos* underwrites scarcity as an ever-present condition. "No matter how great our abundance, we assume it is necessary to make and want more, even if the acquisition of more requires the unjust exploitation of 'less developed lands.'"[101] According to Hauerwas, it is this ontology of self-interest, struggle and competition for limited resources that leads to the assumption that differences and a plurality of traditions must necessarily be conflictual and the attempt to domesticate these conflicts through some form of dialectical or universal logic. However, what such an attempt fails to realize is the violence embedded even within this very attempt itself. For, a social order founded on the assumption that self-interest and competition is always what is going on even in "the beginning" cannot but produce characters that are increasingly mired in "self-assertion, an enjoyment of the arbitrary, and therefore violent power over others—the *libido dominandi.*"[102]

By way of conclusion, we can note that the difference between the two ontologies is, in the final analysis, a difference between two sets of practices, Christian pacifism and liberal competitive struggle. These practices and forms of life are generated by two respective *mythoi* of Creation and Agonistics. Each *mythos* generates a corresponding form of politics in which the practices come to be displayed within a given *telos*. What this conclusion in fact points to is the fact that particular stories can only embody particular visions of society and human flourishing, and accordingly support or give rise to particular excellences that another vision simply may not recognize, given its commitment to an alternative but equally contingent vision. It is this realization that political visions are irreducibly particular which makes the call for witness inevitable.

The consequences for a conception of ethics implied in this defense of witness as a political category are particularly significant. In as much as practices and virtues are at the service of a *telos* embodied within a given ontology, to every politics belongs a corresponding virtue theory. For Hauerwas, this means at least two related things. First, talk about 'natural' or 'human' virtues must proceed with caution, since the nature, number, and meaning of virtues is dependent on the narrative and tradition in which they are inscribed:

> there is a profound sense in which the traditional "theological virtues" of faith, hope and love are "natural." As much as any institution the church is sustained by these "natural virtues." But that does not mean that what is meant by faith, hope, and love is the same for Christians as for other people. For Christians, the sense of what it is in which they have faith, in which they hope, and the kind of love that must be displayed among them derives from the tradition that molds their community. Indeed, because of the character of that story, the nature and meaning of the virtues are essentially changed.[103]

Secondly, but following from the above, this means that there is no virtue theory in general. Rather, the characterizations of the virtues, their content, how they interrelate, etc., will differ from one community and tradition to another. And so, the "recent" enthusiasm for, and revival of "virtue ethics" cannot be uncritically embraced, but must be tempered by the crucial question, "What virtues? Which *telos?*" The significance of this realization for Hauerwas can only become clear by focusing on the critical remarks that Hauerwas has raised against "virtue ethics" in general and MacIntyre's project in particular. Such a focus will make it clear why it would be a mistake to see Hauerwas's work as "virtue ethics." However, in order to appreciate this important qualification, it might prove fruitful to read it alongside two other qualifications about how *not* to understand Hauerwas's work. These three denials—Hauerwas's work is not just virtue ethics, not just communitarian ethics, and not just political theology— flow from the foregoing discussion, and may help to bring this chapter to a conclusion.

4. Beyond Virtue Ethics, Communitarianism, and Political Theology

Not Just a Return to "Virtue Ethics"

Hauerwas has long argued against the "predominant forms of moral theory produced by liberal society exactly because they have, by necessity, been based on a law-like paradigm that ignores the significance of the virtues." However, it would be misleading to see his work as primarily developing a "virtue ethics."[104] For one thing, Hauerwas himself warns that one should not be expected to prefer virtue accounts of ethics to other accounts simply because they are virtue accounts.[105] The reason for this caution in the face of the recent enthusiasm about "virtue ethics"—a revival to which his own work contributed—becomes intelligible within the context of the foregoing discussion to the effect that every account of virtues requires a corresponding politics. But in as much as the recent enthusiasm for virtue ethics has not challenged the liberal social-political arrangement, it continues to be informed by presuppositions which follow from the Enlightenment and thus continues to underwrite the institution of morality. One can identify at least two strategies by which this is achieved.

First, an ethics of virtue is often conceived as complementary or supplementary "to an already well-founded notion of obligation, and so, when recognizing the need to include virtue within their moral systems of thought, these thinkers invariably fashion their 'virtues' so as never directly to interfere with this basic notion."[106] The appeal to virtue, on this reading, becomes a reference to individual traits or character dispositions which can provide motivation (Frankena) or a supererogatory (Foot) supplement to moral obligation.[107] A second strategy is to make the virtues look very much like a list of obligations. This strategy is pursued, for example, by Pincoffs, who, in spite of his strong critique of the standard ethical theories (i.e., utilitarianism, Kantianism, and contract theories), reintroduces the special jurisdiction of obligation when he devises a special category among his many and various virtues called "the mandatory virtues."[108] Both of these strategies, by assuming that the virtues are either a supplement or an alternative to an ethics of principles and rules, continue to reproduce the assumption that there is a separable realm called ethics that led to the ignoring of the virtues in modern moral theory. Thus, both strategies seek to recover the virtues, but without engaging the political implications that an attention to virtue calls for. As a result, both strategies leave liberal democratic politics intact and the "institution of morality" only superficially qualified.

However, even when more thoroughgoing defenses of virtue (like MacIntyre's) have challenged "the institution of morality" and/or the political legitimacy of liberal democracy, a mere defense of virtue is not enough. Given the political implications of every account of virtue, the crucial questions are "What virtues? Which community? Whose politics?" Hauerwas's recent critique of MacIntyre's recovery of virtue helps to illumine the point at stake.

Relying heavily on Milbank's *Theology and Social Theory*, Hauerwas has questioned MacIntyre's attempt to make a universally compelling case for virtue.[109] First, Hauerwas has noted how MacIntyre's account of virtue is not sufficiently historical and concrete:

> Of course for MacIntyre, one must subscribe to some *particular* tradition, some *particular* code of virtue and here he [MacIntyre] identifies himself as 'an Augustinian Christian'. But, all the same, the *arguments* put forward against nihilism and a philosophy of difference [genealogy] are made in the name of virtue, dialectics and the *notion* of tradition in general.[110]

This shortcoming in MacIntyre is connected with what seems to be an uneasy and problematic attempt by MacIntyre to graft the Christian understanding of virtue onto the Greek heritage (defending virtue first and Christianity later!). The crucial turning point is chapter 9 of MacIntyre's *After Virtue*, entitled "Nietzsche or Aristotle?" Even though the Christian tradition is decisive for MacIntyre, and even though in his work MacIntyre talks about Aquinas more than Aristotle, the two really serious options for modern ethics (according to MacIntyre) are: either genealogy (Nietzsche) or tradition (Aristotle–Aquinas). And even though MacIntyre sides with the latter, in so doing and in setting up the debate in the way he has, he does not give Aquinas, the alleged hero, room to significantly disagree with Aristotle. MacIntyre's Aquinas "transcends" Aristotle but remains in his line, in Aristotle's tradition. And so Christianity remains in the line of the Greeks.

This is precisely the problem with MacIntyre. For the deeper implications of the Greek understanding of virtue clash with the political claims of Christianity.[111] While Christian virtue is teleologically ordered to peace, Greek virtue, just like liberal virtue, is ordered to war:

> MacIntyre largely ignores this, and so cannot see that the Christian virtues, represented (ironically) most strongly by Aquinas, actually offer an alternative that radically challenges Greek notions of virtue. For Christians, attaining virtue is not fundamentally a victory, as it is for the Greeks. In that sense, Christianity is not a continuation of the Greek understanding of the virtues, but rather an inauguration of a new tradition that sets the virtues within an entirely different telos in community.[112]

Following Milbank, Hauerwas locates the fundamental points of discontinuity between the Greek and the Christian notions of virtue around the contrast between the Greek *arete* and the Christian *caritas:*

> *Arete* has its sense in relation to a fundamentally heroic image that has no telos other than conflict. The hero vanquishes his foes, and the virtues are his wherewithal, as well as those traits for which he is accorded honor in the *polis* he violently defends. By contrast, *caritas*, the very form of the virtues for Aquinas, sees the person of virtue as essentially standing in mutuality with God and with her fellow human beings.[113]

Another way to characterize the difference between *arete* and *caritas* is to note that the former is founded on a politics of violence and exclusivity.[114] To pursue this claim, Hauerwas calls attention to Aristotle's magnanimous man, his highest embodiment of virtue: "Not only does the magnanimous man seek to be liberal, he seeks to outshine others in liberality, which implies a competition for limited economic resources."[115]

Moreover, when one turns to the formal aspects of Aristotle's ethics, for example, his definition of virtue as lying in a mean between one and the other passion, one detects the central motifs of conflict and control within the Greek *arete.* The virtues—and prudence as their king—are the means by which we control ourselves, conquer, in a way, our own appetitive selves so as to permit us extended control over our contingent circumstances and, if need be, others involved in them. Greek virtue, therefore, is essentially built upon conflict and conquest. And so for Aristotle, just like for the Homeric hero, excellence or *arete* is still in some measure 'effectiveness' which can emerge only by engagement in an *agon*. Thus, in an exclusive Greek *polis* where conquering was constant—if not of Athens, of Sparta, or reason of the appetites or masters of slaves—the only peace imaginable was the absence of conflict.

It is this theme of conquest and victory at the heart of Greek conception of virtue that explains MacIntyre's own constant use of the notions of competition, conflict, and victory. Apart from *Whose Justice?* in which the relation between traditions is depicted in terms of rivalry, crisis (epistemological), and victory[116] in *Three Rival Versions*, MacIntyre acknowledges that his revival of virtue leads to conflict, which he means to "manage" with dialectics.[117] MacIntyre's predilection for these themes reflects the priority he accords to the Greek *arete*, which is fundamentally a "victory."

Moreover, MacIntyre's predilection for the themes of conflict and victory unwittingly confirms his affiliation with the liberal ontology, which he sets out to overcome. It is these themes of conflict and victory which provide fundamental continuity between the liberal ontology of violence and the Greek world.[118] Both liberal society and the Greek *polis* are caught up in this model of exclusivity, conflict, and competition for limited resources. That is why, on this reading, the key liberal virtue of acquisitiveness seems to be patterned on some Aristotelian base of a personal heroic achievement, while the liberal "light-minded ironist"[119] is nothing more than Aristotle's magnanimous man with a modern face. A strange combination of playfulness and violence characterizes both the Greek *polis* and the liberal society.

Caritas, on the other hand, the very form of the virtues for Aquinas, betrays an ontological priority of peace to conflict. Charity cannot be a virtue in the Greek sense of the term. "Unlike the magnanimous man, [Aquinas's] person of charity does not build up a fund of resources and then economically dispense them: instead, her very mode of being is giving, and this constant outgoing paradoxically recruits again her strength."[120] Because the person of *caritas* stands in mutuality with God and with fellow humans, Christian virtue not only transcends, but is a great challenge to, any model of personal heroic achievement and virtue locked in conflict and control. *Caritas* is given and involves giving. It is, as Aquinas would put it, "infused in us by God's grace, which saves us and enables us."[121]

The contrast between *arete* and *caritas* which Hauerwas is invoking here is a contrast between two ontologies that elicit two alternative communities: the Greek *polis*-cum-liberal nation-state, on the one hand, and the Augustinian *Civitas Dei*, on the other. As Hauerwas would have it, it is the latter, which bases political relation and participation on *caritas* (forgiveness and mutuality), rather than on *arete* (competition or acquisitiveness) that offers true (political) possibilities of community and peaceableness that are inconceivable within both the Greek *polis* and the liberal nation-state. It is such a background that helps to make clear why, for Hauerwas, Christian pacifism is not only the decisive form of politics but the best form of Christian social criticism as well.[122]

These critical remarks concerning Aristotelian *arete* do not mean that Hauerwas is about to reject his own (if earlier) reliance on Aristotle in the development of character. The Greek heritage is still significant, even though, from Hauerwas's Christian perspective, only topologically, as a partial anticipation of the Christian *Civitas Dei*. Concretely, this means at least two things. First, that structurally there is no need to reject Aristotle's account of how the virtues are acquired (which MacIntyre helpfully fills out with his notion of practices, communities, and traditions). What is needed, though, is a critical appropriation that is able to note similarities as well as differences between Greek and Christian virtue.

Secondly, Hauerwas thinks that the political implications of an Aristotelian conception of ethics and of virtue are still irreplaceable. In Aristotle, the virtues, their nature, acquisition, individuation, etc., are possible only against the background of a community's practices and the narratives that give those practices intelligibility.[123] From this point of view, the focus on tradition that an Aristotelian conception entails helps to challenge the very paradigms of rationality and correlative political implications that have shaped modern accounts of the moral life.

Not Simply Communitarian Ethics

The foregoing discussion also makes it clear why it would be both misleading and a misreading to see the aim of Hauerwas's reflection as one of defending a communitarian cause.[124] In many ways Hauerwas's sustained critique of liberalism is reminiscent of those formulated by MacIntyre, Sandel, Walzer, and Charles Taylor. In their work, these authors have tried to challenge the liberal foundations of atomistic individualism by calling attention to the constitutive role of the community in self-determination and to the experience of politics as binding individuals into a community of shared values through joint pursuit of the good. Hauerwas is, therefore, aligned with this communitarian cause, and in his earlier work relied heavily upon its logic and rhetoric. However, Hauerwas is not a communitarian.[125]

First of all, Hauerwas has critically noted how communitarians are usually not sufficiently historical or concrete. They rightly argue, against liberalism, that it is only a conception of shared ends that can serve as basis for politics and that these shared ends are to be found in concrete historical practices. However, they usually give no examples of such ends or the concrete historical practices and communities they have in mind. As was noted earlier, Hauerwas has made this criticism in particular of MacIntyre's argument for tradition in general. Given Hauerwas's extensive historical conception, the issue is really not one of 'community or no community' but 'What sort of community?'.

More recently Hauerwas has even come to realize the need to get beyond the "false alternatives of liberalism and communitarianism." The very posing of the issue in terms of "liberalism or communitarianism," he has noted, is sustained by liberal political presuppositions:

> I am uneasy with the contrast between liberalism and communitarianism because that alternative is produced by the very liberal presuppositions that I think are so problematic. I am, accordingly, very sympathetic with Charles Taylor's suggestion that the very terms "liberal" and "communitarian" need to be scrapped.[126]

Behind this conclusion lies a key realization that the 'longing' for community among communitarians is often "the working out of liberal theory and practice." And so, the communities longed for or created by communitarianism tend to reflect the liberal assumption that "men and women wish only to pursue their private purposes and that they form associations only in order to advance these purposes more effectively. . . . solicitude for individual rights extends to the right of association. . . ."[127] Because the communities created or longed for tend to be nothing more than "life-style enclaves" of the lone "individual," their dangers become too real:

> When people are very detached, very devoid of purpose and a coherent world view, . . . people will be attracted to communities that promise them an easy way out of loneliness, togetherness based on common tastes, racial or ethnic traits, or mutual self-interest. There is then little check on community becoming as tyrannical as the individual ego. Community becomes totalitarian when its only purpose is to foster a sense of belonging in order to overcome the fragility of the lone individual.[128]

That is why it is not enough to call for community, for such communities of 'togetherness' fail to serve the traditional socializing functions of conferring a sense of communal belonging, loyalty, and personal identity. Moreover, once the traditioned nature of existence has been accepted, then one realizes that there is nowhere else to stand than within a particular tradition and community. That is why the issue is really not one community or no community, but of which community and whether such a community is substantive enough to offer one a sense of identity as well as forms of cooperation for the achievement of goods otherwise unavailable. For Hauerwas: "That is why of course I am not a communitarian. I am a Christian."[129]

Not Simply Political Theology, But Theological Politics

It should also be clear by now that in spite of the heavily 'politicized' nature of Hauerwas's writing, it would be misleading to characterize his work as political theology. As Rasmusson observes, political theology is in general "an attempt to positively meet the challenges of modernity, characterized by industrialization, urbanization, science, technology, market economy and a growing state and its various ideological backbones in liberalism and socialism, with their common beliefs in progress and in politics as a means for consciously forming the future."[130] Political theology seeks to mediate the Christian tradition in an apologetic fashion to this modern world. In this attempt, political theology accepts not only "the modern idea of religion as a categorical sphere separate from politics and ethics that has gone together with the secularization of knowledge, politics, economy, and so on,"[131] it takes for granted the existence of the liberal nation-state as the primary political actor. However, these are the very assumptions that Hauerwas has consistently challenged. He has therefore welcomed Rasmusson's characterization of his (Hauerwas's) work as "theological politics" but not political theology: "According to Rasmusson, a theological politics understands the church as an alternative *polis* or *civitas*, which is constituted 'by the new reality of the kingdom of God as seen in the life and destiny of Jesus'."[132]

Thus, in contrast with political theology, which makes the political struggle for emancipation the horizon in which the church's theology and practice is interpreted, a theological politics makes the church's story the "counter story" that interprets the world's politics. Making the church the primary locus of politics means that for Hauerwas the labels "church" and "world" do not designate self-regulating subsystems operating within a comprehensive life-world. They name alternative social visions which afford very different possibilities for being and becoming human in the world. In Hauerwas's familiar words,

> The church does not exist to provide an ethos for democracy or any other form of social organization, but stands as a political alternative to every nation, witnessing to the kind of social life possible for those that have been formed by the story of Christ.[133]

For many, even while granting the essential correctness of Hauerwas's tirade against liberal politics as well as the attractiveness of his theological politics, there still remains an uneasiness about his project. Where does the recommendation of the church as a political alternative leave us? Back in the Christendom of the Middle Ages? Such a fear, however, arises out of a superficial (mis)reading of Hauerwas's work, according to which his claim that the church is a political alternative is seen as an attempt (by Hauerwas) to replace liberal state bureaucracy with church bureaucracy. Such a misreading is not only unsustained by a metanarrative conception of politics, it misses the central argument for historically constituted traditions which embody contingent visions and provide witness to one another, without an overarching "tradition of traditions" (liberalism or Christianity). Moreover, seeking to replace liberalism with Christendom would be to miss Hauerwas's re-conception of the 'tactical' existence of the church as a local tradition, by assuming (still) a conception of the church as empire. What this Constantinian conception fails to realize is the historical fact the political character of the salvation made possible by the church was ironically suppressed when the church became a political power. This was in great part because a Constantinian church understands and presents itself as the state. A church that so understands itself cannot but "mimic the procedures of political sovereignty, and invent a kind of bureaucratic management of believers," with the effect that "Christianity has helped to unleash a more 'naked' violence."[134]

The goal of Hauerwas's critical project has been to undermine the foundational epistemological, sociological, and political assumptions that provide any tradition (church or liberal) with such metanarrative singularity. The effect of this singularity is to arrogantly claim for oneself the power "to know not only where we are, but where everyone else is or should be."[135] The violence involved in such an imperialistic self-posturing calls for a critique of the Constantinian church no less than of Enlightenment politics. Accordingly, Hauerwas's claim for the church as an alternative to liberal agonistics has more at stake in those "base communities" where the lines between church and world, spiritual and secular are blurred and relative independence and mutual nurturing within small groups is pursued. Only such local communities, "those cells within each nation that [can] unite in a higher loyalty than nation or class—that are in fact God's international"[136]—might provide an alternative assessment to, and a real option away from, the hegemonic imperialism of a Constantinian Christianity, on the one hand, and the liberal politics of self-interest and nihilistic consumerism, on the other. Only such churched communities may be able to survive liberalism and make a contribution to the world that comes after liberalism.

We hope that with such a background it becomes clear that there can be no more misleading claim than that Hauerwas's ethical-theological reflection involves a withdrawal from *political* engagement. The contrary turns out to be the case, since, as the foregoing discussion has indicated, Hauerwas is far more political than those ethicists and theologians who take the current political reality for granted and only seek ways to contribute relevantly and realistically. Compared to the latter, Hauerwas is engaged in a far more original and challenging form of political thinking, by calling attention to how we should think about the very nature of politics. While such thinking seems, on the surface, to fail us by not addressing the "what must be done" here and now, it nevertheless provides a far more needed service by widening the horizons of our moral and political vision. Such a preoccupation accounts not only for the originality and freshness within Hauerwas's work, but also for its complex and subtle nature.

Conclusion:
Why "Outside the Church There Is No Salvation"

> What manner of a man is the prophet? A student of philosophy who turns from the discourses of the great metaphysicians to the orations of the prophets may feel as if he were going from the realm of the sublime to an area of trivialities. Instead of dealing with the timeless issues of being and becoming, of matter and form, of definitions and demonstrations, he is thrown into orations about widows and orphans, about the corruption of judges and affairs of the marketplace. Instead of showing us a way through the elegant mansions of the mind, the prophets take us to the slums. The world is a proud place, full of beauty, but the prophets are scandalised, and rave as if the whole world were a slum. They make much ado about paltry things, lavishing excessive language upon trifling subjects.
>
> Abraham Joshua Heschel

This study set out to realize one goal, namely, to defend a historical conception of the moral life in general, and of moral reason in particular. We have attempted to do this by exploring two related concerns, notably moral particularity and the 'problem' of religion and ethics. This task obliged us to establish in the first place how these two issues are related. Through a genealogical survey (chapter 1), we were led to discover that the 'problem' of religion and ethics is at home within, and is, in fact, created by, an ahistorical conception of the moral life. The latter, which we have referred to variously as the Institution of Morality, the Moral Point of View, or the Standard Account, is characterized by rational autonomy and universality. However, once ethics has assumed this normative status of autonomy and universality a "problem" is already created, namely how to relate the local, contingent, and timely aspects of one's historical existence to the universality and timelessness of the Moral Point of View. It is therefore not surprising that in an attempt to preserve the "purity" and universality of the Moral Point of View, philosophers and theologians have been keen to assign the historical, particular, and contingent aspects of one's existence to a realm "outside the boundaries of reason," from where they only provide an optional motivational or supererogatory ideal.

What we have found to be ironical, but particularly instructive, is that this ahistorical account of ethics—the one that creates the 'problem' of religion and ethics—itself has historical explanations. This fact is often overlooked by philosophers, who have tended to treat the 'problem' of religion and ethics as "perennial," or as "inevitable," given the "very nature of ethics." A genealogical survey was thus deemed appropriate to show why, on account of its historicity, there is nothing inevitable about the Institution of Morality or about the 'problem' of religion and ethics it gives rise to.

It is against this background that a study of Hauerwas's work was undertaken. This investigation proved helpful in at least two ways. First, Hauerwas's work has helped to provide a critical focus on the various shortcomings within the Institution of Morality, on account of which the latter should be set aside. In our work, we have gathered up these shortcomings around three key areas, namely: (i) an ahistorical (transcendental) conception of the self, (ii) a truncated (quandary) view of the moral life, and (iii) an unconvincing (foundational) account of moral truth and objectivity. Secondly, Hauerwas's work offered an alternative account of the moral life which we found particularly compelling in its historicism.

In the first part of the book we organized this historical account of the moral life around the key categories of Moral Character, Vision, and Narrative. In the second part we sought to make this historical account of the moral life more compelling by defending it against the charges of relativism, fideism-cum-sectarianism, and of social irresponsibility. What, in fact, emerged out of this critical engagement was not only a view of the moral life as inherently historical and particular, but as well a historical conception of truth and objectivity, of religion and of politics. This in itself has been a major discovery which has confirmed that particularity is not just an important aspect within the moral life, it is unavoidable. All human projects are so irreducibly historical that outside the social-linguistic practices of a given way of life, there can be no concept of personal identity (character), of moral vision, moral truth, religion, or even politics. All these become available to one as a participant in a socially embodied way of life and a historically constituted inquiry.

It is only within this broad argument for historical concreteness that one can grasp the meaning and broad significance of Hauerwas's apparently shocking and readily misunderstood essay entitled "Outside the Church

There Is No Salvation."[1] Far from implying an ultraconservative theological agenda, this essay does, in fact, involve defendable moral, epistemological, as well as political claims, all of which confirm the historical conception of the moral life, of religion, and of politics we have outlined in this study. For Hauerwas, religion in general, the church in particular, is nothing but a social-linguistic practice—a particular way of life or community where Christians not only discover their moral identity, draw their vision and account of practical reason, as well as acquire the necessary skills to negotiate the challenges of everyday life (politics). More concretely, this essay provides a radical concretization of how the religious notions of "God," "salvation," "sin"—no less than the moral notion of "the good" or the epistemological notions of "truth" and "objectivity," and the political notion of "justice"—are not foundationally given but only historically learned and creatively employed within a particular social-linguistic form of life. Thus, without the various linguistic, socially embodied, and historically contingent practices associated with a particular community of Church, Christians would have no way of knowing what "salvation" is, or even to "see" that, in fact, one needs "salvation."

The far-reaching implications of this claim, especially the observation that for an individual there is nowhere else to stand than within a particular social-linguistic form of life or tradition, explains three key conclusions that have emerged in the context of this work. First, it vindicates vision as an overriding metaphor for the moral life. What is particularly instructive about the (Hauerwas's) conception of the moral life as a life of vision is the power of language (notions) and ordinary "practices" in forming one's vision. This not only means that one's vision is socially and historically determined, it mitigates against any "neutral" vision of reality. By participating in the social-linguistic practices of a given tradition, one is already drawn into a particular vision.

Secondly, the inability to escape historical contingency altogether underscores the essential fragility of truth and goodness. This realization not only calls into question any exaggerated claims to autonomy and self-determination, it confirms how all one's moral, epistemological, religious, and political projects are tragically dependent on a certain measure of luck—i.e., on historical and contingent events and realities, and on others with whom one happens to share the journey. Self-identity, moral goodness, and objectivity can only be attained within this contingent constellation of social-linguistic practices, through an attentive but constant struggle against self-deception and violence. Yet this, too, depends, in the final analysis, on the fortuitous presence of others, and on finding oneself part of a truthful tradition whose practices encourage and promote this quest for truth and moral goodness in a nondeceptive way.

Thirdly, since particularity cannot be transcended, the traditional debates of "particularity *vs* universality," "is-ought," "religion-ethics" are nothing but misleading and false alternatives. The realization that there is nowhere else to stand than within a particular tradition shifts the philosophical challenge from analytics to ontology. The concern for analytics has been the 'problem' of determining the relation between particularity and universality. The real challenge, however, is how to *be* particular—i.e., a tradition in which the notions of truth, objectivity, and nonviolence remain conceptually and nonideologically intelligible. In this respect, we must register a highly significant aspect of Hauerwas's work, namely, his ability to draw attention to the various elements of phronetic attentiveness and openness which characterize a 'living' tradition. A notable contribution in this line is Hauerwas's rehabilitation of the imagination as a moral and political task by relocating the imagination from a mental faculty to a "pattern of possibilities" generated through the concrete "practices" of a community.

Even more notable is the radically novel category of "witness," which emerges in Hauerwas's overall reflection as both an epistemological and political category. This category is rendered necessary by the realization that the very notion of truth, and any claim thereof, is made possible through and within historically constituted modes of inquiry. However, the absence of any foundational or tradition-independent access to reality makes any tradition's claim to the truth less than absolute. Accordingly, a mark of a 'living' tradition is its willingness to subject its convictions to critical examination and revision. This critical challenge, however, cannot even get off the ground except through the contact and hermeneutical interaction with an "alternative assessment" provided by another equally particular and socially constituted vision.

In this connection, Hauerwas's critical exposition of liberalism's false universalism provides perhaps one of the most concrete expressions of witness as social criticism. This model of social criticism is based on two key premises: first, on the realization that all politics depends on particular narrative configurations or *mythoi* which embody particular visions of the good society and human flourishing. Secondly, it is based on an embodied conception of Christianity as a cultural-linguistic system. In this respect, what Hauerwas has tried to do is to relocate Christianity from the realm of mental "beliefs" and personalized "convictions" by highlighting the potential of the Christian story as a critical political theory capable of inspiring a vision of society that is alternative to the prevailing modernism of liberal agonistics. We find this aspect of social criticism one of Hauerwas's major contributions, but one also which, unfortunately, is the most overlooked or intentionally resisted under the labels of fideism, sectarianism, or social irresponsibility. However, only when this model of social criticism is appreciated is one able to recognize more accurately the critical dimension of Hauerwas's work and its explicitly political purpose and why, in fact, his scholarship defies conventional disciplinary arrangements of academia.

Finally, a word about our own contribution through this argument for moral particularity. A key challenge throughout this study has been to explicate the sort of theoretical framework that is assumed, but not developed, by Hauerwas's account of ethics. In undertaking this task, we have made at least two significant contributions. First, in providing this theoretical framework, our work offers a scheme which makes Hauerwas's wide but disparate scholarship conceptually more clear and its far-reaching implications obvious. Secondly, while Hauerwas's work assumes a historicist conception of ethics, our work has provided the wider epistemological, sociological, and political context that makes this conception of ethics defendable. In this respect, our study has made a contribution towards a historicist conception of truth and objectivity, a cultural-linguistic conception of religion, and an onto-narrative ("in the beginning") account of politics. We realize that our theoretical exploration of these issues has been both preliminary and tentative, and thus calls for a more conscientious and thorough study. However, this exploration does provide a helpful starting point for any headway in the fields of epistemology, sociology of religion, and of political theory, after foundationalism.

This claim may sound immodestly grandiose and self-congratulatory unless it is placed within a key methodological limitation according to which our primary objective in this study has not been a desire to build a "system" out of Hauerwas's work, but to contribute to a certain genre of what might be called "prophetic philosophy." As Heschel implies in the epigraph of this conclusion, such philosophy, "instead of dealing with the timeless issues of being and becoming, of matter and form, of definitions and demonstrations, is thrown into orations about widows and orphans, about the corruption of judges and affairs of the marketplace. Instead of showing us a way through the elegant mansions of the mind, the prophets take us to the slums."[2] The mistake of such prophetic philosophy—and accordingly, our intentionally perpetuated 'mistake' in this study—has been to waste words on what might appear to the academically minded philosopher as trivialities, contingencies and particularities! However, we have found this to be a well-deserving and highly challenging task. Not that we have assumed it begrudgingly like many prophets assume their missions. This has been for us, in many ways, a very interesting and extremely rewarding challenge.

Abbreviations of Key Works Cited

AC   *After Christendom* (Nashville: Abingdon Press, 1991).

AN   *Against the Nations: War and Survival in a Liberal Society* (Minneapolis: Winston-Seabury Press, 1985).

CAV   *Christians among the Virtues: Theological Conversations with Ancient and Modern Ethics*, with Charles Pinches (Notre Dame: University Press, 1977)

CC   *A Community of Character: Toward a Constructive Christian Social Ethic* (Notre Dame: University Press, 1981).

CCL   *Character and the Christian Life: A Study in Theological Ethics* (San Antonio: Trinity University Press, 1975).

CET   *Christian Existence Today: Essays on Church, World, and Living In Between* (Durham: Labyrinth Press, 1988).

DF   *Dispatches from the Front: Theological Engagements with the Secular* (Duke University Press, 1994).

GC   *In Good Company: The Church as Polis* (Notre Dame: University Press, 1995).

PK   *The Peaceable Kingdom: A Primer in Christian Ethics* (Notre Dame: University Press, 1983).

RA   *Resident Aliens: Life in the Christian Colony*, with Will Willimon (Nashville: Abingdon Press, 1989).

SP   *Suffering Presence: Theological Reflections on Medicine, the Mentally Handicapped, and the Church* (Notre Dame: University Press, 1985).

TT   *Truthfulness and Tragedy: Further Investigations in Christian Ethics* (Notre Dame: University Press, 1977).

US   *Unleashing the Scriptures, Freeing the Bible from Captivity to America* (Nashville: Abingdon Press, 1993).

VV   *Vision and Virtue: Essays in Christian Ethical Reflection* (Notre Dame: Fides Press, 1974).

WN   *Why Narrative? Readings in Narrative Theology,* with Gregory
       Jones (Grand Rapids: Eerdmans, 1989).
WW   *Wilderness Wanderings: Probing Twentieth Century Theology and
       Philosophy* (Boulder: Westview Press, 1997.

Notes

Introduction

1. *PK*, xvii.

2. Bartley, *Morality and Religion*, ix.

3. The *bricoleur*, according to Stout, does "odd jobs, drawing on a collection of assorted odds and ends available for use . . . making do with 'whatever is at hand.'" See Stout, *Ethics After Babel*, 74–77.

4. In relation to Milbank, see *DF*, 198 n30; *AC*, 168–69, "Interview." In relation to Lovibond, see *CET*, 10, 20. In relation to Lindbeck, see *AN*, 1, "Embarrassed by God's Presence," 98–99.

5. Great systematic philosophers, Rorty writes, "are constructive and offer arguments. Great edifying philosophers are reactive and offer satires, parodies, aphorisms. They know their work loses its point when the period they were reacting against is over. They are *intentionally* peripheral. Great systematic philosophers, like great scientists, build for eternity. Great edifying philosophers destroy for the sake of their own generation. Systematic philosophers want to put their subject on the secure path of a science. Edifying philosophers want to keep space open for the sense of wonder that there is something new under the sun—something which is not an accurate representation of what was already there, something which (at least for the moment) cannot be explained and can barely be described." See Rorty, *Philosophy and the Mirror of Nature*, 369–70. In making this distinction Rorty identifies Dewey, Wittgenstein, and Heidegger as edifying philosophers, whereas he puts Descartes, Kant, Russell, and Husserl within the systematic camp.

1. Flight from Particularity: Toward a Genealogy of the 'Problem' of the Relation between Religion and Ethics

1. In *The Flight from Authority: Religion, Morality, and the Quest for Moral Autonomy*, Jeffrey Stout undertakes what he calls an ambitious "exercise in conceptual archaeology" with respect to the autonomy of morals in the modern tradition.

2. Stout, *Flight from Authority*, 41.

3. Stout, *Flight from Authority*, 44.

4. Stout, *Flight from Authority*, 237; reference is made to Skinner, *The Foundations of Modern Political Thought*, II, 352.

5. See, for example, Giddens, *The Nation State and Violence*; Skinner, *Foundations of Modern Political Thought*.

6. Stout, *Flight from Authority*, 235.

7. De Certeau, *The Writing of History*, 147–205.

8. De Certeau, *The Writing of History*, 149; 173.

9. De Certeau, *The Writing of History*, 149–150.

10. Only secondarily would the autonomy be connected with the antitraditional rhetoric of the Enlightenment, which would aspire for freedom from all traditional influence whatsoever, or the more sophisticated philosophical denial of having been influenced by tradition. For the latter two forms, see respectively, Gay, *The Enlightenment, An Interpretation*, 2; and MacIntyre, *Whose Justice?* 326–48.

11. Stout, *Ethics After Babel*, 161.

12. Stout, *Flight from Authority*, 238.

13. Stout, *Flight from Authority*, 239. This is one reason why Rawls defines "society" by reference to rules that "specify a system of *cooperation* designed to advance the good of those taking part in it" (Rawls, *A Theory of Justice*, 4).

14. De Certeau, *The Writing of History*, 156–57.

15. De Certeau, *The Writing of History*, 173; 172 n87. De Certeau even makes the interesting connection between the quest for the "usefulness" of religion with other factors like increasing urbanization, commerce, and the development of capitalism, which lead to a "merchant morality" that sought to impose the rule of *utile* everywhere.

16. Lindbeck, *The Nature of Doctrine*, 134.

17. Chapter 4 of De Certeau's *The Writing of History* is significantly entitled, "The Formality of Practices."

18. De Certeau, *The Writing of History*, 175–79. Kant's account of the universal requirement of reason, and the kingdom of ends is, according to Hauerwas, just a secularized version of the Christian Kingdom of God, where peace and not war will characterize the relation between peoples and nations. See, *CC*, 100.

19. Milbank, *Theology and Social Theory*, 126.

20. Musschenga and Van Tongeren, *Does God Matter Morally?*

21. It is therefore misleading to claim, as Bartley does, that "the logical relationship between morality and religion has been a matter of controversy amongst philosophers and theologians from the earliest times . . ." (Bartley, *Morality and Religion*, ix). Similarly it is misleading to claim that this question is structurally and/or substantially the same as the one in Plato's *Euthyphro*: "Do the

gods love what is right because it is right or is it right because the gods love it?" (*Euthyphro* 10d). To so claim (Outka and Reeder, *Religion and Morality*, 1; but also, Hauerwas in one misleading instance, *PK* 11) is to read the *Euthyphro* outside the context of Plato's preoccupation with seeking to discover a universal definition or the Form of the various actions called pious. Moreover, such a claim anachronistically assumes that the Greeks had the same understanding of God(s) as our conception of an absolute and ultimate Creator, the active force of all movement and life. For Plato (the Greeks) the ultimate realities are the Platonic Forms or Ideas, and they remain supreme to the end. However, Plato never called the Forms gods. That name he reserved for those moral personal beings, those more than human forces personified, in whom a person may find guidance in living a good life. As Grube notes, for Plato (Greeks) the separation of the dynamic power of the gods from the eternal reality was not unnatural: "The gods who ruled on Olympus . . . were not creators but created beings. As in Homer, Zeus must obey the balance of Necessity, so the Platonic gods must conform to an eternal scale of values. They did not create them, cannot alter them, cannot indeed wish to do so." See Grube, *Plato's Thought*, 153.

22. Kasper, *Theology and Church*, 39.

23. See, for example, Curran and McCormick, *Readings in Moral Theology*, II.

24. As one of the few exceptions, however, Hans Urs von Balthasar argues that the distinctiveness of Christian ethics derives from the fact that authentic Christian life must be informed by the revelation of God, which is historical and particular, and knowable only from a historical and concrete encounter with the Gospel, and within the living tradition of a Christian community. See Von Balthasar, "Nine Theses in Christian Ethics," 190–206.

25. O'Connell, *Principles for a Catholic Morality*, 39–40

26. McCormick, "Christianity and Morality," 28; Auer, *Autonome Moral*, 191.

27. See, for example, Fuchs, *Human Values*, 57–65; *Christian Morality*, 50–57. According to this reading, which is shared by some current theologies of history, the Incarnation means that God took human nature as it was, put his seal of approval on it, and thereby ratified nature as revelation. Such reading, however, is characterized by both essentialistic reductionism and a unhistorical conception of Incarnation. John Howard Yoder offers a contrary understanding whereby the Incarnation means that God broke through the borders of man's definition of what is human, and gave it a new, formative definition in Jesus. See Yoder, *The Politics of Jesus*. Hauerwas accepts Yoder's understanding of the Incarnation and develops a sustained critique of those theologies that seek to take the language of Incarnation or creation as their starting point. See "Ethics and Ascetical Theology," 91.

28. McCormick, "Christianity and Morality," 28.

29. Fuchs, *Human Values*, 127.

30. Fuchs, *Christian Ethics*, 21–22; For the same position in other key Catholic authors such as Auer and Schüller, see MacNamara, *Faith and Ethics*, 37–55.

31. Descartes's problem was essentially epistemological: How to engage in responsible thought when, following the crisis in authority, the central categories of *scientia* and *opinio* were in such disrepair. For Descartes, as for Luther before him, the basis for truth can no longer be sought in the dimensions of authority and tradition, but in the privacy of subjective illumination. However, once Descartes has assumed an anthropological starting point, then he cannot avoid theological challenge, namely, to justify what role (if any) God played in the self-certifying certainty of the *cogito*. Descartes's own equivocity in the face of this challenge is itself highly instructive. At first Descartes grants that the autonomous *cogito* is independent of God's existence or his nonexistence. It is only at a second stage that Descartes feels compelled to reintroduce the idea of God after discovering that without the idea and reality of God, the "I" cannot be sure either of itself or the world. And so, Descartes grants that in the act of apprehending himself, the human being also apprehends God. See Descartes, "Discourse on Method, Part IV," but particularly "Meditation V" in Anscombe & Geach, *Descartes: Philosophical Writings*, 101–8.

32. Kant's own equivocity in the face of the theological challenge is also notable. The autonomous starting point already ruled out the possibility of God serving as a sanction of moral laws imposed from outside, and even led Kant to reduce God to an extension of the moral law: "Religion is the recognition of all duties as divine commands." Our actions, Kant argued, are binding on us not because they are God's commandments. We see them as God's commandments "because we find them inwardly binding." True religion has no laws except those which we perceive through pure reason. Whatever else "man fancies he can do to become well-pleasing to God is mere religious illusion and pseudoservice of God" (Kant, *Religion within the Limits*, 142, 156, 158). Kant consistently accepted the consequences of this conclusion and argued that morality does not have its end in God, but in the happiness of human beings, which is to be found in the harmony between the moral and the natural order. But when Kant discovers that human beings cannot by themselves guarantee this harmony, he surreptitiously introduces the idea of God as a postulate of practical reason. See Kant, *Critique of Practical Reason*, 128 ff; *Critique of Pure of Reason*, 451 ff.

33. For a case of Christianity being invoked to underwrite the political search for peace and justice, see McDonagh, *Church and Politics*. For Rauschenbusch, the father of the Social Gospel Movement, Christian social ethics was nothing but the exploration of strategies that could best build "a social order in which the worth and freedom of every least human being will be honoured and protected . . ." Rauschenbusch, *A Theology for the Social Gospel*, 224. For Gutiér-

rez, the doyen of liberation theology, "The struggle for liberation is at the same time a struggle for the Kingdom of God," Gutiérrez, *A Theology of Liberation*, 45 ff; 153 ff.

34. In the wake of Hegel, Feuerbach sought for a radical anthropological reading of history as the only way to overcome the alienation of man from himself. As Stout notes, for Feuerbach (Hegel notwithstanding),"history is not the process by which God overcomes his alienation from himself by uniting with humanity but rather the process by which man overcomes his alienation from himself by claiming for himself the attributes of the divine. So long as the divinity of humanity is interpreted theologically, the complete immanence of spirit has not yet been achieved. If God is human nature objectivified in wishful and imaginative representations, he can be nothing more than that without prolonging human self-alienation. A humanity perfectly at one with itself will be post-religious. Theology brought to earth will be Feuerbachian humanism" (Stout, *Flight from Authority*, 139).

35. *PK*, 13.

36. The radical nature of Nietzsche's position should not obscure the fact that Nietzsche was only taking the further step of getting rid of the concept of God, which had increasingly become auxiliary and/or redundant. From this perspective, Nietzsche just radicalized Feuerbach's approach. Like all truth, the idea of God is for Nietzsche "all too human"—a value judgment, a theoretical sketch, a perspective created by human beings themselves. But the God whom the human being has created he can also kill. In fact, the "death of God" for Nietzsche is the real completion of human autonomy, the leap from what is human to what is superhuman. What seems to set Nietzsche apart from the other modern thinkers is that he has the courage to face up to the most extreme consequence of the "death of God." He proclaims a nihilism of strength, an *amor fati* as the formula for human greatness, and a trans-valuation of the traditional categories of good and evil through the freeing up of a heroic will-to-power.

37. "On Keeping Theological Ethics Theological," 18.

38. See, for example, Outka & Reeder, *Religion and Morality*; Bartley, *Morality and Religion*; Reynolds, "A Proposal Concerning the Place of Reason, 156–68; Nielsen, *Ethics Without God*; Graber, "A Critical Bibliography of Recent Discussions," 53–80; Stout, "Redirecting Inquiry in the Religion-Morality Debate," 229–37; Phillips, *Religion and Morality*.

39. "'Analytic' philosophy is one more variant of Kantian philosophy, a variant marked principally by thinking of representation as linguistic rather than mental and of philosophy of language, rather than 'transcendental critique' or psychology, as the discipline which exhibits the 'foundations of knowledge'. . . . For analytical philosophy is still committed to the construction of a permanent, neutral framework for inquiry and thus for all culture." For this, and for a

detailed examination of the transformation by which analytical philosophy becomes a "successor subject" to philosophy as epistemology, see Rorty, *Philosophy and the Mirror of Nature*, 8, 165 ff.

40. Stout, *Flight from Authority*, 184.

41. Thus keeping faithful to Hare's observation to the effect that all logical
relations are analytic and depend for their validity on the meanings of the terms
contained in the concepts related. See Hare, *The Language of Morals*, 83.

42. Bartley, *Morality and Religion*, ix.

43. Stout, *Flight from Authority*, 180–81. Stout draws on Stanley Fish's
analysis of self-consuming artifacts. Self-consuming artifacts, according to Fish
(Self-Consuming Artifacts: The Experience of Seventeenth-Century Literature),
disappear before one's eyes. They announce a topic and begin a refinement of reflection seemingly designed to produce an insight statable as a thesis about the
topic, but the refined turn of thought turns in upon itself, producing not the expected thesis but a new topic altogether.

44. Bell, "Bad Art," 160–71.

45. Frankena, "Is Morality Logically Dependent on Religion?" 295–317.

46. "It is so often asserted, assumed, or clung to; but rarely—if ever—carefully formulated by those who believe in it." Frankena, "Is Morality?" 295, 296.

47. Frankena, "Is Morality?" 313.

48. Frankena, "Is Morality?" 295.

49. Frankena, "Is Morality?" 313.

50. Frankena, "Is Morality?" 314.

51. Rephrasing Nietzsche, *Human, All Too Human*, 14.

52. *PK*, xvii.

53. Nielsen, *Why Be Moral?*

54. This project is what MacIntyre calls the Enlightenment project of providing an autonomous foundation for morality. The "project" is nothing but the attempt to give the moral rules (institutions) inherited from the preceding culture
a systematic justification that would not appeal to any extra-moral (e.g., metaphysical or theological) views about the end or purpose of human existence. See
MacIntyre, *After Virtue*, 35–39. In an earlier work, MacIntyre shows how the attempt to find the needed basis for morality in human physiology was widely undertaken during the seventeenth and early eighteenth century, especially by the
British empiricists. See MacIntyre, *A Short History*, 157–77, 182–83.

55. MacIntyre, *After Virtue*, 56.

56. Stout, *Flight from Authority*, 232, quoting Wolff, *Understanding Rawls*,
114.

57. Kant, *Religion within the Limits*, 36.

58. Kant, *Groundwork*, 59–70.

59. MacIntyre, *After Virtue*, 51.

60. Of parallel development is the rise of Newtonian science and the restric-
tion of the powers of reason to calculative considerations and the assessment of

truths of fact and mathematical relations. "In the realm of practice it [reason] can speak only of means. About ends it must be silent." MacIntyre, *After Virtue*, 52.

61. Kant, *Groundwork*, 65–68, 83–84; Kant, *Critique of Practical Reason*, 26–33.

62. A "peculiar institution," according to Williams, *Ethics and the Limits of Philosophy*, 174 ff.

63. See Toulmin, *An Examination of the Place of Reason in Ethics*, 183.

64. Toulmin, *An Examination of the Place of Reason*, 212–21.

65. Braithwaite, "An Empiricist's View of the Nature of Religious Belief," 53–73; Nowell-Smith, "Religion and Morality," 150–58; Mayberry, "God and Moral Authority," 106–23; Hepburn, "Vision and Choice in Morality," 181–95; Matson, *The Existence of God*, 220–28; Gert, *The Moral Rules*, 231–32.

66. See, e.g., Chisholm, "Supererogation and Offence," 1–14.; Feinberg, *Doing and Deserving*; "Supererogation and Rules," 276–88; Heyd, *Supererogation*; Slote, *Goods and Virtues*; Stocker, "The Schizophrenia of Modern Ethical Theories," 453–66; Clark, "The Meritorious and the Mandatory," 24–37.

67. See, e.g., Blum, *Friendship, Altruism and Morality*; Foot, *Virtues and Vices*; MacIntyre, *After Virtue*; Annas, "Personal Love and Kantian Ethics," 15–31; On sympathy, see particularly Sabin and Mauray, *Moralities of Everyday Life*; Urmson, "Saints and Heroes," 198–216.

68. See, e.g., Strawson, "Social Morality and Individual Ideal," 280–98; Vivas, *The Moral Life and the Ethical Life*; Kupperman, "The Supra-moral in Religious Ethics," 65–71; *Foundations of Morality*. For a contrary argument however, see O'Neil, *Acting on Principle*; Hill, "Kant on Imperfect Duty and Supererogation," 55–76. These latter claim that Kant's theory leaves room for the category of the supererogatory. Marcia Baron argues instead that Kant does not have this category of supererogation and, in fact, does not need it. According to her, Kant's treatment of the category of acts that contemporary ethicists speak of as supererogatory is preferable to the supererogation approach. See Baron, "Kantian Ethics and Supererogation," 237–62.

69. In addition to those mentioned above, see Murdoch, "Vision and Choice in Morality," 195–218; "On 'God' and 'Good'," 46–76.

70. See respectively, Fuchs, "Is There a Specifically Christian Morality?" 1–13; Curran, "Is There a Catholic and/or Christian Ethics?" 60–89; McCormick, "Does Religious Faith Add to Ethical Perception?" 156–75.

71. *VV*, 78.

72. *PK*, 21.

73. "Ethicist as a Theologian," 409.

74. *TT*, 20.

75. *VV*, 79. Inside quotations are a reference to Murdoch, "Vision and Choice," 202.

76. *PK*, 117.

77. MacIntyre, *After Virtue*, 204–5.

78. *TT*, 24. Also, rationality is exactly "that power that allows us to coordinate the many capacities and skills we possess." See "Aristotelian Themes," 12.

2. Moral Character: The Self and Agency within the Limits of History

1. Hauerwas's notion of character is most succinctly developed in his *Character and the Christian Life (CCL)* although we shall examine passages throughout his work for a comprehensive view. *CCL* is a revision of Hauerwas's Ph.D. dissertation, "Moral Character as a Problem for Theological Ethics," Yale, 1968.

2. Toulmin, *An Examination*, 1, emphasis added. For Hare also: "The language of morals is one sort of prescriptive language. And that is what makes ethics worth studying: for the question of "What shall I do?" is one that we cannot for long evade; the *problems* of conduct . . . have to be solved." Hare, *The Language of Morals*, 1, emphasis added.

3. The Situation Ethics debate (sparked off by J. Fletcher's *Situation Ethics*) attracted a great deal of attention during Hauerwas's graduate years at Yale, drawing a number of critical essays in his earlier writings. See particularly Parts I and II of *VV*.

4. The work of Louis Janssens has perhaps been the greatest inspiration for proportionalists (R. McCormick, J. Selling, C. Curran, etc.). At the heart of Proportionalism lies a distinction between "premoral" ("ontic") and "moral" ("ontological") specifications of humanly realized good and evil. It is this distinction that leads to the fundamental claim of Proportionalism, namely that a singular action performed by a moral agent cannot be considered to be evil intrinsically on account of the structure of the exterior act alone, for the moral evaluation of an action can only be had after an assessment of the ends for which, and the circumstances in which, the agent acts. For a general overview of Proportionalism and its intellectual origins, see Hoose, *Proportionalism: The American Debate and Its European Roots*.

5. For the same case made differently, see McDowell, "Virtue and Reason," 331–50; Herman, "The Practice of Moral Judgement, 414–36; Kupperman, *Character*, 67–89.

6. Rawls, *A Theory of Justice*, 136–41.

7. *CC* 82–83; *AC* 60–61; Sandel, *Liberalism and the Limits of Justice*, 15–65; see particularly Sandel, "The Procedural Republic," 81–96.

8. Rawls, *A Theory of Justice*, 255, emphasis added.

9. For Rawls's use of the phrases within quotation marks, see Rawls, *A Theory of Justice*, 46–47, 50, 587. See also, Stout, *Flight from Authority*, 220, 222; Green, *Religious Reason*, 21–23.

10. Rawls, "Kantian Constructivism in Moral Theory: The Dewey Lectures 1980," 515–72. These lectures, recast and revised, appear as Lectures I to III of Rawls's recent book, *Political Liberalism*.

11. See also Rawls, "Justice as Fairness," 223–51. Much of this article has been included in the first chapter of *Political Liberalism* (3–46).

12. O'Connell, *Principles of a Catholic Morality*, 59.

13. O'Connell, *Principles of a Catholic Morality*, 60.

14. O'Connell, *Principles of a Catholic Morality*, 62.

15. *PK*, 41.

16. "The fundamental prejudice of the Enlightenment," writes Gadamer, "is its prejudice against prejudice itself, which deprives tradition of its power." Gadamer, *Truth and Method*, 239–40. Hauerwas's work is in fundamental agreement with the basic direction of Gadamer's project, which is a sustained attempt, against the demystifying intention of the Enlightenment, to rehabilitate the role of prejudice in knowledge by showing that prejudices not only need not distort but can actually be fruitful—as well as being, in any case, simply unavoidable—in all understanding. For Hauerwas's acknowledgement of Gadamer as the Continental philosopher with whom he finds greatest affinity, see "Red Wheelbarrows," 651, 653 n4; Also, "Interview."

17. This shortcoming had already been noted by Hampshire ("Fallacies in Moral Philosophy"), Foot ("Moral Beliefs"), and Anscombe ("Modern Moral Philosophy"). These had suggested, using different arguments, that in its preoccupation with "actions" and "decisions" and "situations" moral philosophy was attempting to do the impossible by proceeding without an adequate moral psychology.

18. *CCL*, 18.

19. *CCL*, 26, 27.

20. *CCL*, 85ff. Hauerwas follows Richard Taylor's analysis according to which Taylor investigates different kinds of action in order to discover what distinguishes them from everything else. He notes different characteristics of action—commandability, directionability, effort, etc., all of which point to an essential reference to an agent. See Taylor, *Action and Purpose*, 99–112.

21. *CCL*, 87.

22. *CCL*, 65; 95–97; *VV*, 55–62.

23. *CCL*, 21, 88.

24. *CCL*, 87.

25. *CCL*, 92–97. Here Hauerwas is drawing on the distinction between purposive and intentional explanation of behavior as made by both Taylor (*Explanation of Behavior*, 5–6, 27–71), and by Hampshire (*Freedom of the Individual*, 52–63). See also, Taylor, *Action and Purpose*, 203–43.

26. *CCL*, 90.

27. *CCL*, 96.

28. This is the gist of Powell Betty's (*Knowledge of Action*) objection. See *CCL*, 89–97.

29. Hauerwas embraces G. Mead's social conception of the self and account of how the self comes to self-awareness. Hauerwas does, nevertheless, criticize

Mead for failing, in *Mind, Self and Society*, to guard sufficiently against the risk that the agent "I" would dissolve in the social "Me" (*CCL*, 103 n25).

30. *PK*, 42.

31. "New Introduction," *CCL*, xx; MacIntyre, *After Virtue*, 209.

32. *TT*, 21.

33. *CCL*, 96.

34. *PK*, 116.

35. *CCL*, 11.

36. References to Aristotle's *Nicomachean Ethics* are given within the text as (*NE*).

37. *CCL*, 40.

38. Contrary to Murray, "Confessional Post Modernism," 83–94.

39. Kupperman conveys the same historical sense of the self we have developed here. However, his language of "constructed self" (*Character*, 40–45) may tend to misleadingly give the impression of character as a 'product', with a clear blueprint (see section 4, below).

40. See, for example, the "New Introduction," *CCL*, xx.

41. *CCL*, 21.

42. *PK*, 39.

43. *CCL*, 117–28.

44. Kant, *Religion within the Limits*, 36.

45. *CCL*, 156.

46. See more concerning the criteria for a truthful story in chapter 4.

47. See, Ogletree, "Character and Narrative," 25; Bondi, "The Elements of Character," 206; Jung, "Sanctification: An Interpretation," 78.

48. *CCL*, 71, emphasis added.

49. *CCL*, 48.

50. *CCL*, 18.

51. Jung, "Sanctification: An Interpretation," 78.

52. *CCL*, 84.

53. *CCL*, 89.

54. Jung, "Sanctification: An Interpretation," 78–79. See also Conway, "The Eyes Have It," 103–13; Haldane, "Some Metaphysical Presuppositions," 296–303.

55. "New Introduction," *CCL* (1985 edition), xvi-xxii; *PK*, 39; *CC*, 277 n55.

56. Lewis, "The Springs of Motion," 275–97.

57. *CCL*, 203, *CC*, 125.

58. Lewis, "The Springs of Motion," 289.

59. Lewis, "The Springs of Motion," 289, 290.

60. Lewis, "The Springs of Motion," 276.

61. Solomon, *The Passions*, 9–10, 129–30, 142.

62. Solomon, *The Passions*, 9.

63. For example, both Nussbaum *(Fragility)* and Sherman *(The Fabric of Character)* emphasize the important role emotions play in Aristotle's understanding of practical reason.

64. *CCL*, 55.

65. *CCL*, 47.

66. *CCL*, 47–48.

67. *CCL*, 52–56.

68. *CCL*, 63. Aquinas, Hauerwas notes, understood the will to be an unusual blend of reason and desire. For Aquinas the intellect and will "include one another in their acts, because the intellect understands that the will wills, and will wills the intellect to understand" *(CCL*, 64). Likewise, "For it is by our intention that the intellect and will are combined in a way that determines the description under which our act is undertaken. 'The will does not order, but tends to something according to the order of reason. Consequently this word intention indicates an act of will, presupposing the act by which the reason orders something to the end.' Therefore, by acting intentionally we not only are able to do what we will, but what we will is not different from what we do" *(CCL*, 66; inside quotation refers to Aquinas, *ST*, I-II, 12,1). For a more thorough treatment of Aquinas's account of the passions, see Simon Harak, *Virtuous Passion*.

69. *CCL*, 47; *CC*, 266.

70. *CC*, 124. Hauerwas still thinks Aristotle and Aquinas had a positive appreciation of the emotions, thus did not subscribe to the myth of the passions. See *CC*, 266.

71. *CC*, 125.

72. Lewis, "The Springs of Motion," 284, 283.

73. *CC*, 266, 267 n55; *PK*, 117.

74. Lewis, "The Springs of Motion," 288–90.

75. *PK*, 117.

76. *CC*, 266.

77. Lewis, "The Springs of Motion," 289, 290.

78. *PK*, 117. See also Nussbaum, "Narrative Emotions," 216–40.

79. Hauerwas himself does not explicitly develop this notion. Our strongest inspiration for this notion comes from Harry G. Frankfurt *(The Importance of What We Care About)*. Bernard Williams also makes some reference to it. See Williams, *Ethics and the Limits*, 182–86.

80. *PK*, 157 n1.

81. "Red Wheelbarrows," 653 n8, emphasis added.

82. *CAV*, 3–54.

83. Frankfurt, *The Importance of*, 85–95.

84. "Red Wheelbarrows," 653 n8.

85. Luther's statement at Worms: "Here I stand; I can do no other" is a radical, but classical example of such helplessness.

86. *CAV*, 31–54.

87. *PK*, 45.

88. *CAV*, 181 n11. However, Hauerwas critically notes that in spite of Aristotle's general attempt to rehabilitate the 'appearances' and thus the inescapability of luck, Aristotle's "account of the high-minded man who is always ready to give but not receive, who wants his friends near him when he has benefited from good fortune but not bad, still manifests the desire to give an account of the moral life that is impervious to fortune." See "Can Aristotle Be a Liberal?" 675–91.

89. *CAV*, 180. While in agreement with many aspects (including this one) of Nussbaum's *Fragility*, Hauerwas has nevertheless raised serious and valid questions concerning Nussbaum's essentialism, which leads Nussbaum to assume that she is dealing with constant 'human' problems which have not changed over the centuries (*Fragility*, 5, 15). The essentialism is also noticeable in other of Nussbaum's writings, like "Non-Relative Virtues," "Human Functioning and Social Justice," and "Recoiling from Reason." As a result of this essentialism, Nussbaum, Hauerwas thinks, effectively avoids the need to deal with the social and political implications of Aristotle's work and how, in particular, these implications are in profound tension with the liberal social and political forms of life. In the absence of any reference to the social-political forms of life that would make luck and tragedy part of an on-going narrative, "fragility" easily becomes just another "insight" for the liberal cultural elite. "Can Aristotle Be a Liberal?" 675–91.

90. *CC*, 106–7.

91. *PK*, 31, 47.

92. *PK*, 32; Niebuhr, *The Nature and Destiny*, 178–79.

93. Audi, "Responsible Action," 304–21.

94. Audi, "Responsible Action," 313, emphasis added.

95. Audi, "Responsible Action," 312.

96. Chalier, "Responsibility and Election," 66, emphasis added.

97. See, e.g., Fischer, *Moral Responsibility*; Schoeman, *Responsibility, Character, and the Emotions*; Scott, *The Metaphysics of Moral Responsibility*.

98. Nagel, "Moral Luck," 24–38.

99. Williams, "Moral Luck," 20–39.

100. The term is Bondi's. See Bondi, "The Elements of Character," 207.

101. Joel Kupperman suggests that part of the problem of character may have to do with the modern (narrow) concept of voluntary, which is generally defined as "immediately controlled or controllable by an act of the will." In spite of Kupperman's apt observation, he himself remains committed to a view of responsibility founded on this narrow concept of voluntary. Accordingly, he has to smuggle in a 'sociological' explanation to justify responsibility for character: The only reason why holding people responsible for their characters even if these are largely involuntary makes sense, Kupperman suggests, is because "it

is an effective and functional" way of modifying and controlling social behavior. See Kupperman, *Character*, 47–64.

102. As we shall shortly make clear, it is the discovery and use of the notions of narrative and tradition that provide a transition away from the early "Kantianism" within Hauerwas's work to a more historical account of ethics in general, and moral character in particular (see "New Introduction," *CCL*, xx). Accordingly, in our work, the designations "early" and "later" in relation to Hauerwas's work roughly correspond to before and after the publication of *Truthfulness and Tragedy* (1977), in which Hauerwas first elaborates the concept of narrative.

103. *CCL*, 48, 68–71, emphasis added. The emphasis clearly shows that any intellectualism in Hauerwas's early account of character is to be explained not in relation to the 'myth of the passions' (Lewis), but in relation to a foundational account of moral responsibility, which agency-theory neatly supports.

104. *CCL*, 49.

105. Meilaender, *The Theory and Practice of Virtue*, x; Quinn, "Is Athens Revived Jerusalem?" 51–56.

106. This explains why Audi ("Responsible Action," 312–16) resorts to the language of 'techniques'; Kupperman's language of "constructed self" also tends to point in this misleading direction (see Kupperman, *Character*, 40–45).

107. "New Introduction," *CCL*, xviii-xxvi.

108. Kosman, "Being Properly Affected," 115; emphasis added. See, however, Hauerwas's most recent qualification in this direction: "the language of choice in Aquinas does not mean, as it does for us, decision. That is, choice is not a chronological state prior to action nor does choice describe a cognitive operation we associate with judging. For the end, for Aquinas, is the principle, not the conclusion, of practical wisdom. For Aquinas, acts shaped by virtuous habits involve judgement and choice but not as if one precedes the other. Aquinas's account of these matters in the *Summa*, I-II, q.6–21, is descriptive and not prescriptive. Thus his circular account of the relation of "will" and "reason" is not vicious since neither "will" nor "reason" name separable faculties but rather descriptions meant to illumine how we become virtuous through God's activity." (Hauerwas, "Gay Friendship," 19).

109. "As men become builders by building and lyre-players by playing the lyre; so too we become just by doing just acts; temperate by doing temperate acts; brave by doing brave acts" (Aristotle, *NE* 1103a28f).

110. Among the interpretations that tend in this direction, see Hardie, *Aristotle's Ethical Theory*; Adkins, *Merit and Responsibility*; Engberg-Perdersen, *Aristotle's Theory of Moral Insight*; Urmson, *Aristotle's Ethics*.

111. Suavé-Meyer, *Aristotle on Moral Responsibility*, 48.

112. We find Suavé-Meyer's *Aristotle on Moral Responsibility* one of the best attempts in this direction.

113. "New Introduction," *CCL*, xx.

114. "New Introduction," *CCL*, xxvii-xxviii; *CAV*, 17–30.

115. The point is made by highlighting the differences between 'journey' and 'trip': "When I go on a trip, I know where I am going , how long it will take, what preparations I need to make, and what I am going to do or hope to accomplish. When I undertake a journey, I often have only a hazy idea of where I am going, how long it will take, how to prepare, or what I hope to accomplish." See *CAV*, 18. Because the success of a 'journey' depends so much on factors (contingent) beyond one's knowledge and planning, it involves a certain measure of "being out of control."

116. "Interview."

117. *PK*, 117.

118. For all of the direct quotations within this paragraph see *PK*, 35–49; *CC*, 144.

119. In a "New Introduction" to the third printing of *Character and the Christian Life* (1985), Hauerwas has acknowledged how the notion of character "was more like a door that, once opened, forced me to see things that I had no idea existed when I first began the work. My emphasis on the importance of vision and the centrality of narrative, together with the stress on the methodological significance of the church [community], are all the result of trying to work out the loose ends and implications involved [in the notion of character]" (*CCL*, xvii).

3. Re-visioning Ethics: 'Unselfing,' Language, and Particularity

1. *VV*, 1.

2. Iris Murdoch has published a number of novels and philosophical essays. The philosophical essays of interest to this chapter are: "On 'God' and 'Good',", "The Idea of Perfection," "The Sovereignty of the Good over Other Concepts," "Against Dryness: A Polemical Sketch," "Vision and Choice in Morality," and "The Sublime and the Good."

3. Murdoch, "Against Dryness," 43.

4. Murdoch, "Sovereignty," 80; "The Idea of Perfection," 30. See Kant, *Groundwork*, 3.

5. *VV*, 34, inside quotation from Murdoch, "On 'God' and 'Good',", 67–68.

6. Murdoch, "The Idea of Perfection," 8; "Sovereignty," 78.

7. Murdoch, "Against Dryness," 49.

8. Murdoch, "Vision and Choice," 202.

9. Murdoch, "Vision and Choice," 211.

10. Murdoch, "Sovereignty," 100–101.

11. Murdoch, "Sovereignty," 93.

12. Murdoch, "On 'God' and 'Good',", 55, emphasis hers.

13. Murdoch, "Sovereignty," 94–95.

14. *VV*, 37.

15. Hauerwas has gradually distanced himself from some of Murdoch's metaphysical and anthropological assumptions, especially the assumption of an aimless existence. We shall pursue these differences in the coming section. Here, it is the affinity between Hauerwas and Murdoch that is stressed.

16. Murdoch, "Sovereignty," 100.

17. Murdoch, "Sovereignty," 79.

18. Murdoch, "Sublime," 52; *VV*, 42–43.

19. *VV*, 32.

20. *VV*, 32; Murdoch, "Against Dryness," 49.

21. Murdoch, "On 'God' and 'Good'," 51.

22. Murdoch, "Sovereignty" 78–79, emphasis added.

23. In her recent work, it is particularly this element that defines Murdoch's "quarrel" with Christianity. The problem with Christianity is not the mythological character of its beliefs, but its tendency, like other totalizing metaphysical theories, to destroy the contingent. By "equating reality with integration in system, and degrees of reality with degrees of integration, and by implying that 'ultimately' or 'really' there is only one system" the contingent character of the particular, which is the source as well as the necessity of mysticism, is lost. Murdoch, *Metaphysics as a Guide*, 196.

24. Murdoch, "Sovereignty," 82.

25. *VV*, 33.

26. Murdoch, "On 'God' and 'Good'," 64. Plato banished the poets because he had come to "believe that all art is bad art, a mere fiction and consolation which distorts reality." Murdoch, "Sovereignty," 88.

27. Murdoch, "Sovereignty," 59.

28. Murdoch, "On 'God' and 'Good'," 55–56.

29. *VV*, 40; Murdoch, "Sovereignty," 95; "The Idea of Perfection," 23.

30. Murdoch, "Sovereignty," 95.

31. Hauerwas, "The Demands of a Truthful Story," 66.

32. Murdoch, "On 'God' and 'Good'," 56.

33. Murdoch, "Sovereignty," 91.

34. Murdoch, "On 'God' and 'Good'," 50; "The Idea of Perfection," 34; Weil, *Waiting on God*, 125–29.

35. *VV*, 58. There is accordingly a kind of flowing-in and flowing-out of clear-sightedness, either way in the direction of goodness. On the one hand, goodness is that which is seen, and hence realized, by the condition of clear-sightedness; on the other, goodness is that which precisely enables one to see, and thus to realize, clear-sightedness. See Stewart-Robertson, "Philosophical Reflections," 59.

36. *PK*, 129; "Hope Faces Power," 456–79.

37. Nussbaum, "Finely Aware and Richly Responsible," 148–67.

38. Bell, "Bad Art," 162–63.

39. Murdoch, "Sovereignty," 87. See also Dunbar, "On Art, Morals and Religion," 522.

40. Murdoch, "On 'God' and 'Good'," 65.

41. "The Novel as a School for Virtue," in *DF*, 31–57.

42. Murdoch, "Sovereignty," 87.

43. *VV*, 39.

44. *VV*, 40, citing Murdoch, "Sublime," 54–55.

45. Hauerwas, "Reflections on the Relation between Morality and Art," [hereafter "Morality and Art"], 14–17.

46. "Morality and Art," 14–15; the quoted portion is from Beardsome, *Art and Morality*, 17.

47. Nielsen, *Why Be Moral?*

48. "Morality and Art," 17. See also Murdoch, "Sovereignty," 86–87.

49. "Morality and Art," 17.

50. "Morality and Art," 17.

51. See his "Murdochian Muddles: Can We Get through Them If God Does Not Exist?" The occasion for the paper was the D. R. Sharpe Lectureship on Social Ethics (organized by the Divinity School, University of Chicago) May 1994. Other papers of this lectureship have recently been published under one title, *Iris Murdoch and the Search for Human Goodness*, ed. Maria Antonaccio and William Schweiker.

52. Murdoch, "On 'God' and 'Good'," 71.

53. "Murdochian Muddles," 194.

54. "Murdochian Muddles," 205 n21. Recent enthusiasm about contingency—as exemplified, for example, in Rorty's *Contingency, Irony, and Solidarity*—stand under critical censure here. However, in relation to Murdoch, one can (even though Hauerwas does not) make a case about her existentialism. Having excluded any teleological framework as a form of "consolation," Murdoch seems to require the individual person—subsumed in contingency and a metaphysically meaningless world—as moral, to reinvent himself or herself out of nothing. This may bring her (in spite of herself) close to Sartre, who, in *Being and Nothingness*, describes the ego as created by itself *ex nihilo*. In fact, in the transcendence of the ego, all that seems to distinguish Murdoch from Sartre is an apparent—but inexplicable—realism about the "good" and her definition of "love," which sharply clashes with Sartre's masochism (love as enjoyment of suppression of one's desires).

55. "Murdochian Muddles," 204.

56. A case concerning Murdoch's intuitionism could rightly be made. Murdoch endorses G. E. Moore's belief that the good is a suprasensible, mysterious, and indefinable quality. See Murdoch, "The Idea of Perfection," 3–4.

57. "Murdochian Muddles," 206.

58. "Murdochian Muddles," 206.

59. "Murdochian Muddles," 192; inside quotation is from Murdoch, "Sovereignty," 33.

60. G. Loughlin, "See-Saying/Say-Seeing," *Theology* 91 (1988): 201–9.

61. Murdoch, "The Idea of Perfection," 33. Murdoch's views on the relation between thought ("a 'private' activity which goes on in our heads") and language are most clearly set out in her early article, "Thinking and Language."

62. *PK,* 117.

63. *TT,* 18.

64. Wittgenstein, *Philosophical Investigations* II, 193e–208.

65. *TT,* 21.

66. "The Demands of a Truthful Story," 66.

67. *VV,* 14–20; Kovesi, *Moral Notions,* 83 ff.

68. See also Lovibond, *Realism and Imagination,* 23–26, 36–45; Wittgenstein, *Philosophical Investigations* I, #97; Pinches, *Describing Morally,* 61 ff.

69. What Wittgenstein denies is the assumption that we can draw an intelligible metaphysical distinction between those parts of assertoric discourse which do, and those which do not, genuinely *describe* reality. The homogeneity of language is not, of course, asserted at the phenomenal level where there are manifestly different kinds of language games. See Wittgenstein, *Philosophical Investigations* I, #486, p. 23.

70. *VV,* 19.

71. Murdoch, "The Idea of Perfection," 37.

72. Murdoch, "The Idea of Perfection," 40.

73. Murdoch, "Sovereignty," 59. See, however, a somewhat more nuanced distinction between imagination and fantasy by Murdoch in "Against Dryness," 48.

74. Hauerwas, "Jesus and/as the Non-Violent Imagination of the Church," [hereafter as "Non-Violent Imagination"], 87. Romanticism is thus the flip side of rationalism. In reaction to rationalists, romanticism made the imagination the supreme faculty.

75. "Non-Violent Imagination," 81, 83.

76. *PK,* 120.

77. "Disciplined Seeing," 250, 251. See also *DF,* 52.

78. *AN,* 55, 52; "Disciplined Seeing," 253.

79. Guevin, "The Moral Imagination," 64.

80. Hauerwas's familiar and favorite example of a craft is bricklaying, the craft of his late father. See "How to Lay Bricks and Make Disciples," *AC,* 93–112; *GC,* 44–49.

81. *RA,* 98.

82. Craig Carr, for example, defends the legitimacy of Kant's notion of political authority. He argues that Kant's appeal to political authority is not inconsistent with his (Kant's) moral philosophy, as it is often supposed. Rather,

Kant's notion of coercion provides the bridge that reconciles his use of political authority with his notion of moral autonomy. "Kant's Theory of Political Authority," 719–31.

83. Gadamer, *Truth and Method*, 297.

84. *AC*, 105; *SP*, 45.

85. In *Deceit, Desire and the Novel*, René Girard develops the mimetic structure of desire by attending to characters in the work of literary authors such as Proust, Dostoevsky, and Flaubert. What is instructive about Girard's overall project is that he is able to finally link this 'universality of mimesis' to the themes of rivalry, violence, and victimization in order to show that human social order is dependent upon the collective violence of periodical victim-making. See Girard, *Things Hidden Since the Foundation of the World*. Milbank *(Theology and Social Theory)* has taken up Girard's thesis in order to show that Christianity 'interrupts' this cycle of violence through an extra-social intervention in the shape of an 'incarnation' and 'forgiveness of sins.' See Fergus Kerr, "Rescuing Girard's Argument?" 385–99. Paul Dumouchel, on the other hand, applies Girard's work to a critical assessment of capitalistic economics. He shows how it is the mimetic stimulation of desire which lies behind the world of commercial advertisement, and leads to the omnipresence of the market through the creation of ever new semiocratic relations and artificial needs. See Dumouchel and Dupuy, *L'enfer des choses*.

86. *PK*, 117.

87. "Red Wheelbarrows," 646–47.

88. *SP*, 40.

89. *AC*, 93–112; *SP*, 39–62. Hauerwas develops this account in relation to MacIntyre's account of crafts in *Three Rival Versions*, and in relation to MacIntyre's understanding of authority as a moral-political concept developed in relation to medicine. See MacIntyre, "Patients as Agents," 197–212.

90. *SP*, 57 n12, quoting MacIntyre, *After Virtue*, 175.

91. *SP*, 44. No doubt, there is always a danger of crafts being obstructed from their goals through domination by the external goods of money, fame, or power.

92. *AC*, 106, citing MacIntyre, *Three Rival Versions*, 64–65.

93. *AC*, 101-2.

94. MacIntyre, *After Virtue*, 177.

95. *AC*, 102; *RA*, 40; *SP*, 43.

96. Aristotle, *NE* 6.11.1143b11–14.

97. *SP*, 80; MacIntyre, *After Virtue*, 76–83.

98. Lovibond, *Realism and Imagination*, 82.

99. *AC*, 98.

100. *AC*, 98.

101. *AC*, 180 n8; see also *AC* 98. This is the dialectical sense of authority and obedience that comes close to Newman's "Illative Sense" *(A Grammar of Assent)*.

102. Lovibond, *Realism and Imagination*, 105. The key text is Wittgenstein's *On Certainty*, #206: "If you learn more, you too will think the same."

103. *CC*, 60–61; *SP*, 43; *AC*, 105.

104. *AC*, 118 n11.

105. *CC*, 62.

106. "The language of 'vision'," Hauerwas claims, "is my attempt to reformulate Aristotle's *phronēsis*." See "Red Wheelbarrows," 647.

107. As Wesley Robbins seems to think. See his "On the Role of Vision in Morality," 623–42.

4. Historicity and Contingency: Narrative Identity and Moral Rationality

1. *TT*, 1.

2. Lauritzen, "Is 'Narrative' Really a Panacea?" 322.

3. Ricoeur's *Time and Narrative* remains perhaps the most philosophically developed argument for narrative.

4. For a good introduction to the trends in narrative theology, see Goldberg, *Theology and Narrative: A Critical Introduction*; Stroup, *The Promise of Narrative Theology*; Nelson, *Narrative and Morality*.

5. George Stroup suggests that part of the reason why the literature on narrative continues to grow without direction or "in every conceivable direction" might lie in the fact that there is no obvious philosophical resource for narrative theology. "Narrative theology does not necessarily need a philosophical 'foundation', but it does need help thinking critically about questions of methodology and epistemology. While process theology has a philosophical conversation partner in Whitehead and Hartshorne and theological existentialism can appeal to Heidegger, narrative theology has no obvious conversation partner in philosophy that can provide it with an epistemology and a methodology." Stroup, "Theology of Narrative," 425.

6. *PK*, xxv. Hauerwas's original interest in story goes back to the influence of Hans Frei and Julian Hartt. *PK*, xxi, xxv

7. *PK*, xxv. See also, Stroup, "Theology of Narrative," 428. Paul Nelson, however, falls into this mistake. See Nelson, *Narrative and Morality*, 111.

8. *PK*, xxv.

9. *TT*, 72; "Introduction," *WN*, 1; Stroup, "A Bibliographical Critique," 134.

10. "Introduction," to *WN*, 4.

11. "Introduction," to *WN*, 5.

12. *TT*, 76.

13. *TT*, 75 (emphasis added), quoting Mink, "History and Fiction," 545.

14. Ricoeur, *Time and Narrative* I, 52–87. See also: Narrative is "the privileged means by which we reconfigure our confused, unformed, and . . . mute temporal existence" (Ricoeur, *Time and Narrative* I, xi).

15. As Steven Crites notes, "Narrative form is primitive in human experience. Only the narrative form can comprehend the tensions, surprises, disappointments, reversals and accomplishments of actual temporal experience." Crites, "The Narrative Quality of Experience," 306.

16. *TT*, 79. Internal quotation is from Hannah Arendt, *The Human Condition*, p. 286.

17. Arendt, *The Human Condition*, 286.

18. *CC*, 144.

19. Allen, "When Narrative Fails," 27, 28.

20. *TT*, 27.

21. Kerby, *Narrative and the Self*, 4.

22. Quingley, "The Ethical and Narrative Self," 43.

23. *TT*, 78, quoting TeSelle, "The Experience of Coming to Belief," *Theology Today* 32/2 (July 1975), 286.

24. *CET*, 25–46.

25. *CET*, 31.

26. *CET*, 36.

27. *TT*, 21–22; *VV*, 72, 116.

28. *TT*, 73.

29. *CC*, 96, emphasis added.

30. *PK*, 45, quoting MacIntyre, *After Virtue*, 206.

31. *PK*, 28, emphasis added.

32. *CC*, 61.

33. *CC*, 60.

34. *PK*, 46, quoting MacIntyre, *After Virtue*, p. 207.

35. *CC*, 14, emphasis added; *PK*, 120.

36. *PK*, 118–19, quoting MacIntyre, "Theology, Ethics," 437.

37. MacIntyre, *After Virtue*, 204.

38. *CC*, 114.

39. *TT*, 42.

40. See, e.g., W. Frankena, "Conversations with Carney and Hauerwas," 45–62; and Robbins, "Narrative, Morality and Religion," 161–76.

41. This is the sense in which Michael Oakeshott rightly refers to rules and obligations as "abridgements of the tradition." Oakeshott, *Rationalism and Politics*, 91–92; 97–98.

42. In a number of related essays Hauerwas has argued that in the absence of a substantive narrative and sustaining community, marriage, the family, parenthood and sex become morally unintelligible, as they become easily captured by liberal and romantic ideals of "rights," "love," personal fulfillment, etc. See for example, "The Politics of Sex" (*AC*, 113–32); "The Moral Value of the Family," (*CC*, 155–66); "The Family: Theological and Ethical Reflections" (*CC*, 167–74);

"Sex in Public: Toward a Christian Ethics of Sex" (*CC*, 175–95); "From Conduct to Character: A Guide to Sexual Adventure," 12–16.

43. *CC*, 168, 172, 174.

44. *CC*, 191.

45. "The Family as a School for Character," 276.

46. *CC*, 190. The reason that singleness made marriage possible within the early Church is that only when we realize we do not have to marry, does marriage between Christians become a vocation rather than a necessity.

47. *CC*, 190, 191.

48. *CC*, 191, 210, emphasis added.

49. *CC*, 227; *SP*, 147–49.

50. *CC*, 165.

51. "The Family as a School for Character," 277.

52. *CC*, 165, 192, 226.

53. Nelson, *Narrative and Morality*, 145–47.

54. Accordingly, the argument developed here in relation to the notions of "family" and "marriage" can be validly extended to other practices and moral notions as well. On Hauerwas's related reflections on the cases of medicine, suicide, euthanasia, and abortion, see the collection of essays in *Suffering Presence: Reflections on Medicine, the Mentally Handicapped, and the Church*; "Memory, Community and the Reasons for Living: Reflections on Suicide and Euthanasia" (*TT*, 101–15); "Having and Learning to Care for Retarded Children" (*TT*, 147–56); "The Retarded and the Criteria for the Human" (*TT*, 157–63); "Why Abortion Is a Religious Issue" (*CC*, 196–211); "Abortion, Why the Arguments Fail" (*CC*, 212–29).

55. Our purpose in this subsection has not been to vindicate the coherency and comprehensiveness of Christian story in relation to liberalism. For this, one would need to appeal to the criteria of a truthful story (see below at chapter 4, section 2), according to which Hauerwas finds the liberal story of marriage as a union between two people "for their mutual fulfillment" deficient on at least two counts. First, such a story is not internally coherent enough to sustain the very "intimacy" and "love" it purports to serve. The kind of family, Hauerwas writes, which is justified in the name of intimacy, ironically finds intimacy impossible to sustain. . . . unless marriage has a purpose beyond being together, it will certainly be a hell" (*CC*, 172). See also, "When families exist for no reason other than their own existence, they become quasi-churches, with sacrifices far too great and for insufficient reasons. The risk of families which demand that we love one another can be taken only when there are sustaining communities with sufficient convictions that can provide means to form and limit the status of the family." "Sex and Politics," 420–21. Secondly, this liberal story cannot sustain the tragic aspects of marriage, especially as these relate to lifelong

fidelity and to the having and caring for children in general and retarded children in particular. See *CC*, 173; *TT*, 147–83.

56. *CC*, 61.

57. *CC*, 13.

58. Adams's *Watership Down* recounts the exodus of a group of rabbits from their well-established warren of Sandleford because it is threatened with destruction. It narrates the hazardous journey that the group is forced to undergo in search of a new warren, ultimately Watership, as well as the dangerous undertaking of securing does from the militaristic warren of Efrafa. See *CC*, 9–35.

59. *CC*, 15, 18.

60. *CC*, 18–22.

61. *CC*, 20, quoting Adams.

62. *TT*, 95.

63. *CC*, 92; See also "Remembering as a Moral Task," in *AN*, 61–90.

64. *AN*, 75, emphasis added.

65. *TT*, 105–6; *CC*, 67; *AN*, 74–76; *PK*, 70.

66. *AN*, 86.

67. *RA*, 100; *TT*, 21.

68. MacIntyre, *Whose Justice?*, 326–69.

69. *CC*, 2.

70. *PK*, 1.

71. *CC*, 4; 289 n8.

72. *CC*, 95.

73. Natural law theorists, in Hauerwas's view, misleadingly (and misreadingly) assume that Aquinas's *Treatise on Law* (*Summa Theologiae* Qa 90–108) is an argument to establish reason as the one overriding role of man that determines and provides criteria to allocate and form other roles. However, according to Hauerwas, natural law in Aquinas is best discussed not in terms of a dominant role (rationality) to determine, allocate, and organize other roles, but in terms of how one is able to find a center for one's life amid the many powers, relations, and roles that lay claim to one. *TT*, 61–62.

74. *TT*, 65.

75. *TT*, 65.

76. As in attempts to justify "the need for morality," or "why be moral," in terms of individual benefit or societal survival and smooth operation proffered under various versions of utilitarianism, naturalism, or biologism. See Mackie, *Ethics*, 105–200.

77. See below, chapter 6, second section.

78. Joseph Dunne *(Back to Rough Ground)* provides a penetrating and invaluable analysis of Aristotle's attempt to resist this tendency. Dunne also examines some key authors in the modern period who have tried to resist the

technicalist tendency, Newman in the sphere of religion, Collingwood in art, Arendt in politics, and Gadamer in philosophy in general. Desmond *(Philosophy and Its Others)* also provides another largely successful (as well as entertaining) attempt to qualify the technicalist way of thinking by calling attention to other valid, albeit different, ways of being mindful.

79. *TT,* 27–28, 64–65.

80. "Ethicist as a Theologian," 409.

81. *TT,* 65.

82. *TT,* 27, 65, 219.

83. *TT,* 35, quoting Aristotle, *NE* 1144a24–1144a37.

84. "Using Aristotle's discriminations as a part of reference is meant to indicate that our thesis could be regarded as a development of his; in fact, we would be pleased to find it judged to be so." *TT,* 27.

85. This intellectual moment of *phronēsis* particularly becomes clear in the passage that comes after this one (*NE* 6.13), when Aristotle dialectically sets out a critique of natural virtue *(phusike arete)* which shows that the latter falls short of true virtue *(kuria arete)* in much the same way that cleverness is shown, in the passage here to fall short of *phronēsis.* There, Aristotle demonstrates that natural virtue is not true virtue because it is not "in accordance with the 'right reason'; 'right reason' being the reason that accords with *phronēsis*" (*NE* 1144b17–1145a6). See also, Richard Sorabji, "Aristotle on the Role of Intellect," 107–12.

86. Our explication of these two strands owes a great deal to Dunne, *Back to the Rough Ground.* Although Hauerwas himself has not referred to Dunne's work in writing, he drew my attention to it in our discussion over these issues ("Interview").

87. 'Practical' in the sense of nontheoretical, the opposite of theoretical, or simply, intellectual activity by which the mind is enabled to draw, following strict logic, inferences from certain principles and premises. This theoretical ideal reaches its highest expression in philosophical wisdom *(sophia),* which combines the power of apprehending first principles *(nous)* with the demonstrative power of tracing other knowledge back to them *(epistēmē).* See Aristotle, *NE* 1141a17–20.

88. "Making and acting are different . . . so that the reasoned state of capacity to act [i.e., *phronēsis*] is different from the reasoned state of capacity to make [i.e., *technē*]" (*NE* 1140a2–5); and again, "*phronēsis* cannot be . . . *technē* . . . because action and making are different kinds of things" (*NE* 1140b1–4).

89. Dunne, *Back to the Rough Ground,* 262.

90. Dunne expresses this difference even more concretely when he notes that "while there is such a thing as excellence in *technē,* there is no such thing as excellence in *phronēsis.*" *Phronēsis* simply *is* an excellence." Dunne, *Back to the Rough Ground,* 264. The difference has to do with the realization that

the excellence in *technē* is in great measure judged by the separable end it produces—a product which might still be appropriated for other purposes. For example, an excellent shoe may be appropriated for other purposes other than
walking. *Phronēsis*, however, simply *is* the excellence, and does not await to be
put to use. *Phronēsis* cannot be appropriated for 'unphronetic' purposes. See
Aristotle, *NE* 1140b21–4,

91. Urmson, *Aristotle's Ethics*, 82.

92. Dunne, *Back to the Rough Ground*, 276, 268.

93. By contrast, works produced by *technē* can be considered apart from
their relationship to their maker. For "they have their goodness in themselves"
(*NE* 1144a13–14).

94. *TT*, 24.

95. "Why the Truth Demands Truthfulness," in *WN*, 303–10.

96. *TT*, 27, emphasis added. Although Aristotle himself does not explicitly
use the image of the "open sea," this image is implied in his (Aristotle's) reference to the art of navigation, particularly by showing how within such an art,
"being circumscribed by no limit" (open sea), the play of chance is ineliminable
(*NE* 1104a2–10; 1096a31).

97. Aristotle, *NE* 1104a2–10; also *NE* 1096a31.

98. Dunne, *Back to the Rough Ground*, 254.

99. That is why we wondered whether one can indeed still refer to them as
technai, for as Aristotle himself admits in another work, "those occupations are
most truly *technai* in which there is the least element of chance," Aristotle,
Politics, 1.11.1258b35.

100. Dunne, *Back to the Rough Ground*, 258.

101. Dunne, *Back to the Rough Ground*, 256.

102. *AC*, 93–112; and see earlier at chapter 3.

103. *PK*, 11; *CC*, 108; *DF*, 152.

104. Nothing could therefore be further from the truth than Albert Musschenga's characterization of a narrative conception of the moral life: "the central ethical question people should ask themselves when taking decisions is not
whether a particular decision is right, but whether it fits into their life story."
See Musschenga, "Narrative Theology and Narrative Ethics," 176, 187–88.

105. *WW*, 89, quoting Nussbaum, *Fragility*, 306.

106. We are aware of, but do not wish to engage, the literature surrounding
the proper interpretation of Aristotle's doctrine of the mean. We are content just
to note with Dunne that this doctrine does not instill an ideal of ultrasobriety or
moderation (a meaning reinforced by some of the associations with prudence,
the word most often used to translate *phronēsis*). See Dunne, *Back to the Rough
Ground*, 311.

107. Aristotle, *NE* 2.6 1107a1–2. Dunne, *Back to the Rough Ground*, 312

108. *TT*, 27. For Hauerwas, the technist tendency within the standard account has been nothing but a seductive temptation, which has only offered a

false sense of security, mastery, and universalizable validity. William Desmond is in agreement when he writes that, "impatient with all obscurity, . . . the technist mind seduces us with secure, definite procedures for tackling issues, procedures to guarantee univocal solutions to troubling ambiguity, unambiguous rules which, if only we follow them, will lead us from the labyrinth of perplexity. . . . it wants to put univocal clarity in what it sees as the equivocity of our being in the middle." Desmond, *Philosophy and Its Others*, 26.

109. *TT*, 35.

110. *CC*, 97.

111. *CC*, 95.

112. *CC*, 149; *TT*, 78.

113. *TT*, 35. "Red Wheelbarrows," 651.

114. According to Terrence Tilley: A "story can be measured by the extent that it re-presents our world (or part of it) in a revealing way; is coherent by being consistent with other facts we recognize, referring and attributing accurately, shows a person ways to overcome self-deception; shows a person how to be honest in shared moral life; and enables a person to be constant (stubborn) in seeking what is true" (cited by Hauerwas at "Why the Truth Demands Truthfulness," 306). Anthony Kerby provides yet another list: "The legitimation of one narrative over another is often due not to its correspondence to 'the way things really are' but to its pragmatic and comprehensive nature. Is it edifying, without being narcissistic or egotistic? Does it make sense of what we otherwise know? Is it useful in furthering other and interesting interpretations? Kerby, *Narrative and the Self*, 97.

115. "I used this notion of 'stepping back', which I got from Stuart Hampshire, but I have left it behind, because I think it reinforces the liberal self"—an unencumbered self that thinks it can always withdraw from its actual commitments into a sort of 'original position' which ensures both its freedom and rationality. That is a mistake, since "you are always stepping back into another tradition" ("Interview").

116. *TT*, 85.

117. *TT*, 85–88; Fingarette, *Self-Deception*, 38ff.

118. Ronald Hepburn rightly points out that the danger of a story ethic lies here. There is great pressure for one living by a story not to violate the unity of his pattern. While this is certainly right, I am not sure about his optimism about the possibility of those who claim to be living by an ethics of principles to be able to readily change them according to their soundness. Hepburn, "Vision and Choice," 193.

119. *AN*, 81 n13. See also "Forgiveness and Political Community," 15–16; "The Holocaust and the Duty to Forgive," 137–39; "Forgiveness and Forgetting," 15–16. On humility as a condition for objectivity, see Kotva, "Christian Virtue Ethics," 46.

120. *CC*, 14; *PK*, 120.

121. *TT,* 78.

122. See also Anthony Kerby: A primary way to overcome, at least in part, the ideological use of narrative is "to open ourselves to alternative viewpoints and world views, and to alternate interpretations." Kerby, *Narrative and the Self,* 97.

123. *TT,* 80 n30; *TT,* 31, 82–98; "Constancy and Forgiveness," in *DF,* 31–57. Significant as it is, fictional contact can never be a surrogate for the hermeneutical necessity of actual contact with real people. This particularly needs to be stressed in the context of the technology-controlled world of cyberspace. In cyberspace, a lonely soul, the product of modern market and liberal individualism, seeks engagement with the other, but without, however, the epistemological and moral challenge such a contact would normally have. No doubt, cyber-friendship may create certain feelings and thoughts, but only in a way which significantly detaches them from their 'normal' context in life. This means that one is neither able to be seriously challenged by, nor himself/herself able to help or hinder, benefit or harm, comfort or dismay, the other. For this danger in fictional literature in general, see John Norton, "Review of *Love's Knowledge,*" 492–95.

124. *TT,* 31–34.

125. Book 6 of the *Confessions* is particularly interesting as it provides a critique of Manicheanism that rings true of modern rationalist pretensions: "From now on I began to prefer the Catholic teaching. The Church demanded that certain things should be believed even though they could not be proved. . . . I thought that the Church was entirely honest in this and far less pretentious than the Manichees, who laughed at people who took things on faith, made rash promises of scientific knowledge, and then put forward a whole system of preposterous inventions which they expected their followers to believe on trust because they could not be proved" (6.5). See *TT,* 34. For a similar argument concerning the 'faith' of science, see Desmond, *Philosophy and Its Other,* 29–34.

126. *TT,* 82–98. See also "Among the Moved," 47–49.

127. *CET,* 199–220.

128. *CC,* 9–35.

Part II: Will the Real Sectarian Stand Up? Reason, Religion, and Politics within the Limits of History

1. See Gustafson, "The Sectarian Temptation," 83–94; Miscamble, "Sectarian Pacifism," 69–77; Holland, "The Problems and Prospects," 157–68; Nelson, *Narrative and Morality,* 130–39; Ogletree, "Character and Narrative," 30.

2. Murphy and McClendon, "Modern and Postmodern Theologies," 192–214.

3. Murphy and McClendon, "Modern and Postmodern Theologies, 199. See also Nuyen, "Postmodern Theology and Philosophy, 67.

5. Phronetic Particularity: Moral Objectivity beyond Subjectivism and Relativism

1. *CET,* 20 n11, emphasis added. See MacIntyre, "Objectivity in Morality," 36–37.

2. Nussbaum, *Fragility,* 248. The context and central argument of Nussbaum's work is very instructive for an appreciation of the issues at stake. Greek *ethos,* according to Nussbaum, was one in which ordinary experience remained fragile, exposed to the vicissitudes of luck *(tuche),* by one's dependence on others, by the chronic possibility of conflict inherent in the plurality of one's engagements, and by the unruly depths within oneself. What was "heroic" but misleading in the Greek philosophy (represented by Plato) was precisely its attempt, centered on the prioritization of the concept of *technē,* to wrest from all this contingency some measure of reliability and control. It is, therefore, Aristotle and not Plato who is the hero of Nussbaum's work. For, against the background of this "heroic" attempt, Aristotle aspired to the task of "saving the appearances," i.e., vindicating, through his concept of *phronēsis,* the 'truth' contained within practices of everyday life. See Nussbaum, *Fragility,* 6–7.

3. McCormick, *Notes on Moral Theology,* 23–27.

4. McCormick, *Notes on Moral Theology,* 25.

5. Childress, "Scripture and Christian Ethics," 371–80.

6. Schüller, "The Debate on," 222.

7. Strawson, "Social Morality and Individual Ideal," 285.

8. See, e.g., Vivas, *The Moral Life and the Ethical Life;* Kupperman, *The Foundations of Morality.*

9. Palmer, *Hermeneutics,* 195.

10. Dunne, *Back to the Rough Ground,* 290. For this reason Dunne finds it desirable to retain *phronēsis* rather than use "practical wisdom" or "practical knowledge," by which it is normally translated.

11. Dunne, *Back to the Rough Ground,* 281, 293.

12. Dunne, *Back to the Rough Ground,* 293.

13. *CC,* 63.

14. Dunne, *Back to the Rough Ground,* 293.

15. Dunne, *Back to the Rough Ground,* 294.

16. *CC,* 26.

17. Dunne, *Back to the Rough Ground,* 305–6.

18. *VV,* 30–47; *AN,* 55, "Disciplined Seeing," 253.

19. *TT,* 84–85.

20. The direct quotations in this paragraph are from *PK,* 46, 120; *CC,* 14.

21. *PK,* 120; 134.

22. *CC,* 92; *PK,* 120.

23. *CC,* 63.

24. See, for example, *CC,* 2, 10, 22–27, 105–6; *PK,* 109. More on the

hermeneutical significance of the presence of the 'stranger' and 'witness' in the fourth section of this chapter.

25. *PK*, 45.

26. *CAV*, 31–51.

27. *DF*, 31–57.

28. "In Praise of Gossip," 5, 23.

29. *PK*, 121.

30. We adopt this somewhat clumsy construction in order to emphasize the notion of objectivity as a process.

31. Schnädelbach, "What Is Neo-Aristotelianism?" 235.

32. Schnädelbach, "What Is Neo-Aristotelianism?" 236. See also p. 234.

33. Schnädelbach, "What Is Neo-Aristotelianism?" 236.

34. Schnädelbach, "What Is Neo-Aristotelianism?" 234, emphasis his.

35. MacIntyre, *After Virtue*, 205–6.

36. *TT*, 24.

37. They thus confirm Thomas Nagel's description of the way one comes to the Moral Point of View, namely, by "stepping outside ourselves" (140); "transcending the appearances" (139); transcending "one's time and place" (187); and escaping "the specific contingencies of one's creaturely point of view" (9). All page references refer to Nagel, *The View from Nowhere*.

38. See chapter 7 below.

39. Gustafson, "The Sectarian Temptation," 88. We shall return to the sociological and political implications of this accusation in the following two chapters of our work.

40. Gustafson, "The Sectarian Temptation," 93.

41. The ambiguous nature of Gustafson's overall ethical and epistemological position is particularly notable from his magisterial *Ethics from a Theocentric Perspective*. Gustafson is critical of the philosophical project which assumes its task is to overcome all historical particularity by anchoring religious and moral beliefs in the fictive community of "all rational individuals." The result of this illusory search for universality, Gustafson notes is to make man, and in particular a parochial view of rationality, the measurer of all things. (Gustafson, *Ethics*, vol. I, 81). Our inherent historical nature and our dependence on tradition make it inevitable that a search for universality can come only by paying close attention to the particular. In spite of this awareness, Gustafson still seeks to find an epistemological high point that can ensure the ability to stand back from our histories, as well as provide the basis for the pursuit of universality and objectivity. See Hauerwas, "God the Measurer," 402–11; "Time and History," in *WW*, 62–81.

42. *CC*, 72.

43. *CET*, 10, 20.

44. Lovibond, *Realism and Imagination*, 45. See Wittgenstein, *Remarks on the Foundations of Mathematics*, 6 #23.

45. Lovibond, *Realism and Imagination*, 19.

46. Lovibond, *Realism and Imagination*, 39.

47. Lovibond, *Realism and Imagination*, 39. The inside quotations refer to Wittgenstein, *Philosophical Investigations* 1 #217. See also *On Certainty*, #204: "Giving grounds, however, justifying the evidence, comes to an end;—but the end is not certain propositions' striking us immediately as true, i.e., it is not a kind of *seeing* on our part; it is our *acting*, which lies at the bottom of the language-game."

48. Richard Rorty, *Philosophy and the Mirror*, 5.

49. Lovibond, *Realism and Imagination*, 42.

50. Lovibond, *Realism and Imagination*, 40, reference to Wittgenstein, *Philosophical Investigations* 1 #241.

51. Wittgenstein, *On Certainty*, ##559; 317.

52. Wong, "Moral Realism without Foundations," 96.

53. Lovibond, *Realism and Imagination*, 33. However, contrary to Lovibond, the induction can never be fully complete.

54. Lovibond, *Realism and Imagination*, 70.

55. "Can one learn this knowledge? Yes, some can. Not, however, by taking a course in it, but through *'experience'*—Can someone else be a man's teacher in this? Certainly. From time to time he gives him the right *tip.*—This is what 'learning' and 'teaching' are like there.—What one acquires here is not a technique; one learns correct judgments. There are also rules, but they do not form a system, and only experienced people can apply them right. Unlike calculating rules." Wittgenstein, *Philosophical Investigations* 2, #227.

56. Lovibond, *Realism and Imagination*, 32–33.

57. This means the rejection of objectivism in the sense that Richard Bernstein defines it, namely "the basic conviction that there is or must be some permanent, ahistorical matrix or framework to which we can ultimately appeal in determing the nature of rationality, knowledge, truth, reality, goodness, or rightness. . . . Objectivism is closely related to foundationalism and the search for an Archimedean point. The Objectivism maintains that unless we can ground philosophy, knowledge, or language in a rigorous manner we cannot avoid radical skepticism." Bernstein, *Beyond Objectivism and Relativism*, 8.

58. Lovibond, *Realism and Imagination*, 33. Collingwood develops this idea of culmination in the context of explaining the notion of a "scale of forms" as understood within the idealist tradition. In defining a philosophical concept, Collingwood shows, our thinking about the subject matter becomes "clearer and more complete." However, wherever we stand in the scale, we stand at a culmination. Collingwood, *An Essay on Philosophical Method*, 100–101.

59. Lovibond, *Realism and Imagination*, 34.

60. Lovibond, *Realism and Imagination*, 58–62.

61. Lovibond, *Realism and Imagination*, 58.

62. Lovibond, *Realism and Imagination*, 65; reference to Wittgenstein, *On Certainty*, #493.

63. *CC*, 133.

64. However, Lovibond misleadingly adopts this Kantian idiom, and confirms our suspicion of a lurking foundationalism in her work. Talking about intellectual authorities, Lovibond suggests that their judgments are authoritative because they embody within the tradition, that standpoint, where "if there really existed an 'ideal spectator of the moral life,' he would have to stand" (Lovibond, *Realism and Imagination*, 59).

65. Lovibond, *Realism and Imagination*, 59.

66. Lovibond, *Realism and Imagination*, 61.

67. Wittgenstein, *Philosophical Investigations* 1, #482.

68. Contrary to Schnädelbach, "What is Neo-Aristotelianism?" 225–29.

69. *CC*, 72; Lovibond, *Realism and Imagination*, 108; MacIntyre, *Whose Justice?* 367.

70. Rorty, *Philosophy and the Mirror*, 321.

71. These critical remarks on algebraic rationality were developed independently of, but seem to be confirmed by, Stanley Fish's remarks on "moral algebra." See Fish, *There Is No Such Thing*, ix, 11, passim.

72. *PK*, xxv; *WN*, 303.

73. Hartt, "Some Theological Investments in Story," in *WN*, 279–92. Hauerwas's response: "Why the Truth Demands Truthfulness: An Imperious Engagement with Hartt," *WN*, 303–10. Hartt's rejoinder: "Reply to Crites and Hauerwas," *WN*, 311–19.

74. Hartt, "Theological Investments," 288.

75. Hartt, "Theological Investments," 289.

76. Hartt, "Theological Investments," 289.

77. There is great affinity here with Collingwood's denial of metaphysics as ontology. According to Collingwood, metaphysics does not say anything about reality, or the way the world *actually* is (pseudo-metaphysics). Metaphysics according to Collingwood is a historical study of "absolute presuppositions" or the way *we* describe, or think/talk about, reality (see Collingwood, *Essay on Metaphysics*). By way of acknowledging a general influence from Collingwood, Hauerwas remarks how he had "become fascinated with . . . Collingwood's analysis of historical investigation and construction" (*PK*, xx). In spite of this affinity and/or influence, there is one key difference between Hauerwas and Collingwood's historical conception of metaphysics. According to Collingwood, metaphysical statements (absolute presuppositions) can be neither true nor false. Collingwood accepts Ayer's logical positivism, according to which only empirical propositions can be verified, and they alone are therefore capable of being true or false. For Hauerwas, however, metaphysical claims can be true or false. However, their truth of falsity does not ultimately depend on how ade-

quately they mirror reality (actuality) but on historico-pragmatic considerations of witness and the richness of social practice and characters they engender.

78. "Why the Truth Demands Truthfulness," 308.

79. *CC*, 90; *PK*, 16, 54.

80. "Murdochian Muddles," 193–94;

81. "Why the Truth Demands Truthfulness," 308; *PK*, 159 n6.

82. *WW*, 192.

83. Lovibond, *Realism and Imagination*, 34.

84. Lovibond, *Realism and Imagination*, 217.

85. Lovibond, *Realism and Imagination*, 217.

86. Lovibond, *Realism and Imagination*, 218–19.

87. Lovibond, *Realism and Imagination*, 218.

88. The later sections of Lovibond's *Realism and Imagination* sit so uneasily with the earlier ones that one gets the impression that the book was written by two different persons. While the Lovibond of the first sections is thoroughly historical, and is driven by both a clearly focused and articulated antifoundational intent, the Lovibond of the later part of *Realism and Imagination* sounds increasingly murky and modernist as she reverts to appeals of a "cosmopolitan rationality." Whereas a clearly articulated Wittgensteinian conception marks the early sections, Hegelian assumptions are at work in the latter sections.

89. Whiteside, "Universality and Violence," 378.

90. *CET*, 61.

91. Hartt, "Theological Investments," 288; Gustafson, "The Sectarian Temptation," 83–94; Miscamble, "Sectarian Pacifism," 69–77; Robins,"Narrative, Morality and Religion," 175; Nelson, *Narrative and Morality*, 122–39.

92. See, e.g., MacIntyre, *Whose Justice?* 352–56.

93. Churchill, "The Bellman's Map," 480–81. Churchill refers to Nozick, *Philosophical Explanations*, 4–5.

94. Wittgenstein, *Philosophical Investigations*, 1, #124.

95. Van Gerwen, "The Church in the Theological Ethics," 55–63.

96. "Red Wheelbarrows," 649.

97. *VV*, 68–92; 222–41. See Strawson, "Social Morality and Individual Ideal," 280–98.

98. "Red Wheelbarrows," 649. Reference is made to MacIntyre, *After Virtue*, 207.

99. *VV*, 86. See R. M. Hare, *Freedom and Reason*; Singer, *Generalization in Ethics*.

100. *PK*, xxi.

101. *TT*, 9–10.

102. "Red Wheelbarrows," 651. McClendon and Smith defend this view of soft perspectivism as a middle position between the two extremes of hard perspectivism and non-perspectivism. While hard perspectivism considers different

traditions to be constituted in such a way that they (traditions) inevitably present radically different and irreducible perspectives of reality, non-perspectivism considers the differences and conflicts between people and communities to be only contingent, trivial, and easily surmountable. What McClendon and Smith consider the balanced position of soft perspectivism "regards convictional differences, and the conflicts flowing out of them, as expected but not inevitable, fundamental but not ultimate, and enduring but not inherently ineradicable. One or more common elements exist, but to discover and use these elements requires measures which cannot be limited along perspectival lines." See McClendon and Smith, *Understanding Religious Convictions*, 6–7.

103. *CC*, 102–3. See Harman, "Moral Relativity Defended," 3–22.

104. Churchill, "The Bellman's Map," 479; Geertz, "Anti-Anti-Relativism," 12.

105. *CC*, 104.

106. The theological importance of witness within Hauerwas's work emerged within the context of questions concerning the Church's social role. Since the primary ethical question for the Church is not *what to do*, but *who to be*, Hauerwas has argued that the primary social task of the Church is to be a people capable of hearing and telling the stories of God as revealed through the life, death, and resurrection of Christ. But since the telling of that story requires that Christians be a particular kind of people in order to hear and tell the story truthfully, then Christians are called, as their primary social task, to witness to the life (of peaceableness, justice, hope, etc.) made possible by their story. There is no need to rehearse here this theological sense of witness (which was sufficiently developed in our "The Distinctiveness of Christian Ethics," 57–65). What perhaps needs to be noted is that John Howard Yoder, a Mennonite theologian who taught at the University of Notre Dame, was the most singularly dominant influence behind this direction, as indeed behind the overall direction of Hauerwas's theological development.

107. *CC*, 105.

108. *AC*, 159.

109. *CC*, 2, 10, 22–27, 105–6; *PK*, 109, et passim.

110. "Learning to See Red Wheelbarrows," 651; *CC*, 48; *PK*, 27, 45.

111. For this historico-pragmatic sense of critique, see Schrag, "Interpretation, Narrative and Rationality," 98–115.

112. *CC*, 14; *PK*, 120.

113. On the factors and resolution of epistemological crisis, see MacIntyre, *Whose Justice?* 361–66; McClendon and Smith, *Understanding Religious Convictions*, 172 ff. However, MacIntyre's language of "victory" in relation to successful resolution of epistemological crisis may be misleading. One should avoid giving the impression of "success" or settling down, for the process dynamically and dialectically reconstitutes itself.

114. *AC,* 168.

115. The citation has been reformulated to fit the context here.

116. In this reconstruction, we are aware that we do make claims that, in some cases, go beyond Hauerwas's own. This is inevitable since, given both his theological (practical) preoccupation and the edifying nature of his work, Hauerwas is not interested in providing a systematic and comprehensive epistemological or metaphysical position. He is rather more interested in raising "the right questions" and challenging the limits of the standard formulations. See, for example, "Why the Truth Demands Truthfulness," 303, where he suggests that epistemological and metaphysical issues "are more appropriately dealt with indirectly."

117. *CET,* 10, 20 n11.

118. Guignon, "Philosophy after Wittgenstein and Heidegger," 668.

6. Cultural Linguistic Prospects: Religion beyond Sectarianism and Fideism

1. Gustafson, "The Sectarian Temptation," 92, 94; Holland, "The Problems and Prospects," 165–67.

2. Quirk, "Beyond Sectarianism," 81–82.

3. Gustafson, "The Sectarian Temptation," 96. Both the substance and language of this critique draws from Kai Nielsen. See Nielsen, "Wittgensteinian Fideism," 191–209. However, as Yon Huang has successfully shown, Nielsen's portrayal of Wittgenstein as a fideist is based on a gross misrepresentation of Wittgenstein's views on religious language. Huang, "Foundation of Religious Beliefs," 252–56.

4. Gustafson, "The Sectarian Temptation," 86. The same fear is behind Joseph Incandela's powerful and successful critique against those who would seek to use Wittgenstein's reference to "language games" or "forms of life" to avoid testing religious language. Incandela, "The Appropriation of Wittgenstein's Work," 457–74.

5. Surin, "Many Religions," 198.

6. For a treatment of various forms of fideism (perceptual, moral, and theological), see Penelhum, *God and Scepticis;* Stump, "Penelhum on Sceptics." On a different distinction between a theological and philosophical form of fideism, see Abraham, *An Introduction to the Philosophy of Religion,* 75–97.

7. Malcolm, "The Groundlessness of Belief," 99.

8. Stout, *Flight from Authority,* 25–94.

9. Stout, *Flight from Authority,* 235.

10. MacIntyre, "The Fate of Modern Theism," 11; Stout, *Flight from Authority,* 97.

11. Stout, *Flight from Authority,* 97.

12. Stout, *Flight from Authority,* 117. See, for example, John Toland's telling

title: *Christianity Not Mysterious* (1696). For a good anthology of seventeenth- and eighteenth-century deism, see Graham Waring, ed., *Deism and Natural Religion*.

13. Hegel clearly saw this danger, and tried, in the wake of Kant and Schleiermacher's reductive interpretations that only encouraged a liberal pietism, to give theism a public standing by subsuming Christianity within a higher synthesis. He was prepared to regard religious mysteries not as paradoxes to be explained away, but as essential truths of religious consciousness. "Religious consciousness attempts to say in symbols and stories what ordinary consciousness cannot say in more direct fashion. . . . Religious paradoxes should not be explained away in terms of ordinary language. Their whole point is to represent *(vorstellen)* what ordinary language consciousness cannot express directly—the underlying unities that escape the essentially rigid and divisive categories to which the understanding *[Verstand]* reduces everything. . . . This is what the new logic and conceptuality of Hegel's mature system are meant to provide: an interpretation of the hard paradoxes that, far from reducing them to the categories of the understanding or mistaking their higher truth for ordinary falsehood, raises them up to the comprehensive intelligibility of reason *[Vernunft]*." Stout, *Flight from Authority*, 136.

14. MacIntyre, "The Fate of Theism," 24; Stout, *Flight from Authority*, 97.

15. See King, "Fideism and Rationality," 441–43; Peterson, *Reason and Religious Belief*, 37–41.

16. Stout, *Flight from Authority*, 142.

17. Stout, *Flight from Authority*, 147.

18. Contrary to Whitmore, "Beyond Liberalism and Communitarianism," 211–12.

19. Hauerwas's continuing debt to Barth must nevertheless be acknowledged. He studied Barth at Yale and discussed his work in his doctoral thesis, even though he criticized Barth for failing, due to his "grace of the moment" theological assumptions, to develop the category of moral character *(CCL*, 169–76.). In all this, however, Hauerwas's greatest lesson from Barth seems to be only inspirational: learning to do theology unapologetically. Otherwise, the two are motivated by completely different concerns and methodological assumptions. Barth sought to find a foundation for the Christian faith against the skeptical challenge and found that ground in the *eternal* veracity of God's Word (Barth, *Church Dogmatics*). Hauerwas, on the other hand, has sought, as his primary concern, to display *narratively* (historically) the truth of Christian convictions, and how they are concretely embodied.

20. 'Revelation', Hauerwas points out, "is not a qualifier of the epistemic status of a kind of knowledge, but rather points to the content of a certain kind of knowledge. We call knowledge about God 'revelation', not because of the rationality or irrationality of such knowledge, but because of what that knowledge is about." *PK*, 66. See also "The Ethicist as Theologian," 408.

21. *PK*, 62.

22. *PK*, 67, emphasis added.

23. *PK*, 66.

24. Steven Lukes, "Relativism: Cognitive and Moral," 158.

25. This has been the major lesson from such diverse authors as MacIntyre, Kuhn, Rorty, and Gadamer.

26. *DF*, 93 n7; 214 n7.

27. *AC*, 134, quoting MacIntyre, *Whose Justice?* 373.

28. MacIntyre, *Whose Justice?* 371. Chapter 19 of *Whose Justice?* is significantly entitled: "Tradition and Translation."

29. Kuhn had set out a similar argument of incommensurability in the field of science, in his denial of a single "algorithm of theory-choice," that can be invoked to decide between rival paradigms in the scientific communities. (Kuhn, *Scientific Revolutions*, 200). That is why Kuhn speaks of a "conversion experience" (Kuhn, *Scientific Revolutions*, 151). In the field of ethics, Nussbaum has shown that Aristotle's approach in the *Ethics* involves a rejection of the 'commensurability thesis' famously propounded by Socrates (or Plato) in the *Protagoras*. As described by Nussbaum, this latter thesis was to the effect that there could be "a *techne* in which all values were commensurable on a single scale" (Nussbaum, *Fragility*, 294), or a "category of value, within which all goods are commensurable, as it were, in terms of a single common coinage" (Burnyeat, "Aristotle on Learning," 87). Dunne confirms this conclusion and notes that Aristotle's explicit denial of commensuration is behind his (Aristotle's) criticism of the Platonic idea of *the* Good and, positively, behind "his careful identification and analysis of several different excellences of character . . . each of which makes its own distinctive and irreducible contribution to the good life— a life, therefore, which only with the greatest good fortune, if at all, can be preserved from painful conflict: conflict that is painful precisely because of the unavailability of any 'common measure' that would unambiguously resolve it" (Dunne, *Back to the Rough Ground*, 46).

30. Davidson, "On the Very Idea," 5–20.

31. *AC*, 185 n4; MacIntyre, *Whose Justice?* 370–71.

32. Stout, *Flight from Authority*, 160; Stout, *Ethics after Babel*, 222–24; Fowl, "Could Horace Talk," 1–20.

33. Stout, *Ethics after Babel*, 66.

34. *AC*, 186–87, quoting Michael Quirk, "Stout on Relativism, Liberalism and Communitarianism," *Ausegung* 17/1 (1991): 1–14.

35. *DF*, 214 n7. For a similar observation by MacIntyre, *Whose Justice?* 371. See the related criticism of linguistics by Giddens, *Social Theory and Modern Sociology*, 79–80.

36. *CC*, 22–27; MacIntyre, *Whose Justice?* 349–69.

37. Otherwise how would MacIntyre himself have attempted to portray 'Justice' as it is understood and operative within the different traditions: Aristotelian,

Augustinian, Thomistic, Scottish-Enlightenment, and Liberal *(Whose Justice?)*, or to successfully portray Encyclopaedia, Genealogy, and Tradition as three 'rival' versions of moral inquiry *(Three Rival Versions)*. See also Hauerwas's comparison of the "Church and Liberalism," *CC*, 72–88; *AC*, 122–31; or his "Tale of Two Stories," in *CET*, 25–46.

38. Gustafson, "The Sectarian Temptation," 86.

39. See Whitmore, "Beyond Liberalism," 208, 213, 222. In fact, Whitmore's criticisms are directed to the strawman that he makes out of Hauerwas's claim for the distinctiveness of Christian ethics.

40. Gustafson, "The Sectarian Temptation," 90.

41. On 'normal' science as a specific cultural-linguistic system, see Kuhn, *Scientific Revolutions*, 43–51.

42. This is the key lesson from chapter 17 of MacIntyre's *Whose Justice?* significantly entitled, "Liberalism Transformed into a Tradition" (326–48).

43. *AN*, 6.

44. Wittgenstein, *Philosophical Investigations*, 1: ##23, 65, 67.

45. Rasmusson, 231, quoting Wogman, *Christian Perspectives on Politics*, 136.

46. Rasmusson, *The Church as Polis*, 233.

47. First published 1913.

48. Rasmusson, *The Church as Polis*, 234–35.

49. If the word "sect" traditionally signified "a challenge to the unity of the Church," today "sect" has come to mean "those who refuse to *act responsibly* for building a just society" (*US*, 154 n2., *AN* 10).

50. Weber, *The Protestant Ethic and the Spirit of Capitalism*, 128–54.

51. "While the church-type's main social function is described as integrative, legitimating, and conservative, the sect-type has often functioned creatively and 'progressively', even if (or because) their aim has not been to directly transform the world. Indeed, according to Troeltsch, the 'non-aggressive' (this is Troeltsch's language) and the least obviously political sects have been more important than the more 'aggressive' sects . . . that more directly aimed at the transformation of society." Rasmusson, *The Church as Polis*, 236, reference to Troeltsch, *The Social Teaching*, 802–20.

52. *CC*, 38–39; "Will the Real Sectarian?" 87.

53. "Jesus' salvation does not have social and political implications, but it is a politics. . . ." *AC*, 58; *CC*, 36–54.

54. Milbank, *Theology and Social Theory*, 75–146.

55. "Interview," See also *DF*, 198 n30; *AC*, 168–69; *WW*, 188–98. Hauerwas is one of six recent authors but for whose work, Milbank says in his preliminary acknowledgements, *Theology and Social Theory* "would not have been conceivable." The other five are: Gilain Rose, Alasdair MacIntyre, René Girard, Gilles Deleuze, and Michel Foucault. If, in spite of this generous tribute, Hauerwas's

work is cited only twice in the whole of Milbank's book, once in support of the critique of Gustavo Gutierrez (241), and again in connection with Aquinas's revision of Aristotle's ethics (362), it is because Hauerwas's contribution to the project of *Theology and Social Theory* is more collaborative, rather than suggesting new lines of argument or constituting a pervasive challenge to the whole project. Milbank's goal is to show that theology can provide a "specifically Christian onto-logic," and thus offer an alternative to the ontology of violence prevalent in secular forms of politics and their corresponding social theories. For this nonviolent practice to be enduring it must take "a collective political form" (395). This is exactly the theme that Hauerwas has been elaborating in his account of the church as a nonviolent political community.

56. Milbank, *Theology and Social Theory*, 92.

57. Milbank, *Theology and Social Theory*, 76–77.

58. Milbank, *Theology and Social Theory*, 83–92.

59. Milbank, *Theology and Social Theory*, 84.

60. Milbank, *Theology and Social Theory*, 84–85.

61. Milbank, *Theology and Social Theory*, 87, quoted in Rasmusson, *The Church as Polis*, 239.

62. Troeltsch, *The Social Teaching*, 257, 295.

63. Milbank, *Theology and Social Theory*, 89.

64. Which Milbank does in the first part of *Theology and Social Theory*, 9–48.

65. *AC*, 58; *PK*, 100; Milbank, *Theology and Social Theory*, 92.

66. Milbank, *Theology and Social Theory*, 92.

67. Milbank, *Theology and Social Theory*, 92.

68. Milbank, *Theology and Social Theory*, 93.

69. Milbank, *Theology and Social Theory*, 97.

70. Milbank treats people like Clifford Geertz, Peter Berger, Thomas Luckmann, Robert Bellah, and Niklas Luhmann, who, in various ways, follow Talcott Parsons. See Milbank, *Theology and Social Theory*, 101–43.

71. A clear example here is Mary Douglas's neo-Kantian assumption that all religions have fundamentally to do with ethical behavior. Douglas, *The Active Voice*, 183–247; Milbank, *Theology and Social Theory*, 123.

72. Talcott Parsons provides an illuminating case. According to him, "society evolves through a process of gradual differentiation into separate social subsystems: gradually art is distinguished from religion, religion from politics, economics from private ethical behaviour. . . ." See Milbank, *Theology and Social Theory*, 126; Parsons, *The Evolution of Societies*, 48–49, 71–82. Although this evolutionary explanation is fairly widespread (implicit in the work of Bellah, Geertz, Berger, and Luhmann), its shortcomings are made obvious: it pretends "that this contingent development represents the essence of the western tradition and the true outcome of human history"—thereby displacing onto the

sociological plane what should be the object of a true historical assessment. Milbank, *Theology and Social Theory*, 113.

73. According to Peter Berger's and Luckmann's theory of social genesis, ". . . the very first social arrangements do not require 'a sacred canopy', but exist only as conventions which have accidentally grown up through the symbolic interaction between individuals. . . . These arrangements are then passed on to the 'second generation', and only at the point of transition to the 'third generation', do questions start to arise about their *rationale*. Questions arise, simply because the circumstances of the genesis of the arrangements have now been forgotten, and instead of the true, forgotten history, a mythical one is substituted which relates existing social facts to some imagined eternal or natural order. Only at *this* stage does society come to require a 'sacred canopy. . . .'" Milbank, *Theology and Social Theory*, 134.

74. Milbank, *Theology and Social Theory*, 109.

75. Weber did of course assume that it was. That is why he defines the state in terms worked out first of all with reference to the modern state, generalizing them backwards, as it were. The state, he says bluntly, "has only in modern times reached its full development," so "it is appropriate to define it in terms appropriate to the modern type of state." Weber, *Economy and Society* I, 56 (cited at Giddens, *The Nation-State and Violence*, 18).

76. Such evolutionary social theories are inspired either by positivism or Marxism. Durkheim and those influenced by him generally represent the positivistic trend in which history—essentially understood as social change—is governed by incremental processes of development. Historical materialism (and to some extent, social Darwinism) represents the Marxist trend. These, too, understand history (as social change) to be marked by a curving upward form. However, unlike the positivist trend, these show the process of development, not as incremental, but as punctuated by phases of rapid transmutation. See Giddens, *The Nation State and Violence*, 31–32.

77. Giddens defends a "'discontinuist' conception of modern history" in which social formations are understood in terms of the contingent discontinuities that separate one from its predecessor. In the case of the modern nation state, Giddens outlines and narrates fourfold "institutional clustering": heightened surveillance, capitalistic enterprise, industrial production, and the consolidation of centralized control of the means of violence. Giddens, *The Nation State and Violence*, 5, 33, et passim.

78. Milbank, *Theology and Social Theory*, 139.

79. Adam, "Review of *Theology and Social Theory*," 510; Milbank, *Theology and Social Theory*, 4.

80. Milbank, *Theology and Social Theory*, 3. In the words of the sociologist Margareta Bertilsson, "Sociology is the theology of the secularised society." See Rasmusson, *The Church as Polis*, 240.

81. Milbank, *Theology and Social Theory*, 2.

82. That is why Richard Roberts's reading of Milbank's "postmodern Augustinian metanarrative" as involving an affirmation of theology as a transcendental sociology is a misreading. See Roberts, "Transcendental Sociology?" 527–35.

83. Milbank, *Theology and Social Theory*, 6.

84. *CC*, 109; *PK*, 99–100.

85. Reviewers have noted the force and brilliance of Milbank's argument. Adam finds it "erudite, intellectually vigorous and theologically passionate," but "extremely dense." He regrets "the complexity and obscurity of Milbank's book, for his subtle, compelling argument deserves a broad and patient audience" (Adam, "Review of *Theology and Social Theory*," 510–12). Loughlin, following Andrew Linzey, notes its "iconoclastic energy and surprise, its provocation, verve and breathless confidence" (Loughlin, "Christianity at the End of the Story," 366). Roberts finds it "the most brilliant, ambitious—and yet questionable" (Roberts, "Transcendental Sociology?" 527). Hütter finds it the "most profound and brilliant theological deconstruction of modernity and postmodernity presently available. . . . an achievement of the very first rate which hopefully will be the catalyst of a long and intense discussion among theologians, philosophers , and social theorists" (Hütter, "The Church's Peace Beyond the Secular," 116). See also Burrell, "An Introduction," 319. The entire issue of *Modern Theology* 8/4 (1992) is, in fact, devoted to a review of Milbank's work.

86. See, *WW*, 188–98; "On Being Placed by Milbank," 199–200. The same critique has been variously made by others. Romand Coles and Gerard Loughlin, for example, wonder whether Milbank's attempt to reclaim for Christian theology its (in Milbank's view) rightful place as a meta-discourse, does not recreate the same violence as the modern metanarrative that he is out to defeat (Coles, "Storied Others," 349; Loughlin, "Christianity at the End of the Story," 375–77). Debra Murphy rightly points out how the metanarrative mode of argument leaves Milbank's argument lacking in the concrete display—through concrete narratives and particular communal practices—of forgiveness, reconciliation, and peace (Murphy, "Power, Politics, and Difference," 137–38). Nicholas Lash wonders whether Milbank does not unwittingly accept Nietzsche's predilection for power and thus reduces all power to violence (Lash, "Not Exactly Power," 358)—a move which, according to Debra Murphy, "betrays Milbank's own debt to the Enlightenment/capitalist/male-identified modes of structuring power that he is seeking to negate?" (Murphy, "Power, Politics," 135). However, Richard Roberts finds Milbank's whole project questionable and counsels both theologians and sociologists to resist (Roberts, "Transcendental Sociology," 533). Although Roberts gives as the reason for rejecting Milbank's work its "abstract, quasi-manichaeistic (yet mutually involuted) opposition of false alternatives that entails abuses of both 'theology' and 'social theory,'" one suspects an intentional misreading as the key motive.

87. No one has argued this more forcefully than Rauschenbusch, the father of the highly influential "Social Gospel" movement. Rauschenbusch's *A Theology for the Social Gospel*, particularly in its diachronic aspect, emplots the coming to be of the church (from ancient Israel, through Jesus to modern secularized Christianity) as the inevitable, but salvific coming to be of a 'democratized' conception of God. This democratized conception of God normatively finds its highest embodiment in the equally 'democratized' social and political setting such that, for Rauschenbusch, the political order is "saved" simply because it is democratic. *DF*, 93–96; *CET*, 175–77; *CC*, 42; "Keeping Theological Ethics Theological," 22–23.

88. In *Christ and Culture* (New York: Harper and Row, 1965) Richard Niebuhr makes a fivefold typological assessment of Christianity's relation to society: Christ-against-culture; Christ-of-culture; Christ-above-culture; Christ-and-culture; and Christ-the-transformer-of-culture. While Niebuhr's assessment presupposes the normative superiority of the Christ-the-transformer-of culture typology, he viewed the Christ-against-culture typology as sectarian, citing the Mennonites as the most pure example. Niebuhr's Troeltschian background is obvious. In fact, Niebuhr sees his book as a supplement and a correction to Troeltsch's *The Social Teaching of the Christian Churches*. See Niebuhr, *Christ and Culture*, xii.

89. *AC*, 72 ff; *DF*, 98–104. Robert Bellah provides one of the best sociological defenses for this civil religion. The Church, according to Bellah, not only sustains a democratic public ethos, it serves as a critical agent within the polity. See Bellah, "Public Philosophy and Public Theology," 79–97. However, the same motivation of a 'civil religion' is behind the theological contributions in Carl Esbeck, *Religious Beliefs, Human Rights and the Moral Foundation of Western Democracy*.

90. *US*, 154; "Will the Real Sectarian Stand Up?" 87; see also: "Christians have not given up the assumption that they have a stake in forming the ethos of societies that embody the *universal* values of the Gospel. Thus 'Constantinianism' is shifted to a new key. No longer able to directly control the governmental apparatus itself, Christians seek to form societies that embody their values on the assumption that those values are *universal*." *AN*, 71, emphasis added.

91. *PK*, 13; *AC*, 88; *DF*, 91–93, 217; *AC*, 26. Also: "Recoiling from Reformation polemics and religious wars, modern ideologies and ethical theorists increasingly had good reason to favor a vocabulary whose sense did not depend on prior agreement about the nature of God and the structures of cosmos and society ordained by him." *AC*, 28, quoting Stout, *Ethics after Babel*, 161.

92. Asad, *Genealogies of Religion*, 39. Asad is commenting on Clifford Geertz's definition of religion as "a system of symbols which act to establish powerful, pervasive, and long-lasting *moods and motivations* in men by formulating conceptions of the general order of existence and clothing these concep-

tions with such an aura of factuality that the *moods and motivations* seem uniquely realistic" (emphasis mine). See Geertz, *The Interpretation of Cultures*, 90.

93. The designation "private" becomes even more questionable within modern liberal societies, as within the dominant market and communication forces the so-called "private" convictions, life-styles, or artistic expressions are re-appropriated within the public sphere and rendered publicly available "commodities" that can however be 'privatized' only as individual preferences. For the notion of religion as a marketable commodity, see Berger, *The Sacred Canopy*, 137ff.

94. *CCL*, 89–96; *VV*, 14–22, 68–70, 76–82; *TT*, 52–53; *PK*, 12–14. Refer also to our treatment in chapter 6 of Lovibond's Wittgenstein-based qualified epistemological realism.

95. Strawson, "Social Morality and Individual Ideal," 285.

96. *AC*, 45–68, 69–92; *CC*, 77; *DF*, 88, 105. See also Barry A. Harvey's well-argued thesis that "the notions of confinement, surveillance, and utilization accurately describe the fate, not only of certain individuals, but also of non-liberal traditions and communities within the disciplinary configurations of liberal cultures and institutions." Harvey, "Insanity, Theocracy, and the Public Realm," 30.

97. *GC*, 210.

98. *AC*, 84.

99. Asad, *Genealogies of Religion*, 27–54.

100. Asad, *Genealogies of Religion*, 40.

101. We have already noted (chapter 2) how even before Kant identified religion with ethics, Lord Herbert of Cherbury had proposed "virtue as the essence of religion" and Montesquieu had noted how "all religions contain principles useful to society." De Certeau, *The Writing of History*, 172–73.

102. Asad, *Genealogies of Religion*, 42.

103. Kant, *Political Writings*, 114.

104. *VV*, 77.

105. *PK*, xvii

106. Lindbeck is a Lutheran theologian from Yale whose *The Nature of Doctrine* has attracted a great deal of attention.

107. *AN*, 1; see also "Embarrassed by God's Presence," 98–99, and "Seeking a Clear Alternative to Liberalism," 109.

108. *AN*, 1–22.

109. A theological goal underpins Lindbeck's theoretical assessment of the various theories of religion, namely, to bring the theories of grammar and sociology into service in ecumenism and in theology. See Lindbeck, *The Nature of Doctrine*, 14.

110. Surin, "Many Religions," 187.

111. Lindbeck, *The Nature of Doctrine*, 16. Classical theodicy, in its preoccupation with proofs of God's existence, assumes this approach. What is at stake in these classical treatises is the contention in Wisdom's famous parable: "Yes or no, is there a gardener (God)?" Flew, *Logic and Language*, 187–207; Phillips, "Wisdom's Gods," 170–203.

112. Lindbeck, *The Nature of Doctrine*, 21.

113. Lonergan, *Method in Theology*, 101–24.

114. Lindbeck, *The Nature of Doctrine*, 31–32.

115. Placher, "Revisionist and Postliberal Theologies," 397. For a highly instructive and almost successful attempt to defend Rahner against Lindbeck's classification of him (Rahner) as a 'hybrid' experiential-expressivist, see Goh, "Tradition, Text, Doctrine, Experience," 68–70.

116. For it assumes that one cannot be religious unless one has had an 'experience' or first felt a 'presence' or sensed a 'something' in the depth of one's heart or in the clarity of one's mind. See, Loughlin, "See-Saying/Say-Seeing," 202.

117. See, e.g., Lovibond, *Realism and Imagination*, 6–26; Sellars, "Empiricism and Philosophy of the Mind," 127–96; Davidson, "On the Very Idea," 5–20; Rorty, *Philosophy and the Mirror*, 257–312; Rorty, *Contingency, Irony, and Solidarity*, 3–22.

118. Lindbeck, *The Nature of Doctrine*, 32.

119. Lindbeck, *The Nature of Doctrine*, 33.

120. Lindbeck, *The Nature of Doctrine*, 18.

121. Lindbeck, *The Nature of Doctrine*, 33.

122. Lindbeck, *The Nature of Doctrine*, 38. For a comprehensive exposition of Wittgenstein's scattered references, see Fogelin, *Wittgenstein*, 153–71.

123. The Yale cultural anthropologist Clifford Geertz is a key influence behind Lindbeck's argument. See especially the former's "Religion as a Cultural System" in Geertz, *The Interpretation of Cultures*, 87–125. "The case of Helen Keller and of supposed wolf children vividly illustrates that unless we acquire language we cannot actualize our specifically human capacities for thought, action, and feeling" (Lindbeck, *The Nature of Doctrine*, 34).

124. Lindbeck, *The Nature of Doctrine*, 36.

125. Lindbeck, *The Nature of Doctrine*, 33–35; Barrett, "Theology as Grammar," 160.

126. Lindbeck, *The Nature of Doctrine*, 40.

127. "Embarrassed by God's Presence," 99; *PK*, 93.

128. As Loughlin notes, "The disciples of Jesus would not have experienced him as the Messiah if they had not first been Palestinian Jews, people whose cultural and religious traditions provided them with the stories, signs and symbols which were the necessary condition for the possibility of their experience." Loughlin, "See-Saying/Say-Seeing," 204–5.

129. Lindbeck, *The Nature of Doctrine*, 35.

130. "Creation, Contingency," 8, 10–11.

131. *AC*, 16, 19, 23–44.

132. For a good introduction, and helpful bibliographical data, see Goh, "Tradition, Text, Doctrine, Experience," 72–93, 100–24. For the major collections of articles about, and in response to, Lindbeck's book, see Marshall, *Theology and Dialogue.*

133. Allik, "Religious Experience," 242.

134. Allik, "Religious Experience," 245–46.

135. Allik, "Religious Experience," 247.

136. Allik, "Religious Experience," 247–80. Ironically in seeking to affirm God's providence by assuming a God-given (invariable) transcendental structure as a sign of this providence, experiential-expressivists compromise faith in God's historical providence.

137. Lindbeck, *The Nature of Doctrine,* 33.

138. Lindbeck, *The Nature of Doctrine,* 118.

139. The work of Hans Frei (a colleague of Lindbeck at Yale) on biblical hermeneutics is of key influence in this reductionistic trend. See especially Frei, *The Eclipse of Biblical Narrative.*

140. Lindbeck, *The Nature of Doctrine,* 127.

141. Lindbeck, *The Nature of Doctrine,* 118.

142. Placher, "Revisionist and Postliberal Theologies," 397; Tracy, "Lindbeck's New Program," 463.

143. For example, "the proper way to determine what 'God' signifies is by examining how the word operates within a religion and thereby shapes reality and experience rather than by first establishing its propositional or experiential meaning and reinterpreting or reformulating its uses accordingly. It is in this sense that theological description is intratextual." Lindbeck, *The Nature of Doctrine,* 114.

144. Tilley, "Incommensurability, Intratextuality," 105.

145. "Seeking a Clear Alternative to Liberalism," 9.

146. This inner dialectic is what is at stake, for example, in the interplay between the two elements of linguisticality and speculativity in Gadamer's hermeneutics. See Gadamer, *Truth and Method,* 438–74.

147. Palmer, *Hermeneutics,* 208.

148. Palmer, *Hermeneutics,* 212.

149. For a rejection of Lindbeck's cultural-linguistic model on the basis that it is devised to fit Lindbeck's 'conservative' theological agenda see Tracy, "Lindbeck's New Program," 465; O'Neil, "The Rule Theory," 426; Wainwright, "Ecumenical Dimension," 124; Goh, "Tradition, Text, Doctrine, Experience," 90. However, for Tina Allik, "anthropological issues, independently of one's concerns about Christian apologetics, might lead one to adopt the cultural-linguistic model." See Allik, "Religious Experience," 255.

150. Lindbeck, *The Nature of Doctrine*, 114–15. Geertz, *The Interpretation of Culture*, 3–30.

151. Lindbeck, *The Nature of Doctrine*, 32, emphasis mine.

7. A Metaphysics of "In the Beginning": Politics beyond Tribalism and Liberal Agonistics

1. Gustafson, "The Sectarian Temptation," 90ff.; Wogaman, *Christian Perspectives*, 135–37; Heeley, "The Ethical Methodology," 277; Nelson, *Narrative and Morality*, 137; Miscamble, "Sectarian Pacifism," 73–74.

2. *AC*, 27–28; *CC*, 110, 217. More specifically, those positive aspects are liberalism's ability to create limitations on state power ("Will the Real Sectarian Stand Up?" 93); a strong sense of moral obligation (*TT*, 26); development of critical skills (*TT*, 26); and a sense of freedom (*TT*, 10).

3. *CC*, 77, 289 n8.

4. *AN*, 18, 81 n14.

5. *AC*, 33–34; Giddens, *The Nation-State and Violence*, 5 et passim.

6. *AC*, 35; see Locke, *The Second Treatise*, nos. 89, 95–99. On Locke's continued influence on modern political thinking see Held, "Central Perspectives on the Modern State," 32–50; Simmons, "Locke's State of Nature," 449–70.

7. *AC*, 34, quoting O'Donovan, "The Loss of a Sense of Place," 40–41.

8. *AN*, 18.

9. *AC*, 33–48; Giddens, *The Nation-State and Violence*, 2, 26, 49. See also Beetham, "The Future of the Nation State," 209.

10. The difference between frontier and border has to do with another key factor that Giddens identifies at the heart of the modern nation-state, namely, heightened surveillance. The latter allows the state to coordinate its administrative scope in a precise fashion within the bounds of a clearly defined territory, its rule sanctioned by law and the direct control (monopoly) of the means of internal and external violence. See Giddens, *The Nation-State and Violence*, 48–50, 121. Bernard Yack is in agreement with Giddens, and according to him, this territorial intensification explains the invention of the "foreigner"—as opposed to the more universal figure of apprehension, the "stranger"—as an object of fear and suspicion. See Yack, "Reconciling Liberalism and Nationalism," 178. See also Brubaker, *Citizenship and Nationhood*, 46–49.

11. *AC*, 167, reference to MacIntyre, "Is Patriotism a Virtue?" 3–20. We realize that Hauerwas's attack against liberalism's failure to account for locality may seem a bit of cliché, particularly from the Western European tradition, where the nation-state has somehow tended to combine the "pre-political" aspects of a shared tradition, historical experiences, language and religion on the one hand, with the Enlightenment ideal of universal rights and democratic principles (see De Wachter, "In Search of a Post-National Identity"). However,

one should realize that Hauerwas's experience of liberal politics is limited to the United States, where, as in Africa, the state is largely an artificial and arbitrary creation. In the absence of any shared history, political rhetoric and philosophy tend to appeal solely to universal and abstract concepts of will, contract, rights, etc.

12. These events have finally drawn political theorists and philosophers to the subject of nationalism. Yack has well noted the dialectical directions within this concern. While on the one hand, such violence and xenophobia have helped to revive considerable sympathy for the much-assailed cosmopolitanism of the Enlightenment, they have, at the same time, made it harder than ever to think of political community as a voluntary association composed of rational, self-interested individuals. See Yack, "Reconciling Liberalism and Nationalism, 166–67. Among the 'recent' attempts to give an account of nationalism within liberal political theory, see Greenfeld, *Nationalism: Five Roads to Modernity;* David Resnick, "John Locke and Liberal Nationalism"; Kristeva, *Nations without Nationalism;* Van De Putte, "Nationalism and Nations"; De Wachter, "In Search of a Post-National Identity."

13. *PK,* 61

14. Loughlin, "Christianity at the End of the Story," 377.

15. *WW,* 198; "On Being 'Placed' by Milbank," 199–200. From this perspective, Milbank's project is still partly determined by Constantinian ambitions. See Gerald Loughlin's insightful assessment of Milbank's project: "Once upon a time, it was theology who wore the crown, theology that carried out the most fundamental reading of *all* other interpretations and *all* other social formations. Theology was social science, it was the *master narrative.* Stolen by secular reason, and worn as 'Social Theory' the master narrative is now sought by its earlier owner. . . . It is not for others to position theology but for theology to *position* them. It is time for theology to reassert its character as a glorious *master-discourse,* to reclaim its crown." Loughlin, "Christianity at the End of the Story," 366–67.

16. *WW,* 198. A familiarity with the argument of Nussbaum's *Fragility* is presupposed in order to appreciate that it is Plato, not Aristotle, who represents the "Greeks" in the above citation.

17. On how a story like "Columbus 'discovered' America" continues to obscure and yet underwrite the merciless extermination of the Native Americans, see *AC* 133–48; 153–61. See Hauerwas's similar accounts of Vietnam and black slavery in America, in "Forgiveness and Political Community," 15–16.

18. The Jewish holocaust remains open to various interpretations. A consciously perpetrated, but (to us) unconvincing account is to see the holocaust as a confirmation of the dangers of particularity—a result of the rejection of the humanistic ideal of human reason or universal humanity; a rejection of a system of rights applicable to all, in the name of the idea that right and morality

were local, particular, and race-related. The account is unconvincing because it is the realization that morality is local and race-related which generates a respect, or at least a tolerance for other particulars and races different from one's own. Accordingly, it was Nazism that destroyed the common, normal moral sensitivity of the average German citizen in the name of what it considered to be the task of rationally organizing universal history. For these dialectical interpretations of the holocaust, see De Wachter, "Postmodern Challenges to Ethics," 80. However, in support of the view of the holocaust as an example of metanarrative violence, see Chansky, "Reflections on *After Virtue* after Auschwitz," 247–56.

19. Mudimbe's *The Invention of Africa* and its sequel, *The Idea of Africa*, provides a most powerful display of how these various discourses have combined to the very formation and conception of an "Africa". See also Appia, *In My Father's House*, 3–27.

20. Van Tongeren, "Morality, Transcendence, Conception of Life," 46, quoting De Dijn, "Trouw en Tolerantie" (unpublished, 4). See also Fish, *There Is No Such Thing*, 134–38. Kerry Whiteside is thus right: "We do not criticize liberalism for being violent; we criticize it for not noticing its violence. . . . By assuming an impersonal Reason, a reasonable Man in general and by proposing itself as a fact of nature not as a historical fact, liberalism assumes that universality has been achieved." Whiteside, "Universality and Violence," 374 quoting Maurice Merleau-Ponty, *Humanisme et terreur* (Paris: Gallimard, 1947), 67.

21. Harvey, "Insanity, Theocracy and the Public Realm," 54; reference is made to De Certeau, *The Practice of Everyday Life*, 62–68.

22. *AC*, 35.

23. Rorty, *Contingency, Irony, and Solidarity*, 22 et passim.

24. On this dialectical danger of the realization of contingency see, Burms, "Disenchantment," 145–55. Rorty's liberal aestheticism (*Contingency*, xv and passim) verges on frivolous fascination. For his romantic nihilism (light-minded irony) is just the inverted image of modernity's arrogance, an act of liberal wistfulness after having been forced finally to accept one's mundane status. As Harvey notes, "This terrible pathos of not being God deeply afflicts us. All because the venue remains unchanged, all because after we have exposed the chimera of an eternal, ahistorical truth, we still perceive and evaluate the realm of the pretensions and retrotensions of time as from the perspective of eternity. . . . So we think of ourselves as being left with 'only' the realities of Being that are disclosed in time, and left 'only' with history." See Harvey, "Insanity, Theocracy, and the Public Realm," 43; See also Poteat, *Philosophical Daybook*, 65.

25. "Will the Real Sectarian Stand Up?" 88; *RA*, 42; *CET*, 18; *CC*, 92; "On the 'Right' to be Tribal," 241.

26. *CET*, 12–13, quoting Brueggemann, "The Legitimacy of a Sectarian Hermeneutic," 22–23.

27. *RA*, 42.

28. *DF*, 93. Hauerwas is in agreement with Fish. Free Speech, Fish argues, is what is left over when a community has determined in advance what it does not want to hear. Fish, *There Is No Such Thing*, 143.

29. "Interview"; see also *CC*, 215; *DF*, 214.

30. *CC*, 108ff. Also, "I am radical in the sense that I do not privilege at all the nation-state as a serious moral actor" ("Interview"). This is Hauerwas's mature position, which represents a development from his very early views when he still considered the democratic process within the nation-state somewhat more positively and thought that within it mutual trust and the aspiration of the good could still be salvaged. See *VV*, 218–19, 229.

31. See chapter 1 of this work. However, Giddens's *The Nation State and Violence* remains in many respects one of the best accounts of the development of the nation-state concept. David Beetham also provides a brief but helpful introduction to the key factors behind the development of the nation-state. Beetham's thesis is particularly instructive and generally successful in showing the contingency of the nation-state by reason of its being a historical product: "just as the nation state became universal, because a combination of economic, military and politico-cultural forces came to consolidate political structures at this particular level, and ensure their success, so a combination of the same forces, at a later stage, is now working to undermine the effectiveness of the political structures at that same level." See Beetham, "The Future of the Nation State," 208–22.

32. "Epilogue," 179. *GC*, 6; "Will the Real Sectarian," 91.

33. *PK*, 119; See also MacIntyre, *After Virtue*, 200–204, and his "Theology, Ethics," 437.

34. *CC*, 79–81, 160. A key indication: with the primacy of the language of "rights" all human relationships assume the form of exchange. Hauerwas cites the U.S. Supreme Court ruling in *Planned Parenthood* vs *Danforth* in which "a husband has no right if his wife wishes an abortion, because 'abortion is a purely personal right of the woman, and the status of marriage can place no limitations on personal rights'" (*CC*, 81).

35. Rasmusson, *The Church as Polis*, 274.

36. Rasmusson, *The Church as Polis*, 277–78; reference is made to Galston, *Liberal Purposes*, 17. For a defense of liberty and equality as the common good of liberalism, see Rawls, "Justice as Fairness," 246. See also Cladis, *A Communitarian Defense of Liberalism*, 136–84.

37. Musschenga, "Universal Morality," 237–38; Rawls, "The Idea of an Overlapping Consensus," 1–25.

38. Musschenga, "Universal Morality," 80.

39. Barber, *The Conquest of Politics*, 151. For a similar critique of liberal "neutrality," see Benhabib, *Situating the Self*, 95–104.

40. McWhorter, "The Event of Truth," 165.

41. *VV*, 224.

42. *VV*, 224.

43. See below in the third section of this chapter.

44. "Foreword," in Duane Friesen, 12.

45. *VV*, 224.

46. *VV*, 224.

47. *GC*, 25.

48. *DF*, 179; *AN*, 12, 51–60.

49. *CET*, 13, quoting Brueggemann, "The Legitimacy of a Sectarian Hermeneutic," 23, emphasis mine.

50. *CC*, 12.

51. In Hauerwas's work, the radical concretization of this embodiment of Church is the Amish and Mennonite forms of Church community (*CC*, 6). But one can also see the Latin American "basic Christian communities" as embodying an alternative, 'anticapitalistic' vision of social arrangement. See Budde, *The Two Churches*, 38–73.

52. For an understanding of liberalism as the form of political culture that regulates or provides procedural mechanisms for the regulation of struggle for power, see Ackerman, *Social Justice*, 53–59.

53. *CET*, 253–66; *RA*, 67.

54. *AC*, 62; Fish, *There Is No Such Thing*, 116.

55. Beiner, "Do We Need a Philosophical Ethics?" 235.

56. Lowi, *The End of Liberalism*, 29. Interest-group liberalism assumes the primary political unit is not the individual but the group.

57. Wolin, "What Revolutionary Action," 20–21; we are indebted to Werpohowski, ("Political Liberalism," 110–11) for this reference.

58. For a similar, "life-style enclave" conception of community see Bellah, *Habits of the Heart*, 71–75.

59. The liberal anthropology is in fundamental tension with the ancient and medieval view to which Hauerwas claims affinity. He notes, following MacIntyre: "The central preoccupation of both ancient and medieval communities was characteristically: how may men work together to realize the true human good? The central preoccupation of modern men is and has been characteristically: how may we prevent men interfering with each other as each of us goes about our own concerns. The classical view begins with the community of the *polis* and with the individual viewed as having no moral identity apart from the communities of kinship and citizenship; the modern view begins with the concept of a collection of individuals and the problem of how out of and by individuals social institutions can be constructed." *TT*, 113, quoting MacIntyre, "How to Identify Ethical Principles."

60. On this discussion as it is taking place in theology, see, e.g., Placher, *Un-*

apologetic Theology; Thiemann, *Constructing a Public Theology*; Browning and Fiorenza, *Habermas, Modernity and Public Theology.*

61. Gustafson, "The Sectarian Temptation," 90; Miscamble, "Sectarian Pacifism," 73; Thiemann, *Constructing a Public Theology,* 19.

62. Lewis, "Toward a NonFoundationalist," 48–49.

63. David Tracy, for example, identifies three "publics" addressed by theology: the Church, the academy, and the wider society. See Tracy, *The Analogical Imagination,* 51–58. However, Tracy's overall concern for the "public" character of Christian convictions, sophisticated as it is, remains in fundamental tension with Hauerwas's work. For Tracy's project seems to be motivated by the assumption that theology still needs—lest it lapse into fideism, tribalism or sectarianism—a foundationalistic notion of universal reason and *the* truth. See Giurlanda, *Faith and Knowledge,* 260, 282.

64. Ackerman, *Social Justice,* 16.

65. See earlier (chapter 6, section 1) for Hauerwas's critical remarks against Davidson's and Stout's appeal to the "very nature of language" to support their case for commensurability. The same observation applys, *mutatis mutandis,* to Habermas's attempt to ground social reason and cooperation on "unstrained conversation" within a communicative theory. See Habermas, "Toward a Theory of Communicative Competence," and his *The Theory of Communicative Action.*

66. By describing the Church as a "tactic" (*AC,* 15–18), Hauerwas is drawing on De Certeau's distinction between strategy and tactic. Strategy is "the calculation (or manipulation) of power relationships that becomes possible as soon as a subject that will empower (a business, an army, a city, a scientific institution) can be isolated. It postulates a *place* that can be delimited as its *own* and serve as the base from which relations with an *exteriority* composed of targets or threats (customers or competitors, enemies, the country surrounding the city, objectives and objects of research, etc.) can be managed. . . . It is the typical attitude of modern science, politics, and military strategy." In contrast, De Certeau describes "tactic" as a "calculated action determined by the absence of a proper locus. No delineation of externality, then, provides it with conditions necessary for autonomy. The space of a tactic is the space of the other, thus it must play on and with the terrain imposed on it and organized by the law of a foreign power." See De Certeau, *The Practice of Everyday Life,* 35–36.

67. *AN,* 17.

68. *AN,* 134.

69. Hauerwas himself admits: "Brought up on the thought of Reinhold Niebuhr, I simply assumed that pacifism, even if it could be justified theologically, could never sustain an intelligible social and political ethic." See "Foreword" in Duane Friesen, 11; see also *PK,* xxiv. This is one reason why in his earlier work, Hauerwas's ambiguous relationship to Yoder is undisguised. See *VV,* 197–221.

70. *PK*, xvii.

71. "Messianic Pacifism," 30; see also *VV*, 199; *PK*, 88.

72. Miscamble, "Sectarian Pacifism," 74–75.

73. The argument is at the heart of the traditional Catholic "just war" tradition. For Hauerwas's more sustained critique of this tradition, see *AN*, 172–79.

74. *CET*, 15; "Will the Real Sectarian," 90.

75. *GC*, 25.

76. *DF*, 120; "Epilogue," 162; *AN*, 16.

77. "Pacifism: Some Philosophical Reflections," 99.

78. "The Sermon on the Mount," 63 ff.

79. "The Sermon on the Mount," 39; Rasmusson, *The Church as Polis*, 305 n9.

80. *DF*, 130. That the Church has often relegated forgiveness to only the personal sphere is, according to Hauerwas, one of its "most glaring failures": "We have failed to exhibit decisively that the Church is a polity of the forgiven and the forgiving. No more important task awaits the Church than a recovery of the significance of forgiveness and reconciliation for our common life." See "Forgiveness and Political Community," 16.

81. "Jesus and/as the Non-violent Imagination," 85; *DF*, 131. Debra Murphy has made an important criticism of Milbank's work which might also apply to Hauerwas. Is it legitimate to reduce all power to violence? (Murphy, "Power, Politics and Difference," 135). Murphy draws on a key distinction between power and violence as made by Hannah Arendt. According to Arendt (*On Violence*, 35–56), power and violence/domination are opposites (56). Although this might be an extreme view, Arendt's description of violence as "instrumentalist" in nature has the ring of truth. Like all means, Arendt argues, violence "always stands in need of guidance and justification through the end it pursues" (51). Power, on the other hand, is an end in itself. One important implication of Arendt's analysis is that power is possible only in community, while violence destroys community. In this case, the issue is not power or no power, but acceptable and unacceptable means of power.

82. *AC*, 196; This theme is well developed by Rasmusson (*The Church as Polis*, 306–13) through attention to the work of the political scientist Jean Elshtain (*Women and War*). The latter reads the history of the nations from Greeks to today as a history of armed civic virtue and Christianity's attempt to disarm this civic virtue. For Hauerwas's very positive assessment of her book, see "Critics' Choices for Christmas," 708.

83. *PK*, 94.

84. Contrary to Gustafson, "The Sectarian Temptation," 93, and Miscamble, "Sectarian Pacifism," 71.

85. Milbank, "Postmodern Critical Augustinianism," 227.

86. Milbank, *Theology and Social Theory*, 5.

87. Milbank, *Theology and Social Theory*, 279.

88. Milbank, *Theology and Social Theory*, 283.

89. Milbank, *Theology and Social Theory*, 279.

90. This is what makes Rawls's recent attempt to deny that his treatment of justice as fairness assumes any comprehensive metaphysical claims about the nature and identity of persons both dubious and unconvincing. See Rawls, "Justice as Fairness," 223–51. This article is integrated (slightly reworked) as Lecture I (3–46) of Rawls's recent book, *Political Liberalism*. However, what becomes even more interesting is the realization that in as much as *mythos* lies at the basis of every politics, every politics is a form of theology. For, in generating a specific form of social praxis, a *mythos* offers, just like any theology does, a set of principles and understandings that give meaning to, define purposes for, and significantly frame the perception of human existence. Moreover, the attention to *mythos* means that the vision of any politics is formed by definite creation narratives ('in the beginning'), in which some "salvation hope" for human flourishing is anticipated. Within liberalism, for example, one can see the determination of the political vision as what is at stake within the writings of the early sixteenth- to seventeenth-century political theorists, who depicted man's primitive condition within a metaphorical State of Nature. The latter should rightly be seen as a type of creation narrative that expresses a particular conception of 'in the beginning'. Moreover, the development of capitalistic production and economics is not only anticipated within these creation narratives (especially in Locke), it is announced as a form of salvation hope, a priestly mediation and harbinger of a not-yet-realized perfect society of human flourishing.

91. *WW*, 188–98.

92. Milbank, *Theology and Social Theory*, 301.

93. *WW*, 190.

94. "Work as Co-creation: A Critique of a Remarkably Bad Idea," in *GC*, 109–24.

95. That is why, as Debra Murphy notes, Milbank makes much of the musical metaphors in Augustine's *De Musica* for the explication not only of creation but the Trinity ("Power, Politics, and Difference," 141 n20). For example, Milbank writes: "the idea of a consistently beautiful, continuously differential and open series is of course the idea of 'music'. In music there must be continuous endings and displacements, yet this is not necessary violence, because only in the recall of what has been displaced does the created product exist. Violence would rather mean an unnecessarily jarring note, a note wrong because 'out of place' or else the premature ending of a development. Perhaps this is partly why, in *De Musica*, Augustine—who realised that creation *ex nihilo* implied the non-recognition of ontological violence, or of positive evil—puts forward a 'musical' ontology." See Milbank, "Postmodern Critical Augustinianism," 228.

96. Milbank, *Theology and Social Theory*, 5–6.

97. *AC*, 40–44; Milbank, *Theology and Social Theory*, 388–92; "Postmodern Critical Augustinianism," 225–37.

98. *WW*, 190, quoting Milbank, *Theology and Social Theory*, 5–6.

99. *WW*, 190.

100. *CAV*, 19.

101. *CC*, 82. Much of the "scarcity" has to do with what Bauman has ana-lyzed as the "creation of risk" in modern and postmodern societies. "'To keep the wheels of the consumer market well-lubricated, a constant supply of new well-publicized dangers is needed. And the dangers needed must be fit to be translated into consumer demand: such dangers as are "made to measure" for privatized risk-fighting'. Accordingly, risk-detection and risk-management are seen as the most precious functions of 'science and technology, with the result that science and technology feed, perversely, on the resilience and vitality of the selfsame disease they are appointed (or self-appointed) to disarm and shackle. *Objectively* and *subjectively* they are a major force in perpetuating, rather than arresting, the risk-generating propensity of the social system'." *GC*, 219 n9, quoting Bauman, *Postmodern Ethics*, 204–5, 207.

102. Milbank, *Theology and Social Theory*, 390.

103. *PK*, 103.

104. As O'Donohoe ("A Return to Virtue," 51–53) suggests.

105. *CAV*, 55–57

106. *CAV*, 58.

107. *CAV*, 58. See Foot, *Virtues and Vices*; Frankena, *Ethics*, 67. See also Hauerwas's earlier engagement with Frankena, *TT*, 40–56, and Frankena's re-sponse, "Conversations with Carney and Hauerwas, " 45–62.

108. *CC*, 117–21; *CAV*, 59; See Pincoffs, *Quandaries and Virtues* and "Quandary Ethics," 92–112.

109. While on the whole appreciative of MacIntyre, Milbank disputes with MacIntyre on points involving the degree to which a universally compelling philosophical case can be made for the ascendancy of virtue. See especially, Mil-bank, *Theology and Social Theory*, 326–79.

110. *CAV*, 61, quoting Milbank, *Theology and Social Theory*, 327.

111. *CAV*, 63.

112. *CAV*, 63.

113. *CAV*, 63–64.

114. For a critique of the Greek *polis* as an exclusive *polis* from which women and slaves were excluded, see Nussbaum, "Recoiling from Reason," 38; Benhabib, *Situating the Self*, 91, 93.

115. Milbank, *Theology and Social Theory*, 352, quoted in *CAV*, 64.

116. See especially, MacIntyre, *Whose Justice?*, 355–69.

117. In the last chapter of *Three Rival Versions*, "Re-conceiving the Univer-sity as an Institution and the Lecture as a Genre" (21–36), MacIntyre uses com-petition for dialectical superiority as the basis for a new vision of the university.

118. Milbank, *Theology and Social Theory*, 329.

119. Light-minded aestheticism or irony, according to Rorty, is the typical/ normative posture to be adopted within liberalism. See Rorty, *Contingency, Irony and Solidarity*, xv et passim. Mark Cladis may thus be right in branding Rorty's "light-minded aestheticism" as a form of "ill-mannered pragmatism." Cladis, "Mild-Mannered Pragmatism," 19.

120. *CAV*, 64, quoting Milbank, *Theology and Social Theory*, 359–60.

121. *CAV*, 68.

122. *CET*, 15; "Will the Real Sectarian Stand Up," 91; *AC*, 149.

123. "A Response to Quinn: Athens May Be a Long Way," 62.

124. As Todd Whitmore does. See Whitmore, "Beyond Liberalism and Communitarianism," 207–25.

125. See Quirk, "Beyond Sectarianism?" 78; Rasmusson, *The Church as Polis*, 273. For Hauerwas's explicit repudiation of the communitarian tradition, see "Communitarians and Medical Ethicists: Why I Am None of the Above" in *DF*, 156–63; "A Communitarian Lament," 45–46.

126. *DF*, 157, reference to Taylor, "Cross-Purposes," 163.

127. Christopher Lasch, "The Community Critique of Liberalism," in *Community in America: The Challenge of Habits of the Heart*, ed. with intro. by Charles H. Reynolds and Ralph Norman (Berkeley: University of California Press, 1988), 183, quoted in *DF*, 159.

128. *RA*, 78.

129. *DF*, 225.

130. Rasmusson, *The Church as Polis*, 11.

131. Rasmusson, *The Church as Polis*, 375–76.

132. *GC*, 6; internal quote is from Rasmusson, *The Church as Polis*, 187–88.

133. *CC*, 12. Elsewhere: "The social task of the Church would not be simply to develop strategies within current political options—though it may certainly include that—but rather to stand as an alternative society that manifests in its own social and political life the way in which a people form themselves when truth and charity rather than survival are their first order of business." See "The Ethicist as a Theologian," 411.

134. Milbank, *Theology and Social Theory*, 408, 432.

135. See "A Response to John Cobb," in *WW*, 25–32.

136. *PK*, 151.

Conclusion: Why "Outside the Church There Is No Salvation"

1. *AC*, 23–44; reprinted in Musschenga, ed., *Morality, Worldview and Law*, 9–26.

2. Heschel, *The Prophets*, 3. The sense of "prophetic philosophy" that we are offering here ties in quite neatly with our earlier reference to Hauerwas's work as a case of "edifying" rather than "systematic" philosophy.

Bibliography

I. HAUERWAS'S WORKS

a. Books:

After Christendom. Nashville: Abingdon Press, 1991.

Against the Nations: War and Survival in a Liberal Society. Minneapolis: Winston-Seabury Press, 1985; rpt. Notre Dame: University of Notre Dame Press, 1992.

Character and the Christian Life: A Study in Theological Ethics. San Antonio: Trinity University Press, 1975; Notre Dame: University of Notre Dame Press, 1989.

Christian Existence Today: Essays on Church, World, and Living in Between. Durham, N.C.: Labyrinth Press, 1988.

Christians among the Virtues: Theological Conversations with Ancient and Modern Ethics. With Charles Pinches. Notre Dame: University of Notre Dame Press, 1997.

A Community of Character: Toward a Constructive Christian Social Ethic. Notre Dame: University of Notre Dame Press, 1981.

Dispatches from the Front: Theological Engagements with the Secular. Durham, N.C.: Duke University Press, 1994.

In Good Company: The Church as Polis. Notre Dame: University of Notre Dame Press, 1995.

Naming the Silences: God, Medicine and the Problem of Suffering. Grand Rapids: Eerdmans, 1990.

The Peaceable Kingdom: A Primer in Christian Ethics. Notre Dame: University of Notre Dame Press, 1983.

Preaching to Strangers. With Will Willimon. Louisville: Westminster, 1992.

Resident Aliens: Life in the Christian Colony. With Will Willimon. Nashville: Abingdon Press, 1989.

Should War Be Eliminated? Philosophical and Theological Explorations. Milwaukee: Marquette University Press, 1984.

Suffering Presence: Theological Reflections on Medicine, the Mentally Handicapped, and the Church. Notre Dame: University of Notre Dame Press, 1986.

Truthfulness and Tragedy: Further Investigations in Christian Ethics. Notre Dame: University of Notre Dame Press, 1977.

Unleashing the Scripture: Freeing the Bible from Captivity to America. Nashville: Abingdon Press, 1993.

Vision and Virtue: Essays in Christian Ethical Reflection. Notre Dame: Fides Press, 1974; Notre Dame: University of Notre Dame Press, 1981.

Wilderness Wandering: Probing Twentieth-Century Theology and Philosophy. Boulder, Colo.: Westview Press, 1987.

b. Edited Books:

Responsibility for Devalued Persons. Springfield, Ill.: Charles Thomas Press, 1984.

Revisions: Changing Perspectives in Moral Philosophy. With Alasdair MacIntyre. Notre Dame: University of Notre Dame Press, 1983.

Schooling Christians: "Holy Experiments" in American Education. With John Westerhoff. Grand Rapids: Eerdmans, 1992.

Theology without Foundations: Religious Practice and the Future of Theological Truth. With Nancey Murphy & Mark Nation. Nashville: Abingdon Press, 1994.

Why Narrative? Readings in Narrative Theology. With L. Gregory Jones. Grand Rapids: Eerdmans, 1989.

c. Articles:

"Among the Moved: Reflections on Speer's *Spandau*." *Worldview* 19/10 (1976): 47–49.

"Casuistry as a Narrative Art." *Interpretation* 37/4 (1983): 377–88.

"Characterizing Perfection: Second Thoughts on Character and Sanctification." In *Wesleyan Theology Today: A Bicentennial Theological Consultation,* ed. Theodore Runyon, 251–63. Nashville: Kingswood Books, 1985.

"A Communitarian Lament: A Review of *The Good Society* [Robert Bellah]." *First Things* 19 (1992): 45–46.

"Critics' Choices for Christmas: Books I Would Recommend Anyone to Read." *Commonweal* 114/21 (1987): 708–9.

"The Demands of a Truthful Story: Ethics and the Pastoral Task." *Chicago Studies* 21/1 (1982): 57–71.

"Disciplined Seeing: Imagination and the Moral Life." With Philip Foubert, *New Catholic World* 225/1350 (1982): 250–53.

"Embarrassed by God's Presence." With William Willimon. *Christian Century* 102/4 (1985): 98–100.

"Epilogue: A Pacifist Response to the Bishops." *Speak Up for Just War or Paci-*

fism: A Critique of the United Methodist Bishop's Pastoral Letter in Defense of Creation, by Paul Ramsey, 149–82. University Park: Pennsylvania State University Press, 1988.

"The Ethicist as Theologian." *Christian Century* 92/15 (1975): 408–12.

"Ethics and Ascetical Theology." *Anglican Theological Review* 61/1 (1979): 87–98.

"The Ethics of Population and Pollution." *The Cresset* 33/9 (1970): 6–9.

"The Faithful Are Not Always Effective." *Gospel Herald* 77/52 (1985): 903.

"Foreword." In *Christian Peacemaking and International Conflict: A Realist Passivist Perspective,* by Duane Friesen, 11–12. Scottsdale, Pa.: Herald Press, 1986.

"Foreword." In *Friendship and the Moral Life,* by Paul J. Wadell, C.P., ix-xii. Notre Dame: University of Notre Dame Press, 1989.

"Forgiveness and Forgetting." *Sh'ma* 11/202 (1980): 12, 15–16.

"Forgiveness and Political Community." *Worldview* 23/1-2 (1980): 15–16.

"From Conduct to Character: A Guide to Sexual Adventure." With Allen Verhey. *Reformed Journal* 36/11 (1986): 12–16.

"The Gesture of a Truthful Story: The Church and 'Religious Education.'" *Theology Today* 42/2 (1985): 181–89.

"God the Measurer: A Review of Gustafson's *Ethics from a Theocentric Perspective.*" *Journal of Religion* 62/4 (1982): 402–11.

"The Gospel's Radical Alternative: A Peace the World Cannot Give." With Michael Cartwright. *The Other Side* 23/6 (1987): 22–27, 45.

"The Grace to Live Contingently." *Reformed Journal* 38/7 (1988): 9–11.

"The Holocaust and the Duty to Forgive." *Sh'ma* 10/198 (1980): 127–39.

"In Praise of Gossip: The Moral Casuistry of Life." *Books and Religion* 3/8&9 (1985): 5; 23.

"Jesus and/as the Non-Violent Imagination of the Church." With Philip D. Kenneson. *Pro Ecclesia* 1/1 (1992): 76–88.

"Language, Experience, and the Life Well-Lived: A Review of the Work of Donald Evans." With Richard Bondi. *Religious Studies Review* 9/1 (1983): 33–37.

"Learning to See Red Wheelbarrows: On Vision and Relativism." *Journal of American Academy of Religion* 45/2 (1977): 225, 644–55.

"The Meaning of Being Human." *Notre Dame Magazine* 1/1 (1972): 26–27.

"Messianic Pacifism." *Worldview* 16/6 (1973): 29–33.

"The Moral Limits of Population Control." *Thought* 44 (1974): 237–49.

"Murdochian Muddles: Can We Get through Them If God Does Not Exist?" In *Iris Murdoch and the Search for Human Goodness,* ed. Maria Antonaccio and William Schweiker. Chicago: University of Chicago Press, 1966.

"A Non-Violent Proposal for Christian Participation in Cultural Wars." *Soundings* 75/4 (1992): 477–92.

"On Being 'Placed' by Milbank: A Response." In *Christ, Ethics, and Tragedy: Essays in Honour of Donald McKennon*, ed. Kenneth Surin, 197–201. Cambridge: Cambridge University Press, 1989.

"On the Right to Be Tribal." *Christian Scholars Review* 16/3 (1987): 238–41.

"Pacifism: A Form of Politics." In *Peace Betrayed? Essays on Pacifism and Politics*, ed. Michael Cromartie, 133–42. Washington: Ethics and Public Policy Center, 1990.

"Pacifism: Some Philosophical Considerations." *Faith and Philosophy* 2/2 (1985): 99–105.

"Peacemaking." *The Furrow* 36/10 (1985): 605–12.

"Reflections on the Relation between Morality and Art: A Review Essay of R. W. Beardsmore's *Art and Morality*." *The Cresset* 39/5 (1976): 14–17.

"A Response to Quinn: Athens May Be a Long Way from Jerusalem, But Prussia Is Even Further." *Asbury Theological Journal* 45/1 (1990): 59–64.

"Review of Alasdair MacIntyre's *After Virtue*." With Paul Wadell. *The Thomist* 46/2 (1982): 313–21.

"Seeking a Clear Alternative to Liberalism: A Review of Lindbeck's *The Nature of Doctrine*." With L. Gregory Jones. *Books and Religion* 13/1 (1985): 7.

"The Sermon on the Mount: Just War and the Quest for Peace." *Concilium* 195 (1988): 36–43.

"Sex and Politics: Bertrand Russell and 'Human Sexuality.'" *Christian Century* 95/14 (1978): 417–22.

"The Significance of the Other." With Bonita Raine. *Catechist* 14 no.7 (1981): 15, 20–21.

"The Significance of the Physical." *Scholastic* 112/12 (1971): 16–19.

"Some Theological Reflections on Gutierrez's Use of 'Liberation' as a Theological Concept." *Modern Theology* 3/1 (1986): 67–76.

"The Sources of Charles Taylor." With David Matzko, *Religious Studies Review* 18/4 (1992): 286–89.

"Testament of Friends: How My Mind Has Changed." *Christian Century* 107/7 (1990): 212–16.

"Virtue." In *The Westminster Dictionary of Christian Ethics*, ed. James F. Childress and John Macquarrie, 648–50. Philadelphia: Westminster Press, 1986.

"Why the Truth Demands Truthfulness: An Imperious Engagement with Hartt." In *Why Narrative? Readings in Narrative Theology*, ed. S. Hauerwas and G. Jones, 303–10. Grand Rapids: Eerdmans, 1989.

"Will the Real Sectarian Stand Up." *Theology Today* 44/1 (1987): 87–94.

d. Unpublished Essays:

"Can a Pacifist Think about War?"

"Christian Ethics in America: Beginning with an Ending," 1–45.

"Gay Friendship: A Thought Experiment in Catholic Moral Theology," 1–27.

"Interview" (of this author) with Stanley Hauerwas at Duke, September 22, 1994.

II. WORKS BY OTHER AUTHORS

Abraham, William J. *An Introduction to the Philosophy of Religion*. Englewood Cliffs, N.J.: Prentice Hall, 1985.

Ackerman, Bruce. *Social Justice in the Liberal State*. New Haven: Yale University Press, 1980.

Ackrill, John L. *Aristotle's Ethics*. London, Faber & Faber, 1973.

Adam, A. K. "Review of *Theology and Social Theory*," *Anglican Theological Review* 74 (1992): 510–12.

Adams, Richard. *Watership Down*. New York: Avon Books, 1972.

Adkins, William A. *Merit and Responsibility*. Oxford: Clarendon Press, 1960.

Alexander, Richard D. "Evolution, Social Behaviour, and Ethics." In *The Roots of Ethics*, ed. C. Callahan & T. H. Engelhardt, Jr., 307–32. New York: Plenum Press, 1981.

Allen, Richard C. "When Narrative Fails." *Journal of Religious Ethics* 21/1 (1993): 27–67.

Allik, Tina. "Religious Experience, Human Finitude, and the Cultural Linguistic Model." *Horizons* 20/2 (1993): 241–59.

Annas, Julia. "Personal Love and Kantian Ethics in 'Effi Briest.'" *Philosophy and Literature*, April 1984: 15–31.

Anscombe, Elizabeth. *Intention*. Oxford: Blackwell, 1958.

———. "Modern Moral Philosophy." *Philosophy* 33 (1958): 1–19.

Antonaccio, Maria and William Schweiker, eds. *Iris Murdoch and the Search for Human Goodness*. Chicago: University of Chicago Press, 1966.

Appia, Kwame Anthony. *In My Father's House: Africa in the Philosophy of Culture*. New York: Oxford University Press, 1992.

Arendt, Hannah. *The Human Condition*. New York, Doubleday Anchor, 1958.

———. *On Violence*. New York: Harcourt, Brace & World, 1969.

Aristotle. *Nicomachean Ethics*. Trans. D. Ross. Oxford: Oxford University Press, 1987.

Asad, Talal. *Genealogies of Religion*. Baltimore: Johns Hopkins, 1993.

Audi, Robert. "Responsible Action and Virtuous Character." *Ethics* 101 (1991): 304–21.

Auer, Alfons. *Autonome Moral und christlicher Glaube*. Düsseldorf: Patmos, 1971.

Augustine. *The Confessions*. Harmonsworth: Penguin Classics, 1971.

Barber, Benjamin. *The Conquest of Politics: Liberal Philosophy in Democratic Times*. Princeton, N.J.: Princeton University Press, 1988.

Baron, Marcia. "Kantian Ethics and Supererogation." *Journal of Philosophy* 84/5 (1987): 237–62.

Barrett, Lee C. "Theology as Grammar: Regulative Principles or Paradigms and Practices." *Modern Theology* 4 (1988): 155–72.

Barth, Karl. *Church Dogmatics*. Trans. A. T. Mickey et al. Edinburgh: T.& T. Clark, 1961.

Bartley, William, III. *Morality and Religion*. London: Macmillan, 1971.

Bauman, Zygmunt. *Postmodern Ethics*. Oxford: Blackwell, 1993.

Beardsome, W. S. *Art and Morality*. London: Macmillan, 1971.

Beetham, David. "The Future of the Nation State." In *The Idea of the Modern State*, ed. Gregor McLennan et al., 208–22. Philadelphia: Open University Press, 1984.

Beiner, Ronald. "Do We Need a Philosophical Ethics? Theory, Prudence and the Primacy of *Ethos*." *Philosophical Forum* 20/3 (1989): 230–43.

Bell, Quentin. "Bad Art." In *Revisions: Changing Perspectives in Moral Philosophy*, ed. S. Hauerwas & A. MacIntyre, 160–71. Notre Dame: University of Notre Dame Press, 1983.

Bellah, Robert, et al. *Habits of the Heart: Individualism, Commitment in American Life*. New York: Harper & Row, 1985.

Bellah, Robert. "Public Philosophy and Public Theology in America Today." In R. Bellah et al., *Civil Religion and Political Theology*, 79–97. New York: Clarendon Press, 1989.

Benhabib, Seyla. *Situating the Self: Gender, Community and Postmodernism in Contemporary Ethics*. Cambridge: Cambridge University Press, 1992.

Berger, Peter. *The Sacred Canopy: Elements of a Sociological Theory of Religion*. New York: Doubleday, 1967.

———. *The Social Construction of Reality*. Harmondsworth: Penguin, 1969.

Bernstein, Richard J. *Beyond Objectivism and Relativism*. Philadelphia: University of Pennsylvania Press, 1983.

Blum, Lawrence. *Friendship, Altruism and Morality*. London: Routledge and Kegan Paul, 1980.

———. *Moral Perception and Particularity*. Cambridge: Cambridge University Press, 1994.

———. "Iris Murdoch and the Domain of the Moral." *Philosophical Studies* 50 (1986): 343–67.

Bondi, Richard. "The Elements of Character." *Journal of Religious Ethics* 12 (1984): 201–18.

Braithwaite, R. B. "An Empiricist's View of the Nature of Religious Belief." In *Christian Ethics and Contemporary Philosophy*, ed. I. T. Ramsey, 53–73. London: SCM, 1966.

Browning, Don S., & F. Fiorenza, eds. *Habermas, Modernity and Public Theology*. New York: Crossroad, 1992.

Brubaker, Rogers. *Citizenship and Nationhood in France and Germany.* Cambridge, Mass.: Harvard University Press, 1992.

Brueggemann, Walter. "II Kings 18-19: The Legitimacy of a Sectarian Hermeneutic." *Horizons in Biblical Theology* 7 (1985): 1–42.

Budde, Michael. *The Two Churches: Catholicism and Capitalism in the World-System.* Durham, N.C.: Duke University Press, 1992.

Bultmann, Rudolf. *Essays: Philosophical and Theological.* Trans. C. G. Greig. London: SCM Press, 1955.

Burms, Arnold. "Disenchantment." *Ethical Perspectives* 1/3 (1994): 145–55.

Burnyeat, Myles. "Aristotle on Learning to be Good." In *Essays on Aristotle's Ethics,* ed. Amelie Rorty, 69–92. Berkeley: University of California Press, 1980.

Burrell, David. "An Introduction to Theology and Social Theory." *Modern Theology* 8/4 (1992): 319–29.

Callahan, D., & T. Engelhardt, Jr., eds., *The Roots of Ethics.* New York: Plenum Press, 1981.

Carr, Craig L. "Kant's Theory of Political Authority." *History of Political Thought* 10/4 (1989): 719–31.

Chalier, Catherine. "Responsibility and Election." In *Ethics,* ed. A. Phillips Griffiths, 63–76. Cambridge: Cambridge University Press, 1993.

Chansky, James. "Reflections on 'After Virtue' after Auschwitz." *Philosophy Today* 37 (1993): 247–56.

Childress, James. "Scripture and Christian Ethics." *Interpretation* 34 (1980): 371–80.

Chisholm, Roderick. "Supererogation and Offence: A Conceptual Scheme for Ethics." *Ratio* 5/1 (1963): 1–14.

Churchill, John. "The Bellman's Map: Does Anti-foundationalism Entail Incommensurability and Relativism?" *Southern Journal of Philosophy* 28 (1990): 469–84.

Cladis, Mark. *A Communitarian Defense of Liberalism.* Stanford: Stanford University Press, 1992.

———. "Mild-Mannered Pragmatism and Religious Truth." *Journal of American Academy of Religion* 60 (1992): 19–34.

Clark, Michael. "The Meritorious and the Mandatory." *Proceedings of Aristotelian Society* 79 (1978/9): 24–37.

Cohen, Joshua. "Moral Pluralism and Political Consensus." In *The Idea of Democracy,* ed. D. Copp et. al., 271–91. Cambridge: Cambridge University Press, 1993.

Coles, Romand. "Storied Others and the Possibilities of Caritas: Milbank and Neo-Nietzschean Ethics." *Modern Theology* 8/4 (1992): 331–51.

Collingwood, R. G. *An Essay on Metaphysics.* Oxford: Clarendon Press, 1939.

———. *An Essay on Philosophical Method.* Oxford: Oxford University Press, 1933.

Conway, D. "The Eyes Have It: Perspectives and Affective Investment." *International Studies in Philosophy* 23/2 (1991): 103–13.

Crites, Steven. "The Narrative Quality of Experience." *Journal of American Academy of Religion* 39 (1971): 291–312.

Curran, Charles. "Is There a Catholic and/or Christian Ethics?" In *Readings in Moral Theology 2: The Distinctiveness of Christian Ethics,* ed. C. Curran & R. McCormick, 156–77. New York: Paulist Press, 1980.

Davidson, David. "On the Very Idea of a Conceptual Scheme." *Proceedings and Addresses of the American Philosophical Association* 47 (1973–74): 5–20.

Davidson, Scott. "The Metaphysics of Moral Responsibility." Diss., University of Notre Dame, 1993.

De Certeau, Michel. *The Practice of Everyday Life.* Trans. Steven F. Rendall. Berkeley: University of California Press, 1984.

———. *The Writing of History* (originally *L'Écriture de l'Histoire*). Trans. Tom Conley. New York: Columbia University Press, 1988.

De Wachter, Frans. "In Search of a Post-National Identity: Who Are My People?" *Canadian Journal of Philosophy,* suppl. vol. 22 (1998): 197–217.

———. "Postmodern Challenges to Ethics." *Ethical Perspectives* 1/2 (1994): 77–88.

Desmond, William. *Philosophy and Its Others: Ways of Being and Mind.* New York: State University of New York Press, 1990.

Douglas, Mary. *The Active Voice.* London: Routledge & Kegan Paul, 1982.

Dumouchel, Paul, & J. P. Dupuy. *L'enfer des choses: René Girard et la logique de l'economie.* Paris: Editions du Seuil, 1979.

Dunbar, Scott. "On Art, Morals and Religion: Reflections on the Work of Iris Murdoch." *Religious Studies* 14 (1978): 515–24.

Dunne, Joseph. *Back to the Rough Ground: 'Phronesis' and 'Techne' in Modern Philosophy and in Aristotle.* Notre Dame: University of Notre Dame Press, 1993.

Edwards, P., ed. *Encyclopedia of Morality.* New York: Macmillan, 1968.

Elshtain, Jean Bethke. *Women and War.* (New York: Basic Books, 1987.

Engberg-Perdersen, T. *Aristotle's Theory of Moral Insight.* Oxford: Clarendon Press, 1983.

Engelhardt, H. T., & S. Spicker. *Philosophical Medical Ethics: Its Nature and Significance.* Dordrecht: Reidel, 1977.

Esbeck, Carl H. ed. *Religious Beliefs, Human Rights and the Moral Foundation of Western Democracy.* Columbia: University of Missouri Press, 1986.

Feinberg, Joel. *Doing and Deserving.* Princeton, N.J.: Princeton University Press, 1970.

———. "Supererogation and Rules." *Ethics* 71 (1961): 276–88.

Fingarette, Herbert. *Self-Deception.* New York, Humanities Press, 1969.

Fischer, John M., ed. *Moral Responsibility*. Ithaca, N.Y.: Cornell University Press, 1986.

Fish, Stanley. *Self-Consuming Artifacts: The Experience of Seventeenth-Century Literature*. Berkeley: University of California Press, 1974.

———. *There Is No Such Thing as Free Speech . . . and It's a Good Thing Too*. New York: Oxford University Press, 1994.

Fletcher, Joseph. *Situation Ethics*. Philadelphia: Westminster Press, 1966.

Flew, Anthony, ed. *Logic and Language*. Oxford: Oxford University Press, 1951.

Fogelin, Robert J. *Wittgenstein*. London: Routledge & Kegan Paul, 1980.

Foot, Philippa. *Virtues and Vices*. Oxford: Basil Blackwell, 1978.

———. "Moral Beliefs." *Proceedings of the Aristotelian Society* 50 (1958): 83–104.

Fowl, Stephen E. "Could Horace Talk with the Hebrews? Translatability and Moral Disagreement in MacIntyre and Stout." *Journal of Religious Ethics* 19/1 (1991): 1–20.

Frankena, William. *Ethics*. Englewood Cliffs, N.J.: Prentice Hall, 1973.

———. "Conversations with Carney and Hauerwas." *Journal of Religious Ethics* 3 (1975): 45–62.

———. "Is Morality Logically Dependent on Religion?" In *Religion and Morality*, ed. Gene Outka & P. Reeder, Jr., 295–317. New York: Anchor Press, 1973.

———. "Obligation and Motivation." In *Essays in Moral Philosophy*, ed. A. I. Melden, 40–81. Seattle: University of Washington Press, 1958.

Frankfurt, Harry G. *The Importance of What We Care About*. Cambridge: Cambridge University Press, 1988.

Frei, Hans. *The Eclipse of Biblical Narrative* (New Haven: Yale University Press, 1974.

Fuchs, Joseph. *Christian Ethics in a Secular Arena*. Dublin: Gill & Macmillan, 1984.

———. *Christian Morality: The Word Becomes Flesh*. Dublin: Gill & Macmillan, 1987.

———. *Human Values and Christian Morality*. Dublin: Gill & Macmillan, 1970.

———. "Is There a Specifically Christian Morality?" In *Readings in Moral Theology 2: The Distinctiveness of Christian Ethics*, ed. C. Curran & R. McCormick, 1–13. New York: Paulist Press, 1980.

Gadamer, H.-Georg. *Truth and Method*, ed. G. Barden and J. Kumming. London: Sheed & Ward, 1975.

Galston, William. *Liberal Purposes: Goods, Virtues and Diversity in the Liberal State*. Cambridge, Mass.: Harvard University Press, 1991.

Gay, Peter. *The Enlightenment, An Interpretation*, vol 2: *The Science of Freedom*. London: Weidenfeld & Nicolson, 1970.

Geertz, Clifford. *The Interpretation of Cultures*. New York: Basic Books, 1973.

———. "Anti-Anti-Relativism." In *Relativism, Interpretation and Confronta-tion*, ed. Michael Krausz, 1–18. Notre Dame: University of Notre Dame Press, 1989.

Gert, Bernard. *The Moral Rules*. New York: Harper & Row, 1966.

Giddens, Anthony. *The Nation State and Violence*. Berkeley: University of California Press, 1987.

———. *Social Theory and Modern Sociology*. Stanford, Calif.: Stanford University Press, 1987.

Girard, René. *Deceit, Desire and the Novel*. London: Athlone Press, 1965.

———. *Things Hidden Since the Foundations of the World*. London: Athlone Press, 1987.

Giurlanda, Paul. *Faith and Knowledge: A Critical Inquiry*. Lanham, Md.: University Press of America, 1987.

———. "The Challenge of Post-liberal Theology." *Commonweal* 64/2 (1987): 40–42.

Goh, Jeffrey C. "Tradition, Text, Doctrine, Experience: Foundations for a Christian Theology of Religions." S.T.L. Thesis, Leuven, 1995.

Goldberg, Michael. *Theology and Narrative: A Critical Introduction*. Nashville: Abingdon, 1982.

Graber, Glenn. "A Critical Bibliography of Recent Discussions of Religious Ethics by Philosophers." *Journal of Religious Ethics* 2 (1974): 53–80.

Green, Ronald M. *Religious Reason: The Rational and Moral Basis of Religious Belief*. Oxford: University Press, 1978.

Greenfeld, Liah. *Nationalism: Five Roads to Modernity*. Cambridge, Mass.: Harvard University Press, 1992.

Griffioen, Sander. "Entering into a Scheme of Belief: MacIntyre's Account of Moral Traditions." In *Morality, Worldview, and Law*, ed. A. Musschenga, B. Voorzanger, & A. Soeteman, 27–38. Maastricht: Van Gorcum, 1992.

Griffiths, A. Phillip, ed. *Ethics*. Cambridge: University Press, 1993.

Grube, G. M. A. *Plato's Thought*. London: Athlone Press, 1980.

Guevin, Benedict. "The Moral Imagination and the Shaping Power of the Parables." *Journal of Religious Ethics* 17 (1989): 63–79.

Guignon, Charles. "Philosophy after Wittgenstein and Heidegger." *Philosophy and Phenomenological Research* 50/4 (1990): 649–72

Gustafson, James. *Ethics from a Theocentric Perspective*, 2 vols. Chicago: University of Chicago Press, 1981, 1984.

———. "The Sectarian Temptation." *Proceedings of the Catholic Theological Society of America* 40 (1985): 83–94.

Gutiérrez, Gustavo. *A Theology of Liberation*. Trans. C. Inda and J. Eagleson. New York: Maryknoll, 1973.

Habermas, Jürgen. *The Theory of Communicative Action*, 2 vols. Boston: Beacon Press, 1985, 1987.

————. "Toward a Theory of Communicative Competence." *Inquiry* 13 (1970): 360–76.

Haldane, John. "Some Metaphysical Presuppositions of Agency." *Heythrop Journal* 35/3 (1994): 296–303.

Hampshire, Stuart. *Freedom of the Individual.* New York: Harper & Row, 1965.

————. *Thought and Action.* New York: Viking, 1960.

————. "Fallacies in Moral Philosophy." *Mind* 68 (1949): 466–82.

Hampton, Jean. "The Moral Commitment of Liberalism." In *The Idea of Democracy*, ed. D. Copp et al., 292–313. Cambridge: Cambridge University Press, 1993.

Harak, Simon. *Virtuous Passion: The Formation of Christian Character.* New York: Paulist Press, 1993.

Hardie, W. F. R. *Aristotle's Ethical Theory.* Oxford: Clarendon Press, 1980.

Hare, R. M. *The Language of Morals.* Oxford: Clarendon Press, 1952.

Harman, Gilbert. "Moral Relativity Defended." *The Philosophical Review* 84 (1975): 3–22.

Hartt, Julian. "Some Theological Investments in Story." In S. Hauerwas and G. Jones, *Why Narrative?* 279–92

Harvey, Barry A. "Insanity, Theocracy, and the Public Realm: Public Theology, the Church, and the Politics of Liberal Democracy." *Modern Theology* 10/1 (1994): 27–58.

Heeley, Gerard F. "The Ethical Methodology of Stanley Hauerwas: An Examination of Christian Character of Ethics." Ph.D. diss., Pontificia Studiorum Universitas A. S. Thomas Aquinas, Rome, 1987.

Held, David. "Central Perspectives on the Modern State." In *The Idea of the Modern State*, ed. Gregor McLennan et al., 32–50. Philadelphia: Open University Press, 1984.

Hepburn, Ronald. "Vision and Choice in Morality." In *Christian Ethics and Contemporary Philosophy*, ed. I. T. Ramsey, 181–95. London: SCM, 1966.

Herman, Barbara. "The Practice of Moral Judgement." *Journal of Philosophy* 82 (1985): 414–36.

Heschel, Abraham J. *The Prophets.* New York: Harper & Row, 1962.

Heyd, David. *Supererogation: Its Status in Ethical Theory.* Cambridge: Cambridge University Press, 1982.

Hill, Thomas E. "Kant on Imperfect Duty and Supererogation." *Kant-Studien* 72 (1972): 55–76.

Hobbes, Thomas. *Leviathan*, ed C. B. Macpherson. Baltimore: Penguin, 1975.

Holland, Scott. "The Problems and Prospects of a 'Sectarian Ethic': A Critique of the Hauerwas Reading of the Jesus Story." *The Conrad Grebel Review* 10 (1992): 157–68.

Hollis, Martin. *The Nature of Man.* Cambridge: Cambridge University Press, 1977.

Hoose, Bernard. *Proportionalism: The American Debate and Its European Roots.* Washington, D.C.: Georgetown University Press, 1987.

Huang, Yon. "Foundation of Religious Beliefs after Foundationalism: Wittgenstein between Nielsen and Phillips." *Religious Studies* 31/2 (1995): 251–67.

Hume, David. *Treatise on Human Nature*, ed. Selby-Bigge and L. Amherst. Oxford: Clarendon Press, 1972.

Hütter, Reinhard. "The Church's Peace Beyond the Secular: A Postmodern Augustinian's Deconstruction of Secular Modernity and Postmodernity" [review essay of John Milbank's *Theology and Social Theory*]." *Pro Ecclesia* 2/1 (1993): 106–16.

————. "Ecclesial Ethics, the Church's Vocation, and Paraclesis." *Pro Ecclesia* 2/4 (1993): 433–50.

Incandela, Joseph. "The Appropriation of Wittgenstein's Work by Philosophers of Religion: Towards a Re-Evaluation and an End." *Religious Studies* 21 (1986): 457–74.

Jung, Patricia. "Sanctification: An Interpretation in Light of Embodiment." *Journal of Religious Ethics* 11/1 (1983): 75–95.

Kant, Immanuel. *The Critique of Practical Reason.* Trans. L. Beck. Indianapolis: Bobbs-Merrill, 1956.

————. *The Critique of Pure Reason.* Trans. J. M. D. Meiklejohn. London: Dent and Sons, 1991.

————. *Groundwork for the Metaphysics of Morals.* In H. J. Paton, *The Moral Law: Kant's Groundwork for the Metaphysics of Morals.* London: Hutchinson, 1958.

————. *Political Writings*, ed. H. Reiss. Cambridge: Cambridge University Press, 1991.

————. *Religion within the Limits of Reason Alone.* Trans. Theodore M. Greene and Hoyt H. Hudson. New York: Harper and Row, 1960.

Kasper, Walter. *Theology and Church.* Trans. [original *Theologie und Kirche*, Mainz, 1987] by Margaret Kohl. New York: Crossroad, 1989.

Katongole, Emmanuel. "The Agent's Perspective: A Study of Stanley Hauerwas' Ethical Project." M.A Thesis in Philosophy, K. U. Leuven, 1983.

————. "The Distinctiveness of Christian Ethics." M.A. Thesis in Religious Studies, K. U. Leuven, 1995.

Kerby, Anthony. *Narrative and the Self.* Bloomington: Indiana University Press, 1991.

Kerr, Fergus. "Rescuing Girard's Argument?" *Modern Theology* 8/4 (1992): 385–99.

King, James. "Fideism and Rationality." *New Scholasticism* 49 (1975): 431–50.

Kosman, L. A. "Being Properly Affected." In *Essays of Aristotle's Ethics*, ed. Amelie Rorty, 103–16. Berkeley: University of California Press, 1980.

Kotva, Joseph. "Christian Virtue Ethics and the Sectarian Temptation." *Heythrop Journal* 35/1 (1994): 35–52.

Kovesi, Julius. *Moral Notions.* New York: Humanities Press, 1975.

Kristeva, Julia. *Nations without Nationalism.* Trans. Leon S. Roudiez. New York: Columbia University Press, 1993.

Kuhn, Thomas. *The Structure of Scientific Revolutions.* Chicago: University of Chicago Press, 1959.

Kupperman, Joel. *Character.* Oxford: Oxford University Press, 1991.

———. *Foundations of Morality.* London: Allen & Unwin, 1983.

———. "The Supra-moral in Religious Ethics." *Journal of Religious Ethics* 1 (1973): 65–71.

Kymlicka, W. *Contemporary Political Philosophy, An Introduction.* Oxford: Clarendon Press, 1990.

Lash, Nicholas. "Not Exactly Politics or Power?" *Modern Theology* 8/4 (1992): 358.

Lauritzen, Paul. "Is 'Narrative' Really a Panacea? The Use of 'Narrative' in the Work of Metz and Hauerwas." *Journal of Religion* 67/3 (1987): 322–39.

Lewis, Paul. "The Springs of Motion: Jonathan Edwards on Emotions, Character and Agency." *Journal of Religious Ethics,* Fall 1994: 275–97.

———. "Toward a NonFoundationalist Christian Social Ethic." *Perspectives in Religious Studies* 22/1 (1995): 45–62.

Lindbeck, George A. *The Nature of Doctrine: Religion and Theology in a Postliberal Age.* Philadelphia: Westminster Press, 1984.

Lloyd, Genevieve. "Iris Murdoch on the Ethical Significance of Truth." *Philosophy and Literature* 6 (1982): 62–75.

Locke, John. *The Second Treatise on Civil Government.* New York: Prometheus Books, 1986.

Lonergan, Bernard. *Method in Theology.* New York: Herder and Herder, 1972.

Loughlin, Gerard. "Christianity at the End of the Story or the Return of the Master Narrative." *Modern Theology* 8/4 (1992): 365–84.

———. "See-Saying/Say-Seeing." *Theology* 91 (1988): 201–9.

Lovibond, Sabina. *Realism and Imagination in Ethics.* London: Blackwell, 1983.

Lowi, Theodore. *The End of Liberalism.* New York: W. W. Norton, 1969.

Lukes, Steven. "Relativism, Cognitive and Moral." In Lukes, *Essays in Social Theory.* New York: Columbia University Press, 1977.

MacIntyre, Alasdair. *After Virtue: A Study in Moral Theory.* London: Duckworth, 1981; Notre Dame: University of Notre Dame Press, 1981; 2nd ed., 1984.

———. *A Short History of Ethics.* New York: Routledge, 1967; Notre Dame: University of Notre Dame Press, 1998.

———. *Three Rival Versions of Moral Enquiry.* Notre Dame: University of Notre Dame Press, 1990.

———. *Whose Justice? Which Rationality?* Notre Dame: University of Notre Dame Press, 1988.

———. "The Fate of Theism." In A. MacIntyre and P. Ricoeur, *The Religious Significance of Atheism*, 3–55. New York: Columbia University Press, 1969.

———. "How to Identify Ethical Principles" prepared for the National Commission for the Protection of Human Subjects of Biomedical and Behavioral Research.

———. "Is Patriotism a Virtue?" Monograph. Lawrence: Kansas Department of Philosophy, 1984.

———. "Objectivity in Morality and Objectivity in Science." In H. T. Engelhardt, Jr., and Daniel C. Callahan, eds., *Morals, Science, and Sociality*, 21–47. Hastings-on-Hudson, N.Y.: Hasting Center, 1978.

———. "Patients as Agent." In H. T. Engelhardt, Jr., and S. F. Spicker, eds., *Philosophical Medical Ethics: Its Nature and Significance*, 197–212. Dordrecht: Reidel, 1977.

———. "Theology, Ethics, and the Ethics of Medicine and Health Care." *Journal of Medicine and Philosophy* 4.4 (December 1979): 428–41.

Mackie, J. L. *Ethics: Inventing Right and Wrong*. London: Penguin Books, 1977.

Macmurray, John. *The Self as Agent*. New York: Harper & Row, 1957.

MacNamara, Vincent. *Faith and Ethics: Recent Catholicism*. Dublin: Gill and Macmillan, 1985.

Malcolm, Norman. "The Groundlessness of Belief." In *Contemporary Perspectives of Religious Epistemology*, ed. Douglas Geivett and Brendan Sweetman, 92–103. Oxford: Oxford University Press, 1992.

Marshall, Bruce D., ed. *Theology and Dialogue: Essays in Conversation with George Lindbeck*. Notre Dame: University of Notre Dame Press, 1990.

Matson, Wallace. *The Existence of God*. Ithaca, N.Y.: Cornell University Press, 1965.

Mayberry, Thomas C. "God and Moral Authority." *Monist* 54 (1970): 106–23.

McClendon, James, and J. Smith. *Understanding Religious Convictions*. Notre Dame: University of Notre Dame Press, 1971.

McCormick, Richard. *Notes on Moral Theology: 1981 through 1984*. Lanham, Md.: University Press of America, 1984.

———. "Christianity and Morality." *Catholic Mind* 75 (1977): 28.

———. "Does Religious Faith Add to Ethical Perception?" In *Readings in Moral Theology* 2: *The Distinctiveness of Christian Ethics*, ed. C. Curran & R. McCormick, 156–75. New York: Paulist Press, 1980.

McDonagh, Enda. *Church and Politics*. Notre Dame: University of Notre Dame Press, 1980.

McDowell, John. "Virtue and Reason." *Monist* 62 (1979): 331–50.

McWhorter, Ladelle. "The Event of Truth: Foucault's Response to Structuralism." *Philosophy Today* 38 (1994): 159–65.

Mead, Herbert G. *Mind, Self and Society.* Chicago: University of Chicago Press, 1934.

Meilaender, Gilbert. *The Theory and Practice of Virtue.* Notre Dame: University of Notre Dame Press, 1984.

Melden, A. I. *Free Action.* New York: Humanities Press, 1964.

Milbank, John. *Theology and Social Theory: Beyond Secular Reason.* London: Blackwell, 1990.

———. "The End of Dialogue." In *Christian Uniqueness Reconsidered,* ed. Gavin D'Costa, 174–91. New York: Orbis, 1990.

———. "Postmodern Critical Augustinianism: A Short *Summa* in Forty-two Responses to Unasked Questions." *Modern Theology* 7/3 (1991): 225–37.

Mink, L. O. "History and Fiction as Modes of Comprehension." *New Literary History* 1.3 (1970).

Miscamble, William. "Sectarian Pacifism." *Theology Today* 44 (1987): 69–77.

Mouffe, Chantal. "Political Philosophy without Politics." *Philosophy and Social Criticism* 13/2 (1987): 105–23.

Mudimbe, V. Y. *The Idea of Africa.* Bloomington: Indiana University Press, 1994.

———. *The Invention of Africa: Gnosis, Philosophy, and the Order of Knowledge.* Bloomington: Indiana University Press, 1988.

Murdoch, Iris. *Metaphysics as a Guide to Morals.* New York: Penguin Press, 1994.

———. "Against Dryness: A Polemical Sketch." In *Revisions: Changing Perspectives in Moral Philosophy,* ed. S. Hauerwas & A. MacIntyre, 43–50. Notre Dame: University of Notre Dame Press, 1983.

———. "The Idea of Perfection." In I. Murdoch, *The Sovereignty of Good,* 1–45. London: Routledge & Kegan Paul, 1970.

———. "On 'God' and 'Good'." In I. Murdoch, *The Sovereignty of the Good,* 46–76.

———. "The Sovereignty of Good over Other Concepts." In I. Murdoch, *The Sovereignty of Good,* 77–104.

———. "The Sublime and the Good." *Chicago Review* 13 (1959), 40–58.

———. "Thinking and Language." *Proceedings of the Aristotelian Society* (Supplementary Volume) 25 (1951): 25–34.

———. "Vision and Choice in Morality." In *Christian Ethics and Contemporary Philosophy,* ed. I. T. Ramsey, 195–218. London: SCM, 1966.

Murphy, Debra D. "Power, Politics, and Difference: A Feminist Response to Milbank." *Modern Theology* 10/2 (1994): 137–38.

Murphy, Nancey, & J. McClendon, Jr. "Distinguishing Modern and Postmodern Theologies." *Modern Theology* 5/3 (1989): 192–214.

Murray, Leslie A. "Confessional Post Modernism and the Process-Relational Vision." *Process Studies* 18/2 (1989): 83–94.

Musschenga, Albert. "Narrative Theology and Narrative Ethics." In *Does God Matter Morally? The Critical Re- Appraisal of the Thesis of Morality's Independence from Religion*, 173–204. Kampen, The Netherlands: Kok Pharos, 1995.

———. "Universal Morality and Moral Tradition." In *Morality, Worldview, and Law*, ed. A. Musschenga et al., 65–82. Maastricht: Van Gorcum, 1992.

Musschenga, A., and P. Van Tongeren, ed., *Does God Matter Morally? The Critical Re- Appraisal of the Thesis of Morality's Independence from Religion.* Kampen, The Netherlands: Kok Pharos, 1995.

Nagel, Thomas. *The View from Nowhere.* New York: Oxford University Press, 1986.

———. "Moral Luck." In T. Nagel, *Mortal Questions*, 24–38. Cambridge: Cambridge University Press, 1979.

Nelson, Paul. *Narrative and Morality: A Theological Inquiry.* University Park: Pennsylvania State University, 1987.

Nelson, Robert. *Reaching for Heaven on Earth: The Theological Meaning of Economics.* Lanham, Md.: University Press of America, 1991.

Newman, John Henry. *An Essay in Aid of a Grammar of Assent.* (1870), ed. and with Introduction by I. T. Ker. Oxford: Oxford University Press, 1985.

Niebuhr, H. Richard. *Christ and Culture.* New York: Harper and Row, 1965.

Niebuhr, Reinhold. *The Nature and Destiny of Man.* New York: Charles Scribner's Sons, 1957.

Nielsen, Kai. *Ethics without God.* New York: Prometheus, 1973.

———. *Why Be Moral?* New York: Prometheus, 1989.

———. "Wittgensteinian Fideism" *Philosophy* 42 (1967): 191–209.

Nietzsche, Friedrich. *Human, All Too Human.* Trans. Marion Faber & Stephen Lehmann. Lincoln: University of Nebraska Press, 1984.

Norton, John. "Review of *Love's Knowledge* [by M. Nussbaum]. *Philosophical Quarterly* 42/169 (1992): 492–95.

Nowell-Smith, "Religion and Morality." In *The Encyclopedia of Morality*, vol. 8, ed. P. Edwards, 150–58. New York: Macmillan, 1968.

Nozick, Robert. *Philosophical Explanations.* Oxford: Clarendon Press, 1981.

Nussbaum, Martha. *The Fragility of Goodness.* New York: Cambridge University Press, 1986.

———. "Finely Aware and Richly Responsible." In M. Nussbaum, *Love's Knowledge: Essays on Philosophy and Literature*, 148–67. Oxford: Oxford University Press, 1990.

———. "Human Functioning and Social Justice: In Defense of Aristotelian Essentialism." *Political Theory* 20/3 (1992): 202–46.

———. "Narrative Emotions: Beckett's Genealogy of Love." in *Revisions: Changing Perspectives in Moral Philosophy*, ed. S. Hauerwas & A. MacIntyre, 216–40. Notre Dame: University of Notre Dame Press,1982.

————. "Non-Relative Virtues: An Aristotelian Approach." *Midwest Studies in Philosophy* XIII: *Ethical Theory: Character and Virtue*, 32–55. Notre Dame: University of Notre Dame Press, 1988.

————. "Recoiling from Reason." *New York Review of Books* 36 (Dec. 7, 1989): 38.

Nuyen, A. T. "Postmodern Theology and Postmodern Philosophy." *International Journal for Philosophy of Religion* 30 (1991): 65–76.

Oakeshott, Michael. *Rationalism and Politics*. New York: Barnes & Noble, 1972.

O'Connell, Timothy. *Principles for a Catholic Morality*. New York: Seabury Press, 1978.

O'Donohoe, James. "A Return to Virtue," *Church* 3/1 (1987): 48–54.

O'Donovan, Oliver. "The Loss of a Sense of Place." *Irish Theological Quarterly* 55 (1989): 39–58.

O'Neil, Colman. "The Rule Theory of Doctrine and Propositional Truth." *The Thomist* 49 (1985): 417–42.

O'Neil, Onora. *Acting on Principle: An Essay on Kantian Ethics*. New York: Columbia University Press, 1975.

Ogletree, Thomas. "Character and Narrative: Stanley Hauerwas' Study of the Christian Life." *Religious Studies Review* 6/1 (1980): 25–31.

Outka, Gene. "Character, Vision and Narrative." *Religious Studies Review* 6/2 (1980): 110–18.

Outka, Gene, and P. Reeder, Jr., eds. *Religion and Morality*. New York: Anchor Press, 1973.

Palmer, Richard E. *Hermeneutics: Interpretation Theory in Schleiermacher, Dilthey, Heidegger, and Gadamer*. Evanston, Ill.: Northwestern University Press, 1969.

Parsons, Talcott. *The Evolution of Societies*. Englewood Cliffs, N.J.: Prentice Hall, 1977.

Penelhum, Terrence. *God and Scepticism: A Study in Scepticism and Fideism*. Dordrecht: Reider, 1983.

Peterson, Michael, William Hasker et al., eds. *Reason and Religious Belief: An Introduction to the Philosophy of Religion*. Oxford: Oxford University Press, 1991.

Phillips, D. Z., ed. *Religion and Morality*. London: Macmillan, 1996.

————. "Wisdom's Gods." In D. Z.Phillips, *Faith and Philosophical Enquiry*, 170–203. London: Routledge & Kegan Paul, 1970.

Pinches, Charles. "Describing Morally." Ph.D. diss., University of Notre Dame, 1984.

Pincoffs, Edmund. *Quandaries and Virtues*. Lawrence: University of Kansas Press, 1986.

————. "Quandary Ethics." In *Revisions: Changing Perspectives in Moral Phi-*

losophy, ed S. Hauerwas and A. MacIntyre, 92–112. Notre Dame: University of Notre Dame Press, 1983.

Placher, William. *Unapologetic Theology.* New York: Westminster Press, 1989.

———. "Revisionist and Postliberal Theologies and the Public Character of Theology." *The Thomist* 49 (1985): 392–415.

Plant, Raymond. *Modern Political Thought.* New York: Blackwell, 1991.

Poteat, William. *Philosophical Daybook: Post-Critical Investigations.* Columbia: University of Missouri Press, 1990.

Powell, Betty. *Knowledge of Action.* London: Allen and Unwin, 1967.

Quingley, T. R. "The Ethical and Narrative Self." *Philosophy Today* 38 (1994): 43–55.

Quinn, Phillip. "Is Athens Revived Jerusalem?" *The Asbury Journal* 45/1 (1990): 51–56.

Quirk, Michael. "Beyond Sectarianism?" *Theology Today* 44 (1987): 78–86.

Ramanathan, Suguna. "The Concept of Good in Four of Iris Murdoch's Later Novels." *Heythrop Journal* 28 (1987): 388–404.

Rasmusson, Arne. *The Church as Polis: From Political Theology to Theological Politics as Exemplified by Jürgen Moltmann and Stanley Hauerwas.* Lund: University Press, 1994; Notre Dame: University of Notre Dame Press, 1995.

Rauschenbusch, Walter. *A Theology for the Social Gospel.* Nashville: Abingdon Press, 1945.

Rawls, John. *Political Liberalism.* New York: Columbia University Press, 1993.

———. *A Theory of Justice.* Cambridge, Mass.: Harvard University Press, 1971.

———. "The Domain of the Political and Overlapping Consensus." In *The Idea of Democracy,* ed. D. Copp, J. Hampton, & E. Roemer, 245–69. Cambridge: Cambridge University Press, 1993.

———. "The Idea of an Overlapping Consensus." *Oxford Journal of Legal Studies* 7 (1987): 1–26.

———. "Justice as Fairness: Political Not Metaphysical." *Philosophy and Public Affairs* 14/3 (1985): 223–51.

———. "Kantian Constructivism in Moral Theory: The Dewey Lectures 1980." *Journal of Philosophy* 77 (1980): 515–72.

Raz, Joseph. "Facing Diversity: The Case of Epistemic Abstinence." *Philosophy and Public Affairs* 19/1 (1990): 3–46.

Rasnick, David. "John Locke and Liberal Nationalism." *History of European Ideas* 15/4-6 (1992): 46–63.

Reynolds, C. "A Proposal Concerning the Place of Reason in Christian Ethics." *Journal of Religion* 50 (1970), 156–68.

Richardson, Robert N. "Christian Community Ethics: Critical Reflections on the Nature and Function of the Church in the Ethics of Stanley Hauerwas." Ph.D. dissertation, University of Natal (Pietermarburg), 1986.

Ricoeur, Paul. *Time and Narrative* 3 vols. Trans. Kathleen McLaughlin and David Pellauer. Chicago: University of Chicago Press, 1984–88.

Robbins, Wesley. "Narrative, Morality and Religion." *Journal of Religious Ethics* 8/1 (1980): 161–76.

———. "On the Role of Vision in Morality." *Journal of the American Academy of Religion*, suppl. 45 (1977): 623–42.

Roberts, Richard. "Transcendental Sociology? A Critique of Milbank's 'Theology and Social Theory'." *Scottish Journal of Theology* 46 (1993): 527–35.

Rorty, Richard. *Contingency, Irony, and Solidarity.* Cambridge: University Press, 1989.

———. *Philosophy and the Mirror of Nature.* Oxford: Basil Blackwell, 1980.

Sabin, John, & S. Mauray. *Moralities of Everyday Life.* New York: Oxford University Press, 1982.

Sandel, Michael. *Liberalism and the Limits of Justice.* Cambridge: University Press, 1982.

———. "The Procedural Republic and the Unencumbered Self." *Political Theory* 12/1 (1984): 81–96.

Sartre, Jean-Paul. *Being and Nothingness.* New York: Pocket Books, 1956.

Schnädelbach, Herbert. "What Is Neo-Aristotelianism?" *Praxis International* 7/3-4 (1987–88): 225–37.

Schoeman, Ferdinand, ed. *Responsibility, Character, and the Emotions.* Cambridge: University Press, 1987.

Schrag, Calvin O. "Interpretation, Narrative and Rationality." *Research in Phenomenology* 21 (1991): 98–115.

Schüller, Bruno. "The Debate on the Specific Character of a Christian Ethics: Some Remarks." In *Readings in Moral Theology 2: The Distinctiveness of Christian Ethics*, ed. C. Curran & R. McCormick, 207–33. New York: Paulist Press, 1980.

Sellars, Wilfred. "Empiricism and Philosophy of the Mind." In W. Sellars, *Science, Perception and Reality*, 127–96. New York: 1967.

Sheehan, Thomas. "The Drama of Karl Rahner." *New York Review of Books*, Feb. 4, 1981: 13–14.

Sheldon, G. Ward. *The History of Political Thought: Ancient Greece to Modern America.* New York: Peter Lang, 1988.

Sherman, Nancy. *The Fabric of Character.* New York: Oxford University Press, 1989.

Simmons, John. "Locke's State of Nature." *Political Theory* 17/3 (1980): 449–70.

Singer, Markus. *Generalization in Ethics.* New York: Knopf, 1961.

Singer, Peter. *The Expanding Circle: Ethics and Sociobiology.* New York: Farrar, Straus & Giroux, 1981.

Skinner, Quentin. *The Foundations of Modern Political Thought.* 2 vols. Cambridge: University Press, 1978.

Slote, Michael. *Goods and Virtues.* Oxford: University Press, 1983.

Smith, John E. *The Works of Jonathan Edwards.* New Haven: Yale University Press, 1959.

Solomon, Robert C. *The Passions: The Myth and Nature of Human Emotion.* Notre Dame: University of Notre Dame Press, 1983.

Sorabji, Richard. "Aristotle on the Role of Intellect in Virtue." *Proceedings of the Aristotelian Society* 74 (1973–74): 107–29.

Stewart-Robertson, C. "Philosophical Reflections on the Obligation to Attend." *Philosophy Today* 31 (1987): 54–68.

Stocker, Michael. "The Schizophrenia of Modern Ethical Theories." *Journal of Philosophy* 73 (1976): 453–66.

Stout, Jeffrey. *Ethics after Babel.* Boston: Beacon Press, 1988.

———. *The Flight from Authority: Religion, Morality, and the Quest for Autonomy.* Notre Dame: University of Notre Dame Press, 1981.

———. "Redirecting Inquiry in the Religion-Morality Debate." *Religious Studies* 16 (1980): 229–37.

Strawson, P. F. "Social Morality and Individual Ideal." In *Christian Ethics and Contemporary Philosophy*, ed. I. T. Ramsey, 280–98. London: SCM, 1966.

Stroup, George. *The Promise of Narrative Theology.* Atlanta: John Knox Press, 1981.

———. "Theology of Narrative or Narrative Theology?: A Response to *Why Narrative?*" *Theology Today* 47 (1991):424–32.

Stump, Eleonore. "Penelhum on Sceptics and Fideists." *Synthese* 67 (1986): 147–54.

Suavé-Meyer, Susan. *Aristotle on Moral Responsibility: Character and Cause.* Oxford: Blackwell, 1993.

Surin, Kenneth. *Christ, Ethics and Tragedy: Essays in Honour of McKennon.* New York: Cambridge University Press, 1989.

———. "'Many Religions and the One True Faith': An Examination of Lindbeck's Chapter Three." *Modern Theology* 4 (1988): 187–209.

Taylor, Charles. *The Explanation of Behavior.* New York: Humanities Press, 1964.

———. "Cross-Purposes: The Liberal-Communitarian Debate." In *Liberalism and the Moral Life*, ed. Nancy Rosenblum, 159–82. Cambridge, Mass.: Harvard University Press, 1989.

Taylor, Richard. *Action and Purpose.* Englewood Cliffs, N.J.: Prentice Hall, 1966.

TeSelle, Sallie. "The Experience of Coming to Belief." *Theology Today* 32.2 (1975): 286.

Thiemann, Ronald. *Constructing a Public Theology: The Church in a Pluralistic Culture.* Louisville: Westminster Press, 1991.

Tilley, Terrence. "Incommensurability, Intratextuality, and Fideism." *Modern Theology* 5/2 (1989): 87–111.

Toulmin, Stephen E. *An Examination of the Place of Reason in Ethics.* Cambridge: University Press, 1960.

Tracy, David. *The Analogical Imagination: Christian Theology and the Culture of Pluralism.* New York: Crossroad, 1981.

———. "Lindbeck's New Program for Theology." *The Thomist* 49 (1985): 460–72.

Troeltsch, Ernst. *The Social Teaching of the Christian Churches.* New York: Macmillan, 1931.

Urmson, J. O. *Aristotle's Ethics.* Oxford: Basil Blackwell, 1988.

———. "Saints and Heroes." In *Essays in Moral Philosophy,* ed. A. Melden, 198–216. Seattle: University of Washington Press, 1958.

Van de Putte, André. "Nationalism and Nations." *Ethical Perspectives* 1/3 (1994): 104–22.

Van Gerwen, Jef. "The Church in the Theological Ethics of Stanley Hauerwas." Ph.D. diss., University of California, Berkeley, 1984.

Van Tongeren, Paul. "Morality, Transcendence, Conception of Life." In *Morality, Worldview and Law,* ed. Musschenga et al., 39–52. Maastricht: Van Gorcum, 1992.

Vivas, Eliseo. *The Moral Life and the Ethical Life.* Chicago: Henry Regnery, 1963.

Von Balthasar, Hans U. "Nine Theses in Christian Ethics." In *Readings in Moral Theology* 2: *The Distinctiveness of Christian Ethics,* ed. C. Curran & R. McCormick, 190–206. New York: Paulist Press, 1980.

Wainwright, Geoffrey. "Ecumenical Dimension of George Lindbeck's 'Nature of Doctrine.'" *Modern Theology* 4 (1988): 121–32.

Waring, Graham, ed. *Deism and Natural Religion.* New York: Ungar, 1967.

Weber, Max. *The Protestant Ethic and the Spirit of Capitalism.* Trans. Talcott Parsons. London: Allen & Urwin, 1985.

———. "The Protestant Sects and the Spirit of Capitalism." In M. Weber, *Economy and Society: An Outline of Interpretative Sociology,* vol. 3, 1204– 1210. Berkeley: University of California Press, 1978.

Weil, Simone. *Waiting on God* [original *Attente de Dieu*]. Trans. Emma Craufurd. London: Routledge and Kegan Paul, 1950.

Werphowski, William. "Political Liberalism and Christian Ethics: A Review Discussion." *The Thomist* (1984): 81–115.

Weston, William J. "The Missing Element in Hauerwas' *A Community of Character.*" *Journal of Religious Studies* 13/2 (1987): 95–105.

Whiteside, Kerry. "Universality and Violence." *Philosophy Today* 35 (1991): 372–89.

Whitmore, Todd. "Beyond Liberalism and Communitarianism in Christian Ethics. A Critique of Stanley Hauerwas." *The Annual of the Society of Christian Ethics,* 1989.

Wildes, Kevin Wm. "After the Fall: Particularism in Bioethics." *Journal of Medicine and Philosophy* 18/6 (1993): 505–29.

Williams, Bernard. *Ethics and the Limits of Philosophy.* Cambridge, Mass.: Harvard University Press, 1985.

———. "Moral Luck." In B. Williams, ed., *Moral Luck,* 20–39. Cambridge: Cambridge University Press, 1981.

Winch, Peter. *The Idea of a Social Science and Its Relation to Philosophy.* (New York: Humanities, 1958.

———. "Understanding a Primitive Society." In *Rationality,* ed. B. R. Wilson, 78–111. Oxford: Oxford University Press, 1970.

Wittgenstein, Ludwig. *On Certainty.* Ed. G. E. M. Anscombe & G. H. von Wright, trans. G. E. M. Anscombe & Denis Paul. New York: Harper & Row, 1969.

———. *Philosophical Investigations.* Trans. E. Anscombe. New York: Macmillan, 1953.

———. *Remarks on the Foundations of Mathematics.* Trans. G. E. Anscombe. Cambridge, Mass.: MIT Press, 1978.

———. *Zettel.* Trans. E. Anscombe. Berkeley: University of California Press, 1967.

Wogaman, Philip. *Christian Perspectives on Politics.* London, 1988.

Wolff, Robert Paul. *Understanding Rawls.* Princeton N.J.: Princeton University Press, 1977.

Wolin, Sheldon. *Politics as Vision.* Boston: Little, Brown, 1960.

———. "What Revolutionary Action Means Today." *Democracy* 2 (1992): 19–32.

Wong, David. "Moral Realism without Foundations." *Southern Journal of Philosophy* 24 Suppl. (1986): 95–113.

Yack, Bernard. "Reconciling Liberalism and Nationalism." *Political Theory* 23/1 (1995): 166–82.

Yoder, John Howard. *The Politics of Jesus.* Grand Rapids: Eerdmans, 1972.

Index

action theory, 52

Adams, Richard, *Watership Down*, 118, 282n.58

affective investment: and moral character, 51–53, 55–59; motivational models and, 27–29

ahistorical approaches: to ethics, 5, 20–21, 28, 29, 253; to the self, 40, 138

Alexander, Richard D., 14

Allen, Richard C., 109

Allik, Tina, 208, 209

analytic philosophy, 16–17, 265–66n.39. *See also* Wittgenstein, Ludwig

anthropological perspective: in Murdoch, 77–78; of religion, 6, 10–16, 265n.34, 300–301n.92, 308n.59

Aquinas, Thomas, 51, 53, 55, 63, 246–47, 271n.68, 273n.108, 282n.73

archetypal stories, 111–12. *See also* metanarrative

Arendt, Hannah, 108, 310n.81

arete, 245–47

Aristotle: on choice (*proairesis*), 64; on the concept of *phronēsis*, xii, 49, 122, 124–31, 141, 146–48, 152, 160, 178, 273n.109, 283nn.85 and 87; on friendship (*philia*), 58; on masters (*phronomoi*), 98; on moral

objectivity, 141–43; *Nicomachean Ethics*, xii, xiv, 35, 64, 125–31, 146; on the passions, 53, 54–55; on virtue, 48–51, 63–67, 244–45, 272n.88, 284n.106, 295n.29

Asad, Talal, on genealogies of religion, 201

attention, 87; *phronēsis* and, 148–49, 150, 177

Audi, Robert, 61–62

Augustine: *City of God* (*Civitas Dei*), 240–41, 247; *Confessions*, 136, 286n.125; *De Musica*, 311n.95

authority: crisis of during Reformation, x–xi, 7–10, 11, 14–15, 182; ethics and, 19, 25–26, 34, 95–96, 99–100

Barber, Benjamin, 224

Barth, Karl, 183, 184, 294n.19

Bartley, William, ix, 18, 262–63n.21

Braithwaite, R. B., 27

Burrell, David, 104

caritas, 245–47

casuistry, 150–51

Catholic Church. *See* church

character. *See* moral character

Childress, James, 145

Christian beliefs, 63, 79, 86–87; the Incarnation or "Christ event," 8,

Fingarette, Herbert, on self-deception, 133

Foot, Philippa, 243–44

Foucault, Michel, 214

foundationalism, xi, 143, 154–57, 167, 179, 184; anti-foundationalist treatises, 186; epistemological, 188–89; relativism and, 168–72; residual, 187, 290n.64

Frankena, William, 57–58, 243

freedom: and moral character, 34, 50, 61; and responsibility, 61–64, 68

friendship, 58–59

Gadamer, H.-Georg, *Truth and Method*, 34, 40, 95, 211, 269n.16

Geertz, Clifford, 171, 212, 300–301n.92

genealogical investigation, xi; of religion, 201; of the religion/ethics problem, 5, 7, 12, 14, 253

Generalization principle, 171

Giddens, Anthony, 216–18, 298n.77, 307n.31

gnosis, 202

God, 16–17, 77–78, 116, 302n.87

good: Murdoch's vision of the, 76–77, 88; Platonic concept of, 74–76, 87

Greek philosophy, 282n.2. *See also* Aristotle; Plato

Greek *polis*, 312n.114

Guevin, Benedict, 93

Gustafson, James: critique of Hauerwas, 154–55, 157, 162, 180, 188, 288n.41; *The Sectarian Temptation*, 286n.1, 293nn.3–4; on tradition, 187, 286n.125

Hampshire, Stuart, 45

Harman, Gilbert, on moral relativity, 170–71

Hartt, Julian, 128, 163–65

Harvey, Barry A., 219

Hauerwas, Stanley, 51–56, 210–13, 281n.1; on the distinctiveness of Christian ethics, 102, 144, 154, 180, 189, 195, 213, 228, 254, 263n.24, 264–65n.33; on ethics and authority, 19, 25–26, 34, 95–96, 99–100; on freedom and moral character, 34, 50, 61; on imagination, 85, 226, 255; on moral character and language or training, 61–64, 68–69, 81–82, 94–103, 124, 130; on moral character and vision, 81–82, 101–3, 230; on moral rationality and particularity, xiii, xv, 29–30, 124–25, 231, 256; on narrative and moral rationality or moral truth, 70, 104–5, 121–22, 127–36, 273n.102; on the notion of sects, 191–92, 198–99; pacifism of, 215–16, 225, 233–38, 309n.69; on the political role of the church, 231–32, 250–51, 309n.63, 313n.133; on rationality and tradition, 154–55, 166, 168, 177–79; on religion as a cultural-linguistic system, 180, 203, 205–6, 207–10, 211, 212–13; on religion or Christianity and liberalism, 199–203, 228, 230–31, 236, 304–5n.11; on vision as learned or contextual, x, xi, xii, 85, 87–91, 93, 94, 102–3; on witness, 172–79, 222, 227–33, 297n.69

—criticisms of: fideism, 180–83, 185, 293nn.3 and 4; moral relativism, 163–65, 167, 168–72; sectarianism, xiii, 139, 144–45, 154–55, 215–16, 294n.13; social withdrawal, 235–36; tribalism, 219–21

—works: *A Community of Character*, 271n.70, 280–81n.42, 281–82n.55,